Dieter W. Storr

Efficient Usage of Adabas Replication

Understanding IT

Autonomous Land Vehicles
by Karsten Berns and Ewald von Puttkamer

Microsoft Dynamics NAV
by Paul M. Diffenderfer and Samir El-Assal jr.

Future of Trust in Computing
by David Grawrock, Helmut Reimer, Ahmad-Reza Sadeghi
and Claire Vishik

Linguistic Identity Matching
by Bertrand Lisbach and Victoria Meyer

Using Microsoft Dynamics AX 2009
by Andreas Luszczak

From Enterprise Architecture to IT-Governance
by Klaus D. Niemann

Efficient Usage of Adabas Replication
by Dieter W. Storr

The New PL/I
by Eberhard Sturm

www.viewegteubner.de

Dieter W. Storr

Efficient Usage of Adabas Replication

A Practical Solution Finder

Edited by Stephen Fedtke

VIEWEG+ TEUBNER

Bibliographic information published by the Deutsche Nationalbibliothek
The Deutsche Nationalbibliothek lists this publication in the Deutsche Nationalbibliografie;
detailed bibliographic data are available in the Internet at http://dnb.d-nb.de.

1st Edition 2011

Editorial Office: Christel Roß | Maren Mithöfer

Vieweg+Teubner Verlag is a brand of Springer Fachmedien.
Springer Fachmedien is part of Springer Science+Business Media.
www.viewegteubner.de

Cover design: KünkelLopka Medienentwicklung, Heidelberg
Printing company: STRAUSS GMBH, Mörlenbach
Printed on acid-free paper

ISBN 978-3-8348-1730-3

Preface

When I presented my experiences with the Event Replicator for Adabas at the International Users' Group Conference in Prague, 2010, Software AG and conference attendees inspired and encouraged me to write a book about replication to share my knowledge.

This book will discuss the basics of the Event Replicator and show how to set-up files for replication and create the definitions for destination, subscription, GFB, initial state and the new ADADBS function.

Not all utility functions can currently be automatically replicated on a non-mainframe platform. An example is file changes that require special handling on the subscription, the replicator engine and the target site. My book will walk you through the process step by step.

From a disaster and recovery standpoint, copying databases to the same or other hardware platforms becomes increasingly important. This book explains the difference between mirroring and replicating and shows the pros and cons of both techniques.

In tests with production-sized data of 160 million records, communication problems occurred, parameters weren't calculated correctly and RPL buffers and SLOG overflowed. The initial-state procedure was too time-consuming and a workaround had to be found.

In production with 1,400 updates per second, the source database showed higher CPU time and batch jobs ran much longer when replication was turned on.

Despite users' statements that the replication works correctly and comparisons between source and target are not necessary, self-written comparison programs sometimes show differences. Three methods will be discussed how to compare source and target files to ensure that both are identical.

Since database data is available in local or wide area networks and on public Web sites, security issues become even more important. One chapter in this book explains the available security software protecting the components during the replication process.

Last but not least, this book will also show the very important recovery function. Normally, the Event Replicator Server restarts automatically after an abnormal end and is able to recover any lost replication. But in some cases, data is lost and the replication must be replayed.

My special gratitude goes out to Larry Frazin, who supported me with replication tests. John Donnelly, Albert Stetson, Victor Tisuela, Hazel Baeza, Gary Walker and Chris Jonas who sent parameter values from their organizations. Roseanna Torretto monitored resources on the mainframe with RMF and Strobe. The team from Software AG, Wolfgang Weiss, Becky Albin, Alex Burggraf and Wil Heynen, who were always available for tuning discussions and product support. My thanks also to Michelle McGowan for her proofreading skills and emotional support.

Dieter W. Storr
Sacramento, California, U.S.A, August 2011

Contents

Table of Figures

1 Replication Basics

1.1 Today's Challenge

In today's world you must keep your enterprise competitive and your customers happy, therefore, it is critically important that your business systems have instant access to changed data.

Some organizations copy their Adabas database data to a data warehouse or to a relational database (RDBMS) located on Linux, UNIX or Windows, and use off-the-shelf software to process the copied data.

Time and cost savings are also reasons to access copied Adabas data on non-mainframe platforms. Some batch jobs run on these platforms faster and cost less compared with running them on the mainframe. But it can be awkward and time-consuming to decompress the data, file transfer it to the open system, compress and reload it.

Other organizations duplicate their Adabas database for disaster and recovery using backups and even protection logs to be up-to-date. This data-copy procedure is only possible on the same hardware platform. Open transactions on protection logs or handling problems with back-ups can easily lead to a corrupted target database.

A third-party software company supports this approach with protection logs and even copies mainframe ADASAV back-ups to non-mainframe platforms. New Adabas releases on the mainframe and non-mainframe platforms makes it difficult or even impossible to keep up with Adabas format changes.

The drawback of these methods is that your customers do not have instant access to the changed data, and the data is not updated in real-time.

Another way is to mirror on a hardware-level your data or disks. Although synchronized mirroring is an update in real-time, you do not have instant access to the mirrored data. In addition, disk data errors will also be mirrored.

Companies who want to copy parts of a file such as sets of records and fields or field values to the target database must write programs for this approach and then maintain this homemade software.

The most practical solution for these problems is the Event Replicator for Adabas, a highly flexible event-publishing tool that efficiently delivers changed data in real-time from Adabas to Adabas and to any RDBMS or middleware. Only committed Adabas modifications on a transaction level will be asynchronously replicated.

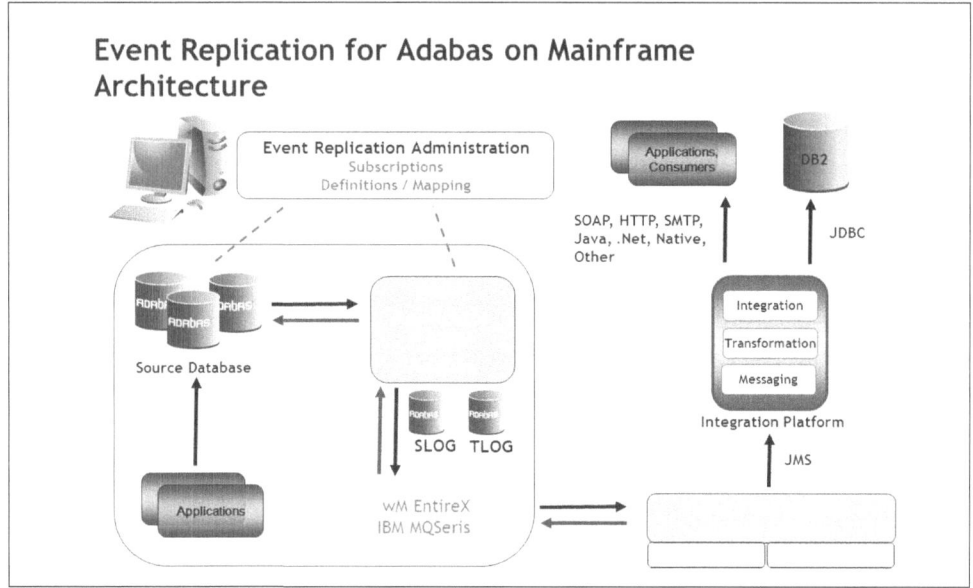

Figure 1: Architecture of Adabas Replication on the Mainframe – Source: Software AG

The following chapters explain in detail the replication process and its parameters, show the architecture of various replication models, and give you guidance for possible problems and their solutions. One chapter is dedicated to security and describes how to protect each level in your replication path. Examples of parameters, Natural and assembler source code complete this book as a guide and support for Adabas replication questions.

- The difference between replication and mirroring: chapter 1.2
- The reasons for replication: chapter 1.3
- What to check before starting and avoid mistakes: chapter 1.4
- Different ways to replicate: chapter 2
- Definitions and parameters: chapter 3
- Compare files of source and target – self-written programs: chapter 4
- Recovery after a crash: chapter 5
- Problems and solutions based on own experiences: chapter 6
- Monitors – self-written and from Software AG: chapter 7
- Security: chapter 8
- Appendix – many programs and parameter examples: chapter 9

1.2 Replicating or Mirroring

For many years, companies backed up their mainframe databases to tapes and stored them at a very safe place, sometimes deep in a mountain storage. In case of a recovery after a disaster, the computer center mostly could not receive the backup tapes because streets, tunnels or bridges are unusable and airplanes are not allowed to fly. In other cases the packages sent by the postal service arrived only with a few tapes. One missing tape out of forty backup tapes is no backup at all. From a security standpoint unacceptable to lose sensitive data, such as social security or credit card numbers.

1.2.1 Mirroring

One possibility to eliminate the above mentioned problem with tapes is to mirror the data from one disk to another disk. Mirroring is based on microcode on a disk array controller or via server software. It is typically a proprietary solution and not compatible between various storage vendors. Examples are EMC 5700 or enterprise storage server ESS Shark from IBM on enterprise servers (mainframes). Using peer to peer remote extended distance (PPRC-XD) from IBM, data will be copied over thousands of miles between two ESS Sharks. SYMMETRIX remote data facility (SRDF) from EMC mirrors synchronized data to a remote back-up site, where the source and the target storage can be located on an enterprise server (mainframe) or on an UNIX box.

Benefits

- **Asynchronous disk mirroring** can provide **better physical protection** by supporting extended physical distances.
- **No loss of committed transactions** in synchronous storage (mirroring/RAID) on a CPU failure.

Limitations

- No protection from data corruption.
- Secondary site is **not guaranteed to be transitionally consistent**, in the case of asynchronous mirroring.
- **Client application must be re-started** after failure and need to be aware of failure.
- **Synchronous mirroring** and RAID devices **can add overhead** to application performance.
- Redundant/specialized high availability hardware/software can be expensive and restricted to use for backup purposes only.
- Secondary copy of data is not available for use – low hardware utilization.
- Need to replicate everything on disk, **no selectivity of data replication**.

IBM's FlashCopy copies nearly instantaneously entire volumes to other volumes (snapshot). It sets pointers and copies later the entire image of volumes. The TimeFinder function from EMC works similar.

The mirror function must be very carefully used in regards to Adabas and its buffer pool. Updated blocks might be still in the buffer pool or disk I/Os are only partially done when the flash copy function is used. The new ADADBS-TRANSACTIONS-SUSPEND function takes care of the buffer flush and new update commands synchronizing it during the snapshot function. Without the transaction-suspend function, the database must be down during flash copy to avoid a database corruption.

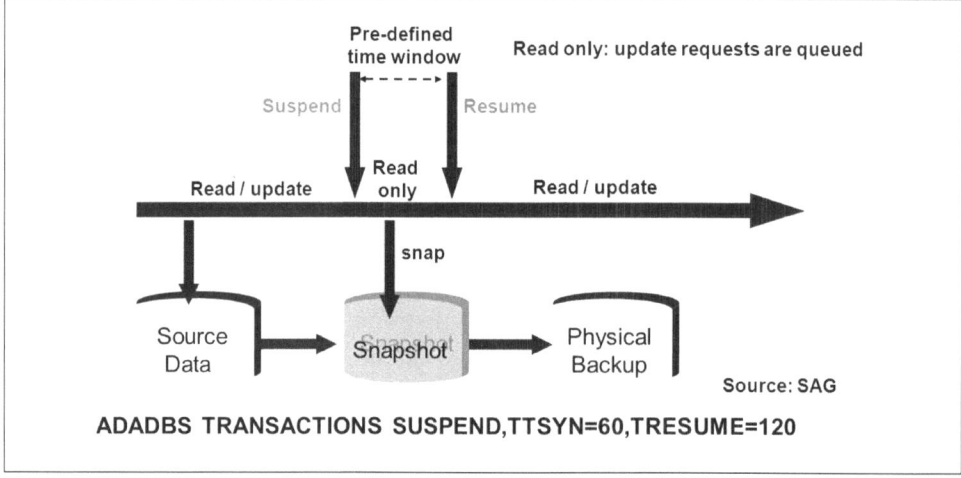

Figure 2: Mirroring – ADADBS TRANSACTION SUSPEND Function

1.2.2 Replication

Mirroring is very often called replication. But there are two main differences, Mirroring copies the tracks of a disk or I/O blocks and the mirrored data cannot be directly used for read-only processes. Replication repeats the database transactions on the target site and the replicated data can be instantly used for read-only processes.

Benefits

- **Warm Standby systems** can be configured over a Wide Area Network, providing protection from site failures.
- **Ability to more quickly swap to the standby system** in the event of failure, as backup database is already on-line.
- **Data corruption is typically not replicated** as transactions are logically reproduced rather than I/O blocks mirrored.

- **Automatic switch over** for clients using a switching mechanism, no client restart needed.
- Originating applications are minimally impacted as **replication takes place asynchronously** after commit of the originating transaction.
- The warm standby database is available for **read-only operations**, allowing better utilization of backup systems.
- **Ability to resynchronize** and easily switch back to primary system when it becomes available without loss of data.
- No need to replicate everything on disk, **data can be selected for replication**.

Limitations

- Warm Standby system will be **out-of-date** by transactions committed at the active database that have not been applied to the standby.
- **Protection is limited** to components supporting Warm Standby (e. g. DBMS data sources may be protected but file systems may not be supported).

1.3 Reasons for Replication

In today's financial environment, many companies and state and federal agencies look at migrating their core applications from the mainframe, Natural and Adabas to newer hardware platforms, database systems and programming languages like Oracle, SQL database, Unix and .NET or Java. However, after a cost analysis, they cannot always justify the expense or get permission from their stockholders to spend a couple of million dollars just to be more in the trend.

There is no proof that such a migration leads to faster processing or is more secure or even easier to use. They also do not take into account the cost of losing all of the expertise in Natural and Adabas and retraining staff members just to be more hype. I can remember back in the 90s, when companies were so proud to own an adaptable database system and a 4GL programming language. Programs developed on the mainframe could easily run under other hardware platforms, as Windows, UNIX, or BS2000.

Some organizations found it is faster and less expensive to program in Natural under MS Windows and use Single Point of Development (SPoD) to coordinate and transport programs between the mainframe and the PC. They decompressed relevant Adabas files on the mainframe, transferred them via FTP to the PC, compressed and re-loaded them into the Adabas database running under Windows. They also found that some batch jobs using Natural and Adabas ran on a PC up to 90% faster and cost less money than on the mainframe. Surprisingly, some other jobs ran 100% slower but this could be that Adabas Fastpath, the optimization tool of SAG, is not available on the PC.

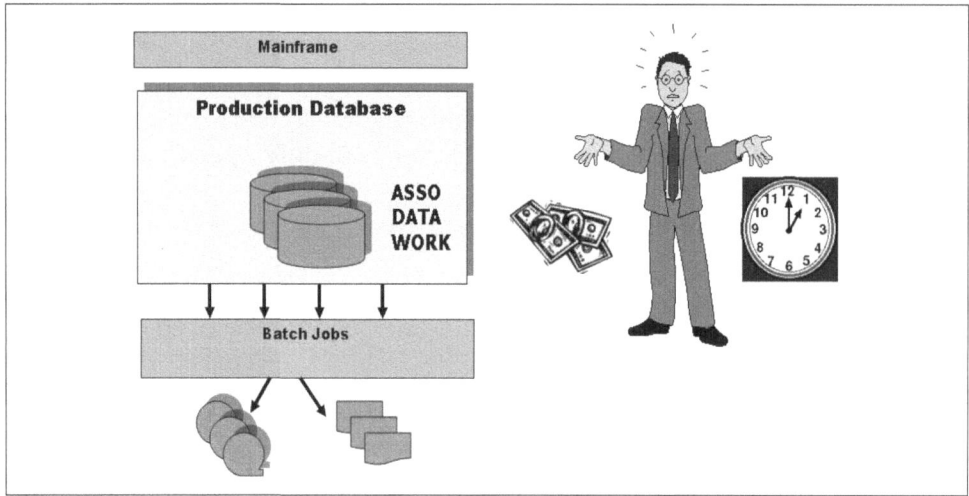

Figure 3:   Reasons for Replication

This type of replication was homemade, very time consuming and left the cost of decompressing jobs on the mainframe site.

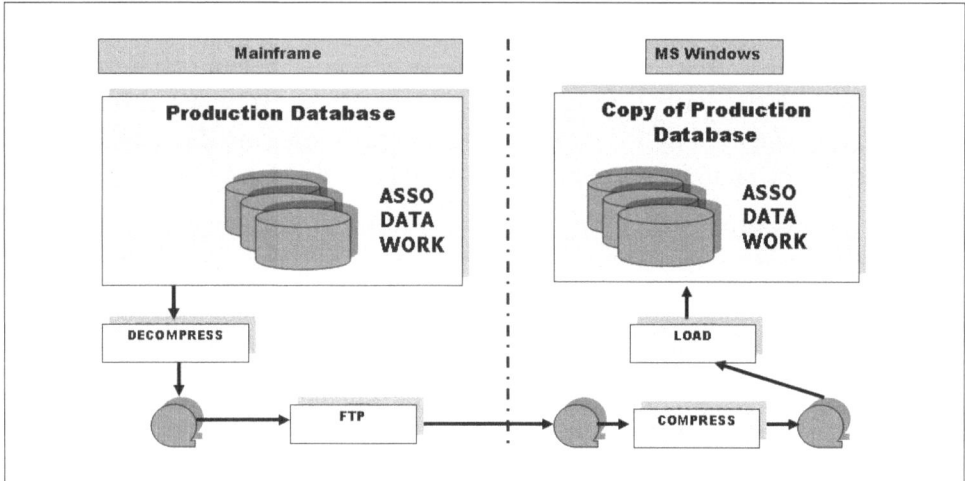

Figure 4:   Homemade Replication

The next challenge was how to populate the latest Adabas data faster from the mainframe to the PC in order to be up-to-date. Replication is the buzzword and some companies advertise products to copy Adabas data by using back-ups and protection logs. Software AG offered to help with their product "Event Replicator for Adabas" to replicate data in real-time from the mainframe to Linux, UNIX and Windows.

For many years, companies have used the Event Replicator for Adabas to replicate for disaster and recovery, development, training, demos and Web access. Off-the-shelf software for non-Adabas databases requires leaving the Adabas databases on the very secure and stable mainframe and replicate its data to non-Adabas databases on Linux, UNIX or Windows (LUW).

1.4   Check Your Intentions Before Starting

1.4.1   Mirroring or Replication?

Chapter 1.2 explains the two main differences between mirroring and replication. Mirroring is often called replication. The updated blocks in the Adabas buffer pool that have not yet been written to the disks can cause problems for mirroring. Adabas read commands receive the updated information from the buffer pool if it is still not written by a buffer flush to the disk. In contrast to the replicated data the mirrored data is not up-to-date. It is disk mirroring and not buffer mirroring.

The replicated target has the benefit that you have instant read-only access to the in real-time delivered data. Can you take advantage of this benefit for your organization? The following questions should help you in your decision process. You also will find in the following chapters detailed explanations to the most important questions about Adabas data replication.

- Do you want to use your copied data in parallel to your original database? You can run batch reports against the replicated database and save money, time, and decrease mainframe workload: see chapter 1.3. If the answer is yes, you must use replication.
- Do you accept the possibility that errors in disk tracks or blocks are copied to the target? Mirroring might already be supported by your hardware (raid technology). If you have a micro-code problem on your source disk and would like to switch your production over to your mirrored target database this won't help because the error was mirrored. There might be an error recovery possible but it will take time. If you accept these errors then mirroring can be the solution.
- Do you want the Adabas transaction to be asynchronously repeated in near real-time on the target database? If you want to use your replicated data instantly then you must use replication.

1.4.2   Usage of Replicated Database

It is important for you to decide what to do with your replicated Adabas database after it is copied from the mainframe. Chapter 2 explains different ways to replicate

- General requirements, basics: chapter 2.1.
- From Adabas to Adabas on the mainframe: chapter 2.2.
- From Adabas on the mainframe to Adabas on Linux, Unix, or Windows: chapter 2.3.
- From Adabas on the mainframe to non-Adabas on Linux, Unix, or Windows: chapter 2.4.

The following questions should help you in your decision process.

- Do you want to provide a real-time database for disaster and recovery and replicate your Adabas database from the mainframe to another Adabas database on the mainframe? Even if it is a replicated database for disaster and recovery, the data can be used instantly for read-only accesses. If the answer is yes, you must use the Event Replicator of Adabas. See chapter 2.2.
- Do you want to reduce the mainframe costs and replicate in real-time your Adabas database from the mainframe to Adabas on Linux, UNIX or Windows? If the answer is yes, the Event Replicator of Adabas is your choice. See chapters 1.3 and 2.3.
- Do you want to create or support a data warehouse with real-time data from your Adabas database on the mainframe? Software AG supports data warehouse appliance vendors and their database architectures, such as for DB2, MS SQL Server, MySQL, Oracle, Sybase, Sybase ASE, and Teradata. If the answer is yes, you must use the Event Replicator of Adabas and its target adapters. See chapter 2.4.
- Do you want to replicate your Adabas database from the mainframe to Linux, UNIX or Windows to a non-Adabas database so you can use your off-the-shelf software, which is written for relational databases only? Software AG supports several target adapters, such as for DB2, MS SQL Server, MySQL, Oracle, Sybase, Sybase ASE, and Teradata. If the answer is yes, you must use the Event Replicator of Adabas. See chapter 2.4.
- Do you want to keep your sensitive data on the secure and stable mainframe and use your existing message-oriented middleware such as MQSeries to copy in real-time all or parts of the data to a RDBMS on the open system? If the answer is yes, the Event Replicator for Adabas is the best solution. See chapter 2.4.

- Do you need Entire Net-Work (WCP) in order to replicate Adabas data from mainframe to mainframe or to Linux, UNIX, or Windows? You must use Entire Net-Work as a broker function. You cannot use webMethods EntireX. For me it makes more sense to use one broker function to replicate Adabas to Adabas and Adabas to non-Adabas databases. In contrast to Entire Net-Work, webMethods EntireX has its own reliable safety mechanism (persistent store). See chapter 2.2.
- Do you need a message-oriented middleware, such as MQSeries, or a broker function, such as webMethods EntireX? Do you already use a broker function and Natural RPC getting mainframe Adabas data from a non-mainframe platform? See chapter 2.4.

1.4.3 Measure/Compute and Determine Your Needs

Moving through the process on the way from the subscription or source database to the destination or target database must be passed, such as middleware, broker, network, router, and firewall. Parameters and the bandwidth of the circuit have to be determined or adjusted. It is therefore a good idea to determine your needs before you start with replication. The following questions will help to determine what information is important to collect and you will find the answers in chapter 3.

- How many Adabas modification commands (new, delete, update) do you expect per second? This information is important to determine buffers in Entire Net-Work as well as a part of the formula to determine the bandwidth (Mbps) to be used for the connectivity. See chapter 3.1.
- How long are the record (RB) and format buffers (FB) per Adabas command? The number of commands per second is part of the formula to determine the bandwidth (Mbps) to be used for the connectivity. See chapter 3.1.
- What line speed (circuit) and what type of connection do you need between the mainframe and Linux, UNIX or Windows servers, such as OC3 or IPSec VPN tunnel? The line speed is crucial for the in real-time replication and should be determined for peak times. See chapter 3.1.
- Do existing lines have sufficient speed and are they shared with other applications, such as Web sites or ftp processes? If you calculate a line needed for 20 Mbps then an OC1 line with 51.8 Mbps can be too slow if used also by other applications. And keep in mind that the replication process sends back an acknowledgement to the Replication Engine. A duplex circuit would be a benefit. See chapter 3.1.
- Are the Adabas modification commands send from batch and/or online programs? Batch programs send Adabas commands faster than online users can hit the enter-key. The number of Adabas commands is important to determine

buffers in Entire Net-Work as well as a part of the formula to determine the bandwidth (Mbps) to be used for the connectivity. See chapter 3.1.

- How many Adabas files should be replicated? The number of files per transaction is a factor in the formula to determine the number of attached buffers (NAB) of the Replication Engine. The Replicator Engine keeps all file updates of one transaction before sending them to the target database. See chapter 3.3.4.
- Do you plan to replicate only some fields of a file? The throughput of data replication to Adabas destinations is improved with version 3.3. SP1 of the Event Replicator for Adabas by filtering format buffers. New parameters allow to specify before (SFFILTERGFBBI) and after-image (SFFILTERGFBAI) format buffers. This will reduce the decompress process time of the entire buffer. See chapter 3.3.9.
- How many records per file? This information is important to determine the time needed for the initial-state process. Files with over 100 million records can take hours. The initial-state function reads record by record and sends store-with-ISN commands (N2) to the target database. Tests showed that based on an Adabas command log on Windows a fast connection can replicate approximately 300 Adabas commands per second. See test results in appendix, chapter 9.4.
- Do you need additional broker software, such as EntireX or Entire Net-Work?

1.4.4 Avoid Mistakes

During many years of experience with replication for Adabas V3.2.1, I ran into some problems and would like to help you to avoid the following mistakes. Problems and solutions are explained in chapter 6.

- Do not create your replicated database on a PC, use a server instead. A local drive (C-drive) on a PC might not handle the traffic, use disk arrays and raid technology (RAID 5) in a SAN box to store the replicated database.
- Do not log or trace your replicated data in a production environment. Depending on the volume of replicated data, it can slow down the replication process.
- Do not log the before image (DSBI=OFF) if it is not necessary. It is an overhead in data transfer between the subscription database and the Replication Engine. Chapter 3.2.3 shows the ADADBS commands.
- Do not use slow lines (circuits) as a connection between the mainframe and open system servers (Linux, UNIX, Windows). A data traffic jam can affect the subscription database and the Replicator Engine, such as CPU time, buffer and SLOG overflow. See chapters 6.2.2 and 6.2.3 for more information.
- Do not define your Adabas and replication buffers too small. It can stop the replication process on the subscription database because there is no overflow area. Only the Replicator Engine has such an area (SLOG).

- Define your SLOG large enough to keep the replicated data for a couple of days if the target database is temporarily not available. Initial-state and/or the REPLAY function are necessary to restore the missed data.
- Do not underestimate the time you will need for the initial-state process, especially if files with large amount of records are involved. Attachment chapter 9.4 gives you an idea of commands per second (cps) going through all the replication components.
- Keep in mind that one Replicator Engine may not be sufficient. The number of update commands per second, the number of files in one transaction, and the number of files to be replicated are responsible for the decision.
- Do not replicate files without a valid destination. It can be a big task to clean-up the SLOG file during an ongoing replication process. See chapter 6.2.9.
- Do not wait to install monitor routines or software to check error messages or response codes reported on the subscription database and Replicator Engine (DDPRINT) – especially for ISNs not replicated. Chapters 4 and 7 explain how to compare and what monitor routines are available.

Plan to have routines in place when file changes must be applied during a program migration. File change replications from Adabas to Adabas won't be done automatically in some cases. Chapter 6.1.5 explains in detail what to do.

2 Different Ways to Replicate

2.1 General Requirements / Basics

The subscription (source) database with the data to be replicated and the replicator engine or Reptor to receive and edit the updates for the destination (target) database are necessary.

Both databases the subscription and the Reptor contain one replication buffer (RPL), defined with the parameter LRPL. Other buffers, also known from regular databases, play an important role during the replication process, such as the Adabas buffer pool (LBP) and the I/O pool (LFIOP) for asynchronous buffer flushes.

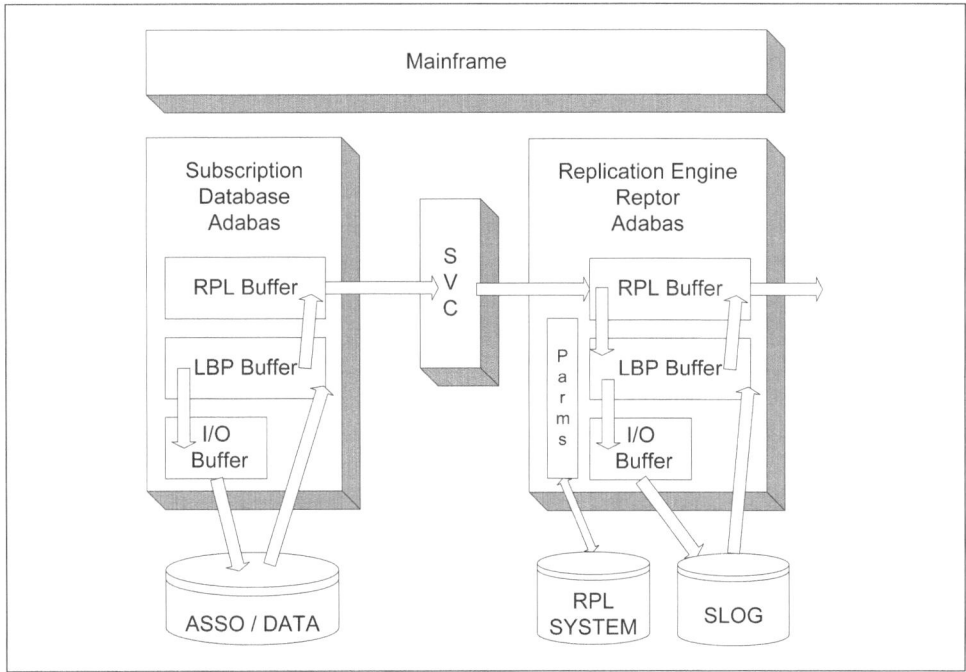

Figure 5: General Requirements – Buffer Usage

In addition to the mandatory Adabas system file, the following files are part of the Replicator Engine (Reptor):

- Replication system file that contains the replication parameters, such as descriptions of destinations, subscriptions and the global formats (GFB).
- Subscription log or SLOG file as the overflow area of the replication buffer should also be defined.

- A transaction log (TLOG) might also be used for performance and tuning. It is the command log of the Reptor and should not be activated at a regular replication process because of the overhead in the system.

Chapter 3 describes the parameters for each database and chapter 6 explains problems and solutions for incorrect defined buffers and parameters.

2.2   From Adabas to Adabas on the Mainframe

The replication from an Adabas database on the mainframe to another Adabas database on the mainframe is mostly used from companies to build a back-up database in real-time for disaster and recovery (D/R).

In contrast to a mirrored database, the replicated database can be used at any time in parallel to the original database in read-only mode. In a case of D/R, all applications can be switched directly to the replicated database and used in read and update mode.

The following components are necessary to replicate:

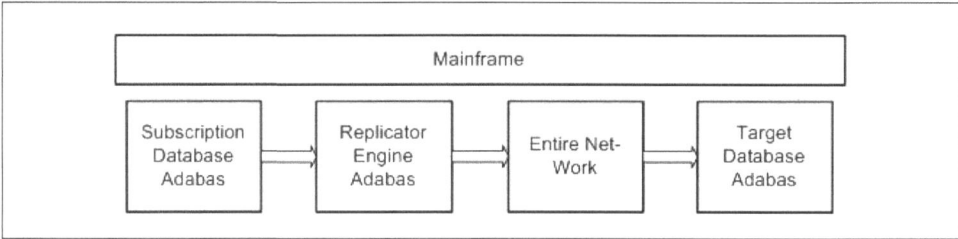

Figure 6:   Replication from Adabas to Adabas on the Mainframe

Source or subscription database

Additional Adabas parameters must be defined and existing ones updated. For more information see chapter 3.

Replicator Engine or Reptor

This is a basic Adabas nucleus loading at start-up some additional replication modules. Adabas parameters should be set-up at least with the same values as the source or subscription database. For more information see chapter 3.

In addition to the known Adabas system file, the following files are part of the database

- Replication system file that contains descriptions of destinations, subscriptions and the global formats (GFB).

- Optional subscription log or SLOG file as the overflow area of the replication buffer.

Entire Net-Work or WCP

Entire Net-Work is also called WCP to differentiate between Net-Work and Net-work. WCP is acting as a broker and passes Adabas direct calls including its buffers to the target database, such as control block, record buffer, and format buffer. For a description see chapter 3 and Figure 12.

You must use at this time Entire Net-Work as a broker function to replicate Adabas to Adabas. You cannot use webMethods EntireX. For me it makes more sense to use one broker function to replicate Adabas to Adabas and Adabas to non-Adabas databases. In contrast to Entire Net-Work, webMethods EntireX has its own reliable safety mechanism (persistent store).

If a connection to the target is no longer available and using Entire Net-Work the transaction will be stored in the subscription log (SLOG) of the Replicator Engine. EntireX will save the transaction in its persistence store, allowing the system to recover to a known point without loss of data.

I had discussions with Software AG and they promised to discuss internally the approach using also EntireX for Adabas to Adabas replication.

Target or destination database

The Adabas target database receives Adabas direct calls from the Replicator Engine through Entire Net-Work (WCP). Values of parameters and buffers should be set in the same way as for source or subscription database.

2.3   From Adabas on the Mainframe to Adabas on Linux, UNIX or Windows (LUW)

The replication from an Adabas database on the mainframe to another Adabas database on Linux, UNIX or Windows is used by companies who use the replicated database to save time and costs for their batch processes. Accessing the replicated database in read-only mode from the Web can also eliminate using networks with all its components between the mainframe and Web servers.

The following components are necessary to replicate:

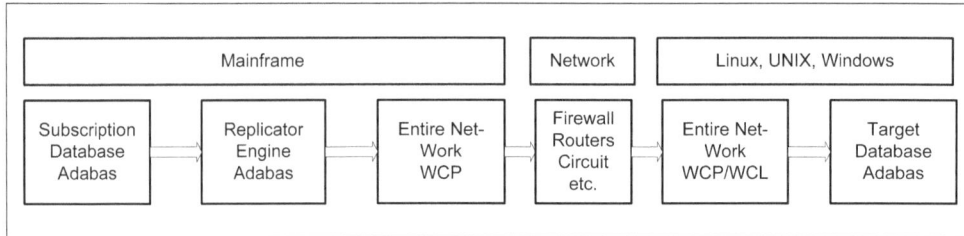

Figure 7:   Replication from Adabas to Adabas on Linux, UNIX or Windows (LUW)

Source or subscription database

Additional Adabas parameters must be defined and existing ones updated. For more information see chapter 3.

Replicator Engine or Reptor

This is a basic Adabas nucleus loading at start-up some additional replication modules. Adabas parameters must be set-up at least with the same values as the source or subscription database. For more information see chapter 3.

In addition to the known Adabas system file, the following files are part of the database

- Replication system file that contains descriptions of destinations, subscriptions and the global formats (GFB).
- Optional subscription log or SLOG file as the overflow area of the replication buffer.

Entire Net-Work or WCP on the mainframe

Entire Net-Work is also called WCP to differentiate between Net-Work and Network. WCP is acting as a broker and transmit Adabas direct calls including its buffers from a client to the remote Adabas target database. The buffers include the Adabas control block, record buffer, and format buffer. For a description see chapter 3 and Figure 12.

Network

The network with its components, such as lines or circuits, firewalls, routers and load balancing system, connects WCP on the mainframe with WCP on LUW.

Entire Net-Work or WCP on LUW

WCP on LUW ships Adabas calls from a client to a database through WCL

Entire Net-Work Client or WCL on LUW

An Entire Net-Work Client uses the Entire Net-Work 7 e-business message protocol to access Adabas databases. The client must be installed on any machine from which you wish to access Adabas databases. A Directory Server is needed to store management data for Entire Net-Work in the form of Universal Resource Locator (URL).

Target or destination database

The Adabas target database receives Adabas direct calls from the Replicator Engine through Entire Net-Work (WCP). Values of Adabas parameters and buffers should be set in the same way as for the source or subscription database.

2.4 From Adabas on the Mainframe to Non-Adabas Databases

The replication from an Adabas database on the mainframe to non-Adabas database on Linux, UNIX or Windows is used with the replicated database for off-the-shelf software or to replicate further with non-Adabas database replication software.

The following components are necessary to replicate:

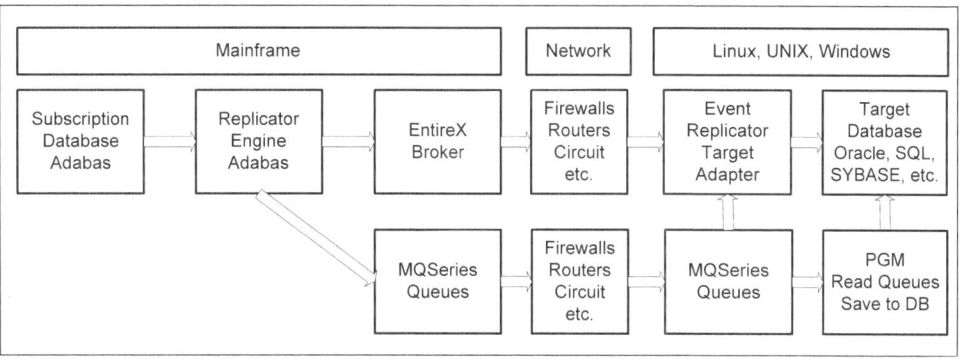

Figure 8: Replication from Adabas to non-Adabas Databases

Source or subscription database

Additional Adabas parameters must be defined and existing ones updated. For more information see chapter 3.

Replicator Engine or Reptor

This is a basic Adabas nucleus loading at start-up some additional replication modules. Adabas parameters must be set-up at least with the same values as the source or subscription database. For more information see chapter 3.

In addition to the known Adabas system file, the following files are part of the database

- Replication system file that contains descriptions of destinations, subscriptions and the global formats (GFB).
- Optional subscription log or SLOG file as the overflow area of the replication buffer.

EntireX Broker (wM EntireX) on the mainframe

EntireX is a message-oriented middleware with broker function.

WebSphere MQ (message queue) on the mainframe

MQ is a message-oriented middleware from IBM transferring data under the control of a queue manager from point A to point B.

One company replicates approximately 50 files from the mainframe over to MQ queues where back-end distributed programs drain the queues and populate to Sybase tables.

WebSphere MQ (with IBM WebSphere MQ Client Attachment Feature enabled) can also use the Event Replicator Target Adapter to replicate data to a relational database.

Event ReplicatorTarget Adapter on Linux, UNIX, or Windows (LUW)

It is necessary to communicate with EntireX Broker on the mainframe and replicate to the non-Adabas target database. The adapter transforms and applies replicated Adabas data to a relational database, such as DB2, MySQL Server, Sybase, or Teradata.

Target or destination database(s)

Any relational database, such as DB2, MySQL Server, Sybase, Teradata, and Oracle.

Program to empty the MQ queues

It needs a program to empty the MQ queues and write it to the target database if WebSphere MQ was only used as a message-oriented middleware (MOM).

3 Definitions and Parameters

3.1 Getting Started

It is necessary to get the following information before your start:

Source database ADARUN parameters, especially

- LBP, the Adabas buffer pool
- LFIOP, <25% of LBP, the Adabas I/O pool, regarding number of buffer flushes
- NAB, the formula in the manual is not correct, can cause NAB overflow
- LRPL, size and how to avoid overflow – there is no SLOG
- ASYTVS=YES, asynchronous Vol-Ser I/Os
- FMXIO= >1, parallel LFIOP I/Os
- REPLICATION=YES

Replicator Engine or Reptor ADARUN parameters, especially

- LBP, the Adabas buffer pool, at least the same as the source database
- LFIOP, the Adabas I/O pool, <10% of LBP, regarding number of buffer flushes
- NAB, the formula in the manual is not correct, can cause NAB
- LRPL, size and how to avoid overflow – there is no SLOG
- ASYTVS=YES, asynchronous Vol-Ser I/Os
- FMXIO= >1, parallel LFIOP I/Os
- REPLICATION=NO

Replicator Engine or Reptor SYSRPTR parameters, especially

- LOGINPUTTRANSACT=70, threshold of RPL buffer before using SLOG

Entire Net-Work (WCP) server ADARUN parameters (mainframe)

- PROG=NETWRK
- TARGETID= unique within the NET-WORK
- NAB= not lower than Reptor DB
- LU=250000, not lower
- NC= number of commands, for example 2000

Entire Net-work (WCP) client parameters (Windows)

Hardware for Adabas on Linux, UNIX, Windows

- Server, not a PC
- Disk arrays / storage area network (SAN), not the C-drive

Bandwidth of the line/circuit between the mainframe and Windows

- Depends of the number of bytes and commands to be sent to the target database
- Best should be a 100 Mbps duplex circuit. Tests with two 60/70 Mbps circuits using IPSec VPN tunnel were not very successful regarding the speed.

To determine the bandwidth of the circuit, the number of bytes passed through Entire Net-Work to the target must be known. The following Apas/Insight request RBLSUM is very helpful to calculate.

```
DBID 00039 REQ RBLSUM    DT 2010-08-26 TIME 13:49:07 TO 16:43:19 LINE    1 OF  24
   FIL          CMD               SUM       MEAN     MAX              SUM       MEAN      MAX
   NUM        COUNT               RBL        RBL     RBL              FBL        FBL      FBL
------ ----------  ------------------ ---------  ------  ------------------ ---------  ------
     0     80,095                   5       0.00       1                   0      0.00        0
     7      8,028          86,100,300  10,725.00   10725           8,373,204  1,043.00     1043
    11    357,788         715,933,788   2,001.00    2001         681,943,928  1,906.00     1906
    14     77,915          33,958,710     435.84    1247          17,444,475    223.89      565
    15     36,527          28,381,479     777.00     777          19,468,891    533.00      533
    20     89,335           8,933,500     100.00     100           4,645,420     52.00       52
    22    228,078         111,530,142     489.00     489          99,213,930    435.00      435
    24    353,108          68,149,844     193.00     193          43,079,176    122.00      122
    25        194             256,086   1,320.03    1524              45,212    233.05      253
    26     36,770         100,345,330   2,729.00    2729          64,273,960  1,748.00     1748
    27  3,351,570         981,290,269     292.79     391         269,795,179     80.50      251
    28        499              86,327     173.00     173              29,940     60.00       60
    29      4,939           7,161,550   1,450.00    1450             938,410    190.00      190
    30      7,595           2,035,460     268.00     268           1,982,295    261.00      261
    31    252,291         143,011,305     566.85    1075          90,377,244    358.23      636
    32     25,243           5,477,731     217.00     217           5,149,572    204.00      204
    33        528              64,668     122.48     255              38,402     72.73      126
    34      6,314           1,059,236     167.76     186             774,982    122.74      135
    35    710,645         152,694,509     214.87     944         167,611,060    235.86     1021
    37      9,082          10,135,512   1,116.00    1116           1,271,480    140.00      140
    38          3                 810     270.00     270                 663    221.00      221
    39      3,515             735,950     209.37     216             533,955    151.91      156
    44  2,444,411       2,001,972,609     819.00     819       1,747,753,865    715.00      715
```

Figure 9:   Determine Length of RBL and FBL

The following is an example of batch traffic by determining the number and type of commands using the performance monitor Apas/Insight from CA.

```
                          PCT    PCT       SUM                 SUM
            QTR      CMD       CMD     TOTAL   TOT      TOT                 TOT
  DATE  HR  HR     COUNT      COUNT     CMDS    IO       IO                  IO
------ -- ---  ---------- ------------ ----- ----- ------------  ----------------
100315 19 78     874,107  |======       11.4  11.2 |======              755,656
100315 19 79   1,488,111  |==========   19.4  18.9 |==========        1,278,291
100315 20 80   1,517,170  |==========   19.8  19.6 |==========        1,324,734
100315 20 81   1,581,223  |==========   20.6  20.5 |==========        1,386,234
100315 20 82   1,467,842  |==========   19.1  19.5 |==========        1,318,488
100315 20 83     740,750  |=====         9.6  10.3 |=====              697,749
100315 21 84      11,484  |              0.1   0.1 |                     9,958
```

Figure 10:   Determine Number of Commands

```
Update  -  "A1"  -  5,250,944
Delete  -  "E1"  -    107,254
Add     -  "N1"  -  8,207,106
Backout- "BT"   -        533
EndTran- "ET"   -  1,912,246
Total              13,565,304  (excluding ET & BT)
```

Figure 11:   Determine Type of Commands

Regarding the number of bytes to be replicated, the replication process will send the following data through the line. Keep in mind that only update commands will be replicated: no search, value, or ISN buffers are used.

The following formula shows that for file 44, at least a 17.3 Mbps line is needed.

```
CBL = Adabas control block length
RBL = Adabas record buffer length
FBL = Adabas format buffer length
BPB = bits per byte = 8
Number of commands per second to be replicated = 1,400

(12 bytes + CBL + RBL + FBL) * BPB

Max value per command for file 7 - only 8,028 commands):
(12 + 10725 + 1906) * 8 = 101,144 bits * 1,400 = 141.6 Mbps

Most commands counted for file 44:
(12 + 819 + 715) * 8 = 12,368 bits * 1,400 = 17.3 Mbps (need at least such bandwidth)
```

Figure 12:   Computation for Mbps Bandwidth

Source database in general

- How many gigabytes of data (ASSO and DATA)
- How many files to be replicated

Expected traffic

- 1,500 update commands per second are considered to be high
- Traffic from online and/or batch

Figure 13 shows the used software versions for tests. The target Adabas database was upgraded to V6.2. It also shows the path from .NET Web programs on Windows to access Adabas data on the mainframe using EntireX Broker and RPC Server.

If the replicated database can be used for read-only Web access then EntireX Broker on Windows would be sufficient.

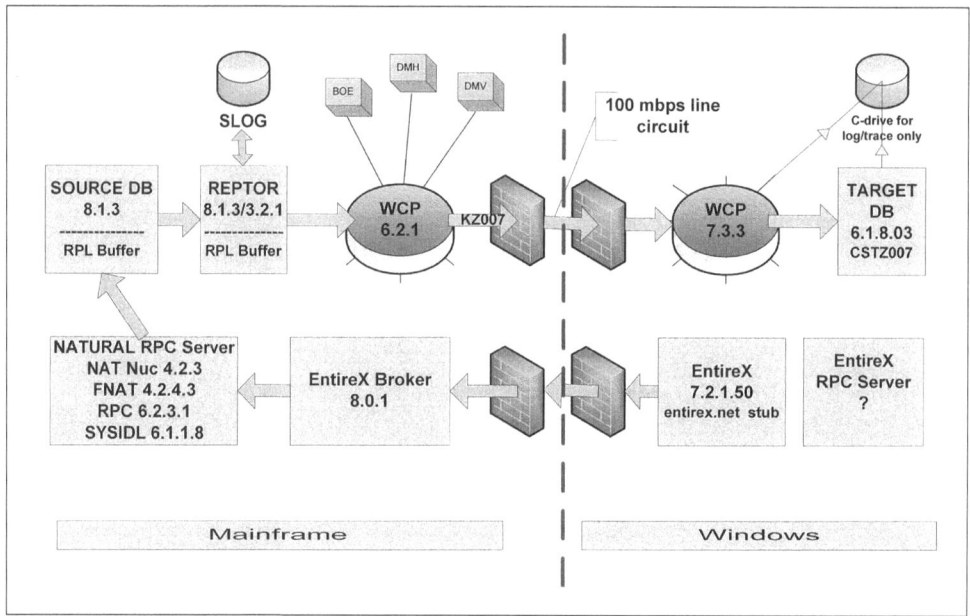

Figure 13:   Used Software Versions

3.2   Source or Subscription Database (V8.1.3)

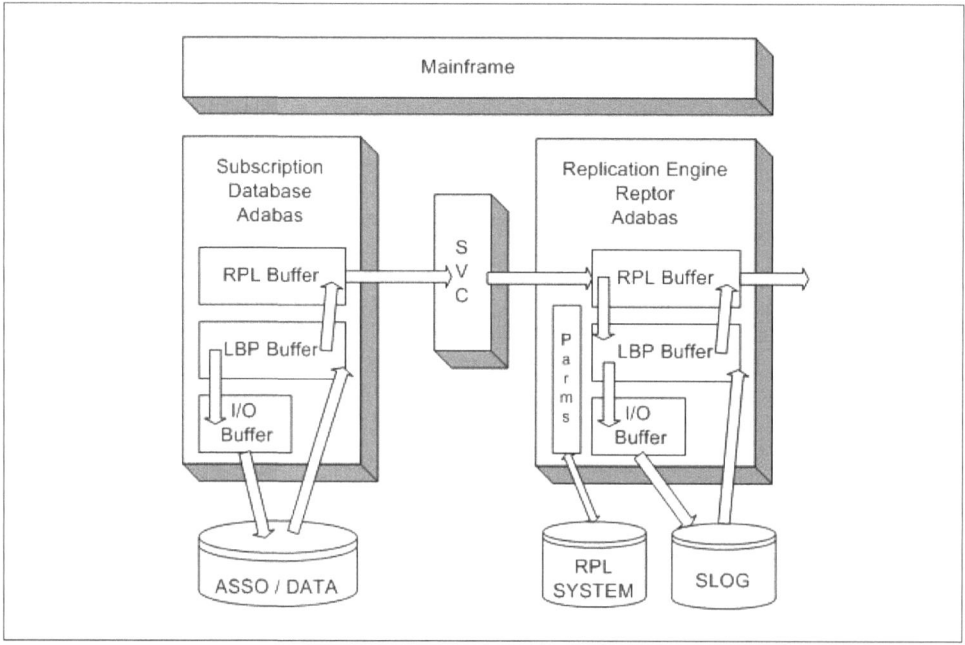

Figure 14:   Buffer Usage in Subscription Database

3.2.1   Workload Manager (WLM)

The subscription or source database must have the same priority as the replicator engine (Reptor).

Source SAG:

"If an Adabas nucleus gets generally CPU constrained, that is it approaches the processor capacity limit and if you are not yet ready to try Parallel Services then put this nucleus into SYSSTC or into a low service class of high importance. Adabas can ill afford to get preempted out of the processor.

If Adabas processes a substantial share of calls originating from batch during high online periods put Adabas into a higher service class of somewhat lower importance than the response time goals of the TP monitor. However this is not recommended, when the TP monitors concurrently executes transactions, which access other databases like DB2. A high CPU consumption in DB2 could then delay transactions doing Adabas calls! With not much batch activity during online periods Adabas and CICS could be in the same importance service class."

3.2.2   ADARUN Parameters

Besides the most important parameters for performance (LBP, LFIOP, NAB, ASYTVS and FMXIO), the following parameters must be defined in addition for the replication process:

Source database ADARUN parameters, especially

- ADARUN REPLICATION=YES
  This parameter loads at start time of the Adabas nucleus the replication module ADARPN.
- ADARUN LRPL=700M,
  The RPL buffer holds the compressed data to be replicated and should be defined larger than LBP and large enough to avoid an overflow because on the source database does not exist an overflow area (SLOG).
- RPLSORT=YES (default)
  Transaction data are sorted by a key consisting of the file number, ISN, and relative update number. All modifications for a given ISN in a file are consolidated before replication occurs. If you do not want to sort to occur, specify RPLSORT=NO.
- RPWARNINCREMENT=1-99 (10 default)
  Warn increment that indicates that the replication pool usage has exceeded the threshold set by the RPWARNPERCENT parameter.
- RPWARNINTERVAL=xxx (60 seconds default)
  Suppress warning messages after xxx seconds.

- RPWARNMESSAGELIMIT=xxx (5 default)

  The number of RPL pool usage warning messages that can be issued to the console before message suppression begins.

- RPWARNPERCENT=0-99 (0 default)

  The threshold for RPL pool usage at which warning messages should be sent.

Appendix, chapter 9.1 and 9.2 shows the ADARUN parameters of a source database used by a company with 57 subscriptions spread across 4 LPARs running on 8 separate Replication STCs.

3.2.3   ADADBS Replicate Files

Run also the ADADBS utility to turn on the files to be replicated and turn off the overhead of the before image log (DSBI).

ADADBS REPLICATION FILE=006,ON,TARGET=302,DSBI=OFF

ADADBS REPLICATION FILE=fnr,ON,TARGET=reptor-db,DSBI=OFF

ADADBS REPLICATION FILE=fnr,ON,TARGET=reptor-db,DSBI=OFF

etc.

The Adabas report displays the replication status of the files and how the before image of updates has been set. In the below example, DSBI was set to the default value ON: 'Collect before images of updates = Yes.' In later tests, it was set to OFF.

```
(snip)
*********************************
*                               *
* File      6 (ST-ADA-CALC-EDAT) *          2010-03-09  13:59:15
*                               *
*********************************
LOB file            No
Contain LOB fields No
RPLUPDATEONLY       No

(snip)

File is replicated:
  Replicator target ID          =    302
  Collect before images of updates = Yes
(snip)
```

Figure 15:   Replication Status in Adabas Report

It is very time consuming to manually check the report of the replication settings for example 200 files. I wrote a parse program in Natural, which displays these flags in a report. See also the chapter describing self-written monitor tools: 7.2.10.

3.3   Replicator Engine – Reptor (V8.1.3/V3.2.1)

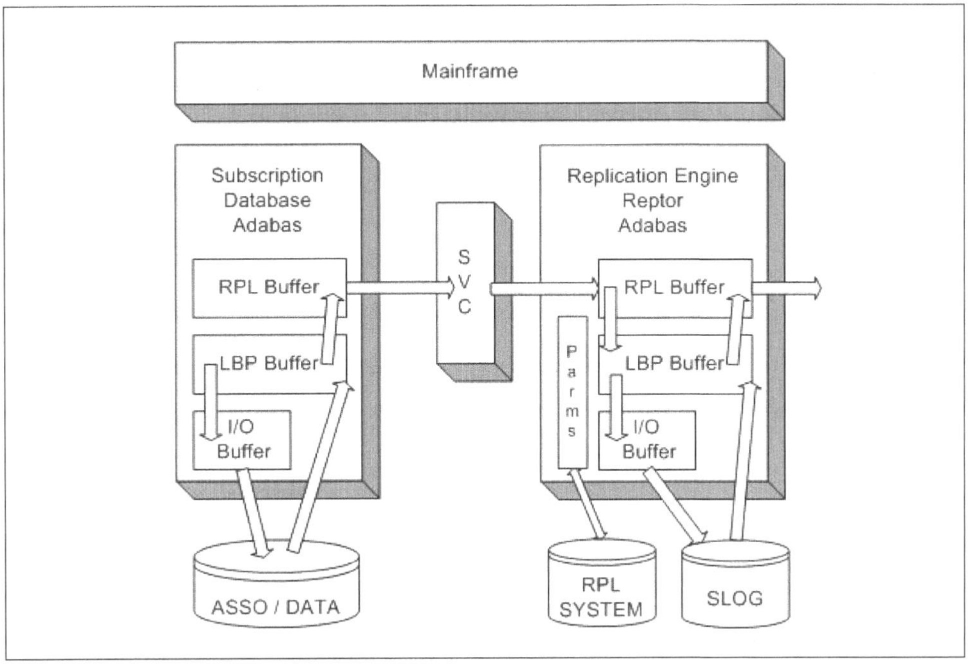

Figure 16:   Buffer Usage in Reptor

3.3.1   Workload Manager (WLM)

The source database must have the same priority as the replicator engine (Reptor).

Source SAG:

"If an Adabas nucleus gets generally CPU constrained, that is it approaches the processor capacity limit and if you are not yet ready to try Parallel Services then put this nucleus into SYSSTC or into a low service class of high importance. Adabas can ill afford to get preempted out of the processor.

If Adabas processes a substantial share of calls originating from Batch during high online periods put Adabas into a higher service class of somewhat lower importance than the response time goals of the TP monitor. However this is not recommended, when the TP monitors concurrently executes transactions, which access other databases like DB2. A high CPU consumption in DB2 could then delay transactions doing Adabas calls! With not much batch activity during online periods Adabas and CICS could be in the same importance service class."

3.3.2   SLOG File

The subscription log file (SLOG) is an Adabas file and is used as an overflow area
if the threshold setting of Reptor's RPL buffer (LRPL) is reached. The size should
be large enough to hold a couple of days not replicated updates (transactions) if
the destination is not available. Many companies reserve an entire 3390 pack for
the SLOG.

```
13:59:16              ***** A D A B A S  BASIC  SERVICES *****        2011-01-05
DBID 312                      - Display File Layout -                 PDRF042
****************
*  File 30      *    SLOG
****************

Records loaded ..... 912665      Date loaded ......... 2008-10-03 13:48:48
TOP ISN ............ 912661      Date of last update .. 2011-01-05 13:28:38
Max ISN expected ... 20000079    Max Compr Rec Lngth .. 5060
Minimum ISN ........ 1           Asso/Data Padding .... 1%/1%
Size of ISN ........ 4 Bytes     Highest Index Level .. 4
Number of Updates .. 1597738     RPLUPDATEONLY. No   Indx Comp ...... Yes
ISN Reusage ........ Yes         USERISN ...... No   PGMREFRESH ..... No
Space Reusage ...... Yes         MIXDSDEV ..... No   NOACEXTENSION .. No
ADAM File .......... No          Spanned rec .. No   MU/PE indices .. 1
Ciphered File ...... No          Replication .. No   Privileged Use . No
Coupled Files ...... None        Universal Encoding ... Yes
Blk per DS Extent .. 0
Blk per UI Extent .. 0
Blk per NI Extent .. 0           Multi Client File .... 0
Free space available for file extents: At least 134  Extents

     I Dev  LiI  Space allocated  I      From          To    I Unused
     I Type TyI  Blocks   / Cyls. I      RABN         RABN   I BLOCKS   / Cyls.
  ---I--------I-----------------I -------------------I------------------
     I        I                 I                        I
ASSOI 3390 ACI    23585       87 I   1221176 -   1244760 I      0         0
ASSOI 3390 UII   135000      500 I   1082447 -   1217446 I  134811       499
ASSOI 3390 NII  1080000     4000 I      2447 -   1082446 I 1065256      3945
     I        I                 I                        I
DATAI 3390 DSI  2250000    15000 I       551 -   2250550 I 1860489     12403
```

Figure 17:   SLOG File Shown in Adabas Report

Once transactions have been written to the SLOG system file, the Event Replicator Server processes them using a throttling mechanism so that only a limited
amount of RPL pool space is used at a time.

3.3.3   Replication System File

The Reptor's system file is an Adabas file and holds all definitions of subscriptions, destinations and global formats for each file to be replicated. This information can be unloaded and reloaded with the utility ADARPD that is located in the
Natural library SYSRPTR.

During the Reptor's start, all information from the system file will be read into its
internal memory.

Parameters can be changed with two different utilities:

- SYSRPTR – ADABAS EVENT REPLICATOR SUBSYSTEM changing permanently values in the system file.
- SYSAOS – changing temporarily values in the internal memory.

After each change in the system file, the refresh function must be executed to update Reptor's internal memory. See Figure 15 – Buffer Usage in Reptor.

3.3.4   ADARUN parameters

ADARUN parameters for the Replicator Engine or Reptor, especially

- LBP, the Adabas buffer pool, at least the same as the source database; with SLOG file, data will be written and read.
- LFIOP, the Adabas I/O pool, <10% of LBP, to avoid long waiting time during buffer flushes; see also ASYNTVS and FMXIO.
- NAB, the formula in the manual is not correct, can cause NAB overflow. The number of files in a transaction must be included into the formula: 410 x number files in one transaction.
- LRPL, define larger size as LBP, at least define the same size as on the source database. To use SLOG as an overflow area, a threshold should be set by using the parameter LOGINPUTTRANS.
- ASYTVS=YES, asynchronous Vol-Ser I/Os; data to be written and read from the SLOG file.
- FMXIO= >1, parallel LFIOP I/Os, determine the value after discussing with your system programmer (most organizations: 6-8).
- REPLICATION=NO, YES should only be used for the source database.
- LU=200000, unload and load Reptor parameters for more than 150 files need this value.
- NT= greater than or equal to 15.
- NC= greater than 10; the maximum number of elements in the command queue.
- NU= greater than the maximum number of users desired; each destination creates one UQE.
- RPLPARMS=FILE, the replication parameters are read from the Replicator system file.
- RPWARNINCREMENT=1-99 (10 default)
  Warn increment that indicates that the replication pool usage has exceeded the threshold set by the RPWARNPERCENT parameter.
- RPWARNINTERVAL=xxx (60 seconds default)
  Suppress warning messages after xxx seconds.

Example of Reptor ADARUN parameters:

```
ADARUN ASYTVS=YES
ADARUN FMXIO=8
ADARUN CT=180              COMMAND LIMIT TIME
ADARUN DBID=200           DATABASE ID NUMNBER FOR REPTOR
ADARUN DEVICE=3390
ADARUN LBP=150000000      LEN BUFR POOL
ADARUN LFP=300000         LEN INTERNAL FB POOL
ADARUN LDEUQP=100000      LEN OF UNIQUE DESCRIPTOR POOL 15K>100K 3/8/01
ADARUN LFIOP=13000000     LEN OF ASYNCH BUFR FLUSH POOL
ADARUN LI=12000           LEN ISN LIST TABLE
ADARUN LOCAL=NO           ALLOW ACCESS FROM OTHER NET-WORK NODES
ADARUN LOGGING=YES        LOG BASIC ADALOG RECORD + ACB
ADARUN LOGCB=YES
ADARUN LOGFB=YES
ADARUN LOGRB=NO
ADARUN LOGSB=YES
ADARUN LOGVB=YES
ADARUN LOGIB=NO
ADARUN LOGIO=NO
ADARUN LP=8000            # PROTECTION BLOCKS - WORK PART 1 - JD 1/18/1
ADARUN LWKP2=5000         WORK PART 2 JD 1/18/1
ADARUN LQ=20000           LENGTH OF SEQUENTIAL COMMAND TABLE
ADARUN LS=150000          SORT AREA    40>60>150 FOR RPULD 2/17/10
ADARUN LU=200000          INTERMEDIATE USER BUFFER
ADARUN LWP=500000         LENGTH OF WORK POOL
ADARUN MODE=MULTI         MULTI FOR V62
ADARUN NAB=420            # ATTACHED BUFFERS 30>50 NSN CLASS 07/02/96
ADARUN NC=120             NUMBER OF CQE'S
ADARUN NH=20000           NUMBER OF HQE'S ALL USERS
ADARUN NISNHQ=5000        # HQE'S EACH USER
ADARUN NONDES=NO          NON-DESCRIPTOR SEARCHES 03/03/03
ADARUN NQCID=50           NUMBER OF ACTIVE CID'S PER USER
ADARUN NT=15              NUMBER OF THREADS
ADARUN NU=4000            NUMBER OF USERS
ADARUN OPENRQ=NO          --->  DEFAULT = YES
ADARUN PLOGRQ=NO          --->  DEFAULT = YES
ADARUN PROGRAM=ADANUC
ADARUN QBLKSIZE=32760
ADARUN SVC=241
ADARUN TT=900             TRANS TIME LIMIT
ADARUN TLSCMD=1800        TIME LIMIT FOR SX COMMANDS
ADARUN TNAA=1800          NON-ACTIVITY TIME LIMIT
ADARUN TNAE=1800          NON-ACTIVITY TIME LIMIT
ADARUN UEX2=EXIT2R        HANDLE BOTH P AND C LOGS
ADARUN DUALCLD=3390,DUALCLS=15000    <--- 100 CYL
*
*   EVENT REPLICATOR PARMS
*
ADARUN REPLICATION=NO
ADARUN LRPL=700M
ADARUN RPLPARMS=FILE
ADARUN RPWARNINCREMENT=1
ADARUN RPWARNMESSAGELIMIT=5
ADARUN RPWARNPERCENT=0
```

Figure 18:   ADARUN Parameters of Reptor

- RPWARNMESSAGELIMIT=xxx (5 default)
  The number of RPL pool usage warning messages that can be issued to the console before message suppression begins.
- RPWARNPERCENT=0-99 (0 default)
  The threshold for RPL pool usage at which warning messages should be sent.
- If SLOG file is used, consider to check the values for ASYTVS, FMXIO, LBP, LDEUQP, LFIOP, LP, NH and NISNHQ.
- If data is sent through Entire Net-Work (WCP), the Entire Net-Work parameters LU, NAB and NC must also set as described for the Reptor.
- See documentation
  http://documentation.softwareag.com / Adabas / Distribution.

Appendix, chapter 8.2 shows the ADARUN parameters of a source database used by a company with 57 subscriptions spread across 4 LPARs running on 8 separate Replication STCs to balance the workload and MQ is LPAR-specific.

3.3.5   Event Replicator Initialization Parameters

Event Replicator initialization parameters can be specified in two ways:

- Defined in an OS dataset or as member of a PDS and read from the DDKARTE statement of the startup job
- Defined online using the Adabas Event Replicator Subsystem and read from the Replicator system file at startup

Each record in the DDKARTE statements must start with ADARPD and using the following parameters:

- DATABASE – ID and DBCONNECT
- DBID (default database ID)
- DESTINATION – DTYPE etc.
- GFORMAT (global format)
- INITIALSTATE
- LOGINPUTTRANSACTION defines the threshold of the RPL buffer before using the SLOG. Tests with values higher than 75% and lower than 50% can cause performance problems, for example Reptor is looping or source DB uses high CPU time.

Depends on the target database, filters and broker functions (EntireX, MQSeries, Entire Net-Work), other parameters must be supported.

- ETBBROKERID (default webMethods EntireX ID
- ETBBROKERNAME (EntireX Broker Stub Program)
- FBVALIDATION
- FILTER
- GLOBALS

- GOPEN
- GQFULLDELAY
- IQUEUE
- IRMSGITERVAL
- IRMSGLIMIT
- MAXOUTPUTSIZE (max output message size)
- MAXRECORDSIZE (max decompressed record length)
- MAXVARRECORDSIZE (max variable decompressed record length)
- MQQMGRNAME (default WebSphere MQ Queue Manager)
- NPADACALLS (number of parallel Adabas calls)
- RECORDPLOGINFO
- RESENDBUFFER
- RETRYCOUNT (number of retry attempts)
- RETRYINTERVAL (retry attempt interval)
- SUBTASKS (number of subtasks)
- SUBTASKWAIT (subtask wait time)
- TLOG (transaction log)
- VERIFYMODE
- See documentation
  http://documentation.softwareag.com / Adabas / Distribution.

In my experience for the Adabas destination, it is easier to define first the parameters for a couple of files by using the Adabas Event Replicator Subsystem (online) and download all parameters. This dataset can be updated and reloaded to
the system file or used as input for the DDKARTE statement. See chapter 3.4, Unload and load parameters. Use for all global formats (GFB) the online system and
create from Predict all fields needed before the unload. Unfortunately, there is no
batch function to create the GFB from Predict. It can be a 'life-time job' to type in
150 fields each for 200 and more files.

From the online 'Main Menu' of the Adabas Event Replicator Subsystem, the
functions destination definitions, subscription definitions and global format buffer definitions must be selected. Files for the initial-state definitions can also be
defined.

I recommend creating the components in the following order. Otherwise, you
will get the error message that the GFB is not defined, for example.

- Global Format Buffer (GFB)
- Destination Definitions
- Subscription Definitions
- Initial-State Definitions (if needed)

```
10:25:48        ***** A D A B A S  EVENT REPLICATOR SUBSYSTEM *****    2009-01-09
Vers 3.1.1                         Main Menu                           M-RP0010


                   Code    Function
                   ----    -------------------------------
                    A      Administrator Functions
                    D      Destination Definitions
                    F      Transaction Filter Definitions
                    G      Global Format Buffer Definitions
                    I      Initial-State Definitions
                    Q      Input Queue Definitions
                    R      Resend Buffer Definitions
                    S      Subscription Definitions
                    ?      Help
                    .      Exit
                   ----    -------------------------------


          Code ... _

Command ==>
Enter-PF1---PF2---PF3---PF4---PF5---PF6---PF7---PF8---PF9---PF10--PF11--PF12---
      Help        Exit
```

Figure 19:   Main Menu Adabas Replicator Subsystem

3.3.6   Define the Global Format Buffer

Before you start, you will need the Adabas view name from Predict to create the
global format buffer (GFB).

```
10:34:01        ***** A D A B A S  EVENT REPLICATOR SUBSYSTEM *****    2009-01-09
                          List of Global Format Buffers                M-RP1130

 Sel   Name        Sel    Name        Sel   Name        Sel   Name
------------       ------------       ------------       ------------
  _   G100589       _                  _                  _
  _   G100591       _                  _                  _
  _   G100592       _                  _                  _
  _   G100593       _                  _                  _
  _   G100594       _                  _                  _
  _   G100595       _                  _                  _
  _   G100596       _                  _                  _
  _   G100597       _                  _                  _
  _   G100598       _                  _                  _
  _   G100599       _                  _                  _
  _                 _                  _                  _
  _                 _                  _                  _
  _                 _                  _                  _


Command ==>
Enter-PF1---PF2---PF3---PF4---PF5---PF6---PF7---PF8---PF9---PF10--PF11--PF12---
      Help  Gen   Exit  Add   Repos      -     +                        Menu
```

Figure 20:   Display Global Format Buffers Using Replicator Subsystem

Add a new format by hitting the <PF4>-key. On the next screen type in the GFB
name, mark Predict parameters with 'S' and press the <Enter>-key.

Companies using the following standard naming convention to define the global format buffer:

GXXXYYY – for example G100590

- G = abbreviation for global format buffer
- XXX = subscription database id, for example 100
- YYY = subscription file number, for example 590

```
10:35:18      ***** A D A B A S  EVENT REPLICATOR SUBSYSTEM *****     2009-01-09
                              Global Format Buffer                    M-RP1120

GFB Name  ..  G100590   Predict Parameters .. s
_____
_____
_____
_____
_____
_____
_____
_____
_____
_____
_____
_____



Command ==>
Enter-PF1---PF2---PF3---PF4---PF5---PF6---PF7---PF8---PF9---PF10--PF11--PF12---
      Help            Exit  Mode  Save         -      +                  Menu
```

Figure 21:   Add Global Format Buffer Using Replicator Subsystem

Mark the selected file with 'S' and press the <PF5>-key to accept this selection.

```
10:41:18      ***** A D A B A S  EVENT REPLICATOR SUBSYSTEM *****     2009-01-09
FDIC=(100,201)                  List of Predict Files                 M-PICKFI


Sel  File ID                          Type  Master File
---  >                                ----  ------------------------------
 _      BS-PRINTER-PROPERTIES           U    BS-PRINTER-PROPERTIES-ADA
 _      BS-PRINTER-PROPERTIES-ADA       A
 _      BS-ST-REQ-LOG                   A
 _      BS-STANDARD-REQUEST             A
 S      DIETER-USER-REQUEST             A
 _      CIS-CNTL-PROCESS                U    CP-CONTROL-ADA
 _      CIS-RUN-CONTROL                 U    CP-RUN-ADA
 _      CIS-RUN-CONTROL-AUDIT           U    CP-RUN-LOG-ADA
 _      CN-REASON-CODE                  U    ST-REVIEW-ADA
 _      CN-REASON-CODE-LOG              U    ST-REVIEW-LOG-ADA
 _      CN-REVIEW-GROUP                 U    ST-REVIEW-ADA
 _      CN-REVIEW-GROUP-LOG             U    ST-REVIEW-LOG-ADA


Command ==>
Enter-PF1---PF2---PF3---PF4---PF5---PF6---PF7---PF8---PF9---PF10--PF11--PF12---
            Exit            Accpt        -      +                  Menu
```

Figure 22:   List and Select Predict Files Using Replicator Subsystem

The next screen shows the Predict Parameter.

```
10:46:29      ***** A D A B A S  EVENT REPLICATOR SUBSYSTEM *****     2009-01-09
FDIC=(100,201)                  Predict Parameters                   M-RP1121

GFB Name ......... G100590

File ID ......... * DIETER-USER-REQUEST_____
Target file ID .. * _____

---------- Generation Information ----------

User .............
Date .............
Time .............
FDIC ............. DBID ..        FNR ..

Adabas version ....
Occurrences used ..
Full format .......


Command ==>
Enter-PF1---PF2---PF3---PF4---PF5---PF6---PF7---PF8---PF9---PF10--PF11--PF12---
     Help         Exit         Exec  Sel   Unlnk                        Menu
```

Figure 23: Select a Predict Files Using Replicator Subsystem

Press the <PF5>-key to EXEC the generation of the GFB for this file number.

```
10:50:48      ***** A D A B A S  EVENT REPLICATOR SUBSYSTEM *****     2009-01-09
FDIC=(100,201)                  Predict Parameters                   M-RP1121

GFB Name ......... G100590

File ID ......... * ST-ADA-CALC-EDATE_____
Target file ID .. * _____

---------- Generation Information ----------
+---------------------------+
| Adabas Version ...* I7     |
| Occurrences used..* Y      |
| Full format ....... Y (Y/N) |
+---------------------------+   FNR ..

Adabas version ....
Occurrences used ..
Full format .......


Command ==>
```

Figure 24: Select a Predict File Using Replicator Subsystem

Accept everything and press the <ENTER>-key.

```
ARF00132: Format buffer generated successfully
10:52:37      ***** A D A B A S  EVENT REPLICATOR SUBSYSTEM *****      2009-01-09
                              Global Format Buffer                      M-RP1122

GFB Name .. G100590  Predict Parameters .. _ +                          1 of 9

Ty L Field ID                       F Cs Length    R K Format Buffer

   1 LOG-COUNTER                     P        15.0  _ _ AA,8,P
   1 ENTITY                          A        50.0  _ _ AB,50,A
   1 LAST-CHGD-DATE-TIME             A        15.0  _ _ AC,15,A
   1 LAST-CHGD-USER                  A         8.0  _ _ AD,8,A
   1 CALC-CODE                       A        10.0  _ _ AE,10,A
   1 EFF-DATE                        A         8.0  _ _ AF,8,A
   1 EFF-DATE-9C                     A         8.0  _ _ AG,8,A
   1 EXP-DATE                        A         8.0  _ _ AH,8,A
   1 DATA                            A       250.0  _ _ AI,250,A




Command ==>
Enter-PF1---PF2---PF3---PF4---PF5---PF6---PF7---PF8---PF9---PF10--PF11--PF12---
      Help          Exit  Mode  Save       -      +                    Menu
```

Figure 25:   Save the Selected Predict File Using Replicator Subsystem

After the format buffer was generated successfully (see ARF00132 message at the top), press the <PF5>-key to save. The message 'ARF00022: New GFB added' will be displayed. Press the <PF3>-key and the new GFB has been added to the list of global format buffers.

```
10:55:01      ***** A D A B A S  EVENT REPLICATOR SUBSYSTEM *****      2009-01-09
                            List of Global Format Buffers               M-RP1130

  Sel    Name          Sel    Name          Sel    Name          Sel    Name
  ------------         ------------         ------------         ------------
    _    G100589        _                     _                    _
    _    G100590        _                     _                    _
    _    G100591        _                     _                    _
    _    G100592        _                     _                    _
    _    G100593        _                     _                    _
    _    G100594        _                     _                    _
    _    G100595        _                     _                    _
    _    G100596        _                     _                    _
    _    G100597        _                     _                    _
    _    G100598        _                     _                    _
    _    G100599        _                     _                    _
    _                   _                     _                    _
    _                   _                     _                    _
    _                   _                     _                    _

Command ==>
Enter-PF1---PF2---PF3---PF4---PF5---PF6---PF7---PF8---PF9---PF10--PF11--PF12---
      Help  Gen   Exit  Add
```

Figure 26:   List Included New Predict File Using Replicator Subsystem

3.3.7 Define the Destinations

Destination definitions can be created for

- Adabas: data is replicated to one or more Adabas files
- webMethods EntireX or EntireX Broker: replicated data is written to an output queue via webMethods EntireX Broker
- WebSphere MQ: replicated data is written to an output queue via IBM WebSphere MQ
- Null: data replication is tested without actually sending the date to a destination
- File: replicated data is written do the CLOG, using TLOG URBLTDOD records

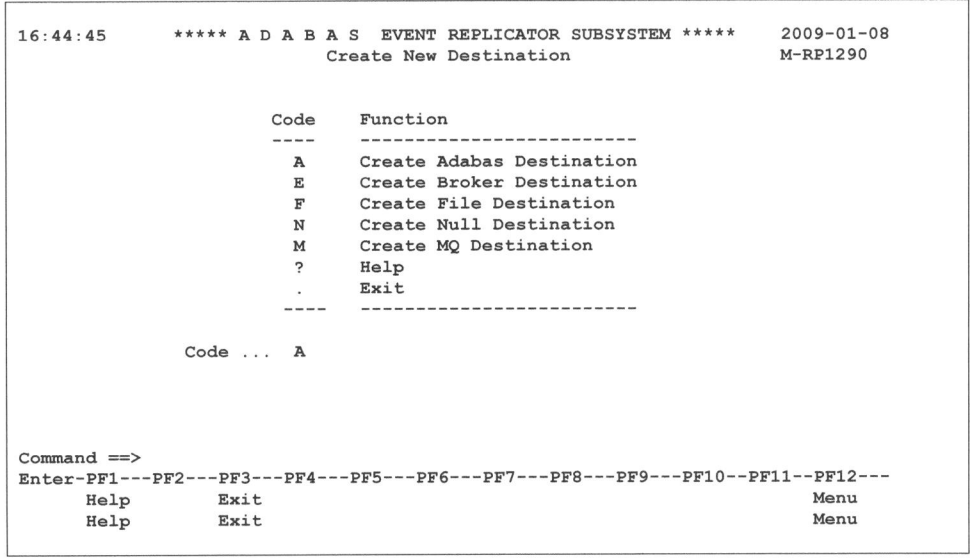

```
16:44:45        ***** A D A B A S  EVENT REPLICATOR SUBSYSTEM *****      2009-01-08
                              Create New Destination                     M-RP1290


                    Code     Function
                    ----     ------------------------
                     A       Create Adabas Destination
                     E       Create Broker Destination
                     F       Create File Destination
                     N       Create Null Destination
                     M       Create MQ Destination
                     ?       Help
                     .       Exit
                    ----     ------------------------

              Code ...  A




Command ==>
Enter-PF1---PF2---PF3---PF4---PF5---PF6---PF7---PF8---PF9---PF10--PF11--PF12---
      Help        Exit                                              Menu
      Help        Exit                                              Menu
```

Figure 27:   Create New Destination Using Replicator Subsystem

Companies using the following standard naming convention to define the destination

DXXXYYY – for example D200590

- D = abbreviation for destination
- XXX = target database id, for example 200
- YYY = target file number, for example 590

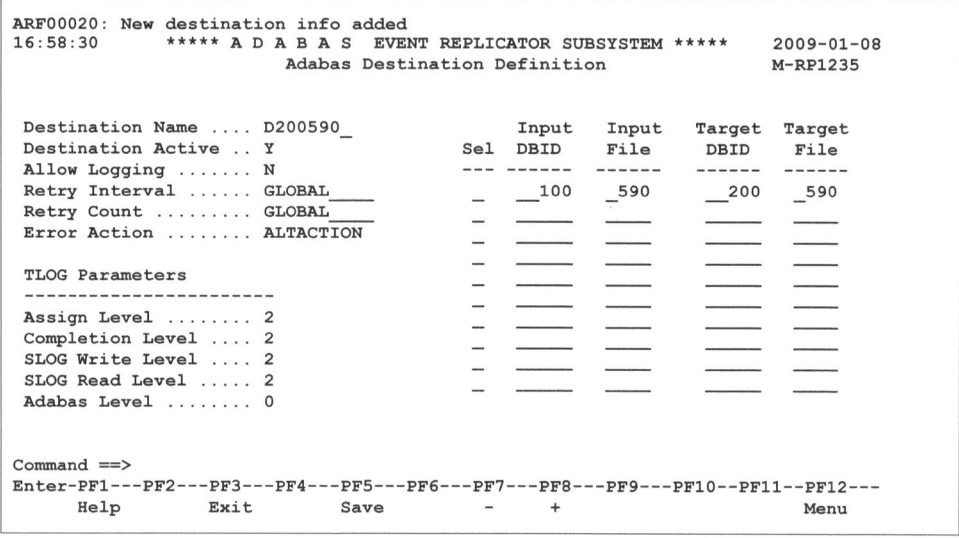

```
ARF00020: New destination info added
16:58:30      ***** A D A B A S  EVENT REPLICATOR SUBSYSTEM *****      2009-01-08
                        Adabas Destination Definition                  M-RP1235


  Destination Name .... D200590_           Input   Input   Target  Target
  Destination Active .. Y           Sel    DBID    File    DBID    File
  Allow Logging ....... N           ---    ------  ------  ------  ------
  Retry Interval ...... GLOBAL____    _     _100    _590    __200   _590
  Retry Count ......... GLOBAL____    _    _____  _____  _____  _____
  Error Action ........ ALTACTION    _    _____  _____  _____  _____
                                     _    _____  _____  _____  _____
  TLOG Parameters                    _    _____  _____  _____  _____
  ----------------------             _    _____  _____  _____  _____
  Assign Level ........ 2            _    _____  _____  _____  _____
  Completion Level .... 2            _    _____  _____  _____  _____
  SLOG Write Level .... 2            _    _____  _____  _____  _____
  SLOG Read Level ..... 2            _    _____  _____  _____  _____
  Adabas Level ........ 0            _    _____  _____  _____  _____


Command ==>
Enter-PF1---PF2---PF3---PF4---PF5---PF6---PF7---PF8---PF9---PF10--PF11--PF12---
      Help      Exit      Save        -       +                        Menu
```

Figure 28:   Define New Destination Using Replicator Subsystem

3.3.8   Define the Subscriptions

Companies using the following standard naming convention to define files of the subscription or source database:

SXXXYYY – for example S100590

- S = abbreviation for subscription or source
- XXX = subscription database id, for example 100
- YYY = subscription file number, for example 590

```
10:05:38      ***** A D A B A S  EVENT REPLICATOR SUBSYSTEM *****      2009-01-12
                        Subscription Definition                        M-RP1410

Description .................. DB100/590 to 200/590_____

Subscription Name ............ S100590_               TLOG Values
User Data Alpha Key ..........  ___0                  ---------------------
Architecture Key .............  ___2                  Input Level ......... 2
Subscription Version .........  __                    Filter Level ........ 0
User Data Wide Key ...........  ___0                  Output Level ........ 2
Resend Buffer Name ...........  _____              Filter Matched ...... 0
                                                      Filter Not Matched ... 0
Destination Name List ........  _                     Filter Ignored ....... 0
File-related Parameters ......  _
                                                      Incomplete Item(s)
Subscription Active ..........  Y                     ------------------
Deactivate if file deactivated  Y                     Destination
Increment Initial State Count   N                     File-Related Parms
                                                      Format Buffer
Command ==>
Enter-PF1---PF2---PF3---PF4---PF5---PF6---PF7---PF8---PF9---PF10--PF11--PF12---
      Help      Exit      Save                                         Menu
```

Figure 29:   Define New Subscription Using Replicator Subsystem

3.3.9   Define the Transaction Filter Definitions

From the SAG V3.3 Guide:

Event Replicator for Adabas 3.3 SP1 introduces two new parameters, SFFILTERGFBAI and SFFILTERGFBBI, that allow you to specify before and after-image format buffers for records selected based on fields defined in the filter definition for a subscription file. This resolves the conflict that occurs when the transaction filter definition for a subscription file (SFILE) definition references a field that is not included in the format buffer (or global format buffer).

These parameters can be used to improve the performance of Event Replicator processing. For example, if most records for a large format buffer are being rejected due to a transaction filter based on the contents of a small number of fields, it may help to specify the key fields in a filter format buffer so that, for most records, only the fields required to make acceptance/rejection decisions are decompressed instead of the entire buffer.

Filter Format Buffers

This information is also stored in the Replicator system file and can be maintained using the Adabas Event Replicator Subsystem.

A transaction filter definition specifies filter conditions for replication, based on the values of fields in the database records.

```
 16:49:53      ***** A D A B A S  EVENT REPLICATOR SUBSYSTEM *****      2010-05-28
                                Filter Condition                        M-RP1155

 Transaction Filter Name ..... MYFILT
            ------- Source ------             ------- Target ------
   Group Field   PE    MU  Image Condition Field    PE    MU  Image
   2nd line:  Begin Length                      Begin Length
   ----- ---------------------- --------- ----------------------
      ___   _   ____  ____   __        __       _   ____  ____  __     or value(s)
                                                       ____  ____
 Target Value 1    ..
 _____
 _____
 _____
 _____
 Target Value 2    ..
 _____
 _____
 _____
 _____
 Command ==>
 Enter-PF1---PF2---PF3---PF4---PF5---PF6---PF7---PF8---PF9---PF10--PF11--PF12---
       Help        Exit        Save        -     +                       Menu
```

Figure 30:   Define New Transaction Filters Using Replicator Subsystem

3.3.10 Define the Initial-State

Before the replication process can begin, the target database must be in synchronization with the source database. The initial-state process will replicate record by record using STORE with ISN (N2) and End-of-Transaction (ET) commands. It can also be initiated by a descriptor but using the ISN seems to be more common to eliminate duplicates.

Depending on the connection between the mainframe and the server, it can take 1–2 days to replicate 150,000,000 ISNs of a file over to the target, as shown by tests. I recommend using a different way of initial-state in this case. Decompress the files of the source or subscription database, transfer (FTP) it over to the open source server and reload it into the target database. For Adabas, it requires a compress before the reload. This process is faster and can be done in a few hours.

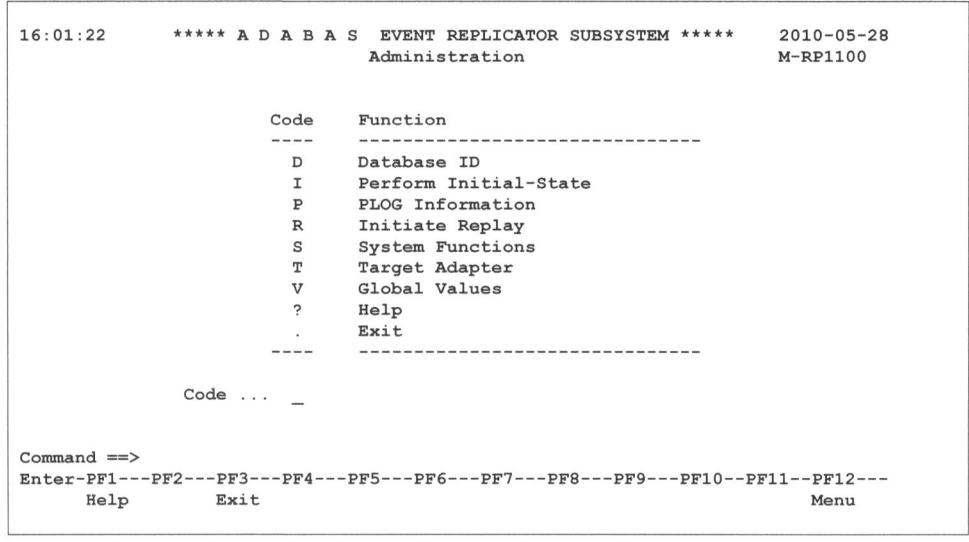

```
 16:01:22       ***** A D A B A S  EVENT REPLICATOR SUBSYSTEM *****       2010-05-28
                              Administration                             M-RP1100


                    Code     Function
                    ----     ------------------------------
                     D       Database ID
                     I       Perform Initial-State
                     P       PLOG Information
                     R       Initiate Replay
                     S       System Functions
                     T       Target Adapter
                     V       Global Values
                     ?       Help
                     .       Exit
                    ----     ------------------------------


              Code ...  _



 Command ==>
 Enter-PF1---PF2---PF3---PF4---PF5---PF6---PF7---PF8---PF9---PF10--PF11--PF12---
        Help       Exit                                                  Menu
```

Figure 31:   Perform Initial-State Using Event Replicator Subsystem

3.4   Unload and load parameters

It is very time consuming to define 200 subscriptions, destinations and global formats by using the online system SYSRPTR. It is preferable to define only a couple of files online and unload this file as a PDS member or a dataset. It is then easy to copy and modify the parameters for other files with ISPF tools.

183 unloaded files will end in more than 142,000 lines of parameters.

Destination parameters

```
LOGON SYSRPTR
ADARPD DESTINATION NAME='D300006'
ADARPD  DTYPE=ADABAS
ADARPD  DREPLICATEUTI=NO
ADARPD  DACTIVE=NO
ADARPD  DTLADABAS=0
ADARPD  DRETRYINTERVAL=GLOBAL
ADARPD  DRETRYCOUNT=GLOBAL
ADARPD  DLOG=YES               <= for SLOG
ADARPD  DTLASSIGN=2            <= 0
ADARPD  DTLCOMP=2             <= 0
ADARPD  DTLSLOGREAD=2         <= 0
ADARPD  DTLSLOGWRITE=2        <= 0
ADARPD  DAIFILE=6,DAIDBID=100,DATFILE=6,DATDBID=300
ADARPD  DAREPLICATEUTI=NO
ADARPD  DAERROR=ALTACTION
(snip)
```

Figure 32:   Destination Parameters

Subscription parameters

```
ADARPD SUBSCRIPTION
ADARPD SSTATUS=CURRENT
ADARPD NAME='S100006'
ADARPD  SDESC='DB100/006 TO 300/006'
ADARPD  SACODE=0
ADARPD  SACTIVE=YES
ADARPD  SDESTINATION='D300006'
ADARPD  SINCREMENTIS=NO
ADARPD  SIDESTINATION='D300006'
ADARPD  STLFILTER=0
ADARPD  STLINPUT=2      <= 0
ADARPD  STLOUTPUT=2     <= 0
ADARPD  SWCODE=0
ADARPD  STLMATCH=0
ADARPD  STLNOMATCH=0
ADARPD  STLIGNORE=0
ADARPD  SDEACTIVATE=YES
ADARPD  SFILE=6,SFDBID=100
ADARPD     SFREPLICATEINSERT=YES
ADARPD     SFREPLICATEUPDATE=YES
ADARPD     SFREPLICATEDELETE=YES
ADARPD     SFREPLICATENOTCHANGED=YES
ADARPD     SGFORMATBI='G100006'
ADARPD     SGFORMATAI='G100006'
(snip)
```

Figure 33:   Subscription Parameters

Filter Format Buffers

Software AG introduced two new subscription parameters with Event Replicator
for Adabas V3.3 allowing you to specify before and after-image format buffers for
records selected based on fields: SFFILTERGFBBI and SFFILTERGFBAI.

Global Formats (from Predict)

```
Global Format G100006
 FB='AA,8,P,AB,50,A,AC,15,A,AD,8,A,AE,10,A,AF'
    ',1,A,AG,10,A,AH,8,A,AI,8,A,AM1,5,P,AM2,5'
    ',P,AM3,5,P,AM4,5,P,AM5,5,P,AM6,5,P,AM7,5'
    ',P,AM8,5,P,AM9,5,P,AM10,5,P,AM11,5,P,AM1'
    '2,5,P,AM13,5,P,AM14,5,P,AM15,5,P,AM16,5,'
    'P,AM17,5,P,AM18,5,P,AM19,5,P,AM20,5,P,AM'
    '21,5,P,AN,2,U,AO,2,U,AP,8,A,AT,8,A,AQ,5,'
    'P,AR,5,P,AV,8,A,AX1,7,P,AX2,7,P,AX3,7,P,'
    'AX4,7,P,AX5,7,P,AX6,7,P,AX7,7,P,AX8,7,P,'
    'AX9,7,P,AX10,7,P,AX11,7,P,AX12,7,P,AX13,'
    '7,P,AX14,7,P,AX15,7,P,AX16,7,P,AX17,7,P,'
    'AX18,7,P,AX19,7,P,AX20,7,P,AX21,7,P,AX22'
    ',7,P,AX23,7,P,AX24,7,P,AX25,7,P,AX26,7,P'
    ',AX27,7,P,AX28,7,P,AX29,7,P,AX30,7,P,AX3'
    '1,7,P,AX32,7,P,AX33,7,P,AX34,7,P,AX35,7,'
    'P,AX36,7,P,AX37,7,P,AX38,7,P,AX39,7,P,AX'
    '40,7,P,AX41,7,P,AX42,7,P,AX43,7,P,AX44,7'
    ',P,AX45,7,P,AX46,7,P.'
```

Figure 34:   Global Formats (GFB) from Predict

It is recommended to back-up weekly all definitions from Reptor's system file. If needed you can reload the saved parameters or use it to build another Replicator Engine.

In example of Figure 35, file 10 is the system file in database 302 (Replicator Engine), which stores destinations, subscriptions and global formats. It unloads all destinations beginning with D191*, subscriptions beginning with S039*, initial-states beginning with I039* and global formats beginning with G039*.

An unloaded system file for 183 files contains more than 142,000 lines of parameters, for example for dataset DIETER.DBID302.DEFIN.TEXT.

```
//RPULD     EXEC NATBT,DEPT=ST,DB=TEST,SYSOUT=*,
// PRM='SYS=STRPTR,AUTO=ON,PROFILE=REPTORT'
//* PRM='MADIO=0,MAXCL=0,MT=0,IM=D,AUTO=ON,EDPSIZE=64'
//* PARM=('IM=D,ID='','',MADIO=0,MAXCL=0,MT=0,',
//*         'EDPSIZE=64,INTENS=1')
//DDPRINT   DD SYSOUT=*
//SYSUDUMP  DD SYSOUT=*
//DDCARD    DD *
ADARUN DB=00302,SVC=214,MODE=MULTI
//CMPRINT   DD SYSOUT=*
//CMWKF01   DD DSN=DIETER.DBID302.DEFIN.TEXT,
//            DCB=(RECFM=FB,LRECL=80),
//            DISP=(NEW,CATLG,DELETE),
//            UNIT=SYSDA,SPACE=(TRK,(25,25),RLSE)
//CMSYNIN  DD *
LOGON SYSRPTR
SYSPROF
RPULD ENTITY=DE,NAME=D191*,DBID=00302,FNR=010,RELATED=N
RPULD ENTITY=SB,NAME=S039*,DBID=00302,FNR=010,RELATED=N
RPULD ENTITY=IS,NAME=I039*,DBID=00302,FNR=010,RELATED=N
RPULD ENTITY=IS,NAME=G039*,DBID=00302,FNR=010,RELATED=N
//
```

Figure 35:   SYSRPTR Unload all Parameters in Batch

Example in Figure 36 loads all unloaded parameters (NAME=*) from dataset 'DIETER.DBID302.DEFIN.TEXT' into RPL system file 10 of Reptor database 302.

```
//STRPULDT JOB (ST345T,ST01,4000T),'RPULDTEST,DIETER',         *
//         MSGCLASS=G,NOTIFY=&SYSUID,TIME=1440
//*MAIN    HOLD=NO,CLASS=P10,LINES=9999
//*FORMAT PR,DDNAME=,DEST=VTAM.STTN8002
//*
//* LOAD DEFINITIONS FROM REPTOR SYSTEM FILE
//* TO WORK FILE 1
//*
//*DELETE EXEC PGM=IEFBR14
//*CMWKF01   DD DSN=DIETER.DBID302.DEFIN.TEXT,
//*             DCB=(RECFM=FB,LRECL=80),
//*             DISP=(MOD,DELETE,DELETE),
//*             UNIT=SYSDA,SPACE=(TRK,(25,25),RLSE)
//*
//RPULD    EXEC NATBT,DEPT=ST,DB=TEST,SYSOUT=*,
// PRM='SYS=STRPTR,AUTO=ON,PROFILE=REPTORT'
//* PRM='MADIO=0,MAXCL=0,MT=0,IM=D,AUTO=ON,EDPSIZE=64'
//* PARM=('IM=D,ID='','',MADIO=0,MAXCL=0,MT=0,',
//*        'EDPSIZE=64,INTENS=1')
//DDPRINT   DD SYSOUT=*
//SYSUDUMP  DD SYSOUT=*
//DDCARD    DD *
ADARUN DB=00302,SVC=214,MODE=MULTI
//CMPRINT   DD SYSOUT=*
//CMWKF01   DD DISP=SHR,DSN=DIETER.DBID302.DEFIN.TEXT
//CMSYNIN  DD *
LOGON SYSRPTR
SYSPROF
RPLOD NAME=*,DBID=302,FNR=10,REPLACE=Y
//
```

Figure 36:   SYSRPTR Load all Parameters in Batch

3.5   Entire Net-Work (WCP V6.2.1) – Mainframe

Entire Net-Work (WCP) is needed to replicate Adabas from the mainframe to Adabas on the mainframe, Windows, Linux or UNIX. It passes Adabas direct commands and its buffers to the target database.

3.5.1   ADARUN parameters

ADARUN parameters for the Entire Net-Work on the mainframe, especially

- CT (default 60), the maximal time in seconds for interregion communication. It should prevent a command queue element and attached buffer from being held for a long period of time for a user who has terminated abnormally. A value up to 180 (seconds) is observed at companies.
- LU, the intermediate user buffer needs a value more than 167,000. A value of 250,000 is necessary with high amount of replicated updates.
- NAB, the number of attached buffers should be set not lower than the value defined in the source database and Replicator Engine.

- NC, the maximum number of command queue elements (CQE). Each call from the Adabas nucleus is assigned a command queue element. In one installation, 1,421 update commands per second were observed and the value was set to 2000.
- SVC, the supervisor call (or router) must correspond to the number used for the Adabas SVC installation.
- TARGETID, the unique Entire Net-Work target ID of a node.
- See documentation
  http://documentation.softwareag.com / Adabas / WCP62 ....

Read by DDCARD DD-statement:

```
The following parameters are in use for this run :

*
*   ADARUN PARMS FOR ADANETXX (ADABAS VERSION 8.1.3)
*
ADARUN PROG=NETWRK
ADARUN TARGETID=7242           /* MUST BE UNIQUE WITHIN NET-WORK   */
*                              /* SHOULD BE 255 < TARGETID < 65535 */
ADARUN SVC=242                 /* SUPPLY ADABAS SVC NUMBER         */
ADARUN NAB=900
ADARUN LU=250000               /* INCR. FROM 65535 FOR REPLICATOR  */
ADARUN NC=2000
ADARUN FORCE=N
(snip)
```

Figure 37:   ADARUN Parameters (DDCARD) for Entire Net-Work (WCP) on Mainframe

3.5.2   Parameter Statements

The Entire Net-Work parameter statements describe the Entire Net-Work environment and the network connection for this node.

- NODE, defines the node's name and operating system
- DRIVER, defines the line driver type, as VTAM, CTCA, TCPI, TCPX, etc.
- LINK, defines the link to another node
- TRANSLAT, heterogeneous platform considerations
- See documentation:
  http://documentation.softwareag.com / Adabas / WCP621mfr/install ....

Read by DDKARTE DD-statement:

```
NODE ONE BUFFERS=(256K,256K,2M)

DRIVER        TCPI API=OES,              -
                    . . . .
LINK SERV008  TCPI ACQUIRE=N,            -
                   INETADDR=nn1.nn2.nn3.n4,-
                   RESTART=(60,5),       -
                   SERVERID=17102,       -
                   WEIGHT=10

TRANSLAT DEFINE ID=(sourceDBID,0),TOASCII=NETUE2A,TOEBCDIC=NETUA2E
```

Figure 38: Parameter Statements (DDKARTE) for Entire Net-Work (WCP) on Mainframe

3.6 Entire Net-Work (WCP V7.3.3) – LUW

Entire Net-Work (WCP) on the open system is necessary to access Adabas on Linux, UNIX or Windows (LUW).

3.6.1 Parameters

- Don't activate the trace. It is an overhead (I/Os) and can slow down the replication process.
- WCP is located on a Win2008 server SERV008. Tests with Win2003 server went very well but this version is no longer supported by Microsoft. Win2008 server experienced some authority problems and all Software AG products cannot be located in one folder (SAG folder).
- Communication parameters see WCP on the mainframe.
- Apply WCP733X003 – WCPv733 Hotfix #3 for Windows, Linux and UNIX to avoid RSP 153 on the Adabas target database.
  Hotfix should be included in WCPv7.3.4

3.6.2 Service.config

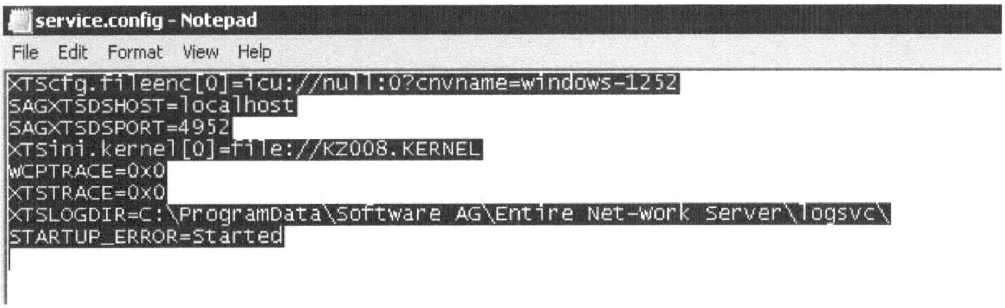

Figure 39: service.config Entire Net-Work (WCP) on Open System

3.6.3   KZ008.KERNEL

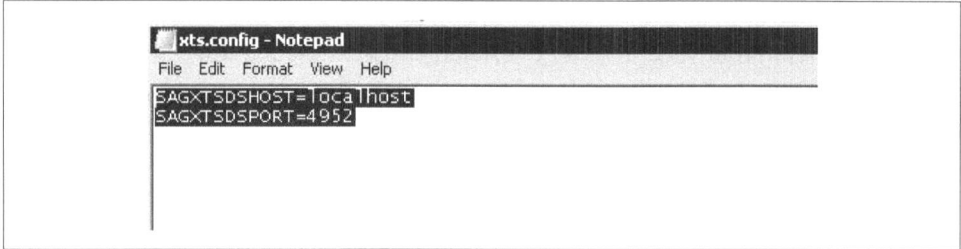

```
KZ008.KERNEL - Notepad
File  Edit  Format  View  Help
xTScfg.fileenc[0]=icu://null:0?cnvname=windows-1252
SAGXTSDSHOST=localhost
SAGXTSDSPORT=4952
NET-WORK=WCP
SERVER_NAME=CSTZ008
xTSlisten.NETWORK73_SMH_KZ008[0]=TCPIP://localhost:0
xTSlisten.NETWORK_SRV_KZ008[0]=TCPIP://localhost:0
xTSlisten.NETWORK_CLN_KZ008[0]=TCPIP://localhost:0?UEY=YES
xTSlisten.NETWORK_RDA_KZ008[0]=RDA://localhost:7869
xTSconnect.NETWORK_KZ008[0]=RDA://134.187.32.5:17102?NODENAME=ADAN5S&RECONNECT=YES&RETRY=3&MANUAL=NO
xTSconnect.NETWORK_KZ008[1]=RDA://134.187.71.1:17103?NODENAME=ADAN7S&MANUAL=YES&RECONNECT=YES&RETRY=3
ACCEPTED_DBIDS=251,134,39,34
RELAY_TRAFFIC=YES
NODEID=1800
WCPTRACE=0x0
XTSTRACE=0
LNKTRACE=0
AUTOSTART=YES
AUTOSTOP=YES
XTSLOGDIR=C:\ProgramData\Software AG\Entire Net-work Server\KZ008\
STARTUP_ERROR=Started
```

Figure 40:   KZ008.KERNEL Entire Net-Work (WCP) on Open System

3.6.4   Xts.config

```
xts.config - Notepad
File  Edit  Format  View  Help
SAGXTSDSHOST=localhost
SAGXTSDSPORT=4952
```

Figure 41:   xts.config Entire Net-Work (WCP) on Open System

3.7   Entire Net-Work (WCL V1.3.1) Client

Entire Net-Work Client is necessary to access Adabas databases. One client per machine is sufficient.

3.7.1   Windows Service

- This is the application stub on Windows client.
- Located on a Win2008 server SERV008.
- Perform the system administration using the System Management Hub (SMH).

- Entire Net-Work uses information stored in a Directory Server to send and receive messages from the client to the database and back. It is critical to the functions of Entire Net-Work V7.
- Software AG also recommends setting ADABAS_TIMEOUT on the client side (WCL) to the same value as the transaction time (TT) on the remote database to avoid RSP 153.

3.7.2 UNIX Daemon

- This is the application stub on UNIX daemon.
- Perform the system administration using the System Management Hub (SMH).
- Entire Net-Work uses information stored in a Directory Server to send and receive messages from the client to the database and back. It is critical to the functions of Entire Net-Work V7.

3.7.3 Xts.config

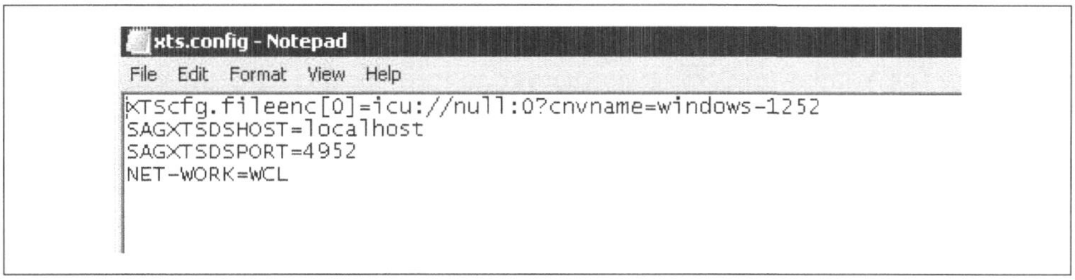

Figure 42: xts.config Entire Net-Work Client (WCL) on Open System

3.7.4 Service.config

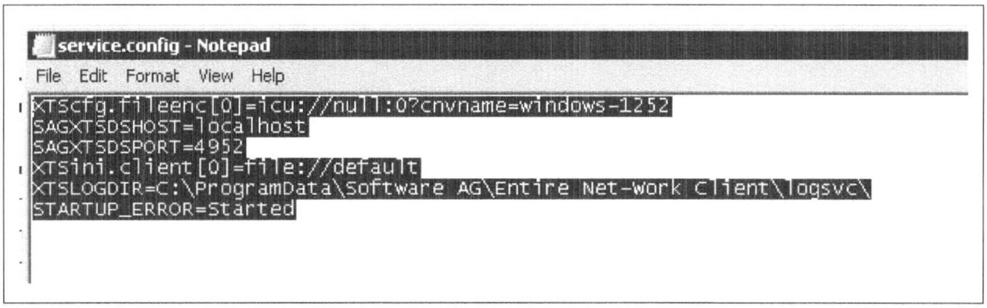

Figure 43: service.config Entire Net-Work Client (WCL) on Open System

3.7.5   Directory Server – xtsurl.cfg

```
xtsurl.cfg - Notepad
File  Edit  Format  View  Help
XTScfg.fileenc[0]=icu://null:0?cnvname=windows-1252
XTSaccess.NETWORK73_SMH_CSTZ008[0]=TCPIP://CSTZ008:49156?WCPSERVICE=ON
XTSaccess.NETWORK73_SMH_KZ008[0]=TCPIP://CSTZ008:49157?WCPKERNEL=ON
XTSaccess.NETWORK_KZ008[0]=TCPIP://CSTZ008:49158?WCPKERNEL=ON
XTSaccess.251[0]=TCPIP://CSTZ008:49159?DBID=LOCAL&KERNEL=KZ008
XTSaccess.NETWORK73_SMH_CSTZ008[1]=TCPIP://CSTZ008:49160?WCLSERVICE=ON
XTSaccess.134[0]=TCPIP://CSTZ008:49159?KERNEL=KZ008
XTSaccess.39[0]=TCPIP://CSTZ008:49159?KERNEL=KZ008
XTSaccess.34[0]=TCPIP://CSTZ008:49159?KERNEL=KZ008
```

Figure 44:   xtsurl.cfg Directory Server Entire Net-Work Client (WCL) on Open System

3.8   Adabas on Windows (V6.2.1.1)

3.8.1   General

- Choose for Adabas on Windows a server and do not use a PC. At least from an installation point of view, Adabas on Win2008 server acts totally different compared with the Win2003 server, for example the ADADIR folder. It is very tricky to define large container files in one contiguous space.

  Database components ASSO, DATA, WORK, TEMP and SORT should be located on disk arrays (raid-5) in the SAN box. A controller should support at least two logical channels. One for the D-drive (ASSO, WORK) and the E-drive (DATA, SORT, TEMP).

- Command log should be activated to observe the speed and to detect response codes. Don't use the C-drive for the command log.

3.8.2   Parameters

Among several Adabas parameters, the following ones are very important

- LBP
  The higher the value for the buffer pool size the better. Values with 400M (419,301,376) were always used to 99%. In contrast to Adabas on the mainframe, Adabas on Windows displays buffer pool statistics.

- WRITE_LIMIT
  This parameter determines the frequency of buffer flushes. Adabas on Windows does not have an I/O buffer for asynchronous I/Os. The buffer flush

therefore should not take too long time. Tests showed that a value of 25% caused a long waiting time for the Reptor to send the next transaction. A value of 5% was more efficient. Observed on the Reptor, a buffer flush on the target database brought the replication process for 23 seconds to a halt and then continued replicating for 37 seconds.

- BFIO=0
  This parameter sets the limit of parallel buffer flush I/Os. Zero (0) means no limit. Tests with different values did not show improvements.

```
                        ADANUC Version 6.2.1.01
           Database 251      High Water Marks       on 12-JAN-2011 20:29:09

Area/Entry                  Size     In Use  High Water      %       Date/Time
----------                  ----     ------  ----------      -       ---------
User Queue                   100          2           2      2 12-JAN-2011 13:43:29
Command Queue                  -          1           3      - 12-JAN-2011 17:26:09
Hold Queue                     -         36          58      - 12-JAN-2011 13:33:39
Client Queue                  50          6           6     12 12-JAN-2011 13:33:39
HQ User Limit             90,000          -          58      0 12-JAN-2011 13:33:39
Threads                       20          2           3     15 12-JAN-2011 17:21:49
Workpool               3,145,728          0     786,448     25 12-JAN-2011 13:32:27
  ISN Sort               393,216          -           0      0
  Complex Search         393,216          -           0      0
Attached Buffer       16,777,216     23,552      31,744      0 12-JAN-2011 16:19:55
ATBX        (MB)              20          0           0      0
Buffer Pool          419,430,400 419,301,376 419,333,120    99 12-JAN-2011 13:32:27
Protection Area          332,790
  Active Area             99,837          -           7      0 12-JAN-2011 16:38:09
Group Commit                  50          1           1      2 12-JAN-2011 13:33:39
Transaction Time             900          -          40      4 12-JAN-2011 15:59:49
```

Figure 45: Adabas Windows Parameters

```
                        ADANUC Version 6.2.1.01
           Database 251    Buffer Pool Statistics    on 12-JAN-2011 20:29:39


Buffer Pool Size    :    419,430,400

Pool Allocation                      RABNs present
---------------                      -------------
Current     ( 99%) :    419,301,376  ASSO              :         67,480
Highwater   ( 99%) :    419,333,120  DATA              :          2,556
Internal    ( 4%) :     19,030,016   WORK              :              0
Workpool    ( 0%) :      2,451,456   NUCTMP            :              0
                                     NUCSRT            :              0

I/O Statistics                       Buffer Flushes
--------------                       --------------
Logical Reads    :     54,038,642    Total             :            480
Physical Reads   :        337,871    To Free Space     :              0
Pool Hit Rate    :          99.4%

                                     Write Limit  ( 5%):     20,971,500
Physical Writes  :      1,805,917    Modified     ( 0%):        665,600
```

Figure 46: Adabas Windows Buffer Pool Statistics

3.9   EntireX Broker (V8.0.1)

webMethods EntireX Broker is needed replicating Adabas data from the mainframe to non-Adabas data on Linux, UNIX and Windows (LUW).

The Event Replicator Target Adapter is also necessary on LUW to communicate with the EntireX Broker. Depends on the target database, different target adapters must be used. Figure 46 shows the target adapter for SQL databases.

EntireX Broker is also used to access Adabas data located on the mainframe with a program located on Windows, for example .NET. On the mainframe site is also a Natural RPC server necessary. But this is not necessary for the replication process. Please see a parameter example of EntireX Broker V8.0.1 in chapter 8.9, EntireX V8.0.1 Parameters. See graphic for RPC process Figure 12.

3.9.1   EntireX Broker (V7.3.4)

```
*************************************************************************
*                                                                     *
*                   EntireX Broker Attribute File v7.3                 *
*                                                                     *
*************************************************************************
*************************************************************************
*MODULE: ETBAMHZ                                                       *
*SOURCE LOCATION: HW.ENTIRE.V734.ATTRB.LOCSRCE.HWDC(ETBAMHZ)           *
*FUNCTION:                                                             *
*    ENTIRE BROKER default attributes                                 *
*************************************************************************
* Broker specific Attributes / Definition of global resources         *
*---------------------------------------------------------------------*

************** v7.3: Global parameters ******************************

DEFAULTS = BROKER
  BROKER-ID              = EXB113

  ACCOUNTING            = 245      * turn on SMF records type 245
  AUTOLOGON             = NO       * ARF recommended
  CLIENT-NONACT         =  15M
  CONV-DEFAULT          = 2000     * CONVERSATIONs per SERVICE
  LONG-BUFFER-DEFAULT   =  500     * LONG BUFFERs per SERVICE - was 300
  NUM-CLIENT            =  400     *
  NUM-CONVERSATION      = 40000    * up from 20K 8/12/09        jac
  NUM-LONG-BUFFER       = 30000    *raise from 15000 04/10/03 db
  NUM-SERVER            =  250     *
  NUM-SERVICE           =  100
  NUM-SHORT-BUFFER      = 40000    * raised from 20000 - db 04/10/03
  NUM-WORKER            =   10     * Dave Hupp recommended 10
  SECURITY              = NO       * No security with ARF
  SERVICE-UPDATES       = YES      * reread ATTRIBUTE file ?
  SHORT-BUFFER-DEFAULT  = 1000     * SHORT BUFFERs per SERVICE
  TRACE-LEVEL           =    0     * trace off if zero but dynamic
  NUM-COMBUF            =  100
  NUM-WQE               =  200
*
  MAX-UOWS              = 50000    * rrf 07/10/07 to match ARF service
  UOW-MSGS              = 500  * alias of MAX-MESSAGES-IN-UOW
  MAX-MSG               = 1000000  *
  DEFERRED              = YES
  STORE                 = BROKER   *
```

```
    PSTORE-TYPE           = ADABAS
    PSTORE                = HOT      * Cold to clear Pstore/Hot to keep
    UWSTATP               = 0        * 0 removes UOW status information ARF
    UWTIME                = 7D       * raised from 10 min.
 *
 *-------------------------------------------------------------------
 * ADABAS Pstore
 *-------------------------------------------------------------------
 DEFAULTS              = ADABAS
    BLKSIZE               = 4096
    DBID                  = 313      * MHO
    FNR                   = 07
    FORCE-COLD            = N        * 'Y' clears the Pstore!
    MAXSCAN               = 20000    * bump up from default 1k 6/11/09 rrf
    OPENRQ                = N
    SVC                   = 214
    TRACE-LEVEL           = 0
 *-------------------------------------------------------------------*
 *
 * High Conv Non-activity Limits for Service Control Manager
 *
    TRBUFNUM = 3
    ABEND-LOOP-DETECTION = YES
    ABEND-MEMORY-DUMP = NO
    NUM-SERVICE-EXTENSION = AUTO
    NUM-SUBSCRIBER-TOTAL = AUTO
    NUM-TOPIC-EXTENSION = AUTO
    NUM-TOPIC-TOTAL = AUTO
    PRIVATE-IPC = NO
    PSTORE-VERSION = 2
    TRANSPORT = NET-TCP

************* v7.3: DIV parameters *********************************

 * DEFAULTS = DIV
************* v7.3: NET parameters *********************************

 DEFAULTS = NET
    ADASVC = 214
    FORCE=NO
    IUBL = 65535
    LOCAL = NO
    NABS = 383
    NCQE = 124
    NODE = 113
    TIME = 90
    NUM-CCOM = 3

************* v7.3: SSL parameters *********************************

 DEFAULTS = SSL
 * PORT = <port_no>
 * HOST = <host_name>
 * KEY-LABEL = <key_label>
 * TRUST-STORE = <trust_store>
 * RESTART = YES|no
 * RETRY-LIMIT = UNLIM|n
 * RETRY-TIME = 10S
 * REUSE-ADDRESS = yes|NO
 * VERIFY-CLIENT = yes|NO

************* v7.3: TCP parameters *********************************

 DEFAULTS = TCP
    HOST = hwdcs1.cahwnet.gov
    PORT = 50513
    STACK-NAME = HWTCP
    RESTART = YES
    RETRY-LIMIT = 20
    RETRY-TIME = 3
    CONNECTION-NONACT = 1H
    REUSE-ADDRESS = YES
```

```
************** v7.3: Security parameters *****************************

DEFAULTS = SECURITY
************** v7.3: Service definitions *****************************

DEFAULTS = SERVICE
  CONV-LIMIT         = UNLIM
  CONV-NONACT        = 5M        * RRF 07/20/05 Changed from 24H
  LONG-BUFFER-LIMIT  = UNLIM
  MAX-UOWS           = 100
  NOTIFY-EOC         = YES       * ensure EOC notification
  SERVER-NONACT      = 30M       * RRF 07/20/05 changed from 200H
  SHORT-BUFFER-LIMIT = UNLIM
  TRANSLATION        = SAGTCHA   * CNM 05/09/00 don't require translation
  UOW-MSGS           = 300
*
* removed CBC server entries 07/20/05
*
  CLASS = MHZ   , SERVER = MHZSVRSC, SERVICE = DATAVAIL
  CLASS = MHZ   , SERVER = MHZSVRSC, SERVICE = DATAWAIT
  CLASS = MHZ   , SERVER = MHZSVRSC, SERVICE = MANAGER
  CLASS = MHZ   , SERVER = MHZSVRSC, SERVICE = PING
*
*-----------------------------------------------------------------------*
*  Replicator Service Definitions                                       *
*-----------------------------------------------------------------------*
*

************** v7.3: Service definitions *****************************

DEFAULTS = SERVICE
  CONV-LIMIT         = UNLIM
  CONV-NONACT        = 120H      * bump up per Victor 6/12/09
  LONG-BUFFER-LIMIT  = UNLIM
  MAX-UOWS           = 50000   * Alex - match broker max!
  NOTIFY-EOC         = YES       * ensure EOC notification
  SERVER-NONACT      = 60M       * Alex
  SHORT-BUFFER-LIMIT = UNLIM
  TRANSLATION        = NO
  DEFERRED           = YES
  UOW-MSGS           = 300
*
  CLASS = DMH , SERVER = REPLICATION , SERVICE = ART
  CLASS = DMH , SERVER = REPLICATION , SERVICE = INIT
*
*-----------------------------------------------------------------------*
* Shorter Conv Non-activity timeouts and MHZ Translation Routine
*

************** v7.3: Service definitions *****************************

DEFAULTS = SERVICE
  CONV-LIMIT         = UNLIM
  CONV-NONACT        = 4M
  LONG-BUFFER-LIMIT  = UNLIM
  MAX-UOWS           = 100
  NOTIFY-EOC         = YES       * ensure EOC notification
  SERVER-NONACT      = 200H
  SHORT-BUFFER-LIMIT = UNLIM
  TRANSLATION        = MHZCTR    * MHZ Translation Routine
  UOW-MSGS           = 300
*
  CLASS = MHZ   , SERVER = MHZSVRTD, SERVICE = TMPLDNL
  CLASS = MHZ   , SERVER = MHZSVRTD, SERVICE = PING
*
  CLASS = MHZ   , SERVER = MHZSVRTU, SERVICE = TMPLUPL
  CLASS = MHZ   , SERVER = MHZSVRTD, SERVICE = PING
*
*
```

```
*-------------------------------------------------------------------*
* Attach Servicer Attributes
*-------------------------------------------------------------------*
*
*-------------------------------------------------------------------*
* Service specific Attributes / tutorial examples:                 *
*-------------------------------------------------------------------*
*

************** v7.3: Service definitions ****************************

DEFAULTS = SERVICE
  CONV-LIMIT          = UNLIM
  CONV-NONACT         = 4M
  LONG-BUFFER-LIMIT   = UNLIM
  NOTIFY-EOC          = YES
  SERVER-NONACT       = 5M
  SHORT-BUFFER-LIMIT  = UNLIM
  TRANSLATION         = SAGTCHA

  CLASS = ACLASS, SERVER = ASERVER, SERVICE = ASERVICE
  CLASS = BCLASS, SERVER = BSERVER, SERVICE = BSERVICE
  CLASS = CCLASS, SERVER = CSERVER, SERVICE = CSERVICE
*
*-------------------------------------------------------------------*
* Service specific Attributes / Tutorial Non-Conversational Services *
*-------------------------------------------------------------------*
*

************** v7.3: Service definitions ****************************

DEFAULTS = SERVICE
  CONV-NONACT         = 1M
  SERVER-NONACT       = 5M
  TRANSLATION         = SAGTCHA

  CLASS=ETB,SERVER=Tutorial,SERVICE=NcDemoMultiSrv1
  CLASS=ETB,SERVER=Tutorial,SERVICE=NcDemoMultiSrv2
  CLASS=ETB,SERVER=Tutorial,SERVICE=NcNoReply
  CLASS=ETB,SERVER=Tutorial,SERVICE=NcWithReply
  CLASS=ETB,SERVER=Tutorial,SERVICE=NcNoReplyAsy
*
*-------------------------------------------------------------------*
* Service specific Attributes / Tutorial Conversational Services    *
*-------------------------------------------------------------------*
*

************** v7.3: Service definitions ****************************

DEFAULTS = SERVICE
  CONV-NONACT         = 4M
  SERVER-NONACT       = 5M
  TRANSLATION         = SAGTCHA

  CLASS=ETB,SERVER=Tutorial,SERVICE=CvBackground
  CLASS=ETB,SERVER=Tutorial,SERVICE=CvDataFromSrvAsy
  CLASS=ETB,SERVER=Tutorial,SERVICE=CvDataToSrvAsy
  CLASS=ETB,SERVER=Tutorial,SERVICE=CvDemoDeregQuies
  CLASS=ETB,SERVER=Tutorial,SERVICE=CvDemoHold
  CLASS=ETB,SERVER=Tutorial,SERVICE=CvParallelAsy
  CLASS=ETB,SERVER=Tutorial,SERVICE=CvUnitOfWork
*
*-------------------------------------------------------------------*
* Service specific Attributes / Tutorial Special Services           *
*-------------------------------------------------------------------*
*

************** v7.3: Service definitions ****************************
```

```
DEFAULTS = SERVICE
  CONV-NONACT    = 8M
  NOTIFY-EOC     = YES
  SERVER-NONACT = 10M
  TRANSLATION    = SAGTCHA
  CLASS=ETB,SERVER=Tutorial,SERVICE=Request
  CLASS=ETB,SERVER=Tutorial,SERVICE=Wait
*
*-----------------------------------------------------------------------*
* Service specific Attributes / NATURAL RPC Services                    *
*-----------------------------------------------------------------------*
*

************** v7.3: Service definitions *****************************

DEFAULTS = SERVICE
  CONV-NONACT    = 5M
  NOTIFY-EOC     = NO
  SERVER-NONACT = 1M
  TRANSLATION    = SAGTCHA

  CLASS=RPC,    SERVER=SRV1,     SERVICE=CALLNAT
  CLASS=RPC,    SERVER=MHZSRV1,  SERVICE=CALLNAT
*
*-----------------------------------------------------------------------*
* ENTIRE/X Attach Manager test services                                 *
*-----------------------------------------------------------------------*
*

************** v7.3: Service definitions *****************************

DEFAULTS = SERVICE
  CONV-NONACT    = 5M
  NOTIFY-EOC     = NO
  SERVER-NONACT = 1M
  TRANSLATION    = SAGTCHA

  CLASS = ATCLASS, SERVER = ATMAN,  SERVICE = ATTACH
  CLASS = EAM,     SERVER = ATTEST, SERVICE = CBCSRCH
  CLASS = EAM,     SERVER = ATTEST, SERVICE = SDLDSTC
  CLASS = EAM,     SERVER = ATTEST, SERVICE = SDLDINT1
  CLASS = EAM,     SERVER = ATTEST, SERVICE = SDLDINT2

*-----------------------------------------------------------------------*
*   END OF DEFINITIONS                                                  *
*-----------------------------------------------------------------------*

****************** END ***********************************************
```

Figure 47:   webMethods EntireX Parameters (V7.3.4)

3.9.2   Event Replicator Target Adapter

The Event Replicator Target Adapter transforms and applies replicated data to one relational database at a time, such as DB2, MySQL, Oracle, SQL Server, Sybase, or Taradata.

Example for SQL Database

```
#sqlrep
#Mon Feb 07 03:15:20 PST 2011
source.rserveraddr=DMH/REPLICATION/ART
deletebeforeinsert=true
messageprefetchcount=20
database.batchcount=0
underscore=true
source.capture=false
sqlerrorcontinue=true
compatible23=false
database.nullfortypedecimal=false
occurrence=true
webdav.cachesize=25
startup.buildnumber=1048
sqlserver.portnumber=1433
source.maxreceivelen=32768
sqlrep.verbose=0
database.connectionreuse=true
sqlserver.hostname=mcalmhsqlc3v1
source.trace=0
source.sserveraddr=DMH/REPLICATION/INIT
broker.rserveraddr=xxxx
broker.capture=false
startup.count=603
quotestring=true
database.dbname=ADT
source.id=hwdcs1.cahwnet.gov\:50513
broker.trace=0
broker.maxreceivelen=32768
broker.id=xxxx
sqlserver.password=xxxx
lowercase=false
database.userdefineemptyvalue=true
broker.waittime=20S
sqlserver.username=sa
source.skipconnection=false
sqlserver.dbname=Adabas
database.nullfortypefloat=false
broker.sserveraddr=xxxx
source.sourcetype=BROKER
```

Figure 48:   Parameters for Target Adapter for SQL Database

3.9.3   Schema and Replicated Data

The XML schema for the data is created from the generated field table (GFB) for the subscription that processed the replicated data. Each of the create, insert, update or delete operation will create the SQL table in the relational database management system (RDBMS).

Generated Field Table GFFT

The field table is created when you generate a global format buffer (GFB) for a subscription in Event Replicator for Adabas. See chapter 3.3.6.

It is generated from Predict file definitions.

```
I T L DB Name                          F      Leng S D Remark
- - - -- -------------- top ------------- - ---------- - - -----------

   1 AA PERSONNEL-ID                    A         8   D
 G 1 AB FULL-NAME
   2 AC FIRST-NAME                      A .      20 N
   2 AD MIDDLE-I                        A         1 N
   2 AE NAME                            A        20   D
   1 AF MAR-STAT                        A         1 F
 *        M=MARRIED
 *        S=SINGLE
 *        D=DIVORCED
 *        W=WIDOWED
   1 AG SEX                             A         1 F
 G 1 A1 FULL-ADDRESS
   2 AJ CITY                            A        20 N D
   2 AK ZIP                             A        10 N
   2 AL COUNTRY                         A         3 N
 G 1 A2 TELEPHONE
   2 AN AREA-CODE                       A         6 N
   2 AM PHONE                           A        15 N
   1 AO DEPT                            A         6   D
   1 AP JOB-TITLE                       A        25 N D
 G 1 A3 LEAVE-DATA
   2 AU LEAVE-DUE                       N       2.0
   2 AV LEAVE-TAKEN                     N       2.0 N
```

Figure 49:   Generate Field Table – Source: SAG

EXAMPLE "Create":

```
<TransactionPart Sub='SUB1' Origin='I' Prefix='N' Part='1'
Id='C0CF513C08C1F20400000000' En='4091'>
     <Event Row='1' File='EMPLOYEES-FILE' Op='Create' Time='2007/06/27-
15:20:42.444665' FNR='10'>
             <Field name='PERSONNEL-ID' ei='1' fmt='string' prc='0' len='8' key='uk'/>
             <Field name='FIRST-NAME' ei='2' fmt='string' prc='0' len='20'/>
             <Field name='NAME' ei='3' fmt='string' prc='0' len='20' key='ky'/>
             <Field name='MIDDLE-NAME' ei='4' fmt='string' prc='0' len='20'/>
             <Field name='MAR-STAT' ei='5' fmt='string' prc='0' len='1'/>
             <Field name='SEX' ei='6' fmt='string' prc='0' len='1'/>
             <Field name='BIRTH' ei='8' fmt='date' prc='0' len='10' key='ky'/>
             <Field name='ADDRESS-LINE' ei='9' fmt='string' prc='0' len='20'
att='mu'/>
             <Field name='CITY' ei='10' fmt='string' prc='0' len='20' key='ky'/>
             <Field name='POST-CODE' ei='11' fmt='string' prc='0' len='10'/>
             <Field name='COUNTRY' ei='12' fmt='string' prc='0' len='3'/>
             <Field name='AREA-CODE' ei='13' fmt='string' prc='0' len='6'/>
             <Field name='PHONE' ei='14' fmt='string' prc='0' len='15'/>
             <Field name='DEPT' ei='15' fmt='string' prc='0' len='6' key='ky'/>
             <Field name='JOB-TITLE' ei='16' fmt='string' prc='0' len='25' key='ky'/>
             <Field name='CURR-CODE' ei='18' fmt='string' prc='0' len='3' att='pe'
gname='INCOME'/>
             <Field name='SALARY' ei='19' fmt='decimal' prc='0' len='10' att='pe'
gname='INCOME'/>
             <Field name='BONUS' ei='20' fmt='decimal' prc='0' len='10' att='mu'
gname='INCOME'/>
             <Field name='LEAVE-DUE' ei='21' fmt='decimal' prc='0' len='2'/>
             <Field name='LEAVE-TAKEN' ei='22' fmt='decimal' prc='0' len='2'/>
             <Field name='LEAVE-START' ei='24' fmt='decimal' prc='0' len='8' att='pe'
gname='LEAVE-BOOKED'/>
             <Field name='LEAVE-END' ei='25' fmt='decimal' prc='0' len='8' att='pe'
gname='LEAVE-BOOKED'/>
             <Field name='LANG' ei='26' fmt='string' prc='0' len='3' att='mu'/>
   <Alias name='INCOME' ei='17'/>
   <Alias name='LEAVE-BOOKED' ei='23'/>
     </Event>
     <TransactionEnd RowCount='1' DBID='44444' Sent='2007/06/27-15:20:58.782005'
Committed='2007/06/27-15:20:58.434591' Version='1.0'/>

</TransactionPart>
```

Figure 50:   Generated XML Schema 'Create' – Source: SAG

EXAMPLE "Insert":

```
<TransactionPart Sub='SUB1' Origin='I' Prefix='N' Part='1'
Id='C0D5D7140B13D3C900000000' En='4091'>
     <E Row='1' File='EMPLOYEES-FILE' ISN='1' Op='Insert' FNR='10'>
           <F ei='1' ai='50005800' key='uk'/>
           <F ei='2' ai='SIMONE'/>
           <F ei='3' ai='ADAM' key='ky'/>
           <F ei='5' ai='M'/>
           <F ei='6' ai='F'/>
           <F ei='8' ai='1952/01/30' key='ky'/>
           <F ei='9' ai='26 AVENUE RHIN ET DA' att='mu' ix='1'/>
           <F ei='10' ai='JOIGNY' key='ky'/>
           <F ei='11' ai='89300'/>
           <F ei='12' ai='F'/>
           <F ei='13' ai='1033'/>
           <F ei='14' ai='44864858'/>
           <F ei='15' ai='VENT59' key='ky'/>
           <F ei='16' ai='CHEF DE SERVICE' key='ky'/>
           <F ei='18' ai='FRA' att='pe' ix='1' gei='17'/>
           <F ei='19' ai='159980' att='pe' ix='1' gei='17'/>
           <F ei='20' ai='23000' ix='1' ix2='1' att='mu' gei='17'/>
           <F ei='21' ai='19'/>
           <F ei='22' ai='5'/>
           <F ei='24' ai='19990801' att='pe' ix='1' gei='23'/>
           <F ei='25' ai='19990831' att='pe' ix='1' gei='23'/>
           <F ei='26' ai='FRE' att='mu' ix='1'/>
           <F ei='26' ai='ENG' att='mu' ix='2'/>
     </E>
     <TransactionEnd RowCount='10' DBID='44444' Sent='2007/07/02-19:51:44.051797'
Committed='2007/07/02-19:51:43.712573' Version='1.0'/>
</TransactionPart>
```

Figure 51:   Generated XML Schema 'Insert' – Source: SAG

EXAMPLE "Update":

```
<TransactionPart Sub='SUB1' Origin='I' Prefix='N' Part='1'
Id='C0D5D7140B13D3C900000000' En='4091'>
     <E Row='1' File='EMPLOYEES-FILE' ISN='10' Op='Update' FNR='10'>
           <F ei='1' bi='50004000' ai='11111111' key='uk'/>
           <F ei='20' bi='8880' ai='0000' ix='1' att='mu' ix2='1' gei='17'/>
           <F ei='18' bi='USD' ai='TWN' att='pe' ix='31' gei='17'/>
           <F ei='26' bi='ENG' ai='CHN' att='mu' ix='2'/>
     </E>
     <TransactionEnd RowCount='1' DBID='44444' Sent='2007/07/08-19:51:44.051797'
Committed='2007/07/08-19:51:43.712573' Version='1.0'/>
</TransactionPart>
```

Figure 52:   Generated XML Schema 'Update' – Source: SAG

EXAMPLE "Delete":

```
<TransactionPart Sub='SUB1' Origin='I' Prefix='N' Part='1'
Id='C0D5D7140B13D3C900000000' En='4091'>
     <E Row='1' File='EMPLOYEES-FILE' ISN='10' Op='Delete' FNR='10'>
     </E>
     <TransactionEnd RowCount='1' DBID='44444' Sent='2007/07/09-19:51:44.051797'
Committed='2007/07/09-19:51:43.712573' Version='1.0'/>
</TransactionPart>
```

Figure 53:   Generated XML Schema 'Delete' – Source: SAG

4 Compare Files of Source and Target

Despite users' statements that the replication works correctly and comparisons between source and target are not necessary, self-written comparison programs sometimes show differences. Many times Adabas response codes are the reason that records or ISNs are not replicated. The system log (DDPRINT) of the subscription database and the Replicator Engine shows response codes but normally, there is no routine in place to check for errors. Chapter 6 points out the reasons and chapter 7 describes the monitor routines to detect response codes, errors and high water marks and how to notify the relevant groups.

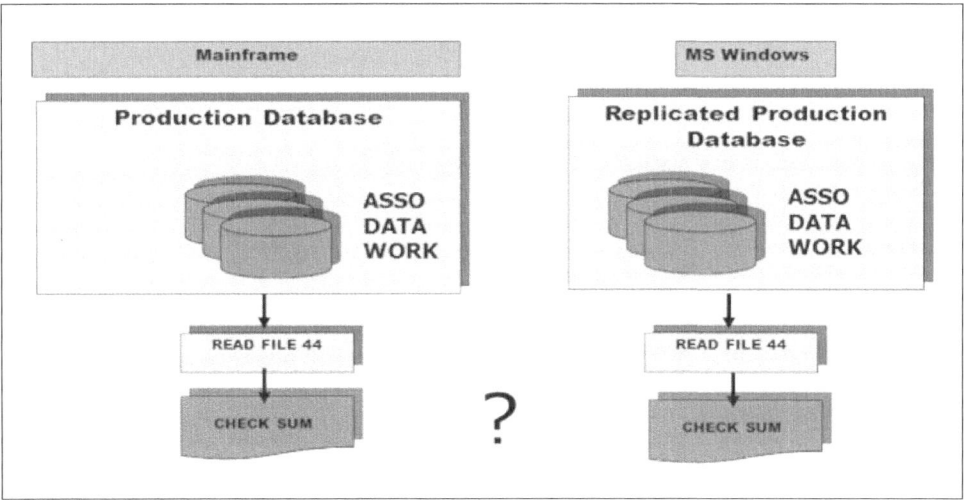

Figure 54:   Compare Source and Target Files – Amount Fields

Three methods will be discussed how to compare source and target files to be sure that both are identical.

4.1   Compare Amount Fields

Counting amount fields of files in both subscription and target databases and compare the result is easy to accomplish. Appendix, chapter 9.5.8 and Figure 211 show the Natural program.

```
<snip>
R1. READ           MULTI-FETCH #MULTIFETCH CONTRIB
   ADD POST-TAX-CNTRB-AMT    TO #POST-TAX-CNTRB-AMT
   ADD PRE-TAX-CNTRB-AMT     TO #PRE-TAX-CNTRB-AMT
   ADD DB-POST-TAX-CNTRB-AMT TO #DB-POST-TAX-CNTRB-AMT
   ADD DB-PRE-TAX-CNTRB-AMT  TO #DB-PRE-TAX-CNTRB-AMT
   ADD LOG-COUNTER           TO #LOG-COUNTER
END-READ
<snip>
```

Figure 55:   Natural Program to Count Amount Fields

```
WINDOWS:
CONTRIBUTION FILE CHECK SUMMARY
   POST-TAX-CNTRB-AMT           27,673,968.59
   PRE-TAX-CNTRB-AMT        29,942,205,909.37
   DB-POST-TAX-CNTRB-AMT       26,347,293.89
   DB-PRE-TAX-CNTRB-AMT     25,380,190,817.46
   LOG-COUNTER                 839,887,724
RECORDS READ:   146,223,112

MAINFRAME:
CONTRIBUTION FILE CHECK SUMMARY
   POST-TAX-CNTRB-AMT           27,658,136.50
   PRE-TAX-CNTRB-AMT        29,942,205,909.37
   DB-POST-TAX-CNTRB-AMT       26,331,461.80
   DB-PRE-TAX-CNTRB-AMT     25,380,189,014.44
   LOG-COUNTER                 840,074,151
Records Read:     146,223,098      read with Multifetch =     800
```

Figure 56:   Result of Natural Program to Count Amount Fields

Figure 56 shows that the file on the target database (Windows) counts 14 records more than the file of the subscription database (mainframe). It can be that the file on the target database was not empty before the initial-state or a replay function was restarted.

4.2   API USR4011N – User Exit

Many files don't contain amount fields and other comparisons must be found. Fortunately, Natural has the capability with its APIs.

The program CHECKSUM uses Natural's API USR4011N to compare two Adabas files.

```
0010 * Sample CHECKSUM
0020 *   1 Provide DBIDs
0030 *   2 Provide file name in #FILE
0040 *   3 provide File Number in #FILE-NBR
0050 *   4 Provide file name in VIEW
0060 *   5 Provide a full DDM definition following VIEW
0070 *   6 Provide the LRECL in #DDM
0080 *
0090 * copy of CHECKSUM as CHKSM006 - File 6
0100 DEFINE DATA LOCAL
0110 1 #DB1 (N5)         INIT <187>               /* <<<<< 1
0120 1 #DB2 (N5)         INIT <250>               /* <<<<< 1
0130 1 #FILE-NBR (N5)    INIT <006>               /* <<<<< 2
0140 1 #FILE (A32)       INIT <'ST-CALC-EDATE'>   /* <<<<< 2
0150 1 DDM   VIEW ST-MC-CALC-EDATE                /* <<<<< 4
0160    2 LOG-COUNTER          (P15.0)            /* <<<<< 5
0170    2 ENTITY               (A50)
0180    2 LAST-CHGD-DATE-TIME  (A15)
0190    2 LAST-CHGD-USER       (A08)
0200    2 CALC-CODE            (A10)
0210    2 EFF-DATE             (A08)
0220    2 EFF-DATE-9C          (A08)
0230    2 EXP-DATE             (A08)
0240    2 DATA                 (A250)
0250                       1 REDEFINE DDM
0260    2 #DDM (A365)                             /* <<<<< 6

(snip)

0490 DEFINE SUBROUTINE HASH-RTN
0500 CALLNAT "USR1040N" #1040
0510 ASSIGN #4011.FUNC = 1
0520 CALLNAT "USR4011N" #4011
0530 ASSIGN #4011.FUNC = 2
0540 ASSIGN #1023.MS   = *CPU-TIME
0550 R.
0560 READ MULTI-FETCH ON DDM BY ISN
0570   ASSIGN #4011.TEXT = #DDM
0580   CALLNAT "USR4011N" #4011
0590 END-READ
0600 ASSIGN #4011.FUNC = 3
0610 CALLNAT "USR4011N" #4011
0620 ASSIGN #1023.MS = *CPU-TIME - #1023.MS
0630 CALLNAT "USR1023N" #1023
0640 DISPLAY 'DBID'    #1040.DB
0650          'Records' *COUNTER (R.)
0660          'Checksum' #4011.HASH
0670          'CPU Time' #1023.TIME (EM=HH:II:SS.T)
0680 END-SUBROUTINE

(snip)
```

Figure 57:   Result of Natural Program to Count Amount Fields

Appendix, chapter 9.5.7 shows the entire Natural program 'CHECKSUM'.

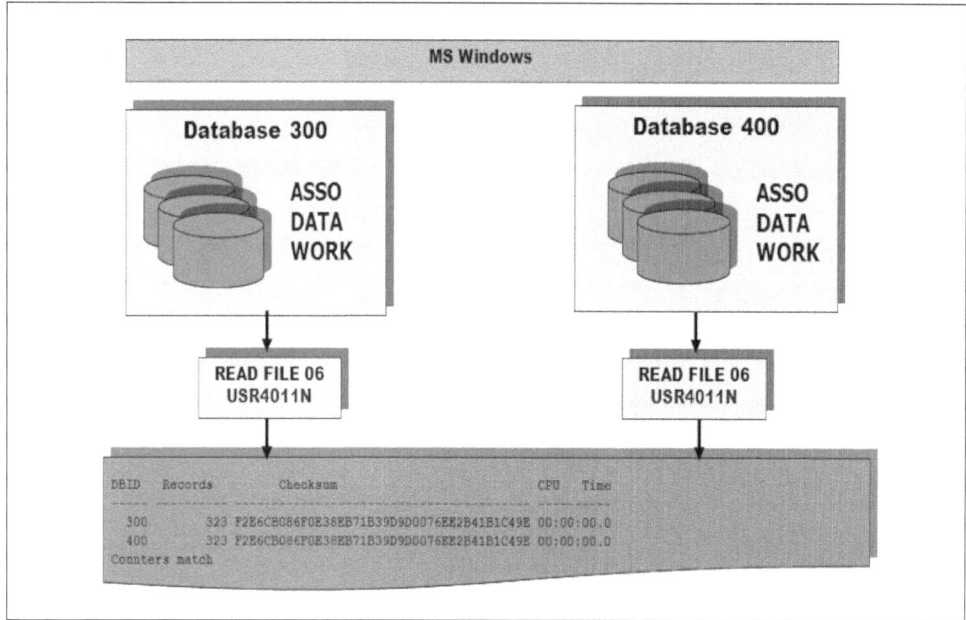

Figure 58:   Result of Natural Checksum Program

The program reads all records of the source and the target database, creates checksums and number of records. Both number of records and the checksums must be identical, see Figure 58.

4.3   Compare Highest ISNs (TOPISN)

Another way to make sure that the source and target files are the same is to com-pare the number of records of both files. But this won't be sufficient because you can have the same number of records in a file but the highest used ISNs are dif-ferent; and this leads to error messages (RSP 113) during the replication process. Also, to compare the MAXISN won't work. MAXISN on both source and target can be the same but the number of records loaded can be different.

The Adabas report shows both the number of loaded records and the maximal used ISNs of each file. Manually comparing Adabas reports of 200 files and more can be too time-consuming. At first, I wrote a parse program to compare pro-grammatically the two reports. I included also in a spread sheet the TOPISN, REUSEISN and MAXISN fields. It showed in later tests that if the target files are not initially loaded with REUSEISN, it is a problem and leads to errors.

	Source Database – Adabas on Mainframe				Target Database – Adabas on Windows			
File Number	Records Loaded	TOP-ISN	MAX-ISN	ISN Reusage	Records Loaded	TOP-ISN	MAX-ISN	ISN Reusage
122	12,434, 148	12,440, 973	12,501, 215	Yes	12,434, 148	12,440, 960	12,449, 279	Enabled

Figure 59: Compare Highest ISN (TOPISN) and Others

The disadvantage of using a full Adabas report in batch is that it can take up to 30 minutes to finish the job with 200 files. In addition, some organizations must pay for used CPU time and I/Os.

Source DB Mainframe

```
09:58:46          ***** A D A B A S
DBID 39                    - Display
****************
*  File 122    *    ST-REVIEW-LOG
****************

Records loaded ..... 12434148
TOP ISN ............ 12440973
Max ISN expected ... 12501215

ISN Reusage ........ Yes
```

Figure 60: Adabas Report Records Loaded, TOPISN and MAXISN (Mainframe)

Target database Windows

```
Database 251, File   122  (ST-REVIEW-LOG  )          26-JAN-2011 10:24:47


Highest Index Level:         4    Padding Factors:      ASSO   5%, DATA   5%
Top ISN:             12,440,960   Maximum ISN expected:        12,449,279
Records loaded:      12,434,148
Last FDT Modification:            03-JAN-2011 11:21:59.055000

ISN reusage:    Enabled, active   Space reusage:     Enabled
Program refresh: Disabled         Ciphering:         Disabled
```

Figure 61: Adabas Report Records Loaded, TOPISN and MAXISN (Windows)

During my researches, I came along with a Natural program written and published on SAG-L in 1999.by Lewis Pritchard that determines the highest ISN in a file. Since there is neither an equivalent Adabas nor a Natural function available (get the highest used ISN), I used this program and adapted it for my client. Now, the Natural program uses the Adabas command 'L1' with an 'F' in command option 2 to get the next highest, unused ISN (thanks to Larry Frazin).

The first parameter is the DBID, the second parameter the starting file number and the third parameter the number of files to be reported.

```
//* -----------------------------------------------------------------
//* Determine the highest used ISNs per file
//* ISNHIGH 112,1,10
//*         --- - --
//*          |   | |
//*          +--------- DBID
//*              | |
//*              +------ start with file number
//*                |
//*                +---- number of files to be reported
//* -----------------------------------------------------------------
//ISNHIGH  EXEC NATBT,DEPT=ST,DB=DEVL,SYSOUT=*,TIME=100,
//          PRM='IM=D,MADIO=0,MAXCL=0,MT=0,LT=999999,AUTO=ON,DU=ABEND'
//SYSOUT   DD SYSOUT=*
//CMPRT01  DD SYSOUT=*
//SYSIN    DD *
LOGON DIETER
ISNHIGH 112,1,10
FIN
//
```

Figure 62:   Compare Highest Used ISN (JCL)

```
NEXT ISNHIGH 112,1,10                                         LIB=DIETER

Page    1                                          03/28/11  08:14:24

DBID:    112 FNR:    1 HIGHEST ISN:        520
DBID:    112 FNR:    2 HIGHEST ISN:        275
DBID:    112 FNR:    3 HIGHEST ISN:          0
DBID:    112 FNR:    4 HIGHEST ISN:       1145
DBID:    112 FNR:    5 HIGHEST ISN:        797
DBID:    112 FNR:    6 HIGHEST ISN:        345
DBID:    112 FNR:    7 HIGHEST ISN:     195690
DBID:    112 FNR:    8 HIGHEST ISN:    1100997
DBID:    112 FNR:    9 HIGHEST ISN:         42
DBID:    112 FNR:   10 HIGHEST ISN:        364
```

Figure 63:   Compare Highest Used ISN (Output)

The Natural program ISNHIGH is located in appendix, chapter 9.5.10.

5 Recovery After a Crash

Normally, the Event Replicator Server restarts automatically after an abnormal end and is able to recover any lost replication. But in some cases, data is lost and the replication must be replayed, as reported in chapter 6 with some response codes from the target database and Entire Net-Work.

The new ADARPL utility and its REPLAY function is similar to the known regenerate function of ADARES. ADARPL needs the protection log of the subscription database and must be run against the subscription database.

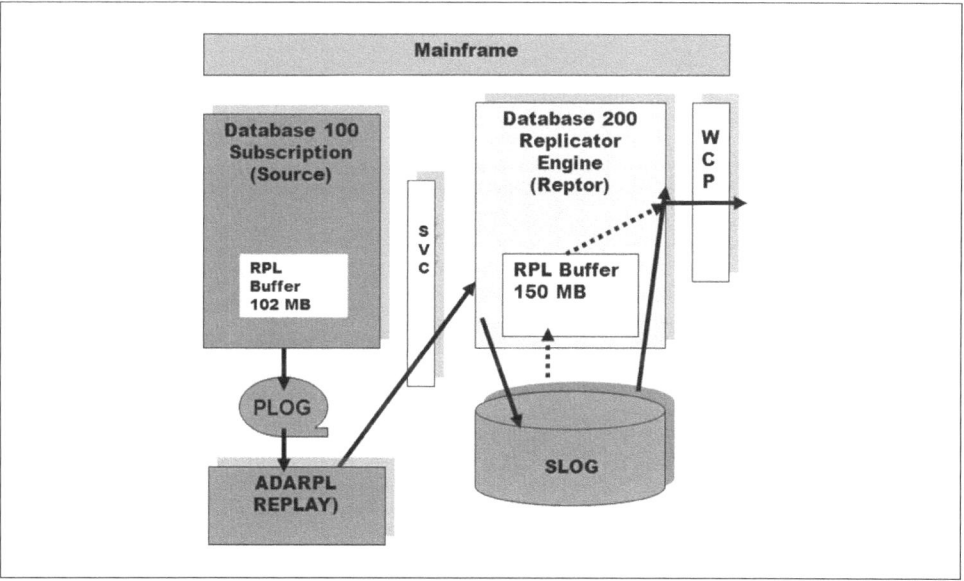

Figure 64: Replay Function and its Components

The replay can be run in the following three modes:

* Synchronized
* Unsynchronized
* Replay-only

```
Code  Allows you to:
R     Run replay processing in Replay-only mode.
S     Run replay processing in synchronized mode.
?     Get help on this menu.
.     Exit the Adabas Event Replicator Subsystem
```

Figure 65: Replay Modes

5.1   Replay with a Token

Initiate Replication Replay

From the 'Event Replication Subsystem' and main menu select 'Administration' and from the administration menu select 'R' for initiate replay.

In synchronized mode – that is Software AG's recommendation – the replay function suspends new Adabas transactions, reactivates files, subscriptions, destinations that are inactive and writes all new data to SLOG. It also synchronizes the data with the new Adabas transactions when processing is complete.

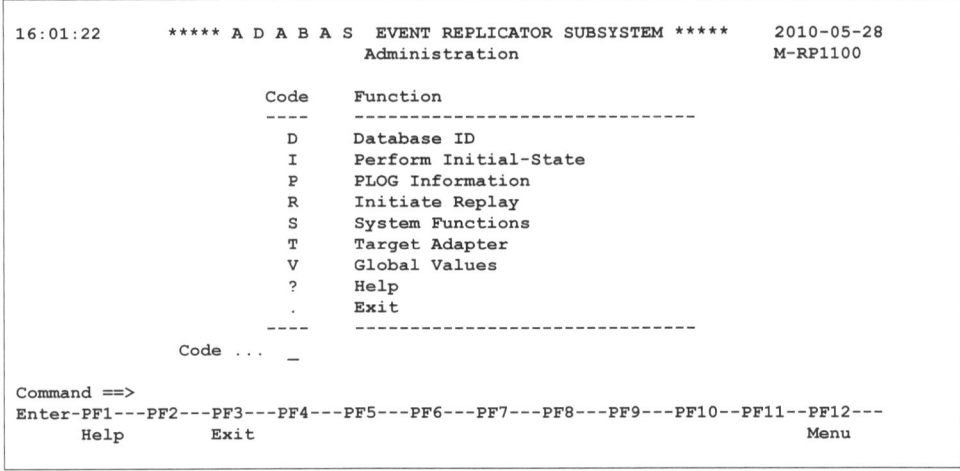

```
16:01:22        ***** A D A B A S  EVENT REPLICATOR SUBSYSTEM *****      2010-05-28
                             Administration                              M-RP1100


                     Code     Function
                     ----     ------------------------------
                      D       Database ID
                      I       Perform Initial-State
                      P       PLOG Information
                      R       Initiate Replay
                      S       System Functions
                      T       Target Adapter
                      V       Global Values
                      ?       Help
                      .       Exit
                     ----     ------------------------------
                Code ...   _


Command ==>
Enter-PF1---PF2---PF3---PF4---PF5---PF6---PF7---PF8---PF9---PF10--PF11--PF12---
     Help       Exit                                                      Menu
```

Figure 66:   Start Replay Using Event Replicator Subsystem

```
ARF00147: Replay process initiated - Token=15828
16:42:38        ***** A D A B A S  EVENT REPLICATOR SUBSYSTEM *****      2010-12-23
                          Initiate Replication Replay                    M-RP2010

                             Synchronized

            DBID ........................... __134
            Automated ...................... N (Y or N)
            Timeout ........................ 900_____

            From Date/Time ................. 2010-12-20  02:00:00
            To Date/Time ...................  _____  _____
            Start Date/Time ................  _____  _____

            Destination Name List ..... _ + * D251009_  D251010_  D251011_
            Subscription Name List .... _   * _____  _____  _____


Command ==>
Enter-PF1---PF2---PF3---PF4---PF5---PF6---PF7---PF8---PF9---PF10--PF11--PF12---
Help       Exit       Sub   Sel                                          Menu
```

Figure 67:   Initiate Replay Using Event Replicator Subsystem

DBID

Specify the database ID of the Adabas database from which you want replicated transactions replayed.

Automated

Indicate whether or not you want the replay automated or not. Valid values are Y (perform an automated replay) or N (do not perform an automated replay). The default is N.

NOTE: If you have set the Record PLOG Information (RECORDPLOGINFO) parameter to N (or NO), you cannot set the Automated field to Y.

If you specify N for the Automated field, there are manual steps you must perform. Specifically, once you have initiated the replay on this screen, a token is generated that must be used in a manually created ADARPL utility job.

In addition, prior to running the ADARPL utility job you might also have to issue a force-end-of-PLOG request to the Adabas database and wait until the resulting PLCOPY job has copied or merged the latest PLOG data set.

If you set the Automated field to Y, none of this manual processing is required.

Timeout

Optionally, specify the length of time, in seconds, at which the replay request should time out. The default is 900 seconds.

From Date/Time

Specify the date and time from which replicated transactions should be replayed. Dates should be specified in YYYY/MM/DD format; times should be specified in HH:MM:SS format. Replay processing will start with transactions in the PLOG that ended at or after this date and time.

From dates and times must be earlier than the current date and time and earlier than the specified end date and time.

To Date/Time

Specify the date and time to which replicated transactions should be replayed. Dates should be specified in YYYY/MM/DD format; times should be specified in HH:MM:SS format. Replay processing will stop with transactions in the PLOG that ended before this date and time. End dates and times must be later than the specified start date and time.

Start Date/Time

The date and time of the PLOG entries that should be used as a starting point for the replay processing. This date and time are used to identify the PLOG with which to start replay processing. Dates should be specified in YYYY/MM/DD format; times should be specified in HH:MM:SS format. Replay processing will search the PLOG with this start date and time first for records that match the other replay processing criteria listed on this screen.

A start date and time must be specified if an automated replay is requested.

Destination Name List

Tab to these fields and type in the names of up to three destinations for replay processing. If you would prefer to select the names from a list, place the cursor on one of the three fields and press PF6. If you need to enter more than three destinations and to review the complete list of destinations, type an X in the single-character space for this field and press Enter. A screen appears on which you can maintain the complete list of destinations. When the replay request is initiated, transactions will be replayed that were originally destined for the destinations on this list.

If you want to select all destinations for replay processing, tab to the first large space for the Destination Name List field and enter an asterisk (*). Note that once you have entered an asterisk in the first field, you can no longer select any specific destinations (errors will occur if you try).

In some versions, the file list is limited, see chapter 6.4, Problems and Solutions.

Subscription Name List

Tab to these fields and type in the names of up to three subscriptions for replay processing. If you would prefer to select the names from a list, place the cursor on one of the three fields and press PF6. If you need to enter more than three subscriptions and to review the complete list of subscriptions, type an X in the single-character space for this field and press Enter. A screen appears on which you can maintain the complete list of subscriptions. When the replay request is initiated, transactions will be replayed that were originally solicited by the subscriptions on this list

If you want to select all subscriptions for replay processing, tab to the first large space for the Subscription Name List field and enter an asterisk (*). Note that once you have entered an asterisk in the first field, you can no longer select any specific subscriptions (errors will occur if you try).

Up to Event Replicator V6.2, the file list is limited, see chapter 6.4, Problems and Solutions.

> *Important info:* do not use the HALT command for Reptor if data is in SLOG. A Reptor restart will delete this leftover.

5.2   Replay Without a Token

Replay without a Token performs an unsynchronized Replay. All files to be replayed must be defined in the job. There are also other parameters that might be necessary, as FROMDATE, FROMTIME, TODATE, and TOTIME.

```
14:33:46  IAT2000 JOB STREPLAY (JOB59127) SELECTED SY7  (In SAR)
14:33:46  IEF403I STREPLAY - STARTED - TIME=14.33.46
14:33:47  IEF188I PROBLEM PROGRAM ATTRIBUTES ASSIGNED
14:36:48  IEF404I STREPLAY - ENDED - TIME=14.36.48

A D A R P L   V8.1  SM1   DBID = 00039  Started          2010-10-20  14:33:45
Parameters:
-----------
ADARPL REPLAY
ADARPL LRPL=600000K
ADARPL FILES=74

Initialization handshake for Reptor 302 successful, token = 15045
Termination handshake for Reptor 302 successful

Total PLOG Blocks Read = 29787
Total replicated transactions = 21285
Highwater mark in replication pool = 1634840
Timestamp of last committed transaction = 2010-10-15 14:28:50

Total replicated transactions sent to Reptor Target ID 302 = 21285


A D A R P L  Terminated normally                         2010-10-20  14:36:47
```

Figure 68:   ADARPL Replay Output without a Token

After the REPLAY, the source and target file 74 were checked with a self-written checksum program, see appendix, chapter 9.5.7.

```
 Page    1                                                   10-10-20  14:55:30

 10/20/2010 14:55:30.0 Started CHKSM074         Checksum Comparison
         File FILE-074                          File#:    74

 DBID    Records                     Checksum                  CPU Time
 -----   ----------  -------------------------------------  ----------

 DBID being accessed:     39
 Key Field AE from File 159 read on WF 2: 1208074666
    39       23866 4946D714D31707A80F5263AAF17068BB655C6AFC 00:00:00.0
 DBID being accessed:    251
   251       23866 4946D714D31707A80F5263AAF17068BB655C6AFC 00:00:00.0

      23866 Counters match

               Checksums match
 10/20/2010 14:56:24.8 Ended
 00:00:54.8
```

Figure 69: Checksum Program to Compare After Replay

5.3 Replay-only Mode

Replay-only mode processing performs replay processing on the replicated transactions in the PLOG, but discards any new Adabas transactions

5.4 Initial-state

In some cases, the target file is corrupted and a Replay won't work. There are two
ways to fix the target file:

- Initial-state using the Adabas Event Replicator Subsystem
  Synchronization will be done automatically.
  Disadvantage: huge files (>100,000,000) can take too long because the replica-
  tion process using Adabas commands to replicate
- Decompress source file, compress file, re-load target file
  Synchronization must be done manually
  Benefit: Adabas utilities are faster than single Adabas commands

From the 'Event Replication Subsystem' main menu select 'Administration' and
from the administration menu 'I' for Perform Initial-State.

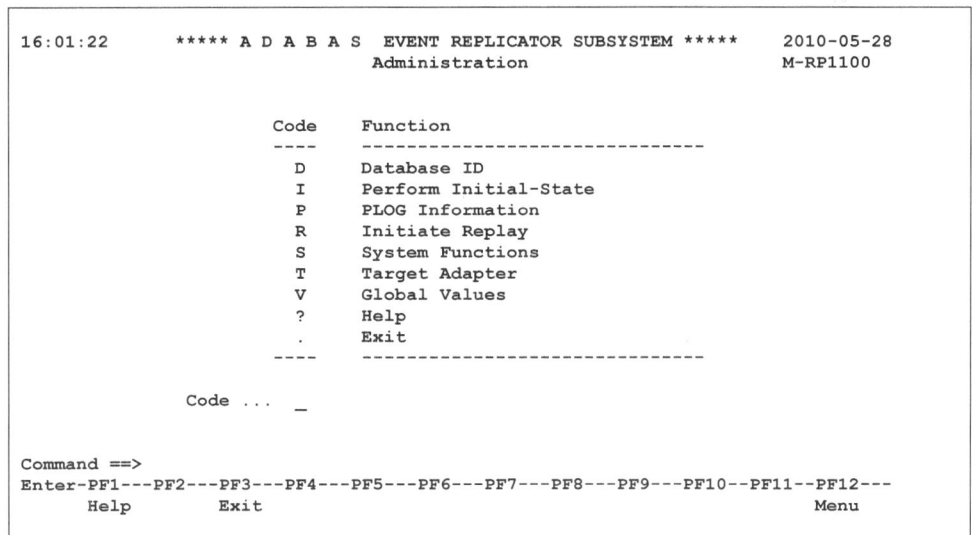

```
16:01:22     ***** A D A B A S  EVENT REPLICATOR SUBSYSTEM *****   2010-05-28
                           Administration                         M-RP1100


                  Code     Function
                  ----     ------------------------------
                   D       Database ID
                   I       Perform Initial-State
                   P       PLOG Information
                   R       Initiate Replay
                   S       System Functions
                   T       Target Adapter
                   V       Global Values
                   ?       Help
                   .       Exit
                  ----     ------------------------------


           Code ...  _



Command ==>
Enter-PF1---PF2---PF3---PF4---PF5---PF6---PF7---PF8---PF9---PF10--PF11--PF12---
     Help       Exit                                                Menu
```

Figure 70: SYSREPTOR – Perform Initial-State

```
16:13:15     ***** A D A B A S  EVENT REPLICATOR SUBSYSTEM *****   2010-05-28
                          Perform Initial-State                   M-RP4012


                  Initial-State Name ....... IS1

Sel  IDBID IFile I      Selection Criteria   or   ISN List
---  ------ ----- - ------------------------------------------------------------
 _   + 0100  1     A
 _   + 0100  3     A
 _
 _
 _
 _
 _
 _
 _



Command ==>
Enter-PF1---PF2---PF3---PF4---PF5---PF6---PF7---PF8---PF9---PF10--PF11--PF12---
       Help       Exit       Sub                                   Menu
```

Figure 71: SYSREPTOR – Perform Initial-State

6 Problems and Solutions

During many replication tests problems occurred in the following areas and here are some solutions based on my own experiences.

- Source or Subscription Database
- Replicator Engine
- Target Database
- Utilities

6.1 Source or Subscription Database

6.1.1 Replicator Buffer (LRPL) Overflow

The Replicator buffer must be defined in the source database and in the Replicator Engine by using the LRPL parameter.

An overflow in the source database leads to a halt of the replication process for the file using this buffer at the time of the overflow happened because no overflow area (SLOG) is available.

In general, the same situation happens with a replication overflow buffer in the Replicator Engine, even if an overflow area (SLOG) is defined but without a threshold. See also chapter 6.2, Replicator Engine.

```
13:47:01           ***** A D A B A S  BASIC  SERVICES *****        2011-01-13
   DBID 134                   -  High Water Marks  -                  PACUH02


   Pool / Queue        I    Size   I    Used   I %Used I   Date        Time    I
   ------------------------------------------------------------------------------
   Attached Buffer(NAB) I    1638400 I     215296 I  13.1 I                      I
   Command Queue   (NC)  I      19200 I       6528 I  34.0 I 2011-01-13 08:10:04 I
   Format Pool     (LFP) I    3000000 I    2999840 I  99.9 I 2011-01-13 10:08:32 I
   Hold Queue      (NH)  I    1134056 I      60088 I   5.2 I 2011-01-11 20:18:43 I
   ISN-List Table (LI)   I       5000 I       1072 I  21.4 I 2011-01-13 11:24:09 I
   Seq. Cmd. Table(LQ)   I      20000 I      12784 I  63.9 I 2011-01-13 09:48:30 I
   User Queue      (NU)  I     312312 I     115500 I  36.9 I 2011-01-13 09:49:06 I
   Unique DE Pool (DUQ)  I      60000 I       6208 I  10.3 I 2011-01-10 19:01:18 I
   Security Pool  (LCP)  I      10000 I          0 I   0.0 I                      I
   UQ File List    (UQF) I      96360 I      39000 I  40.4 I 2011-01-13 09:51:14 I
   ATM Trans. IDs (XID)  I          0 I          0 I   0.0 I                      I
   Work Pool       (LWP) I    1500000 I     687124 I  45.8 I 2011-01-12 13:13:14 I
   Redo Pool      (LRDP) I          0 I          0 I   0.0 I                      I
   Replication    (RPL)  I  524288000 I  462483796 I  88.2 I                      I
```

Figure 72: LRPL Overflow

Tests in January 2011 with mass updates showed that more than 500M should be
set for the LRPL parameter.

6.1.2   High CPU Usage of Source DB

When RPL was switched on in the production database and 9 batch jobs started
in parallel, the CPU time and the EXCPs of the source database increased dramat-
ically. The production database used more than double the CPU time during replication. Also, the 9 batch jobs that would normally finish in 2.3 hours now took
13.3 hours.

Based on statistics, these 9 batch jobs update 6 million records per hour or 1,666
update commands per second.

The table of Figure 73 displays the high CPU time occurring in production on
12 Jan 2011 at 19:00 when the 9 batch jobs started and replication was active. Replication was turned off on 13 Jan 2011 at 8:00 letting the 9 jobs finish before the
online time began.

JOB	PROGRAM	CPU TIME	EXCP TOTL	IN TB TIME
(snip)				
SOURCE DB	ADARUN	0:03:45.83	953,021	12JAN2011:15:00:10.41
SOURCE DB	ADARUN	0:03:03.99	843,886	12JAN2011:16:00:10.41
SOURCE DB	ADARUN	0:02:04.08	629,517	12JAN2011:17:00:10.43
SOURCE DB	ADARUN	0:00:15.25	21,540	12JAN2011:18:00:10.43
SOURCE DB	ADARUN	0:42:11.47	5,053,538	12JAN2011:19:00:10.43
SOURCE DB	ADARUN	0:47:04.52	2,823,878	12JAN2011:20:00:10.43
SOURCE DB	ADARUN	0:41:43.81	1,940,700	12JAN2011:21:00:10.43
(snip)				
SOURCE DB	ADARUN	0:41:37.33	2,278,851	13JAN2011:07:00:10.44
SOURCE DB	ADARUN	0:15:04.88	3,748,049	13JAN2011:08:00:10.44
SOURCE DB	ADARUN	0:11:15.67	5,823,365	13JAN2011:09:00:10.44
SOURCE DB	ADARUN	0:06:54.78	2,749,801	13JAN2011:10:00:10.44
(snip)				

Figure 73:   High CPU Time – 19:00 Start of 9 Batch Programs

Figure 74 compares the both single and total duration of the nine jobs in December 2010 without replication (2:20 hours) and in January 2011 with replication
(13:22 hours).

Job	24 December 2010 Without Replication		12 January 2011 With Replication	
	From – To	Duration	From – To	Duration
5031	19:01 – 21:00	1:59	19:02 – 07:27	12:25
5032	19:01 – 20:58	1:57	19:02 – 21:38	2:36
5033	19:01 – 20:57	1:56	19:01 – 07:11	12:10
5034	19:01 – 21:06	2:05	19:02 – 07:58	12:56
5035	19:01 – 21:21	2:20	19:01 – 08:22	13:21
5036	19:01 – 21:18	2:17	19:01 – 08:23	13:22
5037	19:01 – 20:59	1:58	19:01 – 07:29	12:28
5038	19:01 – 20:59	1:58	19:01 – 07:30	12:29
5039	19:01 – 21:00	1:59	19:01 – 07:33	12:32
TOT	**19:01 – 21:21**	**2:20**	**19:01 – 08:23**	**13:22**

Figure 74:   Duration of 9 Batch Jobs With and Without Replication

After experiencing such a huge difference when replication was turned on, the following tests in a different environment (LPAR) under production-like conditions (database, parameters, etc.) were run with only 20% data.

Figure 75 shows four different tests with parameters of the source or subscription database and the duration (elapsed time) of the 9 parallel running jobs.

Test #	Date	RPL	LBP	LFIOP	LRPL	ASYTVS	FMXIO	9 Jobs Duration
1	01/27/2011	YES	70,000,000	13,000,000	500,000,000	YES	1	79 min
2	01/28/2011	NO	70,000,000	13,000,000	500,000,000	YES	1	40 min
3	01/31/2011	YES	150,000,000	13,000,000	500,000,000	YES	1	74 min
4	02/24/2011	YES	150,000,000	13,000,000	700,000,000	YES	8	61 min

Figure 75:   Duration of 9 Jobs With and Without Replication and Source DB Parameters

Figure 76 shows the CPU time of the source or subscription database with and without replication turned on. The parameters are displayed in Figure 75.

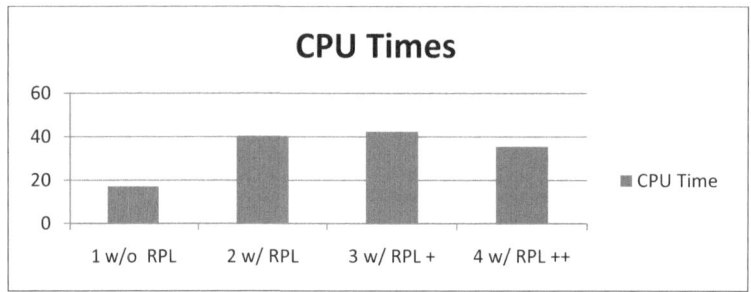

Figure 76:   Duration of 9 Jobs Without and With Replication

The Strobe report (Figure 77) shows that the Adabas module ADANC6, responsible for buffer pool activities, has most activities in the source database (up to 95%) but not in the Replicator Engine. The module ADANC8, responsible for compress and decompress, surprisingly is not shown in the Replicator Engine, even if the decompress process takes place in the Reptor.

Adabas Source Database – Strobe report

MODULE TIME	SECTION	LINE	PROCEDURE/FUNCTION	STARTING	PROCEDURE	CPU
NAME	NAME	NUMBER	NAME	LOCATION	LENGTH	SOLO
.ADABAS	ADANC6	ADANC6	ADABAS BUFFER POOL MNGER			51.49
.ADABAS	ADARPN	ADARPN	ADABAS SYSTEM SERVICES			12.61
.SVC	SVC 114		EXCPVR			.05
.ADABAS	ADANC1	ADANC1	ADABAS THREAD SELECTION			.17
.ADABAS	ADANC8	ADANC8	ADABAS CMPRESS DVT HNDLR			.11
.ADABAS	ADANC0		ADABAS USR/HYP EXIT CALL			.32
.ADABAS	ADAIOS		ADABAS I/O PROCESSING			.21
.ADABAS	ADANC5		ADABAS QUEUE PROCESSING			.10
.ADABAS	ADANC7		ADABAS FORMAT TRANSLATOR			.03
.SUPERVS	IGC0024A		SUPERVISOR SERVICES			.05

Figure 77:   Strobe Report – Adabas Source Database

Adabas Replicator Engine – Strobe report

MODULE TIME	SECTION	LINE	PROCEDURE/FUNCTION	STARTING	PROCEDURE	CPU
NAME	NAME	NUMBER	NAME	LOCATION	LENGTH	SOLO
.ADABAS	ADARPS	ADARPS	ADABAS SYSTEM SERVICES			27.27
.SUPERVS	IGC0024A		SUPERVISOR SERVICES			13.64
.ADABAS	ADANC0	ADANC0	ADABAS USR/HYP EXIT CALL			9.09
.ADABAS	ADANC6	ADANC6	ADABAS BUFFER POOL MNGER			8.18
.ADABAS	ADANC1	ADANC1	ADABAS THREAD SELECTION			7.27
.SVC	SVC 114		EXCPVR			.00
.ADABAS	ADANC7	ADANC7	ADABAS FORMAT TRANSLATOR			3.64
.ADABAS	ADANC5	ADANC5	ADABAS QUEUE PROCESSING			2.73
.NUCLEUS	IEAVESLK		SUSPEND LOCK SERVICE			2.73
.ADABAS	ADAIOS	PSHSTK	ADABAS I/O PROCESSING			2.73

Figure 78:   Strobe Report – Adabas Replicator Engine

LBP and LFIOP at Source and Replicator Engine

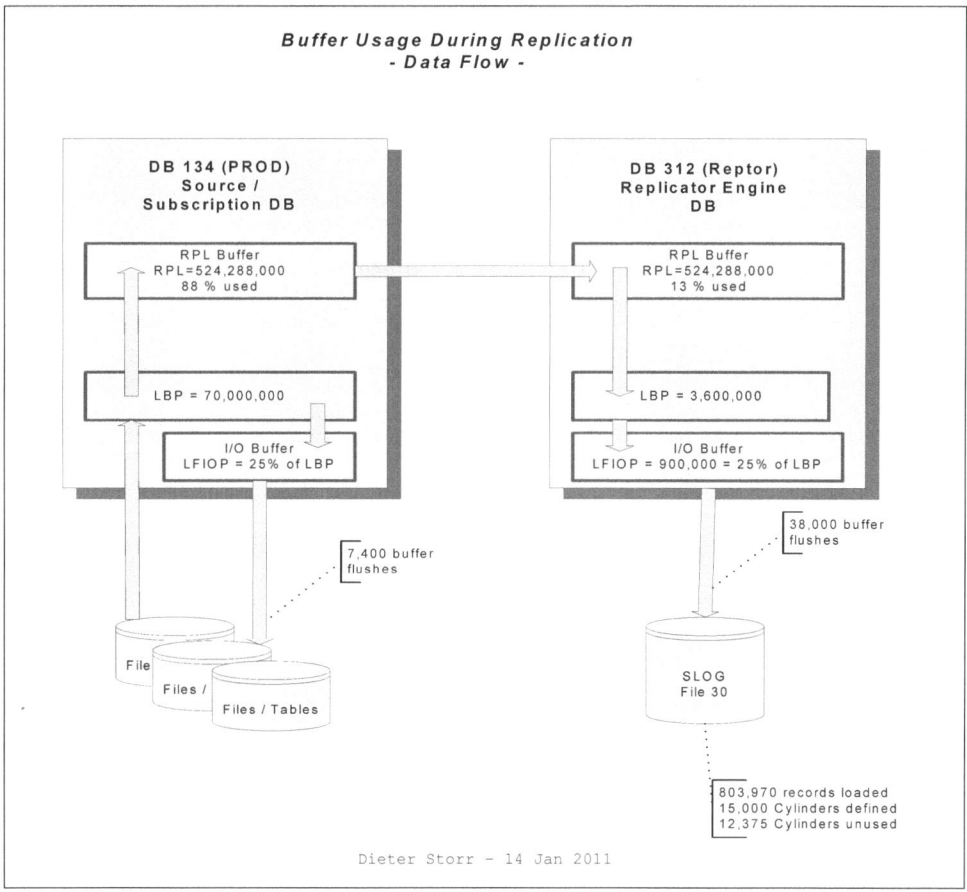

Figure 79:   Buffer Usage Between Source DB and Reptor

The Adabas buffer pool (LBP) on the Replicator Engine was set to a very low value of 3.6M compared with 70M on the Source database. If updates on the Replicator Engine cannot be passed in time from its RPL buffer to the target database then they must be stored into its subscription log (SLOG), an Adabas file. And these updates must be passed through Reptor's buffer pool (LBP) and I/O pool (LFIOP).

If the data to be replicated cannot be passed fast enough from the source database to the Reptor then the RPL buffer of the source overflows. It is also a CPU overhead on the source database to ask very often the Reptor whether to be ready to hand over the next transaction.

Recommendation: LBP size of both source database and Replicator Engine should be the same, at least 150M.

```
12:11:21            ***** A D A B A S  BASIC  SERVICES *****           2011-02-24
DBID 34                    -  Display Parameters  -                     PACPD02


      -------------- Pools --------------    ------------ Queues ------------------
   Sort Area          (LS).. 49920         Command Queue       (NC) .. 100
   Int. User Buffer   (LU).. 500000        Hold Queue          (NH) .. 40500
   Buffer Pool        (LBP).. 150023680    User Queue          (NU) .. 1000
   Format Pool        (LFP).. 5500000      ------------ Time Windows -------------
   ISN List Table     (LI).. 5000          Transaction Time      (TT) .. 300
   Seq. Cmd. Table    (LQ).. 20000         Max Transaction Time (MXTT) .. 3600
   Work Pool          (LWP).. 1500000      Nonactivity ACC-User (TNAA) .. 3600
   Attached Buffer    (NAB).. 400          Nonactivity ET-User  (TNAE) .. 3600
   Security Pool      (LCP).. 10000        Nonactivity EXU-User (TNAX) .. 900
   UQ-DE Pool       (LDEUQP).. 60000       Max Nonactivity Time(MXTNA) .. 3600
   Flush I/O Pool (LFIOP).. 13000000       Time Limit Sx-Cmds (TLSCMD) .. 180
   Err. Recovery (MSGBUF).. 0              Max Time for Sx-Cmds(MXTSX) .. 3600
                                           Command Time          (CT) .. 180
                                           SYNS60 Interval    (INTNAS) .. 3600


   --------- Miscellaneous -----------    -------- User Specific Limits ---------
   Read only session(READONLY) .. NO     Hold Queue Limit  (NISNHQ) .. 10000
   UTI only session  (UTIONLY) .. NO     CIDs per User        (NQCID) .. 50
    OPEN required     (OPENRQ) .. NO       ISN per TBI Element(NSISN) .. 51
   Ignore DIB Entry   (IGNDIB) .. NO     ------------ Buffer Pool --------------
   Local nucleus       (LOCAL) .. NO     Bufferflush Dur.   (TFLUSH) .. 1
    Number of Threads     (NT) .. 30      Parallel LFIOP I/O (FMXIO) .. 8
   Non DE Search      (NONDES) .. YES    Async. by Vol-Ser (ASYTVS) .. YES
   Log AOS/DBS Update (AOSLOG) .. NO     ------------ Replication --------------
   Batch Support       (BATCH) .. NO     Replication (REPLICATION) ... YES
   Data Protection Area   (LP) .. 118000
   Ignore Work Part 4 (IGNDTP) .. NO
   WORK-Part-4 Area     (LDTP) .. 0
   WORK-Part-2 Area    (LWKP2) .. 43000
   SVC                   (SVC) .. 241


   ---- Command Logging ----            --------- Protection Logging ----------
   Command Logging .. YES               PLOG required       (PLOGRQ) .. NO
   LOGCB ............ YES               DUAL PLOG Size      (DUALPLS) .. 13500
   LOGFB ............ YES               DUAL PLOG Device    (DUALPLD) .. 3390
   LOGRB ............ NO                NPLOG ......................... 0
   LOGSB ............ YES               ------------ Other Services ------------
   LOGVB ............ YES               Triggers and Procedures (SPT) .. NO
   LOGIB ............ NO                Delta Save Facility     (DSF) .. NO
   LOGIO ............ NO                Cache Facility        (CACHE) .. NO
   LOGUX ............ NO                Transaction Manager     (ATM) .. NO
   LOGSIZE .......... 32756             TCP/IP Support        (TCPIP) .. NO
   DUAL CLOG Size ... 0                 Ext. Error Recovery    (SMGT) .. NO
   DUAL CLOG Dev. ... 0                 2 Phase Commit Support  (DTP) .. NO
   CLOGMRG .......... NO                Review Support       (REVIEW) .. NO
    NCLOG ........... 0
```

Figure 80:   High CPU Time – Adabas Source Database – Used Parameters

The I/O buffer (LFIOP) is responsible to do asynchronous write I/Os to disk after filled with blocks from the buffer pool (LBP), called buffer flush. It should be smaller than 25% of LBP minimizing Reptor's wait time to do the next buffer flush.

LRPL at Source and Replicator Engine

The RPL buffer of both Source database and Replicator Engine should have at least the same values. If the RPL buffer of the Replicator Engine is also used to store data into the SLOG then the RPL buffer of the Replicator Engine must hold also the data from the SLOG to the target database via the buffer pool (LBP) and the replication pool (LRPL).

Recommendation: LRPL=700M

ADADBS DSBI=OFF

Do not collect before images of data storage for replication during the update of a record on a file. DSBI=ON is only necessary for filtering data in a user exit.

The parameters controlling the replication on the source or subscription database per file should be:

```
ADADBS REPLICATION FILE=006,ON,TARGET=312,DSBI=OFF
ADADBS REPLICATION FILE=007,ON,TARGET=312,DSBI=OFF
ADADBS REPLICATION FILE=008,ON,TARGET=312,DSBI=OFF
etc.
```

Figure 81:   ADADBS REPLICATION and DSBI=OFF

ADARUN ASYTVS=YES and FMXIO=8 (max 16)

The FMXIO parameter sets the limit on the number of I/O operations that can be started in parallel by LFIOP flush processing. The value of FMXIO must be adjusted after discussions with the system programmer if parallel access volumes (PAV) are available and the SLOG file is used causing replication data to be written and read from the SLOG file.

Recommendation: both source database and replicator engine should be set to ASYTVS=YES and FMXIO>1, depends how much parallel I/O activities can be handled for PAVs.

Log Input Transaction / LOGINPUTTRANS

This parameter defines the threshold of Reptor's RPL buffer before using the Adabas file SLOG. It was reduced from 75% to 50%, regarding a former recommendation from Adabas Technical Support to avoid Reptor's lock in stress situations. Now, SAG recommends setting the threshold to 70%.

```
ARF00045: Default info updated
08:22:42      ***** A D A B A S  EVENT REPLICATOR SUBSYSTEM *****      2011-02-08
                              Global Values                           M-RP1110

          General Values                              TLOG Values
--------------------------------------------    -------------------------------
Subtasks ..................... ___3             Maximum RPL Usage ........ _50 %
Max Output Size ............ ____100000         Restart RPL Usage ......... 40 %
EntireX Broker Stub Name ... BKIMBTSO           Input Queue Level ........... 0
Input Request Msg Limit .... _____10         No Match Level .............. 0
Input Request Msg Interval _____60           Queue Completion Level ...... 0
Verify Mode ................ N                   Completion Level ............ 0
Format Buffer Validation ... N                  Request Received Level ...... 0
Record PLOG information .... Y                   Request Rejected Level ...... 0
Max Record Size ............ _____32767         Request Error Level ......... 0
Max Variable Record Size ... _____32767         Status Request Level ........ 0
Retry Interval.............. _____0          I-State Start Request Level .. 0
Retry Count................. _____10          I-State Completion Level ..... 0
Log Input Transaction ...... 070                Retransmit Request Level ..... 0
Subtask Activation Wait .... __10
Open Destinations at Start . Y
Command ==>
Enter-PF1---PF2---PF3---PF4---PF5---PF6---PF7---PF8---PF9---PF10--PF11--PF12---
     Help       Exit      Save                                        Menu
```

Figure 82:   High CPU Time – Event Replicator Subsystem – Global Parameters

Use the Log Input Transaction field to specify whether or not the Event Replicator should use its SLOG system file as a temporary storage location for incoming
compressed replication transactions, before they are queued for processing. Once
transactions have been written to the SLOG system file, the Event Replicator
Server processes them using a throttling mechanism so that only a limited
amount of Event Replicator Server replication pool space is used at a time.

Depends on the RPLPARMS parameter setting (FILE, PARMS, BOTH),
LOGINPUTTRANS can be read from DDPRINT and/or from the system file.

More than one replicator engine (Reptor)

Based on the number of files to be replicated and the number of files in one Adabas transaction, it is recommended to separate heavy updated files for Reptor A
and B. This can be valid for 100 and 200 replicated files or transactions containing
15 and 20 updates.

The Reptor collects all updates for one transaction before it sends to the target
database. Source DB stopped to replicate all files

If you use UTILONLY=YES before you apply mass replication parameters in
batch it will stop all replications.

```
ADADBS REPLICATION FILE=001,MODIFY,DEACTIVATE,TARGET=312
ADADBS REPLICATION FILE=002,MODIFY,DEACTIVATE,TARGET=312
ADADBS REPLICATION FILE=006,MODIFY,DEACTIVATE,TARGET=312
ADADBS REPLICATION FILE=012,MODIFY,DEACTIVATE,TARGET=312
. . . . .
ADADBS REPLICATION FILE=201,MODIFY,DEACTIVATE,TARGET=312
```

Figure 83:   ADADBS REPLICATION DEACTIVATE

Software AG recommends using the SYAOS function 'Modify file parameters' to activate w/o stopping the users.

6.1.3   ADAFRK – Transactions Turned Off

DDPRINT showed the message ADAFRK dbid transaction turned off.

```
14:39:32 ADAFRJ 00302 Use of SLOG for database-related input
14:39:32 ADAFRJ 00302   transactions turned on
15:58:05 ADAFRK 00302 Use of SLOG for database-related input
15:58:05 ADAFRK 00302   transactions turned off
```

Figure 84:   ADAFRK – Transactions Turned Off

This message displays after the last transaction in the SLOG has completed. Regarding to Messages and Codes, no action is required for this informational message.

6.1.4   Source DB didn't come down

ADAEND Replicator Engine – Reptor came down

ADAEND for source database didn't work – received the message:

```
ADAF1E 00134 Waiting for replication data to be
ADAF1E 00134 processed by Reptor   312"
```

Figure 85:   Source DB Waiting for Replication Message

Solution:

- Bring up the Replicator Engine
- Subscription or source database can hand off the replication data
- Subscription or source database comes down automatically from former ADAEND
- The source database must receive ADAEND before the Reptor.

6.1.5   File Changes Won't Replicate

Changes of replicated production files in the source database must also be done at the target database. Adabas does not replicate automatically file changes in Adabas on Windows. The following process must be done manually:

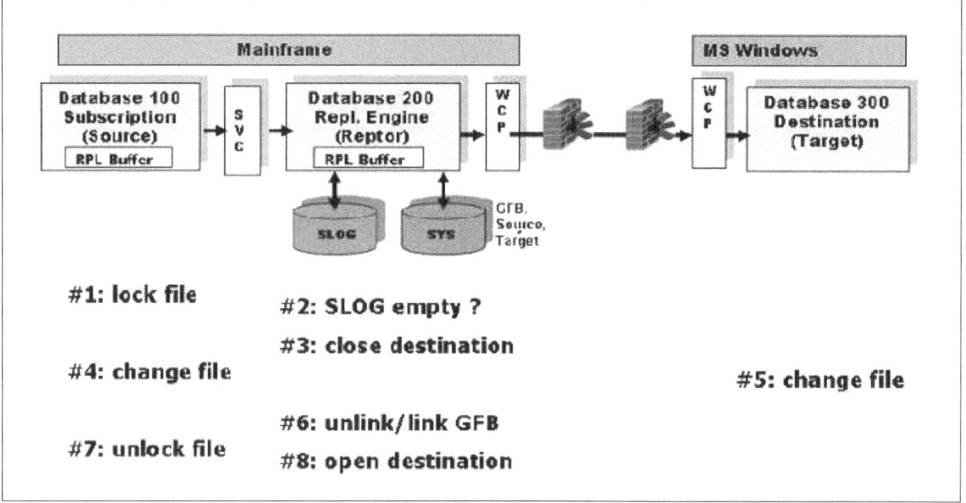

Figure 86:   Manual File Change Procedure – Dataflow

#1: Lock the file in the source or subscription database, effectively stopping replication.

- ADADBS OPERCOM STOPF=file,PURGE stops all users who are using the specified file and delete their user queue elements – don't use STOPI=1,PURGE, logical inconsistencies in the database can occur (see Utilities Manual – OPERCOM: Issue Adabas Operator Commands)
- ADADBS OPERCOM LOCKU=file locks file for all non-utility use

#2 Verify whether Reptor's SLOG is empty or no pending transactions are displayed for the relevant file(s). If not, wait before continue with the next step.

- Display Replicator Statistics
- SYSAOS
- Replicator Management
- F Display Replicator Statistics
- B Replicator Statistics
- SLog statistics for items ... On file .. xxxxx (total on SLOG file)
- PF6 = individual destination SLOG statistics

- Display Destination Statistics
- SYSAOS
- Replicator Management
- F Display Reptor statistics
- D Destination Statistics

```
15:24:17              ***** A D A B A S  BASIC  SERVICES *****        2010-10-14
Replicator 302             - Replicator Statistics -                  PRPTS10

Replicated trans  / messages / bytes   Received from input queues
-----------------------------------    -----------------------------------------
Total trn.                   32,719    Messages ...
Pending ..          18                 Bytes ......
Messages                               Commits ....
Tot msgs .                             Backouts ...
Bytes sent to all destinations
Tot bytes.                             Deleted totals from input queues
                                       -----------------------------------------
SLog statistics for items              Messages ...
-----------------------------------    Bytes ......
Delogged .                   11,146    Commits ....
Logged ...                   13,954    Backouts ...
On file ..           2,839

Replay dbid/token cnt .
Destination slog cnt ..         390                       More: press PF8

PF1--- PF3--- PF4----- PF5-------- PF6-------- PF7--- PF8--- PF12-----
Help   Exit   Refresh  DBID/Token  Dest. SLOG         +      Menu
```

Figure 87: Manual File Change Procedure – SLOG Check

```
15:35:20              ***** A D A B A S  BASIC  SERVICES *****        2010-10-14
Replicator 302             - Destination Statistics -                PRPTS04

Dest Name  Type   Total replicated transactions  Total pending trans
--------   ----   -----------------------------  ------------
 D251018   Abas                             1
 D251035   Abas                           556             2,098
 D251035   Abas                         3,091                18
 D251035   Abas                         5,764                19
 D251035   Abas                         5,954
(snip)
```

Figure 88: Manual File Change Procedure – SLOG Check

#3 **Close the destination** if SLOG is empty

*   SYSAOS
*   Replicator Management
*   A Activate/Deact/Open/Close
*   Y Close Destination

#4 **Implement the file change** in the source or subscription database

*   If not already done: SYSDIC / M Maintenance ET / Extract Maintenance / Add and Build an Extract
*   SYSDICBE / U Unload Migrate, Identification = Extract name / L Load Migrate
*   Start SYSDIC / Generate Adabas File in batch
*   FTP the Predict report from the mainframe to a Windows drive

```
(snip)
000018 //PRDLDFIL EXEC NATBT,DEPT=ST,DB=&ENV,PRM='IM=D,EJ=OFF,AUTO=ON'
000019 //CMPRINT  DD DISP=(,PASS),SPACE=(TRK,(10,10),RLSE),DSN=&&TEMP001
000020 //SYSIN    DD *
000021 LOGON SYSDIC
000022 MENU
000023 GENERATE FDT
000024 FILE-ID=DIETER-TEST-ADABAS%
000025 FNR=999%
000026 DB=STRS-DB112%
000027 DBNR=112%
000028 LOAD=N%
000029 REPLACE-FDT=N%
000030 UPD-FDT=Y%
000031 UPD-PARM=N%
000032 REPLACE-EMPTY=N%
000033 REPLACE-CRIT=N%
000034 RENUMBER=N%
000035 DATAFRM=Y%
000036 LIST=Y%
000037 STOPF=Y
000038 FIN
000039 /*
000040 //FTP      EXEC PGM=FTP,REGION=4M,PARM='(TIMEOUT 100 TRACE EXIT'
000041 //OUTPUT   DD SYSOUT=*
000042 //SYSPRINT DD SYSOUT=*
000043 //SYSTCPD  DD DISP=SHR,DSN=SYS1.TCPIP.PARMLIB(TCPDATA)
000044 //SYSFTPD  DD DISP=SHR,DSN=SYS1.TCPIP.PARMLIB(CFTPDATA)
000045 //FTPIN1   DD DISP=(SHR,PASS),DSN=*.PRDLDFIL.N.CMPRINT
000046 //INPUT    DD DISP=SHR,DSN=DIETER.CCARDS(FTPLOGON)
000047 //         DD *
000048 CD RPL-FILECHANGES
000049 ASCII
000050 PUT //DD:FTPIN1     RPL_UPD_FILES_F999.TXT
000051 QUIT
000052 END
(snip)
```

Figure 89:   Manual File Change Procedure – FTP Predict Changes to Windows

```
13:44:19                ***** P R E D I C T  4.5.2  *****              2010-11-17
                          - Generate Adabas file -
0File ID ............... DIETER-TEST-ADABAS                   PFnr ...   999
 Contained in DA ....... STRS-DB112                          PDBnr ..   112
0Action    Parameter                               Remark
0DEFFDT    FILE=999
           FNDEF='01,AA,80,A,DE'
           Field: FIELD1
           FNDEF='01,AB,10,A'
           Field: FIELD2
           FNDEF='01,AC,PE'
           Field: PE-FIELD
           FNDEF='02,AD,10,U,NU'
           Field: PE-FIELD2
           FNDEF='02,AE,3,U,NU'
(snip)
           Field: FIELD-76
           FNDEF='01,CZ,7,A,NU'
           Field: FIELD-77
           SUPDE='S1=AA(1,80),AB(1,10)'
           Field: SUPER1
 LOADFILE NOACEXTENSION=NO
           MIXDSDEV=YES
           DATAFRM=YES
           MAXISN=1271
           NAME=DIETER-TEST-ADAB
           FILE=999
           MINISN=1
           ASSOPFAC=10
           DATAPFAC=10
           PGMREFRESH=NO
           ISNSIZE=3
           INDEXCOMPRESSION=YES
           ISNREUSE=YES
           DSREUSE=YES
           MAXDS=0
           MAXNI=0
           MAXUI=0
           CIPHER=NO
           MAXRECL=5060
           UISIZE=1B
           NISIZE=1B
           DSSIZE=1B
           DSDEV=3390
  13:44:19                ***** P R E D I C T  4.5.2  *****              2010-11-17
                          - Generate Adabas file -
0File ID ............... DIETER-TEST-ADABAS                   PFnr ...   999
 Contained in DA ....... STRS-DB112                          PDBnr ..   112
 -
           FDT defined successfully
           File loaded successfully
  Page    1                                        11/17/10  13:44:19
013:44:19                ***** P R E D I C T  4.5.2  *****              2010-11-17
                          - Generate Adabas file -
0File ID ...... DIETER-TEST-ADABAS                           PFnr ...   999
 Database ID .. STRS-DB112                                   PDBnr ..   112
 DIC2369 ADABAS FILE ' DIETER-TEST-ADABAS ' GENERATED. IMPLEMENTATION AND DOCU D
 FIELD
 DATA FIN
 NAT9995 Natural session terminated normally.
```

Figure 90:   Manual File Change Procedure – Predict Change Report

#5 Implement the file change in the target database

- Automated process
  An event-driven process will automatically parse the Predict report for
  DEVFDT and LOADFILE information and update the target database.
  Figure 91 – shows the dataflow of the file change process. It can be automated
  on the mainframe site. Updates on the open system site must wait until all
  transactions for the file(s) to be replicated are no longer in the RPL buffer or
  the SLOG file.
  It also should be discussed whether file changes can be done before or during
  a program migration.
  New files: can be done before the program migration.
  New fields, descriptors and superdescriptors: can be done before the program
  migration.
  Adding new fields into a PE group: must be done during program migration.
  Field changes: must be done during program migration.
  Release descriptors: must be done during program migration.

- Manual process
  Remote Desktop Connection
  Adabas DBA Workbench
  Select a Database
  List Files and Select
  Scroll down using the file or descriptor tabs
  Apply all changes

#6 Unlink and link the GFB to get and save the new field formats on Reptor's
system file

- SYSREPTOR
- G Global Format Buffer Definitions
- Select the name of the global format, e. g. G300009
- Mark Predict parameters
- Unlink (PF6)

#7 Unlock the file in the source database to restart the replication

- ADADBS OPERCOM UNLOCKU=file
- Unlock the specified file for utility use and restore it to its pre-locked status for
  non-utility users

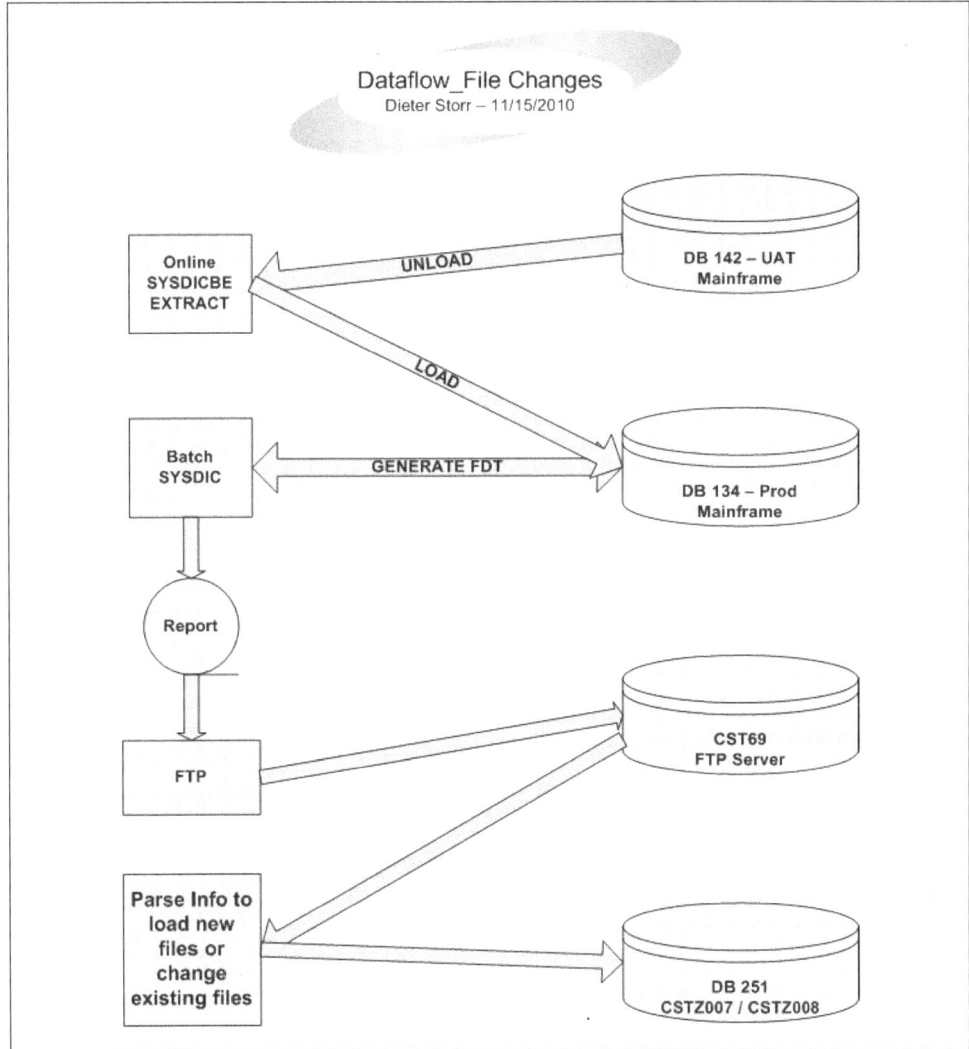

Figure 91: Manual File Change Procedure – Dataflow

#8 Open the destination

- SYSAOS
- Replicator Management
- A Activate/Deact/Open/Close
- K Open Destination

```
10:56:18           ***** A D A B A S  BASIC  SERVICES *****          2010-11-08
Replicator 302     - Replicator Activate/Deact/Open/Close -          PRPT002

    Code    Service                      Code    Service
    ----    --------------------         ----    --------------------
     B      Activate Subscription         R      Deactivate Subscription
     D      Activate Destination          S      Deactivate Destination
     F      Activate DBID/File            U      Deactivate DBID/File
     I      Activate DBID                 X      Deactivate DBID
     K      Open Destination              Y      Close Destination
     O      Open Iqueue                   Z      Close Iqueue
     ?      Help                          .      Exit
    ----    --------------------         ----    --------------------
            Code .......... _
            Subscription ... _____
            Destination .... _____
            Iqueue ......... _____
            Database ID .... _____
            File .......... ____

PF1----- PF2------ PF3------ PF4------ PF6----- PF7----- PF8----- PF12-----
Help               Exit
```

Figure 92:   Manual File Change Procedure – Open the Destination

6.2   Replicator Engine (Reptor)

6.2.1   NAB Overflow

The Replicator Engine uses for each update command (store, update, delete) in one transaction a separate attached buffer (AB). It collects and holds all update commands until the transaction receives an end-of-transaction (ET) command. It sends then all Adabas commands of this transaction to the target database.

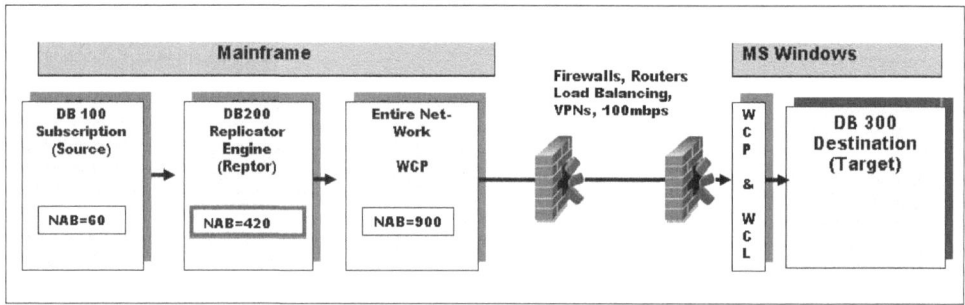

Figure 93:   NAB Overflow on Reptor

```
ADAF18  A1 cmd to DBID   300 FNR    18 RSP    254 subcode    3 ISN        185
```

Figure 94:   NAB Overflow Message

RSP 254 = An internal error occurred during processing of an attached buffer (buffer overflow)

Subcode 3 = CQEFLAG is not equal to CQEFAB plus CQEFW16

Solution:

Replicator: NAB 420 is too small and should be increased. Each update command (store, update, delete) in one transaction (ET) needs one attached buffer.

The formula in the manual is not correct. It must be:

NAB = 41 x 10 x number of source databases (e. g. 1) x number of updates per transaction (e. g. 15)

NAB = 41 x 10 x 1 x 15 = 6,150

The high-water-mark of the attached buffer (NAB) is observed with the AOS command.

```
The actual  h i g h - w a t e r - m a r k s
       for the major pools (except bufferpool)


AREA            ADARUN PARM    HIGH-WATER-MARK
----------------------------------------------------

AB  -POOL    NAB=       420    1715456 ( 99 %)
CQ  -POOL    NC =     23040       1920 (  8 %)
DUQ -POOL    LDE=    100000        871 (  0 %)
FI  -POOL    LFP=    300000      29888 (  9 %)
HQ  -POOL    NH =    560056        700 (  0 %)
RPL -POOL    LRPL= 157286400  149875480 ( 95 %)
SC  -POOL    LCP=     10000          0 (  0 %)
TBI -POOL    LI =     12000        804 (  6 %)
TBS -POOL    LQ =     20000        864 (  4 %)
UQ  -POOL    NU =      4000      17248 (  1 %)
UQF -POOL    NU =      4000       3168 (  0 %)
WORK-POOL    LWP=    500000      53112 ( 10 %)
XID -POOL    XID=                       (  0 %)
```

Figure 95: NAB Overflow High Water Mark

6.2.2 Replicator Buffer (LRPL) Overflow

The Replicator buffer must be defined in the source database and in the Replicator Engine by using the LRPL parameter.

An overflow in the source database leads to a halt of the replication process because no overflow area is available.

In general, the same situation happens with a replication overflow buffer in the Replicator Engine, even if an overflow area (SLOG) is defined. The trick is that you have to set a threshold in Reptor's RPL buffer. If the threshold is reached, for example 75%, all incoming transactions will be stored into the SLOG area.

After new tests in October 2010 with mass updates the parameter LRPL is set in both source database and Replicator Engine to 600MB. The high-water-marks show now for the source database 80% used and for the Reptor 74% used.

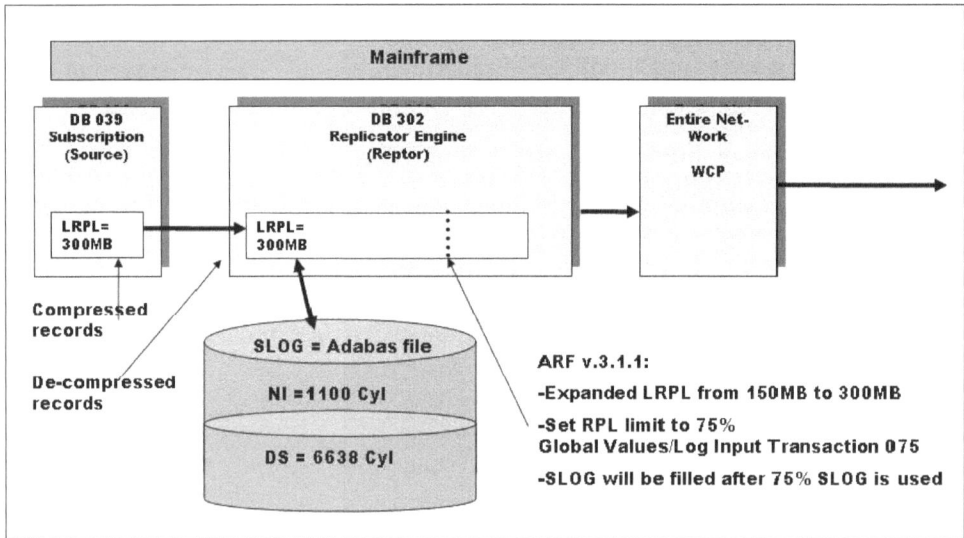

Figure 96:   LRPL Overflow Reptor

The high-water mark of the attached buffer (NAB) is observed with the AOS command.

```
The actual  h i g h - w a t e r - m a r k s
        for the major pools (except bufferpool)


AREA                ADARUN PARM     HIGH-WATER-MARK
-----------------------------------------------------

AB   -POOL     NAB=        420     1715456 ( 99 %)
CQ   -POOL     NC =      23040        1920 (  8 %)
DUQ  -POOL     LDE=     100000         871 (  0 %)
FI   -POOL     LFP=     300000       29888 (  9 %)
HQ   -POOL     NH =     560056         700 (  0 %)
RPL  -POOL     LRPL= 157286400   149875480 ( 95 %)
SC   -POOL     LCP=      10000           0 (  0 %)
TBI  -POOL     LI =      12000         804 (  6 %)
TBS  -POOL     LQ =      20000         864 (  4 %)
UQ   -POOL     NU =       4000       17248 (  1 %)
UQF  -POOL     NU =       4000        3168 (  0 %)
WORK-POOL      LWP=     500000       53112 ( 10 %)
XID  -POOL     XID=                          (  0 %)
```

Figure 97:   LRPL Overflow Reptor High Water Mark

6.2.3   SLOG Overflow

The overflow area of Reptor's replication buffer (SLOG = subscription or source log) should be defined with sufficient space to hold all transactions from the source database for a couple of days in case the network or the target database have problems and the destination is closed.

It is recommended to use an entire 3390-disk for SLOG

```
15:01:52              ***** A D A B A S  BASIC  SERVICES *****        2010-09-24
DBID 302                       - Display File Layout -                PDRF042
****************
* File 30    *   ST-SLOG
****************
Records loaded ..... 35625        Date loaded ......... 2010-01-25 13:55:09
TOP ISN ............ 35532        Date of last update .. 2010-09-24 15:01:08
Max ISN expected ... 5000655      Max Compr Rec Lngth .. 5060
Minimum ISN ........ 1            Asso/Data Padding .... 1%/1%
Size of ISN ........ 4 Bytes      Highest Index Level .. 3
Number of Updates .. 52929        RPLUPDATEONLY. No   Indx Comp ...... Yes
ISN Reusage ........ Yes          USERISN ...... No   PGMREFRESH ..... No
Space Reusage ...... Yes          MIXDSDEV ..... No   NOACEXTENSION .. No
ADAM File .......... No           Spanned rec .. No   MU/PE indices .. 1
Ciphered File ...... No           Replication .. No   Privileged Use . No
Coupled Files ...... None         Universal Encoding ... Yes
Blk per DS Extent .. 0
Blk per UI Extent .. 0            Total Changed Blks ... 37102
Blk per NI Extent .. 0            Multi Client File .... 0
Free space available for file extents: At least 134  Extents

    I Dev  LiI  Space allocated  I      From            To    I Unused
    I Type TyI  Blocks    / Cyls. I     RABN           RABN   I BLOCKS   /  Cyls.
----I--------I------------------I ----------------------I-----------------
    I        I                  I                        I
ASSOI 3390 ACI    5897       21 I    1780 -      7676 I      0        0
ASSOI 3390 UII     200        0 I  304677 -    304876 I    194        0
ASSOI 3390 NII  297000     1100 I    7677 -    304676 I 296556     1098
    I        I                  I                        I
DATAI 3390 DSI  995700     6638 I     551 -    996250 I 892920     5952
```

Figure 98:   Adabas Report SLOG file

Check the following parameters if SLOG is used as an overflow for the RPL buffer on Reptor

- ASYTVS   Async Buffer Flush Based on VolSer#
- FMXIO   Max Number of Parallel I/Os by LFIOP Flush Proc
- LBP   Buffer Pool
- LDEUQP   Unique Descriptor Pool
- LFIOP   Asynchronous Flush Pool
- LP   Work Part 1
- NH   Number of Hold Queue Elements
- NISNHQ   Number of ISNs in Hold Queue for Users

6.2.4   RSP 153 from the Target DB

According Messages and Codes V6.2 SP2, Adabas can only handle one call at a time.

Adabas response code 153 is reported by the Replicator Engine in DDPRINT:

```
11:07:34 ADAF54 00302 Replication error: Adabas destination D251011
11:07:34 ADAF54 00302  Source DBID      39 FNR     11, Target DBID   251 FNR    11
ADAF18  N2 cmd to DBID   251 FNR    11 RSP    153 subcode 16448 ISN      75423
13:00:04 ADAF54 00302 Replication error: Adabas destination D251044
13:00:04 ADAF54 00302  Source DBID      39 FNR     44, Target DBID   251 FNR    44
ADAF18  N2 cmd to DBID   251 FNR    44 RSP    153 subcode 16448 ISN      522015
ADAF54 2010-11-22 13:00:04 Replication error: Adabas destination D251044
ADAF54   Source DBID     39 FNR    44, Target DBID   251 FNR    44
ADAF18  N2 cmd to DBID   251 FNR    44 RSP    153 subcode 16448 ISN      522016
ADAF54 2010-11-22 13:00:04 Replication error: Adabas destination D251044
ADAF54   Source DBID     39 FNR    44, Target DBID   251 FNR    44
ADAF18  N2 cmd to DBID   251 FNR    44 RSP    153 subcode 16448 ISN      522017
ADAF54 2010-11-22 13:00:04 Replication error: Adabas destination D251044
ADAF54   Source DBID     39 FNR    44, Target DBID   251 FNR    44
ADAF18  N2 cmd to DBID   251 FNR    44 RSP    153 subcode 16448 ISN      522018
ADAF54 2010-11-22 13:00:04 Replication error: Adabas destination D251044
ADAF54   Source DBID     39 FNR    44, Target DBID   251 FNR    44
ADAF18  N2 cmd to DBID   251 FNR    44 RSP    153 subcode 16448 ISN      522019
 (snip)
```

Figure 99:   Response Code 153 Shown in Reptor

The command log of the target database shows that the reported ISNs are not replicated. For file 44, the missed 52 ISNs are 522015-522029, 1088638-1088673, and 1088678. Surprisingly, the response code is not reported in the command log of the target database and therefore seems to be set by the ADALINK routine in Entire Net-Work.

```
    DATE                      DUR  USER-ID  NODE-ID  CMD RSP  AD2(HEX)/AD2   FILE      ISN
 IOA IOD IOW
-----------------------------------------------------------------------------------------
 (snip)
2713174 22-NOV-2010 13:00:05    0           ..B...B.  N2   0  00000140/@...    44    522008
2713175 22-NOV-2010 13:00:05    0           .B...B.   N2   0  0000013B/;...    44    522009
2713176 22-NOV-2010 13:00:05    0           ..B...B.  N2   0  0000013E/>...    44    522010
2713177 22-NOV-2010 13:00:05    0           ..B...B.  N2   0  00000135/5...    44    522011
2713178 22-NOV-2010 13:00:05    0           ..B...B.  N2   0  0000013C/<...    44    522012
2713179 22-NOV-2010 13:00:05    0           ..B...B.  N2   0  00000140/@...    44    522013
2713180 22-NOV-2010 13:00:05    0  STCHK251 ..B...B.  OP   0  00000000/....     0         0
2713181 22-NOV-2010 13:00:05    0           ..B...B.  N2   0  0000013C/<...    44    522014
2713182 22-NOV-2010 13:00:05   62  STCHK251 ..B...B.  L1   0  003A012B/+.:.    44         1
2713183 22-NOV-2010 13:00:05    0  STCHK251 ..B...B.  RC   0  00000000/....     0         0
2713184 22-NOV-2010 13:00:05    0  STCHK251 ..B...B.  RC   0  00000000/....     0         0
2713185 22-NOV-2010 13:00:05    0           ..B...B. .N2   0  0000013B/;...    44    522030
2713186 22-NOV-2010 13:00:05    0  STCHK251 ..B...B. .CL   0  00000000/....     0         0
2713187 22-NOV-2010 13:00:05    0           ..B...B. .N2   0  00000150/P...    44    522031
2713188 22-NOV-2010 13:00:05    0           ..B...B. .N2   0  00000150/P...    44    522032
2713189 22-NOV-2010 13:00:05    0           ..B...B. .N2   0  0000013F/?...    44    522033
2713190 22-NOV-2010 13:00:05    0           ..B...B. .N2   0  0000013D/=...    44    522034
 (snip)
```

Figure 100:   Response Code 153 – CLOG Adabas Windows

This response code is caused by a Natural batch program, job STCHK251, reading a record from file 44, and it is the same file as the file to be replicated. In another case, file 231 was read, when file 11 was replicated. As another customer reported, this also happened without active replication and two batch programs try to read records from the replicated Adabas database on Windows.

The following example shows that file 11 of database 251 received response code 153, when trying to store ISN 75423 via a N2-command. The command log shows that ISN 75423 is missing at the same time a LF-command was issued for file 231.

```
From DDPRINT of Reptor:
ADAF18   N2 cmd to DBID    251 FNR     11 RSP    153 subcode 16448 ISN         75423


From the command log of the target database:
REC   DATE                                      CMD RSP
                         DUR    USER-ID               AD2(HEX)/       FILE  ISN    TH IOA IOD
IOW
  79219 22-NOV-2010 11:07:35      0   ..B...B. ....~... N2 0 0000004E/N...    11   75414 3  0  0  0
  79220 22-NOV-2010 11:07:35      0   ..B...B. ....~... N2 0 000000B2/....    11   75415 5  0  0  0
  79221 22-NOV-2010 11:07:35      0   ..B...B. ....~... N2 0 0000006B/k...    11   75416 15 0  0  0
  79222 22-NOV-2010 11:07:35      0   ..B...B. ....~... N2 0 000000CD/....    11   75417 20 0  0  0
  79223 22-NOV-2010 11:07:35      0   ..B...B. ........ OP 0 00000000/.... .   0     0 10 0  0  0
  79224 22-NOV-2010 11:07:35      0   ..B...B. ....~... N2 0 00000075/u...    11   75418 1  0  0  0
  79225 22-NOV-2010 11:07:35      0   ..B...B. ....~... N2 0 000000E9/....    11   75419 16 0  0  0
  79226 22-NOV-2010 11:07:35      0   ..B...B. ....~... N2 0 00000050/P...    11   75420 19 0  0  0
  79227 22-NOV-2010 11:07:35      0   ..B...B. ....~... N2 0 000000D4/....    11   75421 12 0  0  0
  79228 22-NOV-2010 11:07:35      0   ..B...B. ....~... N2 0 00000050/P...    11   75422 17 0  0  0
  79229 22-NOV-2010 11:07:35     16   ..B...B. ........ LF 0 000004F4/.... S  231     0 8  1  0  0
  79230 22-NOV-2010 11:07:35      0   ..B...B. ....~... N2 0 0000008E/....    11   75424 14 0  0  0
  79231 22-NOV-2010 11:07:35      0   ..B...B. ....~... N2 0 000000BB/....    11   75425 18 0  0  0
  79232 22-NOV-2010 11:07:35      0   ..B...B. ....~... N2 0 000000CF/....    11   75426 4  0  0  0
  79233 22-NOV-2010 11:07:35      0   ..B...B. ....~... N2 0 00000085/....    11   75427 6  0  0  0
  79234 22-NOV-2010 11:07:35      0   ..B...B. ....~... N2 0 000000A7/....    11   75428 9  0  0  0
  79235 22-NOV-2010 11:07:35      0   ..B...B. ....~... N2 0 000000B0/....    11   75429 11 0  0
```

Figure 101: Response Code 153 – not shown in CLOG of Adabas Windows

According to Empower, this response code is known since December 2009. What is new that some records as part of a transaction were not replicated, they disappear. It seems at this time that the response code 153 doesn't come from the target database; it is coming from Entire Net-Work. Sending a simple PING from CICS does not create RC153; but sending it from batch, RC153 is repeatable.

Based on the trace, the Adabas session ID contains binary zeroes. This has been solved with WCP733X003 – WCPv733 Hotfix #3 for Windows 2003 Server from 7/31/2009 and Hotfix #4 for Windows 2008 Server. Entire Net-Work's link routine was fixed.

- Adalnkx.dll   v6.2.1.38
- Adamplnk.dll   v6.2.1.38
- and others

The solution is also available for UNIX and Linux.

For v734

- Adalnkx.dll   v6.2.1.48 from 3/4/2010
- Adamplnk.dll   v6.2.1.48 from 3/4/2010
- and others

Software AG also recommends setting ADABAS_TIMEOUT on the client side (WCL) to the same value as the transaction time (TT) on the remote database.

The reason for the RSP 153 seems to be clear now: ISN's are in HOLD state on database, Natural runs with parameter WH=ON and ADABAS_TIMEOUT is lower than TRANSACTION_TIME on Adabas.

But it still doesn't explain why some updates of the transaction did not replicate and others of the same transaction did.

6.2.5   RSP 113 from the Target DB

The error codes are parsed from REPTOR's DDPRINT. The Reptor can determine between three different actions:

- The record will be updated if the record already exists.
- The record will be inserted if an update cannot find the record.
- No action if the record to be deleted does not exist.

```
(snip)

14:37:03 ADAF54 00312  Source DBID   134 FNR   122, Target DBID   134 FNR   122
ADAF18  N2 cmd to DBID   134 FNR   122 RSP   113 subcode      ISN    12440974
ADAFCV  The record to be inserted already exists on the target DBID/file
ADAFCY  The record will be updated.

ADAF54 2011-01-05 16:39:59 Replication error: Adabas destination D251112
ADAF54  Source DBID   134 FNR   112, Target DBID   251 FNR   112
ADAF18  E1 cmd to DBID   251 FNR   112 RSP   113 subcode      ISN       435139
ADAFCU  The record to be deleted does not exist on the target DBID/file

19:13:41 ADAF54 00312  Source DBID   134 FNR   154, Target DBID   251 FNR   154
ADAF18  A1 cmd to DBID   251 FNR   154 RSP   113 subcode      ISN        33
ADAFCU  The record to be updated does not exist on the target DBID/file
ADAFCX  The record will be inserted.

20:16:44 ADAF54 00312  Source DBID   134 FNR   148, Target DBID   251 FNR   148
ADAF18  N2 cmd to DBID   251 FNR   148 RSP   113 subcode      ISN       87430
ADAFCV  The record to be inserted already exists on the target DBID/file
ADAFCY  The record will be updated.

(snip)
```

Figure 102:   Response Code 113 – Message in Reptor

Reasons for RSP 113

ISN REUSAGE was not enabled on the target files. ADAREP displays two values

Enabled, Inactive

It means that ISN REUSAGE is set to this file, and there are no UPDATEs or IN-
SERTs being executed at the moment (no ISNs are being reused at the moment
when ADAREP was run).

Enabled, active

It means that ISN REUSAGE is set to this file, and UPDATEs or INSERTs are being executed at the moment (ISNs are being reused at the moment when
ADAREP was run).

```
Database 251, File   122  (ST-REVIEW-LOG   )          06-JAN-2011 12:35:31


Highest Index Level:          4    Padding Factors:      ASSO    5%, DATA    5%
Top ISN:              12,440,960    Maximum ISN expected:          12,449,279
Records loaded:       12,434,148
Last FDT Modification:             03-JAN-2011 11:21:59.055000

ISN reusage:     Enabled, active    Space reusage:     Enabled
Program refresh: Disabled           Ciphering:         Disabled
```

Figure 103:   Response Code 113 – ISN Reusage

Target files were not refreshed for an initial-state or replay function.

Solution:

- Close all destinations
- Close subscription for file(s)
- Take one file with most activities
- Turn on ISNREUSE for files
- Verify the flag
- Reload file 122 and reset the flag
- Use SYSREPTOR to create a TOKEN (sync) for D251122 and S251122
- FEOFPL in production
- Start PARSEPLOG and determine the PLOG dataset names
- Create the REPLAY job (concatenate the datasets and update the TOKEN #)
- Start the REPLAY job
  REPLAY will open the subscription and destination for file 122 and coordinate
  new updates with updates from the PLOG datasets
- Verify that no more RC113 take place
- If this test was OK, redo it for the other 6 files

MAXISN

An N2 command was issued with ISN larger than the MAXISN in effect for this file in the target database.

Under Windows, Adabas extents only 1 block if the MAXISN is not sufficient.

6.2.6   RSP 98 from the Target DB

Error codes parsed from REPTOR's DDPRINT:

```
(snip)

17:02:11 ADAF54 00312 Replication error: Adabas destination D251080
17:02:11 ADAF54 00312  Source DBID    134 FNR    80, Target DBID    251 FNR    80
ADAF18  N2 cmd to DBID    251 FNR    80 RSP    98 subcode 49622 ISN           1
ADAF54 2011-01-05 17:02:10 Replication error: Adabas destination D251080
ADAF54  Source DBID    134 FNR    80, Target DBID    251 FNR    80
ADAF18  E1 cmd to DBID    251 FNR    80 RSP    113 subcode       ISN           1
ADAFCU  The record to be deleted does not exist on the target DBID/file

(snip)

000001  Start date= 2011-003    Start time= 01:55:02
000002  January  3, 2011, Monday
FNR/RSP/CNT 14 98 23
FNR/RSP/CNT 80 98 280
FNR/RSP/CNT 80 113 280
FNR/RSP/CNT 112 98 224
FNR/RSP/CNT 112 113 10
FNR/RSP/CNT 122 113 8101
FNR/RSP/CNT 148 113 1
FNR/RSP/CNT 154 113 1
FNR/RSP/CNT 221 113 1032
********************************************************
Please check the ADABAS response codes!
********************************************************
The above errors were extracted from the following dataset.
REPTOR.DDPRINT.G0045V00
```

Figure 104:   Response Code 98 Shown in Reptor and Parse Program

Reasons for RSP 98

Uniqueness violation of unique descriptor detected during store/update if subtransactions are not activated, or otherwise at end of subtransaction. The third and fourth bytes of the Additions 2 field contain the name of the descriptor which caused the uniqueness conflict

The descriptor or superdescriptor is defined as unique and the store command tries to add a record with the same existing value.

In this case, file 80 was empty and the first store with ISN 1 resulted into RSP 98.

A test with a Natural program and without the Reptor could not repeat the response code.

6.2.7   RSP 162 from the Target DB

Error codes parsed from REPTOR's DDPRINT:

```
21:05:16 ADAF54 00312 Replication error: Adabas destination D251044
21:05:16 ADAF54 00312  Source DBID    134 FNR    44, Target DBID   251 FNR    44
ADAF18  A1 cmd to DBID   251 FNR    44 RSP   162 subcode 17473 ISN   35249065
21:05:19 ADAF54 00312 Replication error: Adabas destination D251046
21:05:19 ADAF54 00312  Source DBID    134 FNR    46, Target DBID   251 FNR    46
ADAF18  A1 cmd to DBID   251 FNR    46 RSP   162 subcode 17473 ISN    4732732
ADAF54 2011-01-07 21:05:18 Replication error: Adabas destination D251046
ADAF54   Source DBID    134 FNR    46, Target DBID   251 FNR    46
ADAF18  A1 cmd to DBID   251 FNR    46 RSP   162 subcode 17473 ISN    4738881
ADAF54 2011-01-07 21:05:18 Replication error: Adabas destination D251046
ADAF54   Source DBID    134 FNR    46, Target DBID   251 FNR    46
ADAF18  A1 cmd to DBID   251 FNR    46 RSP   162 subcode 17473 ISN    6023043
ADAF54 2011-01-07 21:05:18 Replication error: Adabas destination D251046
ADAF54   Source DBID    134 FNR    46, Target DBID   251 FNR    46
ADAF18  A1 cmd to DBID   251 FNR    46 RSP   162 subcode 17473 ISN    6024172
 (snip)
```

Figure 105:   Response Code 162 Shown in Reptor

RSP 162 means that no additional space was available for the Adabas buffer pool. Increase the value of the LBP parameter. Because the buffer pool overflow is normally caused by too many blocks in the buffer pool waiting to be written to disk, specifying a low value for the WRITE_LIMIT parameter is recommended. This parameter is similar to LFIOP on the mainframe but without I/O pool and I/Os are not done asynchronously.

Solution:

```
Old with RSP 162:
%ADANUC-I-PARSET, setting of LBP=157286400
%ADANUC-I-PARSET, setting of WRITE_LIMIT=25

New:
%ADANUC-I-PARSET, setting of LBP=419430400
%ADANUC-I-PARSET, setting of WRITE_LIMIT=5
```

Figure 106:   Response Code 162 – LBP and WRITE_LIMIT

See also chapter 6.3.6, RSP 162 – LBP Space Problems.

6.2.8   Special characters are not correctly replicated

Comparing one file (27) from the source database (39) with files from the replicated target database (251) showed that the special character, the caret sign or circumflex '^' , was not translated correctly.

```
11/04/2010 14:00:17.7 Started CHKSM027        Checksum Comparison
        File FILE-027                         File#:    27

 DBID   Records                 Checksum                    CPU Time
 -----  ----------  -------------------------------------  ----------

 DBID being accessed:    39
 BV-1 ^PYMT-THRU-DT
 BV-1 B0D7E8D4E360E3C8D9E460C4E3404040404040404040404040404040404040404040
     39        1 6D025E9D31B7EACFD6911FEC9A62D83C734B2A0E 00:00:00.0
 DBID being accessed:   251
 BV-1 ?PYMT-THRU-DT
 BV-1 07D7E8D4E360E3C8D9E460C4E3404040404040404040404040404040404040404040
    251        1 5F1F4D02BAFD221167CE0ABB1BAF778C78CCE025 00:00:00.0

    Counters match

              >>>>>  Checksums do not match  <<<<<
 11/04/2010 14:00:17.8 Ended
 00:00:00.0
```

Figure 107:   Special Character not Translated Correctly

The CCSID of the EBCDIC code page in Entire Net-Work and/or Adabas are responsible for this error and must be changed. From the IBM documentation, with EBCDIC CCSID 37 the caret should be X'B0'. The following parts contain code pages:

- Adabas mainframe
- Replicator mainframe
- Entire Net-Work mainframe
- Entire Net-Work Windows
- Adabas Windows:

6.2.9   Wrong Replicated File in SLOG

At a client-site, we tried to replicate a file in error with a file number not available at the target database. Subscription, destination and global format were defined and the data was saved into the SLOG file waiting until the target file is available. We could not correct the mistakenly defined Reptor definitions because of the waiting SLOG data until we refreshed the SLOG file.

The SLOG file is a system file in Adabas and therefore, it cannot be done if the nucleus is up and running.

To try it online with SYSAOS leads to the error "E09 : Unknown subcode for rsp 064". Also, the ADADBS utility in batch as well as UNLOAD, DELETE and LOAD get an error message.

The following steps are necessary:

- Change the parameter file for the Replicator
  From ADARUN RPLPARMS=FILE
  To ADARUN RPLPARMS=NONE
- Bring down the Replicator (ADAEND)
- Bring up the Replicator (with the adjusted parm)
- Refresh the SLOG file, for example file 30
- Change the parameter file for replicator
  From ADARUN RPLPARMS=NONE
  To ADARUN RPLPARMS=FILE
- Bring down the Replicator (ADAEND)
- Bring up the Replicator (with the old parameter RPLPARMS=FILE)

```
MENFLR05 : File 30  refreshed successfully

17:34:53           ***** A D A B A S  BASIC  SERVICES *****      2010-09-23
DBID 302                     - Display File Layout -             PDRF042
****************
*  File 30    *   ST-SLOG
****************

Records loaded ..... 0           Date loaded ......... 2010-01-25 13:55:09
TOP ISN ............ 0           Date of last update .. 2010-09-23 17:32:25
```

Figure 108: Refresh SLOG

6.2.10 RSP 148 From Target DB

Normally, the response code 148 or NAT3148 means that the database is not active. Is the database in a network and Entire Net-Work (WCP) is used, the following messages can be displayed:

```
<snip>
ADAF54 2009-02-03 11:07:14 Replication error: Adabas destination D187044
ADAF54  Source DBID    134 FNR     44, Target DBID    187 FNR     44
ADAF18  OP cmd to DBID    187 FNR       RSP    148 subcode  8224
ADAF54 2009-02-03 11:07:14 Replication error: Adabas destination D187044
ADAF54  Source DBID    134 FNR     44, Target DBID    187 FNR     44
ADAF18  A1 cmd to DBID    187 FNR     44 RSP    148 subcode  8224 ISN    146148454
11:07:15 ADAFCQ 00312 Destination D187044  is being closed
11:17:46 ADAF8N 00312 Close request received for destination D187044
11:17:46 ADAF8W 00312 Destination D187044  closed on all tasks
<snip>
```

Figure 109: Response Code 148 – Entire Net-Work or DB not Up

```
NAT3148 Database 20251,Network ID 50951 currently not active. Subc 50
```

Figure 110: Response Code 148 – NAT3148

The message is given if

- The database is defined LOCAL=YES in ADARUN and
- Accessed from a node other than the local

The subcode 50 is documented as

- '50: Set in MPM routine MPM12. (mainframe systems)'.
  Neither MPM nor MPM12 are further documented in ADA813 or ADA821 manuals.

Subcodes for RSP-148 will be marked in Manual Messages and Codes as 'Internal Information' in the future, starting with ADABAS 8.2.

Solution:

Check the following and restart if necessary by using the System Management Hub and/or Windows' Computer Management

System Management Hub

- Resources
- Click on Entire Net-Work Server
- Click on Servers
- Click on the + sign to open the server in question, e. g. CST86
- Click on the + sign to open the next level
- Right-click on the server to open a pop-up window
- Click on Start Kernel
- Click on the server one level above to see the status
- The status should be Server xxxxx Status Started

Connectivity

- Click on Kernels
- The kernels with server names displays
- In the right column, the kernel names, server names and the status are displayed
- Click on the kernel name in the left column and you will see the databases and its connections
- Expand databases and click on one to see in the right column the status
- Right-click are to ping, refresh and other functions

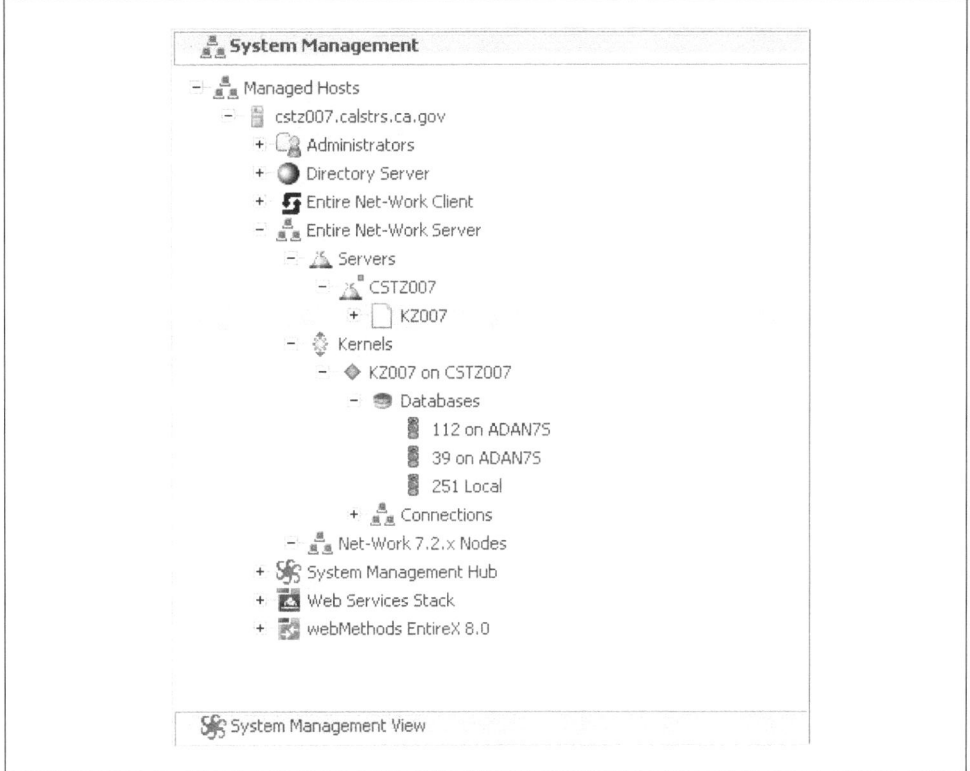

Figure 111: System Management Hub – Connectivity Check

Computer Management

Make also sure that two Windows services of Entire Net-Work are running.

- Right-click on MyComputer / Manage / Services and Applications / Services
- Select (high-light) and a right mouse click
- Software AG Entire Net-Work Client Administration Service
- Software AG Entire Net-Work Server Administration Service
- If necessary select 'Restart'

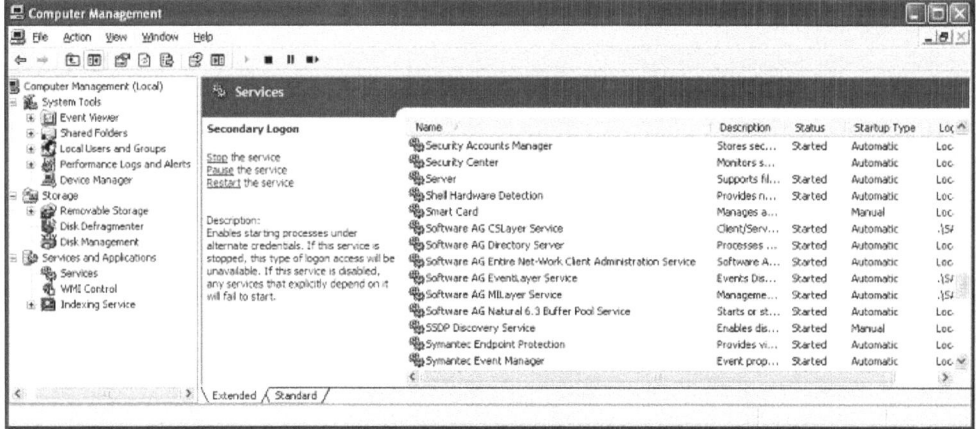

Figure 112:   Computer Management – Services Check

6.2.11 Node is unreachable

```
17:12:35 NET0107I: Link VM006 disconnected from node MVSSY7
```

Figure 113:   Node is Unreachable

Solution:

Use System Management Hub and Windows Computer Management.

See chapter 6.2.10, RSP 148 From Target DB.

6.2.12 Communication Problem

This problem can occur if the target database or the Net-Work (WCP) is down:

RSP 148: Adabas nucleus is not active

RSP 224: Entire Net-Work (WCP) – reply timeout

```
<snip>
ADAF54 2009-02-03 11:07:14 Replication error: Adabas destination D187044
ADAF54   Source DBID   134 FNR    44, Target DBID   187 FNR    44
ADAF18  OP cmd to DBID   187 FNR       RSP   148 subcode  8224
ADAF54 2009-02-03 11:07:14 Replication error: Adabas destination D187044
ADAF54   Source DBID   134 FNR    44, Target DBID   187 FNR    44
ADAF18  A1 cmd to DBID   187 FNR    44 RSP   148 subcode  8224 ISN   146148454
11:07:15 ADAFCQ 00312 Destination D187044  is being closed
11:17:46 ADAF8N 00312 Close request received for destination D187044
11:17:46 ADAF8W 00312 Destination D187044  closed on all tasks
<snip>
```

Figure 114:   Communication Problem

Solution:

Use System Management Hub and Windows Computer Management.

See chapter 6.2.10, RSP 148 From Target DB.

6.2.13 SLOG data disappeared

The Replicator Engine was stopped with a HALT command instead of ADAEND.

6.2.14 Replication is too slow

There are several components in the path from the source to the target database, which can be the reason for the slow replication, especially when you replicate from Adabas on the mainframe to Adabas on Windows:

Replicator Engine or Reptor

The replication buffer can be too small and the parameter LRPL must be increased to minimize the overflow area in SLOG. Check also the Adabas buffer pool (LBP) and the size of the I/O pool (LFIOP).

For SLOG usage check whether asynchronous I/O by volume is activated (ASYTVS=YES) and parallel LFIOP I/Os (FMXIO=x) are set to a value greater than 1. Replication data is written to and read from SLOG.

Make sure that the length of intermediate user buffer area (LU) is set to 200,000. The recommended value of 167,000 is not sufficient to accommodate more than 1,200 update commands per second with a high number of files per transaction.

The number of attached buffers (NAB) must be set to 41 x 10 x 1 x number of files in one transaction. Reptor holds all updates of one transaction before submitting it to the target database. And each file uses one attached buffer.

Entire Net-Work (Mainframe)

The number of attached buffers (NAB) and the length of intermediate user buffer area (LU) should have the same value as defined for Reptor.

Network

Line or circuit between the mainframe and the open system server.

Adabas on Windows

Remove ASSO and DATA from the hard drive C of the PC or server and define both on a SAN box with fast channels and disk arrays (raid-5). For example E-drive for ASSO and WORK and F-drive for DATA and SORT and TEMP.

Reduce the duration of a buffer flush by specifying the percentage of modified blocks permitted in the buffer pool before an implicit buffer flush is taken. Tests showed that a good value is to set WRITE_LIMIT=5. Keep in mind that during a buffer flush no update command will be selected from the command queue and the Reptor waits to submit the next transaction.

Limit the number of parallel I/O requests by a buffer flush and allow earlier processing of concurrent I/Os from other threads by using the parameter BFIO_PARALLEL_LIMIT. Tests in a Windows environment with values between 0 and 50 showed that the value 0 brought the best replication performance and did not result in an I/O error during asynchronous I/Os.

6.2.15 Initial state is too slow

Tests showed that a large file with 17 descriptors and 167 million ISNs would take approximately four days to replicate by using Replicator's 'Initial State' function. To bring the target database in an initial state with 200 files can take weeks. Based on many replication tests, up to 417 records can be replicated per second. Even if you can tune the replication process up to 1000 records per second, it would take approximately 46 hours to have one file at the target.

Another possibility is to decompress 200 files, FTP, compress and reload into the target database. This process takes nearly 3 days. In the meantime, the source database continues to update and the records to be replicated must be collected in SLOG.

A possible solution is ADAMAGIC (distributed by TREEHOUSE) to FTP the compressed backup from the mainframe to Windows, separate DVT and DATA and restore it with ADAMUP into the target database. In December 2010, ADAMAGIC was under development for Adabas 6.2 for Windows. Users would like to have such a tool supported by Software AG.

A decompressed file takes 3–4 hours to FTP. The same compressed file takes only 1 hour to FTP.

It seems at this time, that the backup dataset (VB) can be ftp'ed directly to the Windows server.

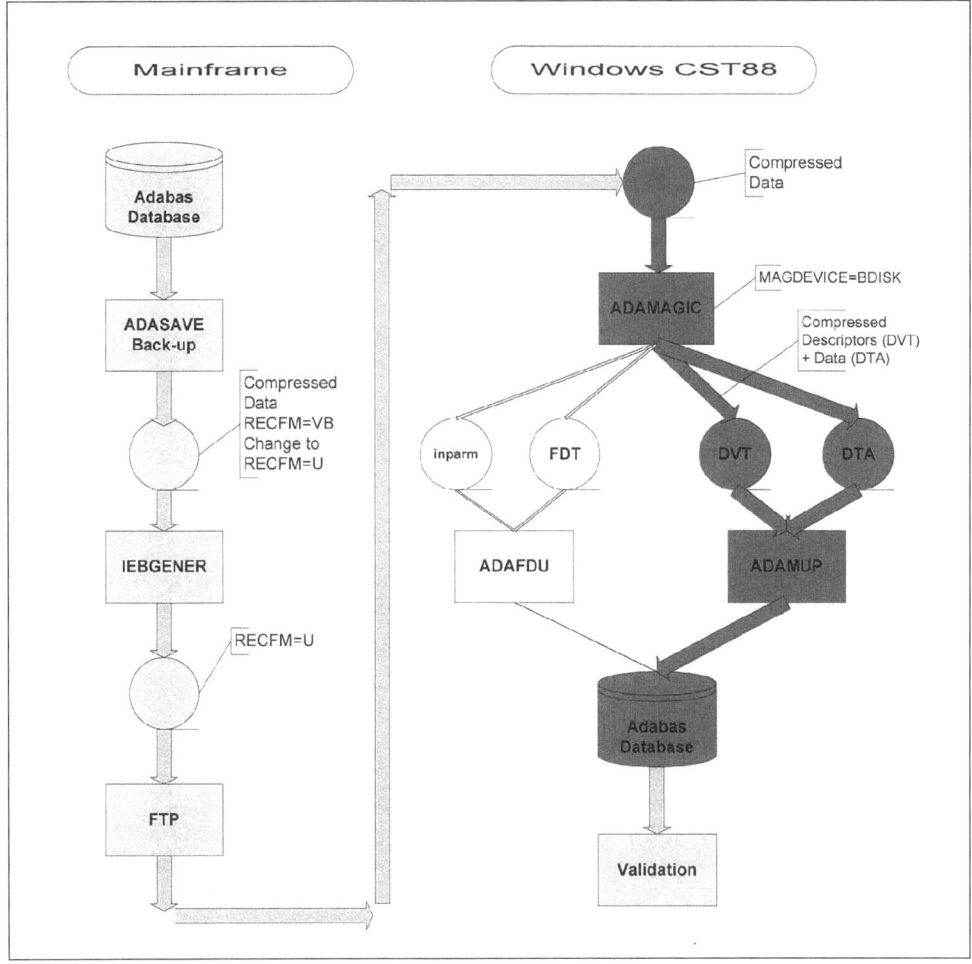

Figure 115: ADAMAGIC – Apply ADASAV from Mainframe Directly to Windows

6.2.16 New ADAFRI Message

Based on messages in DDPRINT, SLOG was turned off without an explanation.

```
ADAFRI 00302 SLOG turned off for destination D191144
```

Figure 116: ADAFRI Message – SLOG Turned Off

There was no reason displayed in the log why SLOG was turned off. The ADAFRI message is also not described in former Error and Messages Manuals.

According to the new Manual ARK331, ADAFRI means the following.

LOGINPUTTRANSACTION is set to ALL or 1-99 and the SLOG system file is not loaded.

You have specified LOGINPUTTRANSACTION as ALL or an integer from 1 to 99, but an SLOG file has not been defined for the Event Replicator Server.

If you really want the LOGINPUTTRANSACTION parameter set to one of these values, define an SLOG file to the Event Replicator Server. For more information, read Setting Up Subscription Logging, in the Event Replicator for Adabas Administration and Operations Guide.

It still does not make sense that the error message points out 'SLOG turned off' and the error message says SLOG not defined. At least this error message needs a clarification from Software AG.

6.2.17 Reptor under Stress

- DB 302, Replicator Engine, was locked and didn't respond
- Used a lot of CPU time – seemed to be in a loop
- ADAREP CPLIST job was in waiting status and ended after timeout
- AOS was locked and must be cancelled, when functions for DB 302 were requested
- The TSO session with the locked AOS must be cancelled
- Nucleus of DB302 couldn't be normally ended (ADAEND)
- Operation tried a couple of times to end with HALT command
- Finally, after a couple of yoyos (recycling), the nucleus started to respond again.
- Then, Replicator Engine continued to empty the SLOG
- Based on the DDPRINT-log, RPL tried to repeat already successfully replicated new records
- See DIETER.RPLTMPM2.DDPRINT.G0689V00 == more than 116,595 lines

From the restarted Reptor DDPRINT:

```
<snip>
ADAF54  Source DBID     39 FNR    55, Target DBID   251 FNR     55
ADAF18  N2 cmd to DBID   251 FNR    55 RSP   113 subcode      ISN     259776
ADAFCV  The record to be inserted already exists on the target DBID/file
ADAFCY  The record will be updated.
17:03:34 ADAM93 00302 User gone Job ADAAFP83 User ID C3D6D9FE000101BE
17:03:34 ADAM93 00302 User gone Job ADAAFP82 User ID C3D6D9FE000101E7
17:11:01 SEFM008 * SAF SECURITY KERNEL (V8.1.2 - BUILD 0002) STARTED
19:29:10 ADAFRK 00302 Use of SLOG for database-related input
19:29:10 ADAFRK 00302  transactions turned off
```

Figure 117:   Reptor Under Stress – User Gone Message

SAG Tech Support recommended setting the threshold of RPL buffer to 50%. After a high CPU time and a slow handshake between the subscription database and Reptor, Becky Albin from Software AG recommended setting it back to 70%.

6.2.18 Replication with wrong FDT/GFB

```
ADAF7F 00312 AI decompression response    55 subcode    0 subscription S134017
```

Figure 118:   Response Code 55 – Wrong FDT/GFB

A decompression failure occurred during the subscription phase of the Event Replicator for Adabas processing. File changes on the subscription database was not applied in Reptor's global format buffer (GFB). The format buffer for the after image (AI) does not fit.

Solution:

Delete the old format and create the new one from Predict.

6.3   Target Database

6.3.1   RSP 52 from the Target DB

FDT on source and target are different. The rightmost two bytes of the ADD2 field contain the sub-code, the leftmost two bytes the name of the field.

This problem can happen during program migrations with file changes and the changes are not done at the target database.

Adabas on Windows does not automatically replicate file changes. A special customized procedure must be developed to synchronize file changes on the source and target database. See also chapter 6.1.5, 'File Changes Won't Replicate'.

The following error messages (ADAF18) are collected from Reptor's active DDPRINT and sent by e-mail to the DBA group to be checked.

```
(snip)
ADAF18  N2 cmd to DBID    191 FNR    116 RSP    52 subcode 49602 ISN      145861
ADAF18  N2 cmd to DBID    191 FNR    116 RSP    52 subcode 49602 ISN      145863
ADAF18  N2 cmd to DBID    191 FNR    116 RSP    52 subcode 49602 ISN      145871
ADAF18  N2 cmd to DBID    191 FNR    116 RSP    52 subcode 49602 ISN      145892
ADAF18  N2 cmd to DBID    191 FNR    116 RSP    52 subcode 49602 ISN      145904
ADAF18  N2 cmd to DBID    191 FNR    116 RSP    52 subcode 49602 ISN      145907
  FNR/RSP/CNT 116 52 7513
  ******************************************************
  Please check the ADABAS response codes!
  ******************************************************
```

Figure 119:   Response Code 52 Showed in Reptor

6.3.2   RSP 176 from the Target DB

The inverted list in the ASSO was corrupted for file 75 in the target database 251. This was probably a sign of later problem with the HP disk arrays – two raid-5 disk arrays failed at the same time.

DDPRINT of Reptor:

```
(snip)
11:38:08 ADAF54 00302 Replication error: Adabas destination D251074
11:38:08 ADAF54 00302  Source DBID      39 FNR     74, Target DBID   251 FNR     74
ADAF18  N2 cmd to DBID    251 FNR     74 RSP    176 subcode 35841 ISN     35320183
ADAF54 2010-10-15 11:38:08 Replication error: Adabas destination D251074
ADAF54  Source DBID      39 FNR     74, Target DBID   251 FNR     74
ADAF18  N2 cmd to DBID    251 FNR     74 RSP    176 subcode 35841 ISN     35320190
ADAF54 2010-10-15 11:38:08 Replication error: Adabas destination D251074
(snip)
```

Figure 120:   Response Code 176 Showed in Reptor

It was also unusual that the target database ended abnormally during the replication process.

Solution:

Unload with ISN and load to re-build the corrupted inverted list.

6.3.3   RSP 98 followed by RSP 113

The target database rejects a store command with ISN 1 (N2) in empty file 80. The following delete command (E1) with ISN 1 results in ISN-1-not-found message. The rest of stores and deletes with ISNs 2-35 ended with RSP 0.

Response Code 98 could not be repeated, as requested from Tech Support of SAG (#5037205). The unique super-descriptor contains of an alphanumeric value and ten asterisks (*), for example 'RISTM0000010183*********'. In former Adabas versions for the mainframe were problems with its unique descriptor pool, defined by LDEUPQ. There is not such parameter in Adabas for Windows but maybe the internal DEUQP has not been cleared or there are problems with the asterisks.

From SAG's messages and Codes:

'Uniqueness violation of unique descriptor detected during store/update if sub-transactions are not activated, or otherwise at end of sub-transaction. The third and fourth bytes of the Additions 2 field contain the name of the descriptor which caused the uniqueness conflict.'

			CMD RSP		FILE	ISN	
2203960 07-JAN-2011 02:53:27	0	ADAN5S	.$...... E1 0 00000000/....		80	34	
2203961 07-JAN-2011 02:53:27	0	ADAN5S	.$...... N2 0 00000068/h...		80	35	
2203962 07-JAN-2011 02:53:27	0	ADAN5S	.$...... ET 0 00000000/....		0		
2203969 07-JAN-2011 02:53:27	0	ADAN5S	.$...... N2 98 4F410000/..AO		80	1	←
2203970 07-JAN-2011 02:53:27	0	ADAN5S	.$...... E1 0 00000000/.... R		80	35	
2203971 07-JAN-2011 02:53:27	0	ADAN5S	.$...... ET 0 00000000/....		0		
(other files)							
2203979 07-JAN-2011 02:53:27	0	ADAN5S	.$...... E1 113 00000000/....		80	1	←
2203980 07-JAN-2011 02:53:27	0	ADAN5S	.$...... N2 0 00000068/h...		80	2	
2203981 07-JAN-2011 02:53:27	0	ADAN5S	.$...... ET 0 00000000/....		0		
(snip)							
2204291 07-JAN-2011 02:53:35	0	ADAN5S	.$...... E1 0 00000000/....		80	33	
2204292 07-JAN-2011 02:53:35	0	ADAN5S	.$...... N2 0 00000068/h...		80	34	
2204293 07-JAN-2011 02:53:35	0	ADAN5S	.$...... ET 0 00000000/....		0		
(other files)							
2204301 07-JAN-2011 02:53:35	0	ADAN5S	.$...... E1 0 00000000/....		80	34	
2204302 07-JAN-2011 02:53:35	0	ADAN5S	.$...... N2 0 00000068/h		80	35	
2204303 07-JAN-2011 02:53:35	0	ADAN5S	.$...... ET 0 00000000/...		0		
(snip)							
2204310 07-JAN-2011 02:53:35	0	ADAN5S	.$...... N2 98 4F410000/..AO		80	1	←
2204311 07-JAN-2011 02:53:35	0	ADAN5S	.$...... E1 0 00000000/.... R		80	35	
2204312 07-JAN-2011 02:53:35	0	ADAN5S	.$...... ET 0 00000000/....		0		
(snip)							
2204320 07-JAN-2011 02:53:35	0	ADAN5S	.$...... E1 113 00000000/....		80	1	←
2204321 07-JAN-2011 02:53:35	0	ADAN5S	.$...... N2 0 00000068/h.		80	2	
2204322 07-JAN-2011 02:53:35	0	ADAN5S	.$...... ET 0 00000000/...		0		
(snip)							

Figure 121: Response Code 98 and 113 Showed in Reptor

Solution:

- Define all files in the target databases to be replicated with REUSEISN and set-up the MAXISN with the same values as in the source database
- Start the initial-state process
- RSP 98 was no longer observed during the replication process.

6.3.4 RSP 113 on several files

The specified ISN was invalid because of

- N2 command was issued with ISN equal to 0 or larger than the MAXISN in effect for the file; Adabas on Windows surprisingly adds only 1 block as a secondary allocation (extent).
- N2 command was issued and the specified ISN was assigned to another record in the file;

- L1/L4, E1, A1 or S1/S2/S4 (with FB) command was issued for a non-existent ISN;
- L3/L6 command found an ISN in the index which did not exist in the Address Converter;
- Replication definitions: source and target DB/FNR were the same, for example from DB134 FNR154 to DB134 FNR154 instead of to DB251 FNR154. There is no check in SYSREPTOR to avoid this.
- Files on the target database were not defined with REUSEISN. Later during the replication process and after closing the destinations, files were correctly defined with REUSEISN.

All files should be defined correctly before the replication process begins.

```
14:37:03 ADAF54 00312  Source DBID    134 FNR    122, Target DBID    134 FNR    122
ADAF18  N2 cmd to DBID    134 FNR    122 RSP    113 subcode        ISN    12440974
ADAFCV  The record to be inserted already exists on the target DBID/file
ADAFCY  The record will be updated.

ADAF54 2011-01-05 16:39:59 Replication error: Adabas destination D251112
ADAF54  Source DBID    134 FNR    112, Target DBID    251 FNR    112
ADAF18  E1 cmd to DBID    251 FNR    112 RSP    113 subcode        ISN    435139
ADAFCU  The record to be deleted does not exist on the target DBID/file

19:13:41 ADAF54 00312  Source DBID    134 FNR    154, Target DBID    251 FNR    154
ADAF18  A1 cmd to DBID    251 FNR    154 RSP    113 subcode        ISN    33
ADAFCU  The record to be updated does not exist on the target DBID/file
ADAFCX  The record will be inserted.

20:16:44 ADAF54 00312  Source DBID    134 FNR    148, Target DBID    251 FNR    148
ADAF18  N2 cmd to DBID    251 FNR    148 RSP    113 subcode        ISN    87430
ADAFCV  The record to be inserted already exists on the target DBID/file
ADAFCY  The record will be updated.
```

Figure 122:   Response Code 113 Showed in Reptor from Target

Solution:

- Define in the target databases all files to be replicated with REUSEISN and set-up the MAXISN with the same values as in the source database
- Start the initial-state process
- RSP 113 was no longer observed during the replication process

6.3.5   RSP 153 – Displayed on Reptor

Adabas response code 153 is reported by the Replicator Engine and the displayed ISNs are not replicated. The command log of the target database doesn't show this response code.

See Software AG ticket SR#5006563 (Adabas on Windows).

Explanation and solution see chapter 6.2.4 – RSP 153.

```
ADAF18  N2 cmd to DBID    251 FNR     11 RSP    153 subcode 16448 ISN         75423


REC   DATE                                        CMD RSP
                              DUR    USER-ID            AD2(HEX)/        FILE  ISN  TH IOA IOD IOW
   79219 22-NOV-2010 11:07:35      0    ..B...B. ....~... N2  0  0000004E/N....    11   75414 3  0  0  0
   79220 22-NOV-2010 11:07:35      0    ..B...B. ....~... N2  0  000000B2/....     11   75415 5  0  0  0
   79221 22-NOV-2010 11:07:35      0    ..B...B. ....~... N2  0  0000006B/k...     11   75416 15  0  0  0
   79222 22-NOV-2010 11:07:35      0    ..B...B. ....~... N2  0  000000CD/....     11   75417 20  0  0  0
   79223 22-NOV-2010 11:07:35      0    ..B...B. ........ OP  0  00000000/....  .   0    0 10  0  0  0
   79224 22-NOV-2010 11:07:35      0    ..B...B. ....~... N2  0  00000075/u...     11   75418 1  0  0  0
   79225 22-NOV-2010 11:07:35      0    ..B...B. ....~... N2  0  000000E9/....     11   75419 16  0  0  0
   79226 22-NOV-2010 11:07:35      0    ..B...B. ....~... N2  0  00000050/P...     11   75420 19  0  0  0
   79227 22-NOV-2010 11:07:35      0    ..B...B. ....~... N2  0  000000D4/....     11   75421 12  0  0  0
   79228 22-NOV-2010 11:07:35      0    ..B...B. ....~... N2  0  00000050/P...     11   75422 17  0  0  0
   79229 22-NOV-2010 11:07:35     16    ..B...B. ........ LF  0  000004F4/....  S  231    0  8  1  0  0
   79230 22-NOV-2010 11:07:35      0    ..B...B. ....~... N2  0  0000008E/....     11   75424 14  0  0  0
   79231 22-NOV-2010 11:07:35      0    ..B...B. ....~... N2  0  000000BB/....     11   75425 18  0  0  0
   79232 22-NOV-2010 11:07:35      0    ..B...B. ....~... N2  0  000000CF/....     11   75426 4  0  0  0
   79233 22-NOV-2010 11:07:35      0    ..B...B. ....~... N2  0  00000085/....     11   75427 6  0  0  0
   79234 22-NOV-2010 11:07:35      0    ..B...B. ....~... N2  0  000000A7/....     11   75428 9  0  0  0
   79235 22-NOV-2010 11:07:35      0    ..B...B. ....~... N2  0  000000B0/....     11   75429 11  0  0
```

Figure 123:   Response Code 153 Showed in Reptor – from WCP/WCL

6.3.6   RSP 162 – LBP Space Problems

This response code is shown in Reptor's DDPRINT:

```
21:05:16 ADAF54 00312 Replication error: Adabas destination D251044
21:05:16 ADAF54 00312  Source DBID   134 FNR    44, Target DBID   251 FNR    44
ADAF18  A1 cmd to DBID   251 FNR    44 RSP   162 subcode 17473 ISN      35249065
21:05:19 ADAF54 00312 Replication error: Adabas destination D251046
21:05:19 ADAF54 00312  Source DBID   134 FNR    46, Target DBID   251 FNR    46
ADAF18  A1 cmd to DBID   251 FNR    46 RSP   162 subcode 17473 ISN       4732732
ADAF54 2011-01-07 21:05:18 Replication error: Adabas destination D251046
ADAF54  Source DBID   134 FNR    46, Target DBID   251 FNR    46
ADAF18  A1 cmd to DBID   251 FNR    46 RSP   162 subcode 17473 ISN       4738881
ADAF54 2011-01-07 21:05:18 Replication error: Adabas destination D251046
ADAF54  Source DBID   134 FNR    46, Target DBID   251 FNR    46
ADAF18  A1 cmd to DBID   251 FNR    46 RSP   162 subcode 17473 ISN       6023043
ADAF54 2011-01-07 21:05:18 Replication error: Adabas destination D251046
(snip)
```

Figure 124:   Response Code 162 Showed in Reptor from Target DB

RSP 162 means that no additional space was available for the Adabas buffer pool. Increase the value of the LBP parameter. Because the buffer pool overflow is normally caused by too many blocks in the buffer pool waiting to be written to disk, specifying a low value for the WRITE_LIMIT parameter is recommended. This parameter is similar to LFIOP on the mainframe but on Adabas for Windows is no I/O pool available and I/Os are not done asynchronously.

To decrease the WRITE_LIMIT parameter from 25% to 5% means that more often a buffer flush takes place but each buffer flush will be done in a shorter time.

Solution:

```
Old with RSP 162:
%ADANUC-I-PARSET, setting of LBP=157286400
%ADANUC-I-PARSET, setting of WRITE_LIMIT=25

New:
%ADANUC-I-PARSET, setting of LBP=419430400
%ADANUC-I-PARSET, setting of WRITE_LIMIT=5
```

Figure 125:   Response Code 162 – LBP and WRITE_LIMIT on Target DB

Buffer usage after expand the LBP parameter

```
ADAOPR-I-STARTED,        24-JAN-2011 14:22:04, Version 6.2.1.01 (Windows)

Database 251, startup at 20-JAN-2011 13:30:44
ADANUC Version 6.2.1.01, PID 3752

                        ADANUC Version 6.2.1.01
         Database 251     Static Parameters      on 24-JAN-2011 14:21:57


Resources:          LAB     :    16,777,216   NT      :          20
                    LBP     :   419,430,400   NU      :         100
                    LWP     :     3,145,728   NCL     :          50

Logging:            NOPLOG
Options:            TRUNCATION, AUTO_EXPAND

Userexits:          8

Cloglayout:         5


%ADAOPR-I-TERMINATED,    24-JAN-2011 14:22:04, elapsed time: 00:00:00
```

Figure 126:   Response Code 162 – LBP and WRITE_LIMIT on Target DB

```
%ADAOPR-I-STARTED,       24-JAN-2011 14:22:04, Version 6.2.1.01 (Windows)

Database 251, startup at 20-JAN-2011 13:30:44
ADANUC Version 6.2.1.01, PID 3752

                        ADANUC Version 6.2.1.01
         Database 251     Dynamic Parameters     on 24-JAN-2011 14:21:57


Resources:          NISNHQ   :      90,000   WRITE_LIMIT:          5%

Time Slices:        TNAA     :       3,000   TNAX     :        3,000
                    TNAE     :       3,000   TT       :          900

Group Commit:       MGC      :          50

Logging:            CLOG     : CB

%ADAOPR-I-TERMINATED,    24-JAN-2011 14:22:04, elapsed time: 00:00:00
```

Figure 127:   Response Code 162 – LBP and WRITE_LIMIT on Target DB

```
%ADAOPR-I-STARTED,      24-JAN-2011 14:25:47, Version 6.2.1.01 (Windows)
Database 251, startup at 20-JAN-2011 13:30:44
ADANUC Version 6.2.1.01, PID 3752

                        ADANUC Version 6.2.1.01
         Database 251     High Water Marks      on 24-JAN-2011 14:25:47

Area/Entry                 Size    In Use  High Water    %      Date/Time
----------                 ----    ------  ----------    -      ---------
User Queue                  100        1           4     4  20-JAN-2011 14:13:37
Command Queue                 -        1           2     -  24-JAN-2011 14:21:57
Hold Queue                    -        0           1     -  20-JAN-2011 15:44:27
Client Queue                 50        4           6    12  20-JAN-2011 14:03:47
HQ User Limit            90,000        -           1     0  20-JAN-2011 15:44:27
Threads                      20        1           4    20  20-JAN-2011 14:14:47
Workpool              3,145,728        0     786,448    25  20-JAN-2011 13:30:45
  ISN Sort              393,216        -           0     0
  Complex Search        393,216        -           0     0
Attached Buffer      16,777,216    4,096      28,672     0  20-JAN-2011 14:13:56
ATBX       (MB)              20        0           0     0
Buffer Pool         419,430,400 22,624,256 32,654,336    7  20-JAN-2011 13:30:45
Protection Area         332,790
  Active Area            99,837        -           2     0  21-JAN-2011 12:13:37
Group Commit                 50        1           1     2  20-JAN-2011 14:03:37
Transaction Time            900        -           0     0
```

Figure 128:   Response Code 162 – LBP and WRITE_LIMIT on Target DB

```
%ADAOPR-I-STARTED,      24-JAN-2011 14:29:48, Version 6.2.1.01 (Windows)
Database 251, startup at 20-JAN-2011 13:30:44
ADANUC Version 6.2.1.01, PID 3752

                        ADANUC Version 6.2.1.01
         Database 251     Buffer Pool Statistics    on 24-JAN-2011 14:29:47

Buffer Pool Size   :   419,430,400

Pool Allocation                      RABNs present
---------------                      -------------
Current    ( 5%) :    22,624,256     ASSO             :        240
Highwater   ( 7%) :    32,654,336     DATA             :          4
Internal    ( 4%) :    19,030,016     WORK             :          0
Workpool    ( 0%) :     2,453,504     NUCTMP           :          0
                                      NUCSRT           :          0

I/O Statistics                       Buffer Flushes
--------------                       --------------
Logical Reads      :        4,359     Total            :         12
Physical Reads     :          252     To Free Space    :          0
Pool Hit Rate      :        94.2%

                                      Write Limit  ( 5%):   20,971,500
Physical Writes    :           24     Modified     ( 0%):      104,448


%ADAOPR-I-TERMINATED,   24-JAN-2011 14:29:48, elapsed time: 00:00:00
```

Figure 129:   Response Code 162 – LBP and WRITE_LIMIT on Target DB

6.4   Utilities

6.4.1   Replay with more than 60 files

Version 3.2.1 cannot REPLAY more than 60 files. Software AG recommends starting multiple REPLAY jobs with 60 files each in parallel and setting the disposition
of the PLOG dataset to SHR. It is planned from Software AG to change it in a future release.

```
A D A R P L   V8.1  SM1   DBID = 00039  Started          2010-04-28  18:16:06
Parameters:
-----------
 ADARPL REPLAY
 ADARPL FILES=006,007,009,010,012,013,016,019,021,023,028,033,034,037
 ADARPL FILES=039,040,041,043,047,048,051,058,059,060,061,063,066,066
 ADARPL FILES=067,068,071,072,076,077,078,080,081,082,083,084,086,088
 ADARPL FILES=090,091,092,093,094,096,097,099,103,104,105,106,109,110
 *** ADARPL FILES=111,113,116,119,123,124,125,130,131,133,135,137,138,140
                                   ***
 ERROR-009, Parameter error, too many values in a list
            Check the parameter input.
            Supply no more than the maximum number of parameter
            values permitted, and rerun the job.

A D A R P L   Terminated                                2010-04-28  18:16:06
```

Figure 130:   ADARPL Replay > 60 Files

6.4.2   Replay with ERROR-139

REPLAY received ERROR-139. ADARPL has exceeded the replication pool size
allocated via the LRPL parameter.

Both RPL of the target database and the Reptor are only 2% used, according to the
HWM.

The utility ADARPL has its own RPL buffer.

Increase the default value of LRPL from 100,000 to 300,000K. Tests with many
files to be replayed showed that a value of 600,000K is better.

```
ERROR-139, ADARPL replication pool overflow
           Increase LRPL parameter and rerun the job.
```

Figure 131:   ADARPL Replay ERROR-139

6.4.3   Replay with ERROR-140 RSP 254

REPLAY received ERROR-140 with response code 254 and sub-code 6 at location 1.

```
A D A R P L:  Error occurred during execution:
ERROR-140, Unexpected REPTOR response 254 subcode 6 location 1
A D A R P L  Terminated                      2010-05-03  17:39:25
```

Figure 132:   ADARPL Replay ERROR-140 RSP 254

The attached buffers (NAB) can be too small defined. Based on the high-water-marks of the source database and the Replicator Engine, NAB is only up to 20% used. The Replication Utility Manual Version 3.3.1 does not describe a related parameter to the attached buffers.

Subcode 6 means that the low-order 6 bytes of CQECKSUM (checksum of command queue element) do not equal UBCKSUM (checksum of user block check). This information seems to be not very helpful for a DBA.

It also can be that the CT parameter limit was exceeded (tested with CT=180), the nucleus terminates the user, generated the equivalent of a BT command internally, released the CQE and attached buffer space, and issued ADAM93 or similar message. This message was not detected during this ERROR-140.

No solution or explanation has been found to solve this problem.

6.4.4   Replay with ERROR-140 RSP 131 Subcode 70

The following REPLAY was running without a TOKEN:

```
A D A R P L   V8.1  SM1   DBID = 00134  Started        2010-12-23  12:38:28



  Parameters:
  -----------


  ADARPL REPLAY
  ADARPL LRPL=600000K
  ADARPL FILES=006,007,008,009,010,011,012,013,014,015,016,017,018,019,020
  ADARPL FILES=021,022,023,024,025,026,027,028,029,030,031,032,033,034,035
  ADARPL FILES=036,037,038,039,040,041,042,043,044,045,046,047,048,049,050
  ADARPL FILES=051,052,053,054,055,056,057,058,059,060,061,062,063,064,065

A D A R P L:  Error occurred during execution:
ERROR-140, Unexpected REPTOR response 131 subcode 70 location 2
A D A R P L  Terminated                      2010-12-23  12:38:29
```

Figure 133:   ADARPL Replay ERROR-140 RSP 131 SC 70

RSP 131 has up to 111 subcodes but subcode 70 is not found in Messages and Codes V3.3.2, nucleus response codes.

Subcode 69 means that a replay for the same DBID/FNR is already running.

ADARPL was running with the following version:

```
ADARPL              Date 2007-07-13, Version 3.1, SM 1, Base AZ311000
                    Zaps AZ311001 AZ311008 AZ311017 AZ311054 AZ311071
                         AZ311073 AZ311074 AZ311084
```

Figure 134:   ADARPL Version and Zap Level

6.4.5   Replay with ERROR-140 RSP 131 Subcode 61

```
ARF00156: Response 131 Subcode 61
```

Figure 135:   ADARPL Replay ERROR-140 RSP 131 SC 61

Subcode 61 means that an invalid request sent to Event Replicator Server. RBL is insufficient, no FB provided on Init handshake or other such error. Notify your Software AG technical support representative.

Solution:

Just restart the job.

6.4.6   Replay with ERROR-148 – Token

Token 19655 was created.

```
ARF00147: Replay process initiated - Token=19655
   12:12:34      ***** A D A B A S  EVENT REPLICATOR SUBSYSTEM *****    2010-12-23
                         Initiate Replication Replay                   M-RP2010

                              Synchronized

            DBID ...........................  __134
            Automated ......................  Y (Y or N)
            Timeout ........................  600_____

            From Date/Time ................. 2010-12-20  02:00:13
            To Date/Time ................... 2010-12-23  11:55:00
            Start Date/Time ............... 2010-12-20  02:00:13

            Destination Name List ..... _ + * *_____  _____  _____
            Subscription Name List .... _    *  _____  _____  _____


A D A R P L   V8.1  SM1   DBID = 00134  Started         2010-12-23  12:31:57
```

Figure 136:   ADARPL Replay – Create Token

The Token 19655 was not found. There are no replay processes active with the token number listen in the message.

```
Parameters:
-----------

ADARPL REPLAY TOKEN=19655
ADARPL RPLTARGETID=312
ADARPL LRPL=600000K

A D A R P L:  Error occurred during execution:

ERROR-148, TOKEN 19655 not found in Reptor.

          Investigate the cause of the error.
          Correct it and rerun the job.

A D A R P L  Terminated                    2010-12-23  12:31:58
```

Figure 137:   ADARPL Replay ERROR-148

Solution:

Deleted the TOKEN, created a new one and started the replay with the new TOKEN number.

Reason: The field 'Automated' (Figure 136: ADARPL Replay – Create Token) should be marked with N and not Y.

6.4.7   Replay Abended with S0C4

Created token 15825 with 183 destinations and subscriptions. The started ADARPL utility ended abnormally with error code S0C4 and reason code 10. This is normally caused because of protection exception, incorrectly linked modules, invalid pointer value, wrongly concatenated Adabas library, etc.

```
A D A R P L   V8.1  SM1   DBID = 00134  Started        2010-12-23  14:51:27


  Parameters:
  -----------

ADARPL REPLAY TOKEN=15825
 ADARPL RPLTARGETID=312
 ADARPL LRPL=600000K

 (snip)

 14:51:57   END OF SYMPTOM DUMP
 14:51:57   IEF450I STREPLAA ST1 REPLAY - ABEND=S0C4 U0000 REASON=00000010
 14:51:57           TIME=14.51.57
 14:51:57   IEF404I STREPLAA - ENDED - TIME=14.51.57
```

Figure 138:   ADARPL Replay S0C4

Restarted the replay job with the latest Adabas steplib and with a new Token 15826 but received the same S0C4. The dump can be viewed in appendix, chapter 8.7.

Solution:

Cleaned up 15826.

```
16:24:35              ***** A D A B A S   BASIC   SERVICES *****           2010-12-23
 Replicator 312            - Replicator Management -                        PRPT002

                       Code   Service
                       ----   -------------------------
                        A     Activate/deact/open/close
                        D     Display Reptor definitions
                        F     Display Reptor statistics
                        H     Perform RPLCheck
                        L     Perform RPLCleanup
                        P     Perform RPLRefresh
                        *     Parameter subsystem
                        ?     Help
                        .     Exit
                       ----   -------------------------

            Code ......... _
            Database ID .. 312    (RPLPB-DATA-BASE)

 ERPT001 : Issue RPLCleanup function completed
  Command ==>
 PF1----- PF2------ PF3------ PF4------ PF6----- PF7----- PF8----- PF12-----
 Help      File Serv Exit                                          Menu
```

Figure 139:   ADARPL Replay S0C4 – RPL Cleanup

Solution:

Created multiple TOKENs with only a couple of files.

```
ARF00147: Replay process initiated - Token=15828
16:42:38         ***** A D A B A S   EVENT REPLICATOR SUBSYSTEM *****       2010-12-23
                      Initiate Replication Replay                           M-RP2010

                              Synchronized

            DBID ......................... __134
            Automated ..................... N (Y or N)
            Timeout ....................... 900_____

            From Date/Time ................ 2010-12-20  02:00:00
            To Date/Time .................. _____  _____
            Start Date/Time ............... _____  _____

            Destination Name List ..... _ + * D251009_  D251010_  D251011_
            Subscription Name List .... _    * _____  _____  _____




 Command ==>
 Enter-PF1---PF2---PF3---PF4---PF5---PF6---PF7---PF8---PF9---PF10--PF11--PF12---
```

Figure 140:   ADARPL Replay S0C4 – Create Multiple Token

Solution:

Ran multiple Replay jobs in parallel, each with different TOKEN, and with the same shared PLOGs.

6.4.8   Replay with Response 131 Subcode 61

It seems that you cannot define more destinations than fit on one selection page (PF6).

```
ARF00156: Response 131 Subcode 61 Received from replicator
  17:56:56      ***** A D A B A S  EVENT REPLICATOR SUBSYSTEM *****      2010-12-23
                        Initiate Replication Replay                      M-RP2010

                              Synchronized

           DBID ..........................  __134
           Automated .....................  N (Y or N)
           Timeout .......................  900_____

           From Date/Time ................  2010-12-20  02:00:00
           To Date/Time ..................  _____  _____
           Start Date/Time ...............  _____  _____

           Destination Name List .....  _  +  *  D251130_  D251131_  D251132_
           Subscription Name List ....  _     *  _____  _____  _____




  Command ==>
  Enter-PF1---PF2---PF3---PF4---PF5---PF6---PF7---PF8---PF9---PF10--PF11--PF12---
        Help         Exit         Sub   Sel                             Menu
```

Figure 141:   ADARPL Replay S0C4 – RPL Cleanup

A valid TOKEN was given when only a few files were selected to be replayed.

7 Monitors

7.1 What can be monitored?

Assume that you replicate from Adabas on the mainframe to Adabas on Windows, you can monitor the following parts:

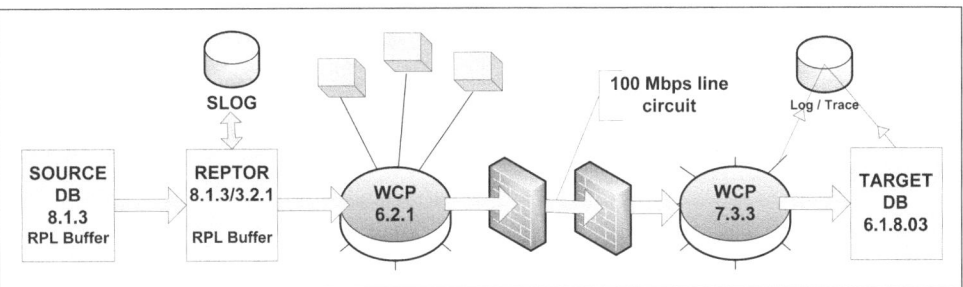

Figure 142: Monitoring Replication Parts – Graphic

#	Software	Version	Monitor	Comments
1	Adabas on the mainframe	8.1.3	SYSAOS / Apas/Insight / TRIM / Review	
2	Replicator on the mainframe	8.1.3 3.2.1	SYSAOS / Apas/Insight / TLOG transaction log	
3	Entire Net-Work or WCP on the mainframe	6.2.1	Trace Hourly Snapshot	Trace is very costly; snapshots are recommended
4	Network / line or circuit	100 Mbps duplex	NetQoS	Always active
5	Firewalls / routers / load balancing systems		Different	Ask network people
6	Entire Net-Work or WCP on Windows	7.3.3	Trace / Log	Very costly, might be placed on a SAN box – not C-drive
7	Adabas on Windows	6.2.1	Command log	Costly, no async I/Os

Figure 143: Monitoring Replication Parts – Tools

Why is it necessary to monitor components in the path from the subscription to the target database?

The following test scenario (test #14) shows that the subscription database sends 1,186 commands per second (cps) to the Reptor but the Reptor sends only 292 cps to Entire Net-Work (WCP). Based on the command log from the target database, the same amount of Adabas commands arrived. The question is, where is the bottleneck?

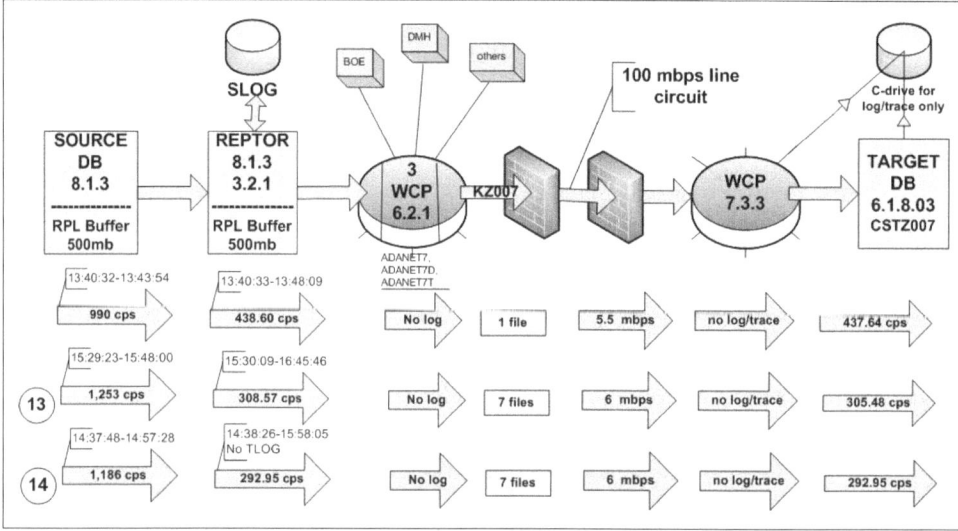

Figure 144:   Monitoring – Number of Commands per Second

In this case, the following measurements will improve the throughput:

- Increase the Adabas buffer pool (LBP) on both subscription database and Replicator Engine. LBP on Reptor should not be defined smaller than on the subscription database
- Increase the replication buffer (LRPL) on both subscription database and Replicator Engine. LRPL on Reptor should not be defined smaller than on the subscription database
- Increase the threshold of the replication buffer (LOGINPUTTRANS) on Reptor from 50% to 70%. Adabas commands can be longer replicated out of the RPL buffer and the usage of the overflow area SLOG can be delayed or avoided.
- The number of updates and files per Adabas transaction from multiple users (online and batch) cannot be handled in time from one Reptor. Heavily used files should be dedicated to special Replicator Engines. One company is using for example 8 Replicator Engines.
- Activate on the Replicator Engine asynchronous Vol-Ser I/Os (ASYTVS=YES) and decide to set the parallel LFIOP I/Os (FMXIO) to a value greater than 1 (normally 6-8) if data to be written and read from the SLOG file.

7.1.1   Source DB on the Mainframe

SYSAOS shows the high water marks (HWM) of some Adabas queues and buffers.

A Session monitoring / U display resource utilization / H   high water marks

Critically important for the replication process is using the attached buffers (NAB) and the replication buffer (LRPL). An overflow of these buffers on the source or subscription database will stop the replication process and an INITIAL-STATE or REPLAY is necessary.

```
11:43:44            ***** A D A B A S  BASIC  SERVICES *****          2010-09-24
DBID 39                     -  High Water Marks   -                   PACUH02


  Pool / Queue        I    Size    I    Used    I %Used I   Date        Time    I
--------------------------------------------------------------------------------
Attached Buffer(NAB) I    245760 I    49920 I  20.3 I                          I   ←
Command Queue   (NC)  I     76800 I      960 I   1.2 I 2010-09-24 11:29:48 I
Format Pool     (LFP) I   2500000 I        0 I   0.0 I 2010-09-24 11:19:59 I
Hold Queue      (NH)  I    560056 I     8428 I   1.5 I 2010-09-24 11:31:41 I
ISN-List Table  (LI)  I      4000 I        0 I   0.0 I 2010-09-24 11:19:59 I
Seq. Cmd. Table (LQ)  I      9000 I       68 I   0.7 I 2010-09-24 11:35:14 I
User Queue      (NU)  I    466312 I     6160 I   1.3 I 2010-09-24 11:30:54 I
Unique DE Pool  (DUQ) I     60000 I        0 I   0.0 I                          I
Security Pool   (LCP) I     10000 I        0 I   0.0 I                          I
UQ File List    (UQF) I    144360 I      576 I   0.3 I 2010-09-24 11:30:54 I
ATM Trans. IDs  (XID) I         0 I        0 I   0.0 I                          I
Work Pool       (LWP) I   1500000 I    59908 I   3.9 I 2010-09-24 11:29:49 I
Redo Pool       (LRDP)I         0 I        0 I   0.0 I                          I
Replication     (RPL) I 314572800 I 137375292 I  43.6 I                          I   ←
```

Figure 145:   Monitoring – High Water Marks – Source DB

SYSAOS with the HWM function also runs in batch and a Natural parse program analyzes programmatically the data (see chapter 7.2).

7.1.2   Replicator on the Mainframe

SYSAOS

The Replicator Engine or Reptor contains of the Adabas nucleus and some Replicator modules. SYSAOS can also be used to show the high water marks (HWM) of some Adabas queues and buffers.

A   Session monitoring / U display resource utilization / H   high water marks

Critically for the replication process is using the attached buffers (NAB) and the replication buffer (RPL, parameter LRPL). An overflow of the attached buffers (NAB) will stop the replication process and an INITIAL STATE or REPLAY is necessary.

A replication buffer (RPL) overflow will deactivate the destination if no SLOG is defined or activated. The parameter 'LOGINPUTTRANSACTION' can be set to use its SLOG system file as temporary storage location for incoming compressed replication transactions, before they are queued for processing. A value set to 70%, for example, will automatically switch to the SLOG if the threshold is reached. Without setting a threshold, the SLOG won't be used, even if the SLOG is created and available.

The Adabas buffer pool (LBP) is also important but its usage cannot be displayed with SYSAOS on the mainframe, in contrast to Adabas on Windows, see Figure **199**.

```
 11:14:45            ***** A D A B A S  BASIC  SERVICES *****        2010-09-24
 DBID 302                   -  High Water Marks  -                   PACUH02


   Pool / Queue        I   Size    I   Used    I %Used I   Date        Time    I
  ----------------------------------------------------------------------------------
   Attached Buffer(NAB) I   1720320 I    45312 I   2.6 I                       I  ←
   Command Queue   (NC) I     23040 I      576 I   2.5 I 2010-09-23 17:34:44 I
   Format Pool     (LFP) I   300000 I    10944 I   3.6 I 2010-09-24 11:09:02 I
   Hold Queue      (NH) I    560056 I     5712 I   1.0 I 2010-09-24 07:43:56 I
   ISN-List Table  (LI) I     12000 I        0 I   0.0 I                       I
   Seq. Cmd. Table(LQ) I      20000 I      276 I   1.3 I 2010-09-24 07:48:28 I
   User Queue      (NU) I   1236312 I     4928 I   0.3 I 2010-09-24 11:13:14 I
   Unique DE Pool (DUQ) I    100000 I        0 I   0.0 I                       I
   Security Pool  (LCP) I     10000 I        0 I   0.0 I                       I
   UQ File List   (UQF) I    384360 I      288 I   0.0 I 2010-09-24 11:13:14 I
   ATM Trans. IDs (XID) I         0 I        0 I   0.0 I                       I
   Work Pool      (LWP) I    500000 I    53060 I  10.6 I 2010-09-24 07:49:30 I
   Redo Pool      (LRDP)I         0 I        0 I   0.0 I                       I
   Replication    (RPL) I 314572800 I 213229780 I  67.7 I                       I  ←
```

Figure 146:   Monitoring High Water Marks – Reptor

TLOG

The transaction log (TLOG) will be activated on the subscription level by using SYSRPTR and the 'Subscription Definition' for each file logging is needed – see TLOG Values.

```
 12:03:39      ***** A D A B A S  EVENT REPLICATOR SUBSYSTEM *****    2010-11-09
                         Subscription Definition                    M-RP1410

 Description .................. DB039/144 TO 251/144_____

 Subscription Name ............ S039144_  Current      TLOG Values
 User Data Alpha Key ..........  ___0                 -----------------------
 Architecture Key .............  ___2                 Input Level ......... 2
 Subscription Version .........   __                  Filter Level ........ 0
 User Data Wide Key ...........  ___0                 Output Level ........ 2
 Resend Buffer Name ...........  _____             Filter Matched ....... 0
                                                      Filter Not Matched ... 0
 Destination Name List ........ _ +                   Filter Ignored ....... 0
 File-related Parameters ....... _ +

 Subscription Active .......... Y
 Deactivate if file deactivated Y
 Increment Initial State Count  N
```

Figure 147:   Monitoring TLOG – Adjustments

The program ADARPR selects and prints the transaction log, the Adabas command log of the Replicator.

```
//PRITLOG    EXEC PGM=ADARUN
//STEPLIB    DD DISP=SHR,DSN=ADABAS.ARF.V321.TEST.LOADLIB
//           DD DISP=SHR,DSN=ADABAS.V81.USER.ADALOAD
//           DD DISP=SHR,DSN=ADABAS.V81.TEST.LOADLIB
//           DD DISP=SHR,DSN=ADABAS.ADAUTL.V81.UTLIB
//DDCARD     DD *
ADARUN PROGRAM=ADARPP,SVC=241,DEVICE=3390,DB=302
//DDCLOG     DD DISP=SHR,DCB=BUFNO=60,UNIT=(CTAPE,2),
//              DSN=DIETER.CLOG.RPLT2.D092410.T150704
//           DD DISP=SHR,DSN=REPTOR.CLOG.RPLT2.D092410.T151639,
//              DCB=BUFNO=60,UNIT=AFF=DDCLOG
//           DD DISP=SHR,DSN=REPTOR.CLOG.RPLT2.D092410.T153749,
//              DCB=BUFNO=60,UNIT=AFF=DDCLOG
//DDDRUCK    DD SYSOUT=*
//DDPRINT    DD SYSOUT=*
//SYSUDUMP   DD DUMMY      SYSOUT=*
//DDKARTE    DD *
ADARPP TLINPUT=3                    *RECORDS ASSIGNED QUEUE EVENTS
*                                   *0 = PRINT NO OUTPUT FOR THE EVENT
*                                   *1 = PRINT EVENT REC AND INPUT TRANS
*                                   *2 = SAME AS 1 + FILE/ISN INFO
*                                   *3 = 1 + 2
ADARPP TLCOMP=1                     *RECORDS LOGGED WHEN TRANSACT. COMPLET
*                                   *0 = NO OUTPUT
*                                   *1 = INPUT AND OUTPUT
**ADARPP DESTINATION='D251144'       *W/O = ALL
**ADARPP SUBSCRIPTION='S039144'      *W/O = ALL
ADARPP FROMDATE=20100924            *YYYYMMDD
ADARPP FROMTIME=14300000            *HHMMSSTH
**ADARPP TODATE=20100924             *YYYYMMDD
**ADARPP TOTIME=15045999             *HHMMSSTH
ADARPP PRINT=FORMAT                 *DUMP / FORMAT / BOTH
ADARPP STATE=YES                    *YES / NO
//


Output:

(snip)
 URBLQEYE: URBLQ   URBLQFNR: 144     URBLQISN: 11,135          URBLQRSN: 35
 URBLQBFZ: 2,497,940     URBLQTTM: 2010-09-24 14:56:53.60
 URBLQIMT:    URBLQUPT: I  URBLQRSP: 0       URBLQSUB: 0
 URBLQFMT: 2010-09-24 14:56:53.57  URBLQLMT: 2010-09-24 14:56:53.57

 URBLEYE:  URBL    URBLLEN: 64      URBLTLEN: 128     URBLVER:  01
 URBLTIME: 2010-09-24 14:56:53.60   URBLTYPE: AC      URBLPTYP: 5
 URBLDNAM:           URBLSNAM: S039144

 URBLQEYE: URBLQ   URBLQFNR: 144     URBLQISN: 11,136          URBLQRSN: 36
 URBLQBFZ: 2,497,941     URBLQTTM: 2010-09-24 14:56:53.60
 URBLQIMT:    URBLQUPT: I  URBLQRSP: 0       URBLQSUB: 0
 URBLQFMT: 2010-09-24 14:56:53.57  URBLQLMT: 2010-09-24 14:56:53.57

 URBLEYE:  URBL    URBLLEN: 64      URBLTLEN: 128     URBLVER:  01
 URBLTIME: 2010-09-24 14:56:53.60   URBLTYPE: AC      URBLPTYP: 5
 URBLDNAM:           URBLSNAM: S039144
(snip)
```

Figure 148:   Monitoring TLOG – ADARPP

Explanation of different TLOG elements

```
URBC -- Continuation element
URBD -- Data element
URBE -- End-of-transaction element
URBH -- Message header
URBI -- Input element
URBL -- Reptor Transaction Log Record Definition   (size F0F1
URBP -- Subscription user exit parameter list
URBQ -- User Exit Program Parameter Block
URBS -- Reptor status/response element
URBT -- Transaction element
URBU -- ADARPE Extract Header User Element
URBX -- Subscription user exit parameter block
URBZ -- User Exit Program Parameter Block
```

Figure 149:   Monitoring TLOG – Explaining Elements

Another way to determine the activities on Replicator Engine is to display the destinations statistics. Figure 130 shows the time the first transaction D251018 (DB251 file 018) was committed at 2010/11/02 16:26:45 and the last ET was done at 2010/11/02 16:51:07. In 1,462 seconds, 21,556 transactions were committed. These are 14.7 transactions per second for file 18.

The command log can show how many Adabas commands contain in one transaction (from ET to ET).

```
17:31:31          ***** A D A B A S  BASIC  SERVICES *****          2010-11-02
Replicator 302       - Selected Destination Statistics -            PRPTS04

Selected Dest Name : D251018
Selected Dest Type : Adabas                             Time tran committed
Total replicated transactions .          21,556 2010/11/02 16:26:45
Total pending transactions ....               0
Total messages sent ..........                0
Total commits ................                0
Slog logged count ............                0
Slog de004 count ..........                   0
Items for destination on slog .               0
Items to delete from slog .....               0
Bytes sent to destination .....               0
Pending bytes for destination .               0
Pending messages .............        0
Number of BT's ...............                0 Time of last ET
Number of ET's ...............           21,556 2010/11/02 16:51:07
```

Figure 150:   Monitoring Destination Statistics on Reptor

7.1.3   Entire Net-Work (WCP) on the Mainframe

The trace function is an overhead and slows down the replication process. Therefore, it is recommended not to activate it. Hourly snapshots are not helpful because they cannot show the real number of Adabas calls per second. The display shows only 18 Adabas calls per second during approximately 3 hours.

The calculation: 202005 api calls / 10855.943 secs = 18.6 per second

```
15:55:25 NETP063I: + Statistics For Link CSTZ007    Period     3:00:55 ( 10855.943 Secs)  +
15:55:25 NETP063I: + -------------  ---Bytes----  --Messages--  -Api Calls--  ----------- +
15:55:25 NETP063I: + Writes           321.869M        202,005      202,005  Total         +
15:55:25 NETP063I: +                   30.363K             18           18  Per Second    +
15:55:25 NETP063I: + Reads            29.281M         202,005      202,006  Total         +
15:55:25 NETP063I: +                    2.761K             18           18  Per Second    +
15:55:25 NETP063I: + -------------  ---Total----  ----Task----  ---Other----  ----------- +
15:55:25 NETP063I: + Write Cmd's      202,005        202,005            0  Total         +
15:55:25 NETP063I: +                       18             18            0  Per Second    +
15:55:25 NETP063I: + Read Cmd's       202,006        202,006            0  Total         +
15:55:25 NETP063I: +                       18             18            0  Per Second    +
15:55:25 NETP063I: +-------------------------------------------------------------------+
15:58:13 NETT003I: Dbid 251 Inactive  on Node KZ007
```

Figure 151:   Monitoring Entire Net-Work (WCP) – Mainframe

Based on the Adabas command log, the target database received over 400 Adabas commands per second during the above mentioned time.

The System Management Hub is not very helpful to determine the throughput of Entire Net-Work (WCP) on the mainframe. The statistics for a connected database shows the number of Adabas calls since WCP startup. It seems to be the same as displayed in Figure 131.

There are also two Entire Net-Work diagnostic utilities:

- NETPFIL1
- NETPFIL2

NETPFIL1 is used to select the information to be printed from WCP NETPRNT file, which contains tracing, logging and dump output. Selection parameters can be used to select **a certain time and day, as well as logging, dump and trace records that match** the title or any portion of the title.

NETPFIL2 is used to search for a control block or storage area snapped by either the logging function or a dump.

```
//YOURJOB  JOB (0),'NET-WORK',
//         CLASS=A,MSGCLASS=X,MSGLEVEL=(1,1)
//FILTER1  EXEC PGM=NETPFIL1
//STEPLIB  DD   DSN=NETWRK.vrs.LOAD,DISP=SHR        load lib for WCP
//         DD   DSN=WAL.vrs.LOAD,DISP=SHR           load lib for Adabas
//NETFILE  DD   DSN=NETWRK.vrs.NETPRNT,DISP=SHR     created by WCP
//DDCARD   DD   *
  THIS COMMENT WILL BE PRINTED AT THE BEGINNING OF THE OUTPUT
  DATE=20000316
  STARTTIME=12570000
  ENDTIME=12580000
  LOG=T R A C E
* LOG=IDDDATA
  TRACE=
* TRACE=SENDOUT
//DDPRINT  DD   SYSOUT=*,DCB=(LRECL=121,BLKSIZE=1210,RECFM=FBA)
/*
```

Figure 152:   Entire Net-Work (WCP) – Mainframe – Diagnostic Utilities (JCL)

As pointed out at the beginning of this chapter, tracing and logging is an over-head in WCP during replication and should only be used debugging errors.

In a next release after V6.2, Software AG will drop support for both utilities NETPFIL1 and NETPFIL2.

7.1.4   Network – Line or Circuit

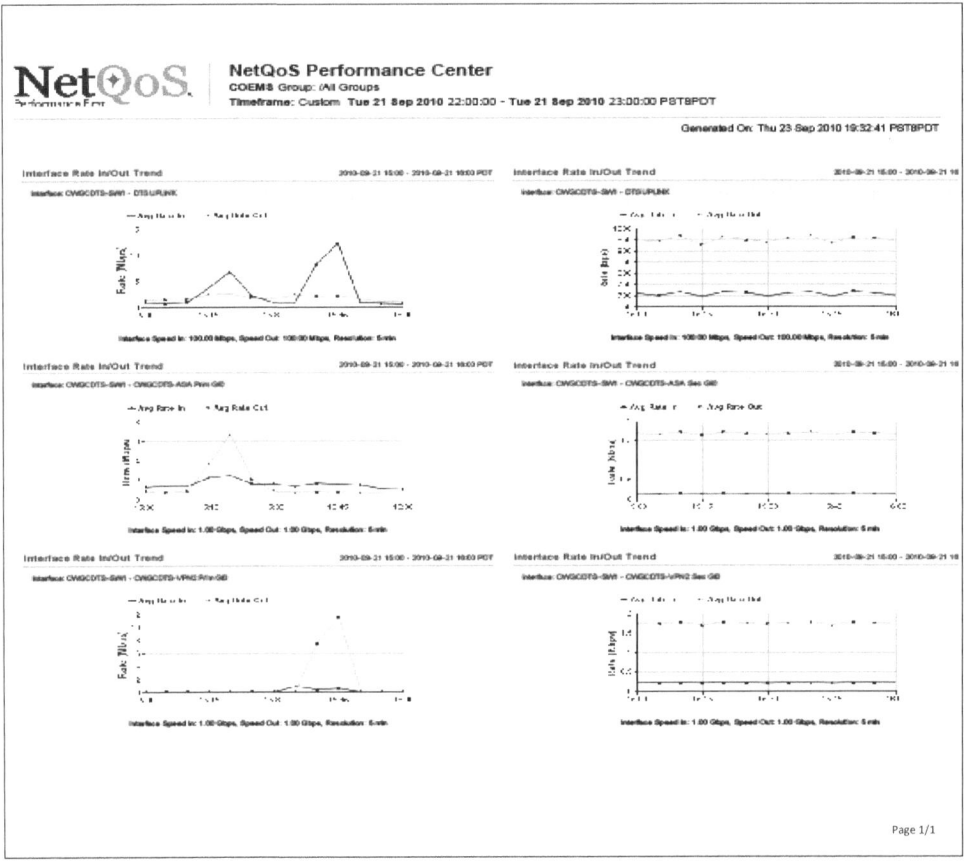

Figure 153:   Monitoring Network – NetQoS

Several tools allow you to monitor and optimize your network bandwidth. You need for your replication process a fast line to guaranty real-time data on your target database.

Some of the monitors offer user interfaces based on browser, Windows GUI and iPhone application.

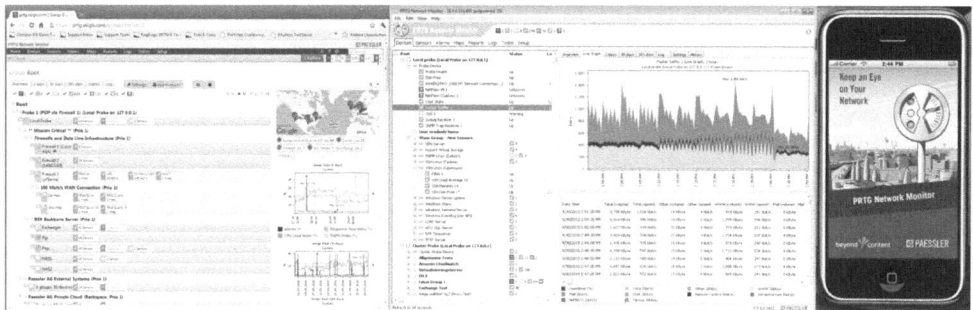

Figure 154:   Monitoring Network – Browser, GUI, iPhone

7.1.5   Firewalls, Routers, Load Balancing Systems

A Firewall is an important perimeter defense tool that protects your network from attacks. Security tools like Firewalls, VPN, and Proxy Servers generate a huge quantity of traffic logs, which can be mined to generate a wealth of security information reports.

ManageEngine Firewall Analyzer is a web-based, cross-platform, log analysis tool that helps network administrators and managed security service providers (MSSP) to understand how bandwidth is being used in their network. Firewall Analyzer analyzes logs received from different firewalls and generates useful reports and graphs. Trend analysis, capacity planning, policy enforcement, and security compromises are some of the critical decisions that are made simpler using Firewall Analyzer.

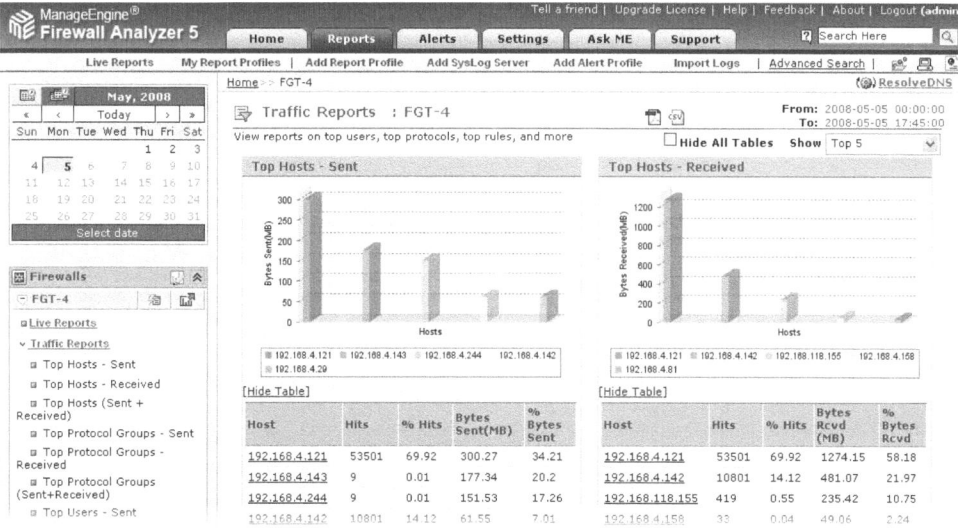

Figure 155:   Monitoring Firewall Analyzer – ManageEngine

7.1.6   Entire Net-Work (WCP) on Windows

Each Adabas command in the WCP log starts with the eye catcher

======= New ADABAS call ======= New ADABAS call =======

And continues for example with

- Start LCL call
- Calling A1 local extended_adabas DBID=251 rc=0
- Format and record buffers

```
15:53:08.630 ba7560 LNK: (EA) ======= New ADABAS call ======= New ADABAS call =======
15:53:08.630 ba7560 LNK: (EA) - ACB content Length=80/0x50 Buffer=0xbe68a8

(snip) obfuscated data

    0310:  F2F1F23E FDFA1619 36004F44 4D1C0000  *òñò>ýú..6.ODM...*
    0320:  000000F2 F0F0F3F0 F9F0F1F2 F0F0F3F0  *...òðñòòñòñòðñòðð*
    0330:  F9F3F0                               *ùòð             *
15:53:08.646 4b5ab0 LNK: (FIRST) thread block 00BD5168
15:53:08.646 4b5ab0 LNK: (EA) ADALNKX Version: 6.2.1.23 - Build-Number 0 and ARCH BYTE 0x'21'
15:53:08.646 4b5ab0 LNK: ADALNKX Compilation Date: Oct  1 2008 Time: 15:18:31
15:53:08.646 4b5ab0 LNK: (EA) ======= New ADABAS call ======= New ADABAS call =======
(snip)
```

Figure 156:   Entire Net-Work (WCP) on Windows Log

The entire WCP log can be viewed in appendix, chapter 8.6.

The Natural parse program RDWCPLOG checks for the eye catcher '=======
New ADABAS call ======= New ADABAS call =======' and counts the number
of calls for each second. The report shows that 81 Adabas calls took place between the time 15:53:17.005 and 15:53:18.005 (one second).

```
Page    1                                                        10-09-13  17:23:26

Adabas Calls
Total   per sec
    1       0 15:53:09.068 ba7660 LNK: (EA) ======= New ADABAS call ======= New ADABAS call ==
   77      76 15:53:10.005 ba7560 LNK: (EA) ======= New ADABAS call ======= New ADABAS call ==
  157      80 15:53:11.005 ba7560 LNK: (EA) ======= New ADABAS call ======= New ADABAS call ==
  236      79 15:53:12.005 ba7660 LNK: (EA) ======= New ADABAS call ======= New ADABAS call ==
  313      77 15:53:13.005 4b5ab0 LNK: (EA) ======= New ADABAS call ======= New ADABAS call ==
  393      80 15:53:14.005 4b5ab0 LNK: (EA) ======= New ADABAS call ======= New ADABAS call ==
  470      77 15:53:15.005 4b58b0 LNK: (EA) ======= New ADABAS call ======= New ADABAS call ==
  544      74 15:53:16.005 4b59b0 LNK: (EA) ======= New ADABAS call ======= New ADABAS call ==
  621      77 15:53:17.005 ba7660 LNK: (EA) ======= New ADABAS call ======= New ADABAS call ==
  702      81 15:53:18.005 ba7560 LNK: (EA) ======= New ADABAS call ======= New ADABAS call ==
  782      80 15:53:19.005 ba7560 LNK: (EA) ======= New ADABAS call ======= New ADABAS call ==
  861      79 15:53:20.005 ba7660 LNK: (EA) ======= New ADABAS call ======= New ADABAS call ==
  942      81 15:53:21.005 ba7560 LNK: (EA) ======= New ADABAS call ======= New ADABAS call ==
 1022      80 15:53:22.005 ba7560 LNK: (EA) ======= New ADABAS call ======= New ADABAS call ==
 1100      78 15:53:23.021 4b58b0 LNK: (EA) ======= New ADABAS call ======= New ADABAS call ==
 1179      79 15:53:24.005 4b59b0 LNK: (EA) ======= New ADABAS call ======= New ADABAS call ==
 1258      79 15:53:25.005 4b5ab0 LNK: (EA) ======= New ADABAS call ======= New ADABAS call ==
 1322      64 15:53:26.005 ba7560 LNK: (EA) ======= New ADABAS call ======= New ADABAS call ==
 1378      56 15:53:27.005 4b5ab0 LNK: (EA) ======= New ADABAS call ======= New ADABAS call ==
 1458      80 15:53:28.005 4b5ab0 LNK: (EA) ======= New ADABAS call ======= New ADABAS call ==
 1537      79 15:53:29.005 ba7560 LNK: (EA) ======= New ADABAS call ======= New ADABAS call ==
 1615      78 15:53:30.005 4b58b0 LNK: (EA) ======= New ADABAS call ======= New ADABAS call ==
Page    2                                                        10-09-13  17:23:26

Adabbas calls    1619
```

Figure 157:   Natural Parse Program for WCP on Windows Log

7.1.7   Adabas on Windows – Command Log

As explained in chapter 7.1, it is very helpful to determine the number of Adabas commands per second on the target database to analyze bottlenecks.

```
ADAF18  N2 cmd to DBID   251 FNR   11 RSP   153 subcode 16448 ISN     75423


REC  DATE                                      CMD RSP
                       DUR    USER-ID              AD2(HEX)/      FILE  ISN   TH IOA IOD IOW
  79219 22-NOV-2010 11:07:35    0    ..B...B. ....~... N2  0 0000004E/N...    11   75414 3  0  0  0
  79220 22-NOV-2010 11:07:35    0    ..B...B. ....~... N2  0 000000B2/....    11   75415 5  0  0  0
  79221 22-NOV-2010 11:07:35    0    ..B...B. ....~... N2  0 0000006B/k...    11   75416 15 0  0  0
  79222 22-NOV-2010 11:07:35    0    ..B...B. ....~... N2  0 000000CD/....    11   75417 20 0  0  0
  79223 22-NOV-2010 11:07:35    0    ..B...B. ........ OP  0 00000000/....  .  0     0 10 0  0  0
  79224 22-NOV-2010 11:07:35    0    ..B...B. ....~... N2  0 00000075/u...    11   75418 1  0  0  0
  79225 22-NOV-2010 11:07:35    0    ..B...B. ....~... N2  0 000000E9/....    11   75419 16 0  0  0
  79226 22-NOV-2010 11:07:35    0    ..B...B. ....~... N2  0 00000050/P...    11   75420 19 0  0  0
  79227 22-NOV-2010 11:07:35    0    ..B...B. ....~... N2  0 000000D4/....    11   75421 12 0  0  0
  79228 22-NOV-2010 11:07:35    0    ..B...B. ....~... N2  0 00000050/P...    11   75422 17 0  0  0
  79229 22-NOV-2010 11:07:35   16    ..B...B. ........ LF  0 000004F4/.... S  231   0  8 1  0  0
  79230 22-NOV-2010 11:07:35    0    ..B...B. ....~... N2  0 0000008E/....    11   75424 14 0  0  0
  79231 22-NOV-2010 11:07:35    0    ..B...B. ....~... N2  0 000000BB/....    11   75425 18 0  0  0
  79232 22-NOV-2010 11:07:35    0    ..B...B. ....~... N2  0 000000CF/....    11   75426 4  0  0  0
  79233 22-NOV-2010 11:07:35    0    ..B...B. ....~... N2  0 00000085/....    11   75427 6  0  0  0
  79234 22-NOV-2010 11:07:35    0    ..B...B. ....~... N2  0 000000A7/....    11   75428 9  0  0  0
  79235 22-NOV-2010 11:07:35    0    ..B...B. ....~... N2  0 000000B0/....    11   75429 11 0  0
```

Figure 158:   Adabas Command Log on Windows

Using a self-written Natural program, you can parse through the Adabas command log and count the Adabas commands per second. You can also use a text editor for Windows with search capabilities, such as display number of lines with '22 NOV 2010 11:07:35' or 'N2' commands. A selection function by columns (from/to) is beneficiary to search a command log size of 200 MB and more.

7.2   Self-Written

7.2.1   RPL and NAB Buffer Overflow

The length of the replication buffer (LRPL) and the number of attached buffers (NAB) can overflow on both the subscription or source database and the Replicator Engine. To automate the check of these buffers, the following job creates the high water marks by using SYSAOS in batch (statements 33-36) and a following Natural program parses the values (statements 48-50) and sends e-mails (statements 56-80) to the data base administration (DBA).

```
000001 //STHWM302 JOB
000002 //          NOTIFY=&SYSUID,TIME=NOLIMIT
000003 //*MAIN     HOLD=NO,SYSTEM=SY5,CLASS=P10,USER=DIETER
000004 //*FORMAT   PR,DDNAME=,FORMS=41,FCB=A8,CHARS=G125
000005 //*----------------------------------------------------------------*
000006 //* This job is scheduled to run every 4 hours, as Becky Albin from
000007 //* Software AG recommended. ESP = DIETER.DB302HWM
000008 //*
000009 //* This job creates and checks the high water marks of the
000010 //* Replicator Engine DB 312 and sends emails if HWM > 65%
000011 //*
000012 //* DIETER.CNTL(RPLHW302)
000013 //*
000014 //* Date        Name      Changed
000015 //* ----------  --------  ------------------------------------------
000016 //* 17 Mar 2009 DSTORR    copied from RPLHW134
000017 //* 19 Mar 2009 DSTORR    HWM msg from 50% to 65%
000018 //* 23 Dec 2009 DSTORR    copied from RPLHW312
000019 //*
000020 //*----------------------------------------------------------------*
000021 //* Create High Water Marks DB302 using AOS / PROD source    SY5
000022 //*----------------------------------------------------------------*
000023 //RPLHWM   EXEC PGM=NATBATCH,REGION=0M,
000024 // PARM='PARM=SYPROD,SYS=STRSY5,AUTO=ON,IM=D,STACK=(LOGON SYSAOS;MENU)'
000025 //STEPLIB    DD DISP=SHR,DSN=ADABAS.ALIAS.SYPROD.LOADLIB    ADABAS
000026 //           DD DISP=SHR,DSN=ADABAS.ALIAS.SYPROD.PGMLIB     NATURAL
000027 //           DD DISP=SHR,DSN=ADABAS.ALIAS.SYPROD.PARMLIB    NATPARM
000028 //DDCARD     DD DISP=SHR,DSN=ADABAS.CONTROL.CARD(PRODN)
000029 //CMPRINT    DD DSN=DIETER.HWM.RPL302,
000030 //**            RECFM=FBA,LRECL=133,BLKSIZE=0,UNIT=MISCDA,  by AOS
000031 //             DISP=(,CATLG),SPACE=(TRK,(10,10),RLSE)
000032 //CMSYNIN    DD *
000033 A,302
000034 U
000035 H
000036 ,,,FIN
000037 //*----------------------------------------------------------------*
000038 //* Check High Water Marks of DB302 - Replicator Engine (REPTOR)
000039 //*----------------------------------------------------------------*
000040 //RPLCHECK EXEC NATBT,DEPT=ST,DB=DEVT,SYSOUT=*,TIME=100,
000041 //          PRM='IM=D,MADIO=0,MAXCL=0,MT=0,LT=999999,AUTO=ON,DU=ABEND'
000042 //CMWKF01    DD DISP=SHR,DSN=DIETER.HWM.RPL302       input
000043 //CMWKF02    DD DSN=DIETER.HWM.PROD.RPL302,          output
000044 //             RECFM=FB,LRECL=79,BLKSIZE=0,UNIT=MISCDA,
000045 //             DISP=(,CATLG),SPACE=(TRK,(10,10),RLSE)
000046 //CMPRINT    DD SYSOUT=*
000047 //CMSYNIN    DD *
000048 LOGON DIETER
000049 DWSLOGHW
000050 FIN
000051 //*
000052 //*        IF RPLCHECK.N.RC=0 THEN
000053 //* -------------------------------------
000054 //* E-mail High Water Marks Lower Than 65%
000055 //* -------------------------------------
000056 //*EMAIL1  EXEC PGM=IKJEFT01,REGION=4096K,DYNAMNBR=50
000057 //SYSTSIN  DD *
000058     SMTPNOTE TO(DSTORR@STORRCONSULTING.COM) -
000059       SUBJECT(High Water Marks Lower Than 65% - DB302) BATCH -
000060       DATASET('DIETER.HWM.PROD.RPL302')
000061 //SYSPROC  DD DSN=SYS2.CLIST,DISP=SHR
000062 //SYSTSPRT DD SYSOUT=*
000063 //         ENDIF
000064 //         IF RPLCHECK.N.RC=12 THEN
000065 //** -------------------------------------
000066 //** E-mail High Water Marks Greater Than 65%
000067 //** -------------------------------------
000068 //EMAIL2   EXEC PGM=IKJEFT01,REGION=4096K,DYNAMNBR=50
000069 //SYSTSIN  DD *
```

```
000070     SMTPNOTE TO(DSTORR@STORRCONSULTING.COM) -
000071       SUBJECT(High Water Marks Greater Than 65% - DB302) BATCH -
000072       DATASET('DIETER.HWM.PROD.RPL302')
000073     SMTPNOTE TO(ADMIN@STORRCONSULTING.COM) -
000074       SUBJECT(High Water Marks Greater Than 65% - DB302) BATCH -
000075       DATASET('DIETER.HWM.PROD.RPL302')
000076     SMTPNOTE TO(INFO@STORRCONSULTING.COM) -
000077       SUBJECT(High Water Marks Greater Than 65% - DB302) BATCH -
000078       DATASET('DIETER.HWM.PROD.RPL302')
000079 //SYSPROC  DD DSN=SYS2.CLIST,DISP=SHR
000080 //SYSTSPRT DD SYSOUT=*
000081 //         ENDIF
000082 //DELETE   EXEC PGM=IEFBR14
000083 //DD1       DD DISP=(SHR,DELETE),DSN=DIETER.HWM.RPL302
000084 //DD2       DD DISP=(SHR,DELETE),DSN=DIETER.HWM.PROD.RPL302
000085 //
```

Figure 159:   Check NAB and RPL Overflow (JCL)

See the code of the Natural parse program in appendix, chapter 9.5.3 RPL and NAB Buffer Overflow.

Output of the e-mail:

```
Subject: High Water Marks Greater Than 65% - DB302

13:47:57          ***** A D A B A S  BASIC  SERVICES *****          2010-10-14
  DBID 302                    -  High Water Marks  -                PACUH02


   Pool / Queue        I    Size   I    Used   I %Used I   Date        Time    I
-------------------------------------------------------------------------------
Attached Buffer (NAB) I   2457600 I   126464 I    5.1 I                         I
Command Queue   (NC)  I     23040 I      384 I    1.6 I 2010-10-08 15:47:04 I
Format Pool     (LFP) I    300000 I    54880 I   18.2 I 2010-10-14 12:47:52 I
Hold Queue      (NH)  I    560056 I      644 I    0.1 I 2010-10-08 16:45:46 I
ISN-List Table (LI)   I     12000 I     1072 I    8.9 I 2010-10-13 01:00:20 I
Seq. Cmd. Table (LQ)  I     20000 I      884 I    4.4 I 2010-10-08 16:45:42 I
User Queue      (NU)  I   1236312 I     8624 I    0.6 I 2010-10-11 10:23:35 I
Unique DE Pool  (DUQ) I    100000 I      328 I    0.3 I 2010-10-08 16:45:46 I
Security Pool   (LCP) I     10000 I        0 I    0.0 I                         I
UQ File List    (UQF) I    384360 I     1152 I    0.2 I 2010-10-11 10:23:35 I
ATM Trans. IDs  (XID) I         0 I        0 I    0.0 I                         I
Work Pool       (LWP) I    500000 I   129188 I   25.8 I 2010-10-13 01:00:20 I
Redo Pool       (LRDP)I         0 I        0 I    0.0 I                         I
Replication     (RPL) I 524288000 I 368520896 I  70.2 I                         I

NAB or RPL reached 65%
```

Figure 160:   Check NAB and RPL Overflow (Output)

7.2.2 SLOG check on Reptor

The following job submits SYSAOS in batch to get the Replicator statistic of the
SLOG file. The online display of SYSAOS must be simulated in batch because the
software does not know keyword commands, for example O,302 / X / F / B / „FIN.

The Natural program DWSLOGCK parses the output of the 'Replicator Statistic'
for not yet replicated transactions. It creates a report with the Replicator Statistic.

If the SLOG is empty then it sets the condition code 0 and writes 'SLOG is empty.'
If the SLOG is not empty then it sets the condition code to 12 and writes 'SLOG is
not empty – open the destination.'

```
//job card
//*-----------------------------------------------------------------*
//* Delete datasets from prior run
//*-----------------------------------------------------------------*
//DELETE   EXEC PGM=IDCAMS
//SYSPRINT  DD SYSOUT=*
//SYSIN     DD *
  DELETE DIETER.SLOG302        PURGE
//*-----------------------------------------------------------------*
//* Create SLOG report by using SYSAOS / Replication Maintenance ---*
//*-----------------------------------------------------------------*
//RPLSTAT1 EXEC PGM=NATBATCH,REGION=0M,
// PARM='PARM=SYPROD,SYS=STRSY7,AUTO=ON,IM=D,STACK=(LOGON SYSAOS;MENU)'
//STEPLIB    DD DISP=SHR,DSN=ADABAS.ALIAS.SYPROD.LOADLIB    ADABAS
//           DD DISP=SHR,DSN=ADABAS.ALIAS.SYPROD.PGMLIB     NATURAL
//           DD DISP=SHR,DSN=ADABAS.ALIAS.SYPROD.PARMLIB    NATPARM
//DDCARD     DD DISP=SHR,DSN=ADABAS.CONTROL.CARD(TESTY)
//CMPRINT    DD DSN=DIETER.SLOG302,
//              DISP=(,CATLG),SPACE=(TRK,(10,10),RLSE)
//CMSYNIN    DD *
O,302
X
F
B
,,FIN
/*
//* -----------------------------------------------------------
//* Check SLOG for empty (RC=0) or not empty (RC=12)
//* -----------------------------------------------------------
//SLOGREP1 EXEC NATBT,DEPT=ST,DB=DEVL,SYSOUT=*,TIME=100,
//           PRM='IM=D,MADIO=0,MAXCL=0,MT=0,LT=999999,AUTO=ON,DU=ABEND'
//SYSOUT     DD SYSOUT=*
//CMWKF01    DD DISP=SHR,DSN=DIETER.SLOG302
//CMPRT01    DD SYSOUT=*
//SYSIN      DD *
LOGON DIETER
DWSLOGCK
FIN
//
```

Figure 161:   SLOG Check on Reptor (JCL)

The Natural parse program DWSLOGCK is located in the appendix, chapter 9.5.4.

The following shows the Replicator Statistics to be parsed:

```
17:00:01           ***** A D A B A S  BASIC  SERVICES *****           2011-02-24
Replicator 312            - Replicator Statistics -                   PRPTS10

Replicated trans  / messages / bytes   Received from input queues
-------------------------------------   -------------------------------------
Total trn.                    43,607   Messages ...
Pending ..          6,400              Bytes ......
Messages                               Commits ....
Tot msgs .                             Backouts ...
Bytes sent to all destinations
Tot bytes.                             Deleted totals from input queues
                                       -------------------------------------
SLog statistics for items              Messages ...
-------------------------------------   Bytes ......
Delogged .                       216   Commits ....
Logged ...                    17,639   Backouts ...
On file ..          17,639

Replay dbid/token cnt .
Destination slog cnt ..          190                      More: press PF8

PF1---   PF3---   PF4-----   PF5--------   PF6--------   PF7---   PF8---   PF12-----
Help     Exit     Refresh    DBID/Token    Dest. SLOG             +       Menu
```

Figure 162:   SLOG Check on Reptor (Input)

The following shows the output of the program DWSLOGCK:

```
17:00:01           ***** A D A B A S  BASIC  SERVICES *****           2011-02-24
Replicator 312            - Replicator Statistics -                   PRPTS10

Replicated trans  / messages / bytes   Received from input queues
-------------------------------------   -------------------------------------
Total trn.                    43,607   Messages ...
Pending ..          6,400              Bytes ......
Messages                               Commits ....
Tot msgs .                             Backouts ...
Bytes sent to all destinations
Tot bytes.                             Deleted totals from input queues
                                       -------------------------------------
SLog statistics for items              Messages ...
-------------------------------------   Bytes ......
Delogged .                       216   Commits ....
Logged ...                    17,639   Backouts ...
On file ..          17,639

Replay dbid/token cnt .
Destination slog cnt ..          190                      More: press PF8

SLOG is not empty - open the destination.
```

Figure 163:   SLOG Check on Reptor (Output)

7.2.3   Compare two SLOGs and Open Destination

Similar to the prior chapter 7.2.2, this job compares two Replicator Statistics and open destinations if necessary.

See detailed description of the job – see JCL comments:

```
//STSLOGCT JOB (ST345T,ST01,ST),DBA,MSGCLASS=1,
//         NOTIFY=&SYSUID,TIME=NOLIMIT     ,TYPRUN=SCAN
//*MAIN    HOLD=NO,SYSTEM=SY5,CLASS=P10,USER=DIETER
//*FORMAT  PR,DDNAME=,FORMS=41,FCB=A8,CHARS=G125
//*-----------------------------------------------------------------*
//* Replicator Destination Check - DIETER.CNTL(RPLSLOG2)
//* Job will be daily started by ESP on SY5: DIETER.SLOGCHECK-T
//* At this time: DB039 / DB302 / DB251
//*
//* Step Name   Check  Function
//* ----------- ------ ----------------------------------------
//* RPLCHECK    Set CC  0 if destination and DB are OK
//*             Set CC 12 if not OK
//* ---- if rplcheck.n.rc = 12 then
//* EMAIL1      CC 12  Send e-mail and stop job
//* ---- if rplcheck.n.rc = 0 then
//* RPLSTAT1    Create SLOGREP1 by using AOS
//* SLOGREP1    Check  SLOGREP1 whether SLOG is emtpy
//*             Set CC  0 if SLOG is empty
//*             Set CC 12 if SLOG is not empty
//* ---- if slogrep1.n.rc = 0 then
//* EMAIL2      Send e-mail everything is OK and stop job
//* ---- if slogrep1.n.rc = 12 then
//* RPLOPEN     Open destination by using AOS
//* WAIT        Wait for 1 minute
//* RPLSTAT2    Create SLOGREP2 by using AOS
//* SLOGREP2    Compare datasets SLOGREP1 and SLOGREP2
//*             Set CC  0 if SLOG is empty
//*             Set CC 12 if SLOG is not empty
//* ---- if slogrep2.n.rc = 0 then
//* EMPTY       Sent e-mail that SLOG is empty and stop job
//* ---- if slogrep2.rc = 12 then
//* NOTEMPTY    Sent e-mail that destin opened but SLOG is not empty
//* ---- endif
//*
//* Date        Name     Reason
//* ---------- -------- ------------------------------------------
//* 2009-01-27 Dstorr   copied from RPLSLOG1 and modified for TEST
//* 2009-12-23 Dstorr   updated for a new test with COEMS PROD
//*
//*-----------------------------------------------------------------*
//* Delete datasets from prior run
//*-----------------------------------------------------------------*
//DELETE EXEC PGM=IDCAMS
//SYSPRINT  DD SYSOUT=*
//SYSIN     DD *
  DELETE DIETER.MSG6          PURGE
  DELETE DIETER.MSG7          PURGE
  DELETE DIETER.MSG8          PURGE
  DELETE DIETER.SLOGREP3      PURGE
  DELETE DIETER.SLOGREP4      PURGE
//*-----------------------------------------------------------------*
//* Check whether Net-Work is open and DB 191 is available (RC148)
//* Available: RC = 0; unavailable: RC 12; other errors: RC 16
//*-----------------------------------------------------------------*
//RPLCHECK EXEC NATBT,DEPT=ST,DB=DEVT,SYSOUT=*,TIME=100,
//         PRM='IM=D,MADIO=0,MAXCL=0,MT=0,LT=999999,AUTO=ON,DU=ABEND'
//SYSOUT    DD  SYSOUT=*
//CMPRINT   DD  DISP=(,CATLG),DSN=DIETER.MSG6,
//              RECFM=FB,LRECL=120,BLKSIZE=0,UNIT=MISCDA,
```

```
//           SPACE=(TRK,(10,50),RLSE)
//CMSYNIN  DD *
LOGON DIETER
DWSRD44R 251
FIN
//       IF RPLCHECK.N.RC=12 THEN
//** ----------------------------------------------------------------
//** E-mail Network and DB are down
//** ----------------------------------------------------------------
//EMAIL1   EXEC PGM=IKJEFT01,REGION=4096K,DYNAMNBR=50
//SYSTSIN  DD *
  SMTPNOTE TO(DSTORR@STORRCONSULTING.COM) -
    SUBJECT(RPL: DESTINATION DATABASE 191 OR NETWORK IS DOWN) BATCH -
    DATASET('DIETER.MSG6')
//SYSPROC  DD DSN=SYS2.CLIST,DISP=SHR
//SYSTSPRT DD SYSOUT=*
//       ENDIF
//       IF RPLCHECK.N.RC=16 THEN
//** ----------------------------------------------------------------
//** E-mail Network problems - RC 224
//** ----------------------------------------------------------------
//EMAIL1   EXEC PGM=IKJEFT01,REGION=4096K,DYNAMNBR=50
//SYSTSIN  DD *
  SMTPNOTE TO(DSTORR@STORRCONSULTING.COM) -
    SUBJECT(NETWORK: RespTime longer than defined REPLYTIM) BATCH -
    DATASET('DIETER.MSG6')
//SYSPROC  DD DSN=SYS2.CLIST,DISP=SHR
//SYSTSPRT DD SYSOUT=*
//       ENDIF
//       IF RPLCHECK.N.RC=0 THEN                 network open
//*----------------------------------------------------------------*
//* Create SLOG report by using SYSAOS / Replication Maintenance ---*
//*----------------------------------------------------------------*
//RPLSTAT1 EXEC PGM=NATBATCH,REGION=0M,
// PARM='PARM=SYPROD,SYS=STRSY5,AUTO=ON,IM=D,STACK=(LOGON SYSAOS;MENU)'
//STEPLIB   DD DISP=SHR,DSN=ADABAS.ALIAS.SYPROD.LOADLIB     ADABAS
//          DD DISP=SHR,DSN=ADABAS.ALIAS.SYPROD.PGMLIB      NATURAL
//          DD DISP=SHR,DSN=ADABAS.ALIAS.SYPROD.PARMLIB     NATPARM
//DDCARD    DD DISP=SHR,DSN=ADABAS.CONTROL.CARD(PRODN)
//CMPRINT   DD DSN=DIETER.SLOGREP3,
//             DISP=(,CATLG),SPACE=(TRK,(10,10),RLSE)
//CMSYNIN   DD *
O,302
X
F
B
,,FIN
/*
//* ----------------------------------------------------------------
//* Check SLOG for empty (RC=0) or not empty (RC=12)
//* ----------------------------------------------------------------
//SLOGREP1 EXEC NATBT,DEPT=ST,DB=PRST,SYSOUT=*,TIME=100,
//         PRM='IM=D,MADIO=0,MAXCL=0,MT=0,LT=999999,AUTO=ON,DU=ABEND'
//SYSOUT   DD SYSOUT=*
//CMWKF01  DD DISP=SHR,DSN=DIETER.SLOGREP3
//CMPRT01  DD DSN=DIETER.MSG7,
//            DISP=(,CATLG),SPACE=(TRK,(10,10),RLSE)
//SYSIN    DD *
LOGON PDSTUTIL
DWSLOGCK
FIN
//       ENDIF
//       IF SLOGREP1.N.RC = 0 THEN
//** ----------------------------------------------------------------
//** E-mail Network and DB are available
//** ----------------------------------------------------------------
//EMAIL2   EXEC PGM=IKJEFT01,REGION=4096K,DYNAMNBR=50
//SYSTSIN  DD *
```

```
   SMTPNOTE TO(DSTORR@STORRCONSULTING.COM) -
      SUBJECT(RPL: Destination DB 191 and Net-Work is available) BATCH -
      DATASET('DIETER.MSG7')
//SYSPROC  DD DSN=SYS2.CLIST,DISP=SHR
//SYSTSPRT DD SYSOUT=*
//        ENDIF
//*
//      IF SLOGREP1.N.RC = 12 THEN
//** ----------------------------------------------------------------
//**  OPEN the destination - SLOG was not empty
//** ----------------------------------------------------------------
//RPLOPEN EXEC PGM=NATBATCH,REGION=0M,
// PARM='PARM=SYPROD,SYS=STRSY5,AUTO=ON,IM=D,STACK=(LOGON SYSAOS;MENU)'
//STEPLIB    DD DISP=SHR,DSN=ADABAS.ALIAS.SYPROD.LOADLIB    ADABAS
//           DD DISP=SHR,DSN=ADABAS.ALIAS.SYPROD.PGMLIB     NATURAL
//           DD DISP=SHR,DSN=ADABAS.ALIAS.SYPROD.PARMLIB    NATPARM
//DDCARD     DD DISP=SHR,DSN=ADABAS.CONTROL.CARD(PRODN)
//CMPRINT    DD SYSOUT=*
//CMSYNIN    DD *
O,302
X
A
K,,D251006
K,,D251007
K,,D251008
K,,D251009
K,,D251010
K,,D251011
K,,D251012
K,,D251013
K,,D251014
K,,D251015
K,,D251016
K,,D251017
K,,D251018
K,,D251019
K,,D251020
K,,D251021
K,,D251022
K,,D251023
K,,D251024
K,,D251025
K,,D251026
K,,D251027
K,,D251028
K,,D251029
K,,D251030
K,,D251030
K,,D251032
K,,D251033
K,,D251034
K,,D251035
K,,D251036
K,,D251037
K,,D251038
K,,D251039
K,,D251040
K,,D251041
K,,D251042
K,,D251043
K,,D251044
K,,D251045
K,,D251046
K,,D251047
.
.
,,FIN
/*
//*-------------------------------------------------------------------*
```

```
//* Wait 1 minute before creating the SLOG report #2
//*-----------------------------------------------------------------*
//WAIT     EXEC PGM=SLEEP,PARM='00:01:00.00'          (HH:MM:SS:TH)
//STEPLIB  DD  DISP=SHR,DSN=DIETER.ASM.LOADLIB
//DDPRINT  DD  SYSOUT=*
//SYSUDUMP DD  DUMMY
//ABENDAID DD  SYSOUT=*
//*-----------------------------------------------------------------*
//* Create SLOG report #2 using SYSAOS / Replication Maintenance ---*
//*-----------------------------------------------------------------*
//RPLSTAT2 EXEC PGM=NATBATCH,REGION=0M,
// PARM='PARM=SYPROD,SYS=STRSY5,AUTO=ON,IM=D,STACK=(LOGON SYSAOS;MENU)'
//STEPLIB    DD DISP=SHR,DSN=ADABAS.ALIAS.SYPROD.LOADLIB    ADABAS
//           DD DISP=SHR,DSN=ADABAS.ALIAS.SYPROD.PGMLIB     NATURAL
//           DD DISP=SHR,DSN=ADABAS.ALIAS.SYPROD.PARMLIB    NATPARM
//DDCARD     DD DISP=SHR,DSN=ADABAS.CONTROL.CARD(PRODN)
//CMPRINT    DD DSN=DIETER.SLOGREP4,
//              DISP=(,CATLG),SPACE=(TRK,(10,10),RLSE)
//CMSYNIN    DD *
O,302
X
F
B
,,FIN
/*
//* ------------------------------------------------------------------
//* Check SLOG for empty (RC=0) or not empty (RC=12)
//*   - Sum SLOG report 1 and SLOG report 2 empty = (RC=0) SLOG empty
//*   - Sum SLOG report 1 = ' ' and rep 2 EQ ' '  = (RC=0) emptied
//*   - Sum SLOG report 1 GT sum SLOG report 2     = (RC=0) empty in prog
//*   - Sum SLOG report 1 EQ sum SLOG report 2     = (RC=12) open destin
//*     open did not work
//* ------------------------------------------------------------------
//SLOGREP2 EXEC NATBT,DEPT=ST,DB=DEVT,SYSOUT=*,TIME=100,
//         PRM='IM=D,MADIO=0,MAXCL=0,MT=0,LT=999999,AUTO=ON,DU=ABEND'
//SYSOUT   DD SYSOUT=*
//CMWKF01  DD DISP=SHR,DSN=DIETER.SLOGREP3
//CMWKF02  DD DISP=SHR,DSN=DIETER.SLOGREP4
//CMPRT01  DD DSN=DIETER.MSG8,
//            DISP=(,CATLG),SPACE=(TRK,(10,10),RLSE)
//SYSIN    DD *
LOGON DIETER
DWSLOGC2
FIN
//       ENDIF
//       IF SLOGREP2.N.RC = 0 THEN              SLOG was empty
//** --------------------------------------------------------------
//**  EMAIL SLOG EMPTY
//** --------------------------------------------------------------
//EMPTY   EXEC PGM=IKJEFT01,REGION=4096K,DYNAMNBR=50
//SYSTSIN DD *
 SMTPNOTE TO(DSTORR@STORRCONSULTING.COM)    -
    SUBJECT(Replicator: SLOG DB302 is empty) BATCH -
    DATASET('DIETER.MSG8')
  SMTPNOTE TO(LFRAZIN@CALSTRS.COM) -
    SUBJECT(Replicator: SLOG DB302 is empty) BATCH -
    DATASET('DIETER.MSG8')
  SMTPNOTE TO(ADABASSERVERADMINISTRATORS@CALSTRS.COM) -
    SUBJECT(Replicator: SLOG DB302 is empty) BATCH -
    DATASET('DIETER.MSG8')
//SYSPROC  DD DSN=SYS2.CLIST,DISP=SHR
//SYSTSPRT DD SYSOUT=*
//       ENDIF
//       IF SLOGREP2.N.RC = 12 THEN
//** --------------------------------------------------------------
//**  EMAIL SLOG NOT EMPTY
//** --------------------------------------------------------------
//NOTEMPTY EXEC PGM=IKJEFT01,REGION=4096K,DYNAMNBR=50
//SYSTSIN  DD *
```

```
 SMTPNOTE TO(DSTORR@STORRCONSULTING.COM) -
  SUBJECT(Repl DB312: SLOG is not empty - Open destin. failed) BATCH -
  DATASET('DIETER.MSG8')
 SMTPNOTE TO(LFRAZIN@CALSTRS.COM) -
  SUBJECT(Repl DB312: SLOG is not empty - Open destin. failed) BATCH -
  DATASET('DIETER.MSG8')
 SMTPNOTE TO(ADABASSERVERADMINISTRATORS@CALSTRS.COM) -
  SUBJECT(Repl DB312: SLOG is not empty - Open destin. failed) BATCH -
  DATASET('DIETER.MSG8')
//SYSPROC  DD DSN=SYS2.CLIST,DISP=SHR
//SYSTSPRT DD SYSOUT=*
//        ENDIF
//
```

Figure 164:   Compare two SLOGs Open Destination (JCL)

Appendix, chapter 9.5.5 shows the Natural compare program and chapter 9.8.1 displays the assembler program Sleep/Wait. Appendix chapter 9.8.2 shows an assembler program to determine the dataset name via the DDNAME as part of the JCL. The routine can be called from a Natural program or as part of a job stream.

7.2.4   SLOG Check for Logged Files

It is important to know in case of pending file changes what files are still in the SLOG before you update fields in the global format buffer (GFB) and the target database.

In some versions and SM-levels of SYSAOS, the replicator statistics show that files are on the SLOG but hitting the PF6-key shows nothing. This function worked in prior replicator and AOS versions.

```
 17:00:01            ***** A D A B A S  BASIC  SERVICES *****        2011-02-24
 Replicator 312            - Replicator Statistics -                 PRPTS10

 Replicated trans  / messages / bytes   Received from input queues
 -----------------------------------    ------------------------------------------
 Total trn.                  43,607  Messages ...
 Pending ..         6,400             Bytes ......
 Messages                             Commits ....
 Tot msgs .                           Backouts ...
 Bytes sent to all destinations
 Tot bytes.                           Deleted totals from input queues
                                      ------------------------------------------
 SLog statistics for items            Messages ...
 -----------------------------------  Bytes ......
 Delogged .                    216  Commits ....
 Logged ...                 17,639  Backouts ...
 On file ..        17,639

 Replay dbid/token cnt .
 Destination slog cnt ..             190                        More: press PF8

 PF1---  PF3---  PF4-----  PF5--------  PF6--------  PF7---  PF8---  PF12-----
 Help    Exit    Refresh   DBID/Token   Dest. SLOG           +       Menu
```

Figure 165:   SLOG Check for Logged Files

Another function 'Destination Statistics' shows 'Total pending trans' but it is not clear whether these pending transactions are located in the replication buffer or in SLOG.

```
15:35:20              ***** A D A B A S   BASIC   SERVICES *****            2010-10-14
Replicator 302              - Destination Statistics -                     PRPTS04

Dest Name  Type   Total replicated transactions  Total pending trans
--------   ----   -----------------------------  -------------
 D251018   Abas                               1
 D251035   Abas                             556            2,098
 D251035   Abas                           3,091               18
 D251035   Abas                           5,764               19
 D251035   Abas                           5,954
(snip)
```

Figure 166:   Manual File Change Procedure – SLOG Check

Based on this problem, I wrote a Natural program as a workaround until Software AG can fix the bug. It reads the SLOG file and displays the long name of files.

See the Natural program READF30P at appendix, chapter 9.5.12.

Output of program READF30P in SYSPRINT:

```
Page      1                                                    12/15/10  10:38:33
          File Name        ISN SLOG
--------------------    --------

No records found in SLOG file 30 in DB 312
```

Figure 167:   Monitor Program: SLOG Check for Logged Files – READF30P

7.2.5   SLOG Space and Number of Records Check

The subscription log (SLOG) is an Adabas file and used as an overflow area for the RPL buffer of the Reptor. To make sure that the SLOG does not overflow, the space and the number of records must be manually checked based on the Adabas report. File 30 is in this example the SLOG file (see Figure 168) and I wrote a Natural program to parse the Adabas report and display the space and the number of records. The program can set a condition code if the size reaches a special threshold and an additional job step can send out an e-mail to the DBA group.

The Natural monitor program is located in appendix, chapter 9.5.11.

```
//STRP030P JOB (ST345T,ST01,ST),DBA,MSGCLASS=1,
//         NOTIFY=&SYSUID,TIME=NOLIMIT
//*MAIN    HOLD=NO,SYSTEM=SY7,CLASS=P10,USER=STADBA
//*FORMAT  PR,DDNAME=,FORMS=41,FCB=A8,CHARS=G125
//*-----------------------------------------------------------------*
//* This job creates an online report of file 30 and parses it for
//* - Number of records
//* - Free space
//*
//* DIETER.CNTL(RPL30REP)
//*
//* Date          Name     Changed
//* -----------   -------  --------------------------------------------
//* 15 Dec 2010   DSTORR   created
//*
//*-----------------------------------------------------------------*
//* Delete datasets from prior run
//*-----------------------------------------------------------------*
//DELETE  EXEC PGM=IDCAMS
//SYSPRINT  DD SYSOUT=*
//SYSIN     DD *
  DELETE DIETER.REPF30.DB312     PURGE
  DELETE DIETER.RPFF30.DB312     PURGE
  DELETE DIETER.RINF30.DB312     PURGE
//*-----------------------------------------------------------------*
//* Create High Water Marks DB312 using AOS / PROD source     SY5
//*-----------------------------------------------------------------*
//RPLHWM    EXEC PGM=NATBATCH,REGION=0M,
// PARM='PARM=SYPROD,SYS=STRSY5,AUTO=ON,IM=D,STACK=(LOGON SYSAOS;MENU)'
//STEPLIB   DD DISP=SHR,DSN=ADABAS.ALIAS.SYPROD.LOADLIB    ADABAS
//          DD DISP=SHR,DSN=ADABAS.ALIAS.SYPROD.PGMLIB     NATURAL
//          DD DISP=SHR,DSN=ADABAS.ALIAS.SYPROD.PARMLIB    NATPARM
//DDCARD    DD DISP=SHR,DSN=ADABAS.CONTROL.CARD(PRODN)
//CMPRINT   DD DSN=DIETER.REPF30.DB312,
//**           RECFM=FBA,LRECL=133,BLKSIZE=0,UNIT=MISCDA,  by AOS
//            DISP=(,CATLG),SPACE=(TRK,(10,10),RLSE)
//CMSYNIN   DD *
R,312
F,30,312

,,FIN
//
//*-----------------------------------------------------------------*
//* Check the SLOG report for number or records and used space
//*-----------------------------------------------------------------*
//SLOGHECK EXEC NATBT,DEPT=ST,DB=DEVT,SYSOUT=*,TIME=100,
//          PRM='IM=D,MADIO=0,MAXCL=0,MT=0,LT=999999,AUTO=ON,DU=ABEND'
//CMWKF01  DD DISP=SHR,DSN=DIETER.REPF30.DB312           input
//CMWKF02  DD DSN=DIETER.RPFF30.DB312,                   output AOS report
//            RECFM=FB,LRECL=79,BLKSIZE=0,UNIT=MISCDA,
//            DISP=(,CATLG),SPACE=(TRK,(10,10),RLSE)
//CMWKF03  DD DSN=DIETER.RINF30.DB312,                   output of RPL30REP
//            RECFM=FB,LRECL=080,BLKSIZE=0,UNIT=MISCDA,
//            DISP=(,CATLG),SPACE=(TRK,(10,10),RLSE)
//CMPRINT   DD SYSOUT=*
//CMSYNIN   DD *
LOGON STDBAUTI
RPL30REP
FIN
//

DIETER.REPF30.DB312 output of SYSAOS report
DIETER.RPFF30.DB312 relevant lines, input for RPL30REP
DIETER.RINF30.DB312 output of program RPL30REP
```

Figure 168:   SLOG Number of Records and Space Check (JCL)

```
DIETER.RINF30.DB312
******************************* Top of Data *********************************
2010-12-16 - 17:55:03.7 - Report of SLOG File 30 DB312 - RPL30REP
Records loaded ..... 0
UI space allocated (blk):    135000 UI space unused (blk):    134999
NI space allocated (blk):   1080000 NI space unused (blk):   1080000
DS space allocated (blk):   2250000 DS space unused (blk):   2250000
***************************** Bottom of Data ********************************
```

Figure 169:   SLOG Number of Records and Space Check (Output)

7.2.6   Check Messages on DDPRINT

Under z/OS, it is normally not possible to check the output queue of an active job. To check messages of DDPRINT, the IBM utility EJESLNK can locate the job name and DD name and save the content to a dataset. A Natural program parses the dataset for error messages, warnings and response codes and saves it to another dataset.

```
000010 //EJESLNK EXEC PGM=EJESLNK
000011 //* EJESEXT DD SYSOUT=*
000012 //EJESEXT DD DSN=ADABAS.EXTRACT.DDPRINT,
000013 //            DISP=(NEW,CATLG,DELETE),VOL=(,,,20),
000014 //            UNIT=MISCDA,BUFNO=20,RECFM=FB,LRECL=240,
000015 //            SPACE=(240,(100,50),RLSE),AVGREC=K,RETPD=30
000016 //EJESOUT DD SYSOUT=*,RECFM=VB,LRECL=240
000017 //EJESIN  DD *
000018   ST REPTMPM
000019   FIND RETMPM
000020   :S
000021   FIND DDPRINT
000022   :E
000023 //
```

Figure 170:   Read Output Queue of Active Job – EJESLNK (JCL)

See the parse program at the appendix, chapter 9.5.2.

The report of the parse program:

```
<snip>
017528  ADAF18  ET cmd to DBID    187 FNR        RSP   254 subcode   3
017529  ADAF18  A1 cmd to DBID    187 FNR     18 RSP   254 subcode   6 ISN          186
017530  ADAF18  ET cmd to DBID    187 FNR        RSP   254 subcode   3
017531  ADAF18  ET cmd to DBID    187 FNR        RSP   254 subcode   3
017532  ADAF18  A1 cmd to DBID    187 FNR     18 RSP   254 subcode   3 ISN          185
017533  ADAF18  E1 cmd to DBID    187 FNR     14 RSP   113 subcode     ISN       237158
017534  ADAF18  E1 cmd to DBID    187 FNR     14 RSP   113 subcode     ISN       237186
****************************************************
017534  AB  -POOL    NAB=        420    1715456 ( 99 %)
****************************************************
****************************************************
017534  RPL -POOL    LRPL= 157286400  149875480 ( 95 %)
****************************************************
FNR/RSP/CNT:   0 254 4
FNR/RSP/CNT:  14 113 224
FNR/RSP/CNT:  15 113 4
FNR/RSP/CNT:  18 113 11
FNR/RSP/CNT:  18 254 4
FNR/RSP/CNT:  20 113 25
FNR/RSP/CNT:  22 113 6
```

Figure 171:   Output of Natural Parse Program

EJESLNK and the parse program can be used to check DDPRINT of the source database and the Replicator Engine.

7.2.7   Target Check – Ping

The following job is scheduled to run every hour to check whether the target database, Adabas on Windows, is reachable and the files are available.

A Natural program reads one record of one file on the target database and set based on the Adabas response codes a condition code for the batch job. See Natural program in appendix chapter 9.5.1, Ping Target Database.

```
//PING JOB (ST345T,ST01,ST),DBA,MSGCLASS=1,TIME=NOLIMIT
//*MAIN     HOLD=NO,SYSTEM=SY5,CLASS=P10,USER=DIETER
//*FORMAT   PR,DDNAME=,FORMS=41,FCB=A8,CHARS=G125
//** ------------------------------------------------------------ **
//** SCHEDULED FOR DAILY EVERY HOUR -- DIETER.RPLSRVCHECK (TEMP OFF)**
//**                                                              **
//** CHECK WHETHER TARGET DB IS UP AND RUNNING - SEND EMAIL       **
//**                                                              **
//** DATE           NAME    REASON                                **
//** ------------   -----   ------------------------------------  **
//** 2010/12/06     DSTORR  PREPARED FOR SY5                      **
//** 2010/11/09     DSTORR  ELIMINATED STEP EMAIL1 WITH RC=0 CHECK **
//** 2010/11/02     DSTORR  DATABASE AND MESSAGE DATASET, EP EVENT **
//** 2009/12/01     DSTORR  CREATED                               **
//**                                                              **
//** ------------------------------------------------------------
//RPLCHECK EXEC NATBT,DEPT=ST,DB=DEVL,PRM='IM=D,AUTO=ON'
//SYSOUT   DD  SYSOUT=*
//CMPRINT  DD DISP=(,CATLG),DSN=DIETER.DB251CHK,
//            RECFM=FB,LRECL=120,BLKSIZE=0,UNIT=MISCDA,
//            SPACE=(TRK,(10,50),RLSE)
//CMSYNIN  DD *
LOGON DIETER
DWSRD44R 251
FIN
//** -------------------------------
//       IF RC=0 THEN
//*** -------------------------------
//EMAIL1  EXEC PGM=IKJEFT01,REGION=4096K,DYNAMNBR=50
//SYSTSIN DD *
  SMTPNOTE TO(DSTORR@STORRCONSULTING.COM) -
  SUBJECT(RPL: DESTINATION DATABASE 251 AND NETWORK IS UP) BATCH -
  DATASET('DIETER.DB251CHK')
//SYSPROC  DD DSN=SYS2.CLIST,DISP=SHR
//SYSTSPRT DD SYSOUT=*
//     ENDIF
//** -------------------------------
//      IF RC GT 11 THEN
//** -------------------------------
//EMAIL2  EXEC PGM=IKJEFT01,REGION=4096K,DYNAMNBR=50
//SYSTSIN DD *
  SMTPNOTE TO(DSTORR@STORRCONSULTING.COM) -
   SUBJECT(RPL: DESTINATION DATABASE 251 OR NETWORK IS DOWN) BATCH -
   DATASET('DIETER.DB251CHK')
//SYSPROC  DD DSN=SYS2.CLIST,DISP=SHR
//SYSTSPRT DD SYSOUT=*
//     ENDIF
//** -------------------------------
//DELETE EXEC PGM=IEFBR14
//DD1     DD DISP=(OLD,DELETE),DSN=DIETER.DB251CHK
//
```

Figure 172:   WCP, Network and Target DB Check – PING – (JCL)

7.2.8   Destination Report

The following job submits SYSAOS in batch and creates a report, which will be parsed by a Natural program.

```
000001 //STDES302 JOB (ST345T,ST01,ST),DBA,MSGCLASS=1,
000002 //         NOTIFY=&SYSUID,TIME=NOLIMIT     ,TYPRUN=SCAN
000003 //*MAIN    HOLD=NO,SYSTEM=SY7,CLASS=P10,USER=DIETER
000004 //*FORMAT  PR,DDNAME=,FORMS=41,FCB=A8,CHARS=G125
000005 //*----------------------------------------------------------------*
000006 //* Replicator Subscription Check - DIETER.CNTL(DEST302)
000007 //* ADA813
000008 //*----------------------------------------------------------------*
000009 //* Delete datasets from prior run
000010 //*----------------------------------------------------------------*
000011 //DELETE EXEC PGM=IDCAMS
000012 //SYSPRINT DD SYSOUT=*
000013 //SYSIN    DD *
000014   DELETE DIETER.DEST302        PURGE
000015 //*----------------------------------------------------------------*
000016 //* Create SUBS report by using SYSAOS / Replication Maintenance ---*
000017 //*----------------------------------------------------------------*
000018 //RPLSTAT1 EXEC PGM=NATBATCH,REGION=0M,
000019 // PARM='PARM=SYPROD,SYS=STRSY7,AUTO=ON,IM=D,STACK=(LOGON SYSAOS;MENU)'
000020 //STEPLIB   DD DISP=SHR,DSN=ADABAS.ALIAS.SYPROD.LOADLIB    ADABAS
000021 //          DD DISP=SHR,DSN=ADABAS.ALIAS.SYPROD.PGMLIB     NATURAL
000022 //          DD DISP=SHR,DSN=ADABAS.ALIAS.SYPROD.PARMLIB    NATPARM
000023 //DDCARD    DD DISP=SHR,DSN=ADABAS.CONTROL.CARD(TESTY)
000024 //CMPRINT   DD DSN=DIETER.DEST302,
000025 //             DISP=(,CATLG),SPACE=(TRK,(10,10),RLSE)
000026 //CMSYNIN   DD *
000027 O,302
000028 X
000029 F
000030 D
000031
000032
000033
000034
000035
000036
000037
000038
000039
000040
000041
000042
000043
000044
000045 ,,FIN
000046 //

Remark: blank lines are for each screen to be displayed with destination info
```

Figure 173:   SYSAOS Batch – Display Reptor Statistics – Destinations (JCL)

```
15:35:20          ***** A D A B A S  BASIC  SERVICES *****        2010-10-14
Replicator 302          - Destination Statistics -               PRPTS04

Dest Name  Type   Total replicated transactions  Total pending trans
--------   ----   -----------------------------  -------------
 D251018   Abas                              1
 D251035   Abas                            556              2,098
 D251035   Abas                          3,091                 18
 D251035   Abas                          5,764                 19
 D251035   Abas                          5,954
 D251144   Abas                          4,000
 D251158   Abas                              1
 D251167   Abas                              1
 D251168   Abas                              1
 D251249   Abas                              1
 D251227   Abas                          2,000
 D251228   Abas                          2,000
 D251229   Abas                          2,000
 D251230   Abas                          2,000
 D251231   Abas                          2,000
 D251232   Abas                          2,000
 D251249   Abas                              1
```

Figure 174: SYSAOS Batch – Display Reptor Statistics – Destinations – Output

```
14:53:06          ***** A D A B A S  BASIC  SERVICES *****        2010-10-14
Replicator 302       - Selected Destination Statistics -         PRPTS04

Selected Dest Name : D251035
Selected Dest Type : Adabas                            Time tran committed
Total replicated transactions .           1,062 2010/10/14 14:51:16
Total pending transactions ....           1,592
Total messages sent ..........                0
Total commits ................                0
Slog logged count ............                0
Slog delogged count ..........                0
Items for destination on slog .               0
Items to delete from slog .....               0
Bytes sent to destination .....               0
Pending bytes for destination .               0
Pending messages .............. 0
Number of BT's ................                0 Time of last ET
Number of ET's ................           1,062 2010/10/14 15:03:29
```

Figure 175: SYSAOS Batch – Select one Destination – Output

7.2.9   Subscription Report

The following job submits SYSAOS in batch and creates a report, which will be parsed by a Natural program.

```
000001 //STSUB302 JOB (ST345T,ST01,ST),DBA,MSGCLASS=1,
000002 //          NOTIFY=&SYSUID,TIME=NOLIMIT    ,TYPRUN=SCAN
000003 //*MAIN     HOLD=NO,SYSTEM=SY7,CLASS=P10,USER=STADBA
000004 //*FORMAT  PR,DDNAME=,FORMS=41,FCB=A8,CHARS=G125
000005 //*----------------------------------------------------------------*
000006 //* Replicator Subscription Check - DIETER.CNTL(SUBS302)
000007 //* ADA813
000008 //*----------------------------------------------------------------*
000009 //* Delete datasets from prior run
000010 //*----------------------------------------------------------------*
000011 //DELETE EXEC PGM=IDCAMS
000012 //SYSPRINT  DD SYSOUT=*
000013 //SYSIN     DD *
000014   DELETE DIETER.SUBS302        PURGE
000015 //*----------------------------------------------------------------*
000016 //* Create SUBS report by using SYSAOS / Replication Maintenance ---*
000017 //*----------------------------------------------------------------*
000018 //RPLSTAT1 EXEC PGM=NATBATCH,REGION=0M,
000019 // PARM='PARM=SYPROD,SYS=STRSY7,AUTO=ON,IM=D,STACK=(LOGON SYSAOS;MENU)'
000020 //STEPLIB    DD DISP=SHR,DSN=ADABAS.ALIAS.SYPROD.LOADLIB    ADABAS
000021 //           DD DISP=SHR,DSN=ADABAS.ALIAS.SYPROD.PGMLIB     NATURAL
000022 //           DD DISP=SHR,DSN=ADABAS.ALIAS.SYPROD.PARMLIB    NATPARM
000023 //DDCARD     DD DISP=SHR,DSN=ADABAS.CONTROL.CARD(TESTY)
000024 //CMPRINT    DD DSN=DIETER.SUBS302,
000025 //              DISP=(,CATLG),SPACE=(TRK,(10,10),RLSE)
000026 //CMSYNIN    DD *
000027 0,302
000028 X
000029 F
000030 R
000031
000032
000033
000034
000035
000036
000037
000038
000039
000040
000041
000042
000043
000044
000045 ,,FIN
000046 //

Remark: blank lines are for each screen to be displayed with subscription info
```

Figure 176:   SYSAOS Batch – Display Reptor Statistics – Subscriptions (JCL)

```
14:15:38          ***** A D A B A S  BASIC  SERVICES *****      2010-11-08
Replicator 302         - Subscription Statistics -             PRPTS04

Mark   Subscription  Total replicated transactions
       Name
 -     --------      --------------------------
 _     S039144                        2,126
 _     S039145
 _     S039146
 _     S039147
 _     S039148
 _     S039149
 _     S039150
 _     S039151
 _     S039152
 _     S039153
 _     S039158
 _     S039159
 _     S039160                            Select detail information
 _     S039162                            by marking with 'S'
```

Figure 177:   SYSAOS Batch - Display Reptor Statistics – Subscriptions – Output

```
14:15:38          ***** A D A B A S  BASIC  SERVICES *****      2010-11-08
Replicator 302      - Selected Subscription Statistics -       PRPTS04

Selected Subscription Name: S039144

Total replicated transactions .......             2,126
Total C5 data ......................                  0
Initial-state completed .............                0
Initial-state data ..................                0
User transactions ...................             2,126
UTI function .......................        0
Lost data count ....................        0
   DBID ..........................  39
   File ..........................  144
   Number of deletes ...............               0
   Number of initial state ..........             0
   Number of inserts ...............         200,000
   Number of updates ...............             126

Press 'Enter' to continue       Displaying 1   of 1
```

Figure 178:   SYSAOS Batch – Select one Subscription – Output

7.2.10   RPL Flag Check in ADAREP

It is very awkward to scan manually an Adabas report with 200 files and check for the value of the RPL flags and whether before images are collected.

The following job submits an Adabas Report in batch with NOFDT and NOSTD to get the inactive and active RPL flags per file. The Natural program DWSRPLRP parses the output and send a compressed report the Adabas DBA group. See the parse program DWSRPLRP at the appendix, chapter 9.5.8.

```
000001 //STREP039 JOB (ST345P,ST01,STLXF,6230T),229-4945,
000002 //         MSGCLASS=2,NOTIFY=&SYSUID,
000003 //**      RESTART=RPLREP.N
000004 //        RESTART=DELETE1
000005 //*MAIN    SYSTEM=SY7,CLASS=P10,USER=STADBA,LINES=9999
000006 //*FORMAT PR,DDNAME=,DEST=TEALE2.RT185,FORMS=8511,CARRIAGE=LD8
000007 //*FORMAT PR,DDNAME=,CHARS=ST15
000008 //* ----------------------------------------------------------
000009 //* DELETE 1
000010 //* ----------------------------------------------------------
000011 //DELETE1 EXEC PGM=IEFBR14
000012 //DD1     DD  DSN=DIETER.ADAREP39,
000013 //             DISP=(MOD,DELETE),
000014 //             SPACE=(TRK,(1,1),RLSE)
000015 //* ----------------------------------------------------------
000016 //* ADABAS REPORT V8 - DIETER.CNTL(ADAREPV8)
000017 //* ----------------------------------------------------------
000018 //REP039     EXEC ADAUSRM,DB=STST9,UTILITY=ADAREP,QUAL=MPM,VER=V81
000019 //DDTEMPR1    DD DUMMY
000020 //DDSORTR1    DD DUMMY
000021 //ST1.DDPRINT DD DUMMY
000022 //ST1.DDDRUCK DD DISP=(,CATLG),SPACE=(TRK,(100,10),RLSE),
000023 //             DSN=DIETER.ADAREP39
000024 //SYSIN       DD *
000025    ADAREP REPORT
000026    ADAREP NOFDT,NOSTD
000027 //* ----------------------------------------------------------
000028 //* DELETE
000029 //* ----------------------------------------------------------
000030 //DELETE2 EXEC PGM=IEFBR14
000031 //DD1     DD  DSN=DIETER.RPLREP,
000032 //             DISP=(MOD,DELETE),
000033 //             SPACE=(TRK,(1,1),RLSE)
000034 //* ----------------------------------------------------------
000035 //* CHECK DB FOR INACTIVE AND ACTIVE RPL FLAGS PER FILE
000036 //* ----------------------------------------------------------
000037 //RPLREP   EXEC NATBT,DEPT=ST,DB=DEVL,SYSOUT=*,TIME=100,
000038 //             PRM='IM=D,MADIO=0,MAXCL=0,MT=0,LT=999999,AUTO=ON'
000039 //SYSOUT     DD SYSOUT=*
000040 //**CMWKF01  DD DISP=SHR,DSN=*.REP039.ST1.DDDRUCK
000041 //CMWKF01  DD DISP=SHR,DSN=DIETER.ADAREP39
000042 //CMWKF02  DD SYSOUT=*
000043 //CMPRT01  DD DISP=(,CATLG),DSN=DIETER.RPLREP,
000044 //             RECFM=FBA,LRECL=081,BLKSIZE=0,UNIT=MISCDA,
000045 //             SPACE=(TRK,(10,50),RLSE)
000046 //SYSIN    DD *
000047 LOGON DIETER
000048 DWSRPLRP
000049 FIN
000050 //** ---------------------------------------------------------
000051 //** ADD THE DATE TO THE DATASETS AND FTP - #1 OF 2
000052 //** ---------------------------------------------------------
000053 //        IF RC = 0 THEN
```

```
000054 //DATEUPD1 EXEC NATBT,DEPT=ST,DB=DEVL,SYSOUT=1,TIME=100,
000055 //          PRM='IM=D,MADIO=0,MAXCL=0,MT=0,LT=999999,AUTO=ON'
000056 //SYSOUT   DD SYSOUT=*
000057 //CMPRINT  DD SYSOUT=*
000058 //CMWKF01  DD DISP=SHR,DSN=DIETER.CNTL(FTPLOG08) FDT STMT
000059 //SYSIN    DD *
000060 LOGON DIETER
000061 COWP10DT DIETER.ADAREP39 ADAREP ADAREP39_FILE_RPL_ DATE
000062 FIN
000063 //FTP1     EXEC PGM=FTP,REGION=4M,PARM='(TIMEOUT 100 TRACE EXIT'
000064 //OUTPUT   DD SYSOUT=*
000065 //SYSPRINT DD SYSOUT=*
000066 //SYSTCPD  DD DISP=SHR,DSN=SYS1.TCPIP.PARMLIB(TCPDATA)
000067 //SYSFTPD  DD DISP=SHR,DSN=SYS1.TCPIP.PARMLIB(CFTPDATA)
000068 //INPUT    DD DISP=SHR,DSN=DIETER.CNTL(FTPLOG08)
000069 //*
000070 //** --------------------------------------------------
000071 //** ADD THE DATE TO THE DATASETS AND FTP - #2 OF 2
000072 //** --------------------------------------------------
000073 //DATEUPD2 EXEC NATBT,DEPT=ST,DB=DEVL,SYSOUT=1,TIME=100,
000074 //          PRM='IM=D,MADIO=0,MAXCL=0,MT=0,LT=999999,AUTO=ON'
000075 //SYSOUT   DD SYSOUT=*
000076 //CMPRINT  DD SYSOUT=*
000077 //CMWKF01  DD DISP=SHR,DSN=DIETER.CNTL(FTPLOG09) FDT STMTS
000078 //SYSIN    DD *
000079 LOGON DIETER
000080 COWP10DT DIETER.RPLREP   ADAREP RPLREP39_FILE_ DATE
000081 FIN
000082 //FTP2     EXEC PGM=FTP,REGION=4M,PARM='(TIMEOUT 100 TRACE EXIT'
000083 //OUTPUT   DD SYSOUT=*
000084 //SYSPRINT DD SYSOUT=*
000085 //SYSTCPD  DD DISP=SHR,DSN=SYS1.TCPIP.PARMLIB(TCPDATA)
000086 //SYSFTPD  DD DISP=SHR,DSN=SYS1.TCPIP.PARMLIB(CFTPDATA)
000087 //INPUT    DD DISP=SHR,DSN=DIETER.CNTL(FTPLOG09)
000088 //* -----------------------------------------------------------
000089 //*  EMAIL THE RPL STATUS REPORT                             **
000090 //* -----------------------------------------------------------
000091 //SUCCESS EXEC PGM=IKJEFT01,REGION=4096K,DYNAMNBR=50
000092 //SYSTSIN  DD *
000093  SMTPNOTE TO(DSTORR@STORRCONSULTING.COM) -
000094        SUBJECT(DB39: RPL STATUS REPORT) BATCH -
000095        DATASET('DIETER.RPLREP')
000096  SMTPNOTE TO(LFRAZIN@CALSTRS.COM) -
000097        SUBJECT(DB39: RPL STATUS REPORT) BATCH -
000098        DATASET('DIETER.RPLREP')
000099 //SYSPROC  DD DSN=SYS2.CLIST,DISP=SHR
000100 //SYSTSPRT DD SYSOUT=*
000101 //         ENDIF
000102 //
000103 //DEL1     DD DISP=(OLD,DELETE),DSN=DIETER.ADAREP39
000104 //DEL2     DD DISP=(OLD,DELETE),DSN=DIETER.RPLREP
000105 //
```

Figure 179:   Check RPL Flag (JCL)

Output of ADAREP DDDRUCK – NOFDT,NOSTD

```
Output of ADAREP DDDRUCK - NOFDT,NOSTD

(snip)
*********************************
*                               *
* File     6 (ST-ADA-CALC-EDAT) *                    2010-03-09  13:59:15
*                               *
*********************************



TOP-ISN             =          333    Highest Index Level =  3
MAX-ISN Expected    =        1,271    Padding Factor ASSO = 10%
Records Loaded      =          333    Padding Factor DATA = 10%
MIN-ISN             =            1    Length of Client NR =  0
Number of Updates   =           44    ISNSIZE             =  3

MAX COMP REC LEN    =        5,060    Date Loaded         = 2007-10-20
BLK/ADD DS   EXT    =            0    Time Loaded         = 12:17:32
BLK/ADD UI   EXT    =            0    Date of last update = 2010-03-09
BLK/ADD NI   EXT    =            0    Time of last update = 12:03:48

ADAM File           No
Ciphered File       No
ISN Reusage         Yes
Space Reusage       Yes
Coupled Files       None
Expanded File       No
USERISN             No
NOACEXTENSION       No
MIXDSDEV            No
PGMREFRESH          No
Multi Client File   No
Privileged usage    No
Online INVERT       None
Index Compressed    Yes
Spanned Rec Supp    No
Two Byte MU/PE      No
LOB file            No
Contain LOB fields  No
RPLUPDATEONLY       No

File is replicated:
  Replicator target ID               =     302
  Collect before images of updates   = Yes

(snip)
```

Figure 180:   Adabas Report RPL Flag Check – (Output)

Output of parse program DWSRPLRP with RPL flag and DSBI status

```
--------------------------------------------------------------------------------
2010-03-09 14:15:36          Adabas Replicator Report              Page     1
DWSRPLRP                                                           DIETER
--------------------------------------------------------------------------------
A D A R E P   V8.1  SM3   DBID = 00039  Started          2010-03-09  13:59:15
FNR  RPL STATUS    TDB  DSBI
----  ---  --------  ---  ----
   6  YES active    302  On
   7  YES active    302  On
   8  YES active    302  On
   9  YES active    302  On
  10  YES active    302  On
  11  YES active    302  On
  12  YES active    302  On
  13  YES active    302  On
  14  YES active    302  On
(snip)
 131  YES active    302  On
 132  YES active    302  On
 133  YES active    302  On
 134  YES active    302  On
 135  NO  n/a
 137  NO  n/a
 138  NO  n/a
 139  NO  n/a
 140  NO  n/a
 141  NO  n/a
 142  NO  n/a
(snip)
```

Figure 181: RPL Flag Check Report – (Output))

7.2.11 Analyze WCP Log

The program RDWCPLOG (ReaD WCP Log) counts the number of Adabas commands per second in the Entire Net-Work log of the client side.

```
Page    1                                                      10-09-13  17:23:26

Adabas Calls
Total   per sec
    1       0 15:53:09.068 ba7660 LNK: (EA) ======= New ADABAS call ======= New ADABAS call ==
   77      76 15:53:10.005 ba7560 LNK: (EA) ======= New ADABAS call ======= New ADABAS call ==
  157      80 15:53:11.005 ba7560 LNK: (EA) ======= New ADABAS call ======= New ADABAS call ==
  236      79 15:53:12.005 ba7660 LNK: (EA) ======= New ADABAS call ======= New ADABAS call ==
  313      77 15:53:13.005 4b5ab0 LNK: (EA) ======= New ADABAS call ======= New ADABAS call ==
  393      80 15:53:14.005 4b5ab0 LNK: (EA) ======= New ADABAS call ======= New ADABAS call ==
  470      77 15:53:15.005 4b58b0 LNK: (EA) ======= New ADABAS call ======= New ADABAS call ==
  544      74 15:53:16.005 4b59b0 LNK: (EA) ======= New ADABAS call ======= New ADABAS call ==
  621      77 15:53:17.005 ba7660 LNK: (EA) ======= New ADABAS call ======= New ADABAS call ==
  702      81 15:53:18.005 ba7560 LNK: (EA) ======= New ADABAS call ======= New ADABAS call ==
  782      80 15:53:19.005 ba7560 LNK: (EA) ======= New ADABAS call ======= New ADABAS call ==
  861      79 15:53:20.005 ba7660 LNK: (EA) ======= New ADABAS call ======= New ADABAS call ==
  942      81 15:53:21.005 ba7560 LNK: (EA) ======= New ADABAS call ======= New ADABAS call ==
 1022      80 15:53:22.005 ba7560 LNK: (EA) ======= New ADABAS call ======= New ADABAS call ==
 1100      78 15:53:23.021 4b58b0 LNK: (EA) ======= New ADABAS call ======= New ADABAS call ==
 1179      79 15:53:24.005 4b59b0 LNK: (EA) ======= New ADABAS call ======= New ADABAS call ==
 1258      79 15:53:25.005 4b5ab0 LNK: (EA) ======= New ADABAS call ======= New ADABAS call ==
 1322      64 15:53:26.005 ba7560 LNK: (EA) ======= New ADABAS call ======= New ADABAS call ==
 1378      56 15:53:27.005 4b5ab0 LNK: (EA) ======= New ADABAS call ======= New ADABAS call ==
 1458      80 15:53:28.005 4b5ab0 LNK: (EA) ======= New ADABAS call ======= New ADABAS call ==
 1537      79 15:53:29.005 ba7560 LNK: (EA) ======= New ADABAS call ======= New ADABAS call ==
 1615      78 15:53:30.005 4b58b0 LNK: (EA) ======= New ADABAS call ======= New ADABAS call ==
```

Figure 182: Analyze WCP Log

Using a self-written Natural program, you can parse through the WCP log and count the Adabas calls per second. You can also use a text editor for Windows with search capabilities, such as display number of lines with '====== New ADABAS call ====== New ADABAS call ='. A selection function by columns (from/to) is beneficiary to search a command log size of 200 MB and more.

7.2.12 Determine Highest ISN Currently Used

The program ISNHIGH reads files of a database and reports the highest ISN currently used.

The Natural program is described at chapter 4.3, Compare Files of Source and Target DB, and is located at appendix, chapter 9.5.10.

7.2.13 Compare File Components After Replication

The following job creates an Adabas report on the mainframe with NOFDT and NOSTD and FTP it to a Windows server. The Adabas on Windows report is created and saved directly to the Windows server to be compared.

```
//STREP039 JOB . . .
//         MSGCLASS=2,NOTIFY=&SYSUID,TIME=1440
//*  . . . .
//* -----------------------------------------------------------------
//* DELETE 1
//* -----------------------------------------------------------------
//DELETE1 EXEC PGM=IEFBR14
//DD1      DD  DSN=ST.ADADBA.ADAREP39,
//             DISP=(MOD,DELETE),
//             SPACE=(TRK,(1,1),RLSE)
//* -----------------------------------------------------------------
//* ADABAS REPORT V8 - DIETER.CNTL(ADARP039)
//* -----------------------------------------------------------------
//REP039     EXEC ADAUSRM,DB=STST9,UTILITY=ADAREP,QUAL=MPM,VER=V81
//DDTEMPR1    DD DUMMY
//DDSORTR1    DD DUMMY
//ST1.DDPRINT DD DUMMY
//ST1.DDDRUCK DD DISP=(,CATLG),SPACE=(TRK,(1000,10),RLSE),
//             DSN=DIETER.ADAREP39
//SYSIN       DD *
   ADAREP REPORT
   ADAREP NOFDT,NOSTD
//* -----------------------------------------------------------------
//* FTP TO THE Z-DRIVE
//* -----------------------------------------------------------------
//FTP1       EXEC PGM=FTP,REGION=4M,PARM='(TIMEOUT 100 TRACE EXIT'
//OUTPUT     DD SYSOUT=*
//SYSPRINT   DD SYSOUT=*
//SYSTCPD    DD DISP=SHR,DSN=SYS1.TCPIP.PARMLIB(TCPDATA)
//SYSFTPD    DD DISP=SHR,DSN=SYS1.TCPIP.PARMLIB(CFTPDATA)
//FTPIN1     DD DISP=SHR,DSN=DIETER.ADAREP39
//INPUT      DD DISP=SHR,DSN=DIETER.CCARDS(FTPLOGON)
//           DD *
ascii
CD ADAREP
put //DD:FTPIN1   ADAREP39_FILE_RPL.20110127.txt
quit
end
//
```

Figure 183:   Create and FTP an Adabas Report to a Windows Server

The program RPL-P002 reads both Adabas reports and creates a list with TOPISN, Records Loaded, and MAXISN of both source (DB039) and target (DB251) databases.

See the Natural program at appendix, chapter 9.5.13.

```
FILE-NR  TOPISN 039 TOPISN 251 RECLOD 039 RECLOD 251 MAXISN 039 MAXISN 251
-------  ---------- ---------- ---------- ---------- ---------- ----------
000006          341        341        341        341      1,271      1,279
000007      195,637    195,637    195,635     95,635  1,000,427    196,095
000008    1,098,767  1,098,767  1,098,767  1,098,767  1,251,011  1,114,879
000009           42         38         38         38      1,271      2,047
000010          364        364        364        364      3,815        511
000011   25,665,942 25,665,942 25,191,478 25,191,478 30,000,119 25,673,727
000012      250,289    250,289    249,229    249,229  1,000,427    257,279
000013            5          5          5          5        635      8,191
000014    6,004,159  6,004,159  6,003,833  6,003,833  8,000,243  6,004,735
000015    2,439,377  2,439,377  2,439,314  2,439,314  6,000,023  2,441,215
000016        3,887      3,887      3,673      3,672      5,087      8,191
```

Figure 184: Create Adabas Report and FTP to a Windows Server

The report shows differences in highest ISN (TOPISN), records loaded (RECLOD) and the maximum set ISNs (MAXISN). One record of file 16 received RSP 113 and was therefore not replicated, as pointed out in Reptor's log dataset DDPRINT.

7.3 Optimize for Infrastructure (O4I)

7.3.1 General

Currently, companies have to write or purchase several monitor programs to gather statistical data to evaluate the performance of Software AG products. They use this data to improve their processes.

To make this more efficient, Software AG and other vendors offer single monitor software on the mainframe such as Review, Adabas Statistic Facility, Adabas Online System, Adabas Event Replicator Subsystem, Apas/Insight, System Management Hub, and Trim.

Some customers find it very awkward to get performance data from a green screen on the mainframe and then switch over to the PC for additional information on Windows-based Software AG products. For example, if you monitor Event Replication for Adabas on the mainframe, you must close the Adabas Event Replicator Subsystem screen and open the Adabas Online System screen to get additional information for the same product.

In 2009 Software AG introduced their 'new tool' <u>Optimize for Infrastructure: the</u> <u>Mainframe Edition</u>. For many years, webMethods used their Business Activity Monitoring (BAM) tool, which includes Optimize for Process, Optimize for SAP, and Optimize for B2B. After the merge, Software AG updated and improved the existing Optimize product for monitoring their enterprise products in real time. This tool is UNIX or Windows-based and collects data from Software AG's products such as Adabas, EntireX, Event Replicator for Adabas, Adabas Delta Save, Natural, Entire Net-Work and Adabas Fastpath.

The benefit of this solution enables you to observe your performance data from a single web-based dashboard using your favorite Web browser.

The Software AG products Adabas, Event Replicator for Adabas, Com-plete, Entire Net-Work, Natural, Entire System Server, ApplinX and EntireX are already equipped with 'hooks' to get performance data if the latest versions are installed. In some cases, small system modifications (ZAPs) are necessary.

One or more special Natural RPC servers on the mainframe are necessary to get the data from the above-mentioned products through EntireX Broker (webMethods server) to a JMS Queue and on to the Analytic Engine for interpretation and application for KPI rules. The Analytic Engine stores the data into a relational database. For example, a batch Natural RPC server monitors all global Natural components: a CICS Natural RPC server monitors all global Natural components: a CICS Natural RPC server monitors in general only local environment-specific Natural components. If EntireX Broker is not available on one of the monitored platforms, the EntireX Broker stubs (EntireX Mini Runtime) must be installed.

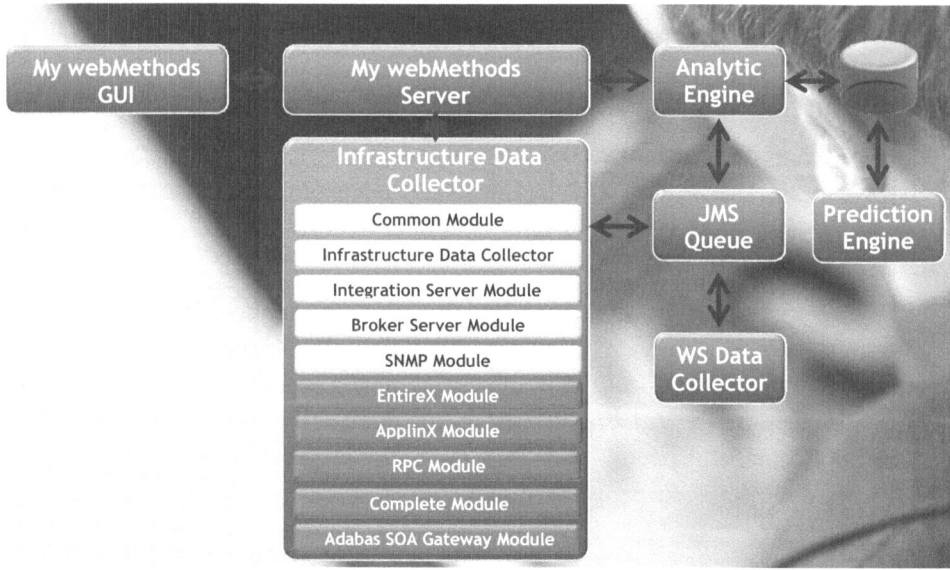

Figure 185:   Analyze WCP Log (Source: SAG)

Optimize for Infrastructure comes with over 600 predefined Key Performance Indicators (KPIs), which can be selected and activated to collect the data you want to monitor and analyze. You can also create rules, send predefined alerts or start activities by using Web services.

In addition to the data collection, Optimize implementation performs other main functions such as data communication, data processing and analysis, data storage and data presentation.

Optimize for Infrastructure uses the following parameters to monitor Adabas Event Replicator: Dimensions, KPIs and Built-in Rules.

7.3.2 Dimensions

Administration Name	Displayed Value
Host	The name of the host.
Product	The product component name "Adabas Event Replicator".
AdabasEventRep	The ID and name of the Event Replicator server.

7.3.3 KPIs of Event Map AdabasEventRep

Administration Name	KPI Name	Unit	Type	Description
RepBytesSentTotal	Bytes Sent Total	count	delta	The total number of bytes sent in the messages.
RepFreeSLOGAssoSpace	SLOG – ASSO Free Blocks	percent	last value	Free space on ASSO for SLOG entries.
RepFreeSLOGDataSpace	SLOG – DATA Free Blocks	percent	last value	Free space on DATA for SLOG entries.
RepHWMRepPool	High-Water Mark – Replication Pool (RPL)	percent	last value	The high-water mark of the Replication Pool (RPL).
RepMessagesTotal	Replicated Messages Total	count	delta	The number of replicated messages.
RepPendTransactions-Total	Pending Transactions Total	count	last value	The number of pending transactions.
RepSLOGEntriesTotal	SLOG – Number of Entries	count	last value	The total number of entries in the SLOG file.
RepState	Replicator – State	state	state	The state of the Event Replicator (online/offline). This KPI is automatically monitored.
RepTransactionsTotal	Replicated Transactions Total	count	delta	The number of replicated transactions.

7.3.4   Built-In Rules

Administration Name	Expression	Severity	Description
Adabas Event Replicator Not Active	Adabas.RepState = 0	2 – High	The Event Replicator is not active.
Adabas Event Replicator SLOG ASSO Full	Adabas.RepFreeSLOGAssoSpace < 10	2 – High	Less than 10% of the SLOG ASSO space is free.
Adabas Event Replicator SLOG DATA Full	Adabas.RepFreeSLOGDataSpace < 10	2 – High	Less than 10% of the SLOG DATA space is free.

7.3.5   Dimensions – Destination

Administration Name	Displayed Value
Host	The name of the host.
Product	The product component name "Adabas Event Replicator".
AdabasEventRep	The ID and name of the Event Replicator server.
AdabasEventRepDest	The Event Replicator destination.

7.3.6   KPIs of Event Map AdabasEventRepDest

Administration Name	KPI Name	Unit	Type	Description
RepDestBytesSent	Bytes Sent	count	delta	The number of bytes sent.
RepDestCommands Committed	Commands Committed	count	delta	The number of commands committed.
RepDestCommands Pending	Commands Pending	count	last value	The number of commands pending.
RepDestLatency	Latency Time of Last Transaction	ms	last value	Latency time of last transaction. This value is only available for Adabas destinations.
RepDestMessagesSent	Messages Sent	count	delta	The number of messages sent.
RepDestPendingTransactions	Pending Transactions	count	last value	The number of pending transactions.
RepDestReplicated Transactions	Replicated Transactions	count	delta	The number of replicated transactions.
RepDestSlogDelog	SLOG – Delogged Count	count	delta	SLOG delogged count.
RepDestSlogEntries	SLOG – Number of Entries	count	last value	Number of SLOG entries for this destination.

Administration Name	KPI Name	Unit	Type	Description
RepDestSlogLog	SLOG – Logged Count	count	delta	SLOG logged count.
RepDestState	State of the Event Replicator Desti-nation	state	state	State of the Event Replicator destination (active or not). This KPI is automatically monitored.

7.3.7   Built-In Rules – Destination

Administration Name	Expression	Severity	Description
Adabas Event Replicator Destination Not Active	Adabas.RepDestState = 0	2 – High	The Event Replicator destina-tion is not active.

7.3.8   Dimensions – Input Queue

Administration Name	Displayed Value
Host	The name of the host.
Product	The product component name "Adabas Event Replicator".
AdabasEventRep	The ID and name of the Event Replicator server.
AdabasEventRepInQueue	The Event Replicator input queue name.

7.3.9   KPIs of Event Map AdabasEventRepInQueue

Administration Name	KPI Name	Unit	Type	Description
RepInQBackouts	Number of Back-outs	count	delta	The number of backouts.
RepInQBytes	Number of Bytes Received	count	delta	The number of bytes re-ceived.
RepInQCommits	Number of Commits	count	delta	The number of commits.
RepInQMessages	Number of Mes-sages	count	delta	The number of messages.
RepInQPendingBytes	Number of Pending Bytes	count	last value	The number of pending bytes.
RepInQPendingMessages	Number of Pending Messages	count	last value	The number of pending mes-sages.
RepInQState	State of the Event Replicator Input Queue	state	state	The state of the Event Repli-cator input queue. This KPI is automatically monitored.

7.3.10 Built-In Rules

Administration Name	Expression	Severity	Description
Adabas Event Replicator Input Queue Closed	Adabas.RepInQState = 0	2 – High	The Event Replicator input queue is closed.

7.3.11 Dimensions – Subscription

Administration Name	Displayed Value
Host	The name of the host.
Product	The product component name "Adabas Event Replicator".
AdabasEventRep	The ID and name of the Event Replicator server.
AdabasEventRepSubscr	The Event Replicator subscription name.

7.3.12 KPIs of Event Map AdabasEventRepSubscr

Administration Name	KPI Name	Unit	Type	Description
RepSubInitialStateCompleted	Initial-State Transactions Completed	count	delta	The number of initial-state transactions completed.
RepSubLostData	Lost Data Count	count	delta	The number of lost data.
RepSubRepTransactions	Replicated Transactions	count	delta	The number of replicated transactions.
RepSubRepUtilityFunctions	Utility functions	count	delta	The number of replicated utility functions.
RepSubState	State of the Event Replicator Subscription	state	state	The state of the Event Replicator subscription (active or not). This KPI is automatically monitored.
RepSubUserTransactions	User Transactions	count	delta	The number of replicated user transactions.

7.3.13 Built-In Rules

Administration Name	Expression	Severity	Description
Adabas Event Replicator Subscription Not Active	Adabas.RepSubState = 0	2 – High	The Event Replicator subscription is not active.

7.3.14   How to Monitor a Component

After you run the discovery process to ascertain the products running in your environment, select product-instances and KPIs you want to see, you can monitor the KPIs and display details.

Figure 186 shows Analytics Overview of the Adabas Event Replicator and some KPIs of destinations, subscriptions, input queue, etc.

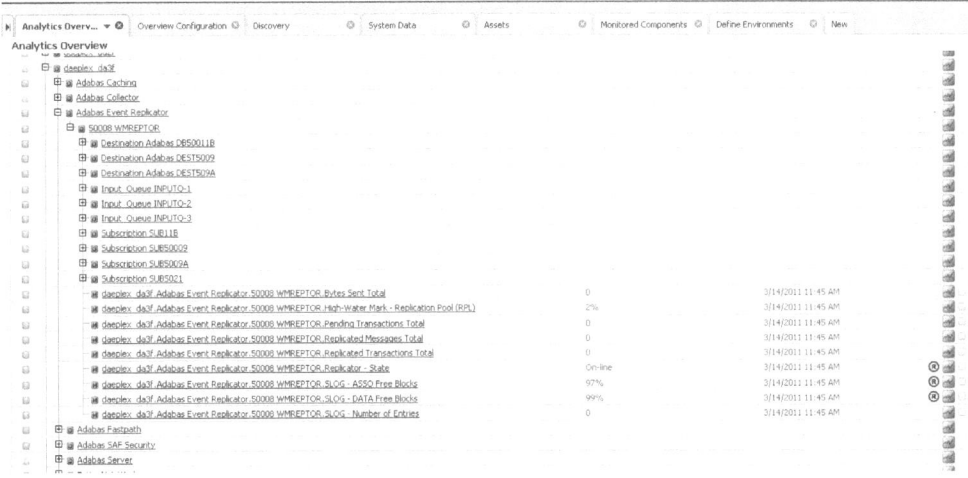

Figure 186:   Optimize for Infrastructure (O4I) – Analytics Overview

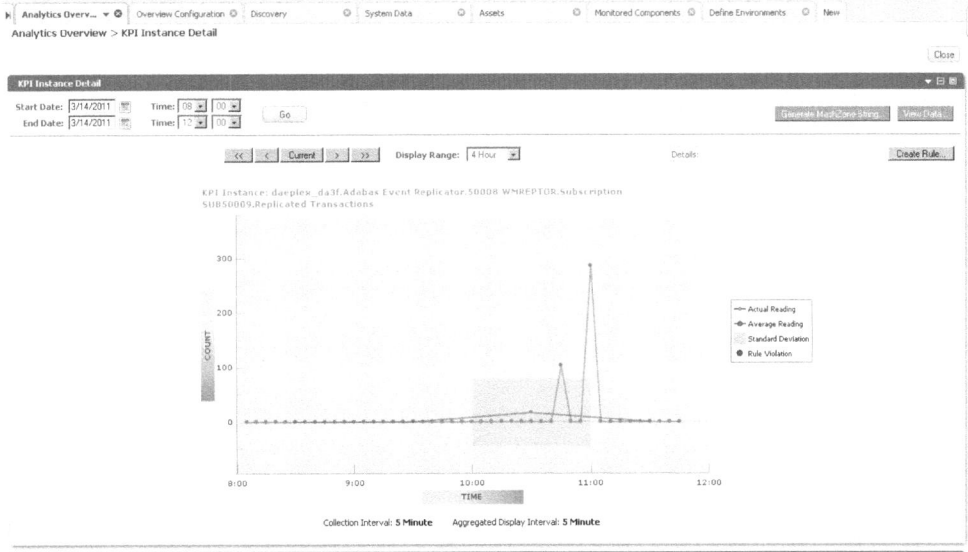

Figure 187:   Optimize for Infrastructure (O4I) – KPI Subscription User Transaction

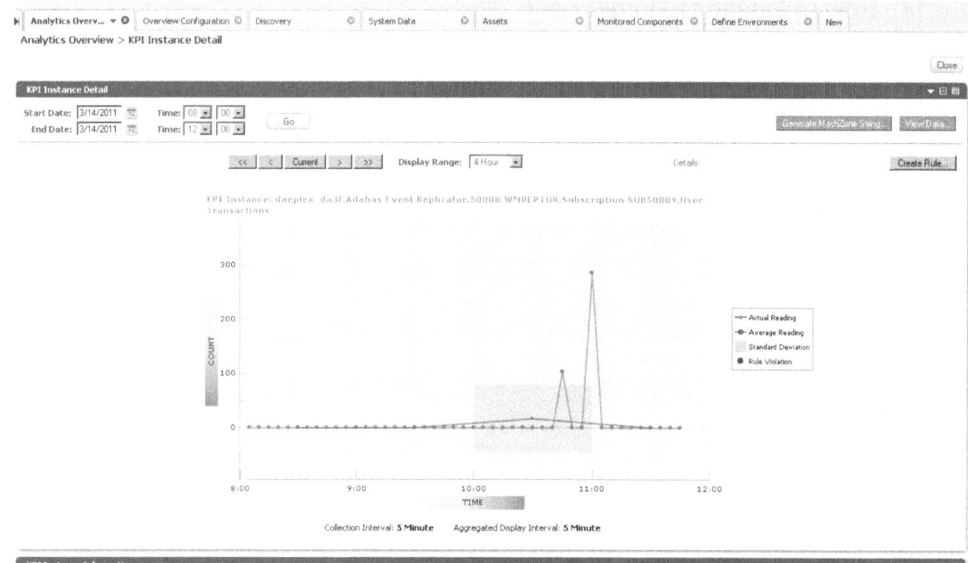

Figure 188:   Optimize for Infrastructure (O4I) – KPI Destination Replicated Transactions

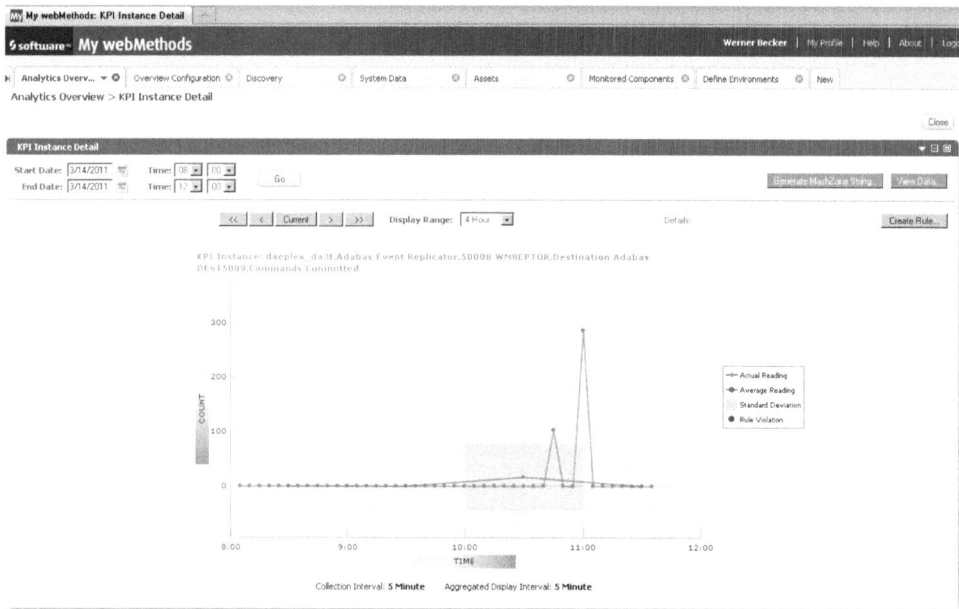

Figure 189:   Optimize for Infrastructure (O4I) – Destination Adabas Calls Committed

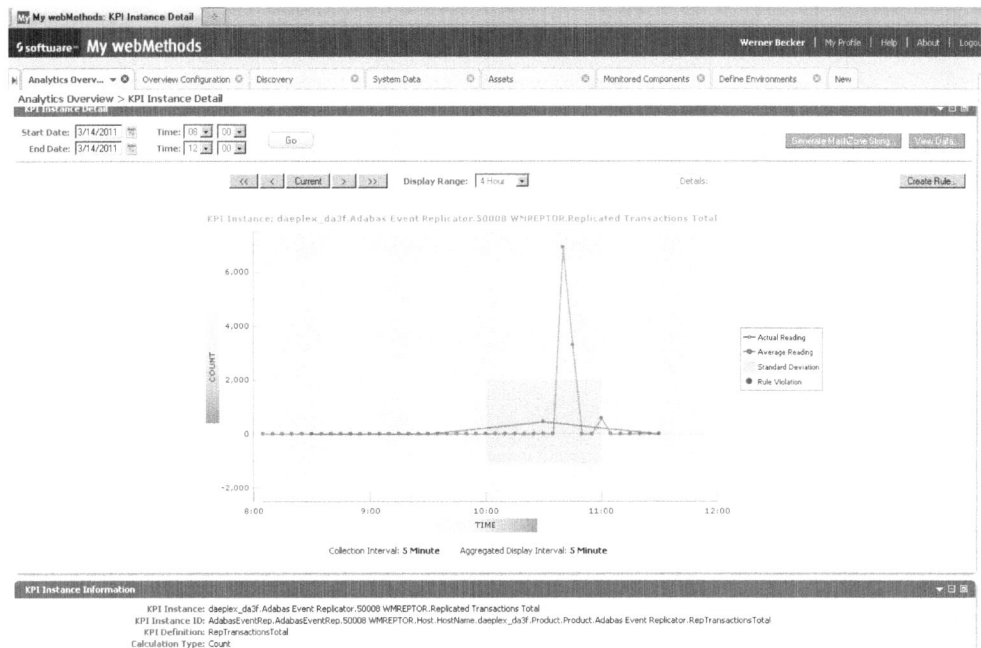

Figure 190: Optimize for Infrastructure (O4I) – Total Replicated Transactions

8   Security

Databases are designed to provide open and flexible access to data. But this open access makes them vulnerable to malicious activities.

Adabas databases on enterprise servers (mainframes) are in general very safe and has not been reported (as far as I know) that hackers successfully accessed or manipulated this data. However, as database data is available in local or wide area networks (WAN, LAN) and on Web sites, security becomes increasingly important.

The System Authorization Facility (SAF) is used by z/OS and compatible sites to provide rigorous control of the resources available to a user or group of users. Security packages such as RACF, CA-ACF2, and CA-Top Secret allow the system administrator to maintain user identification credentials such as User ID and password. SAF establish also profiles determining the datasets, storage volumes, transactions, and reports available to a user.

Software AG offers several security products to enhance the effectiveness of the SAF central security repository.

Using the SAF repository, the following Software AG products can be secured:

- Adabas SAF Security protects Adabas
- Adabas SQL Server SAF Security protects Adabas SQL Server (ESQ)
- Entire Net-Work SAF Security protects Entire Net-Work version 5.6 and above
- EntireX Security protects EntireX, Entire Broker, Broker Services – also Natural RPC using Entire Broker. It protects Entire Broker (pre-EntireX) operating in z/OS, UNIX, and Windows environments (the security built into webMethods EntireX now protects EntireX Broker and Broker Services as well)
- Natural SAF Security protects Natural

The Entire Security SAF Gateway protects client/server, peer-to-peer, and standard application systems.

The following chapters will show how data from the source to the replicated target can be protected.

8.1   Source Database Adabas

8.1.1   Adabas SAF Security (ADASAF)

Adabas SAF Security (ADASAF) enhances the scope of SAG-based security packages by integrating Adabas resources into the central security repository.

ADASAF enables a single control and audit system for all resources and industry-standard protection of Adabas data. See also description to SAF in chapter 8, Security introduction.

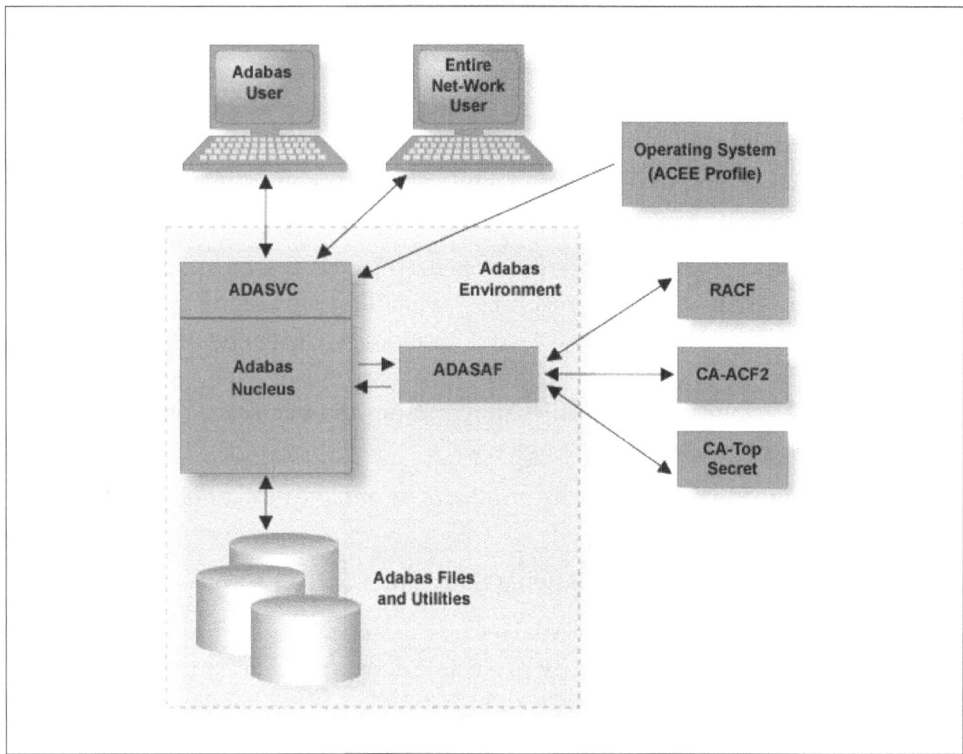

Figure 191:   Adabas SAF Security (ADASAF) – Source: SAG

8.1.2   Adabas Security (ADASCR)

Adabas Security and the related security utility ADASCR is part of Adabas without additional costs and provides selective user access and update protection at a file, field, and field value level. The documentation is only available on special request at Software AG.

The feature 'Value Level Protection' or 'Security by Value' can be an overhead in the system, as tests from customers have proved.

8.1.3   Adabas Data Encryption (Ciphering)

Data encryption is an integral feature of Adabas and requires no options or extra modules. It encrypts at this time only the DATA component of Adabas but not the ASSO. An Adabas user exit is available to control the cipher code and protects the file from corruption if data is added with the wrong cipher code.

8.1.4   Adabas Multi-client Files

The feature 'Multi-client Files' is part of Adabas without additional costs and controls access to records in a file. The owner ID is assigned to a user ID. A user ID can have only one owner ID, but an owner ID can belong to more than one user. Each user can access only the subset of records that is associated with the user's owner ID.

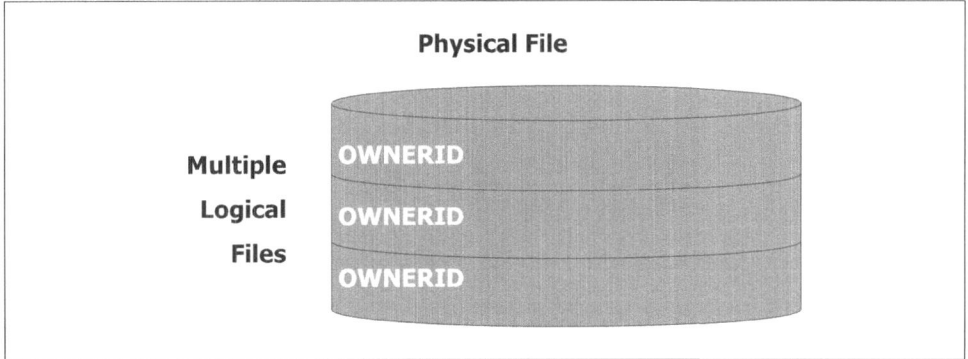

Figure 192:   Adabas Multi-client File

8.2   Replicator Adabas

8.2.1   Adabas SAF Security (ADASAF)

The Replicator is basically an Adabas nucleus and Adabas SAF Security (ADASAF) is available to protect its resources, as described in chapter 8.1.1.

Adabas Security (ADASCR) and data encryption for Reptor's system files inclusively SLOG and TLOG does not make sense and may slow down the replication process.

8.3   Entire Net-Work (WCP) Mainframe V6.2.1

8.3.1   Entire Net-Work SAF Security (NETSAF)

Entire Net-Work SAF Security is a separate, optional product for z/OS environments and protects Entire Net-Work (WCP) version 5.6 and above. It allows Entire Net-Work clients to access SAF-secured data sources (targets): for example Adabas, EntireX Communicator, and Entire System Server. See also the description to SAF in chapter 8, Security, introduction and chapter 8.1.1, Adabas SAF Security (ADASAF).

8.3.2   Encryption V1.1.2

Encryption is a Software AG product option that provides support for the Secure Socket Layer (SSL) management that is provided for and installed on both mainframe and open systems.

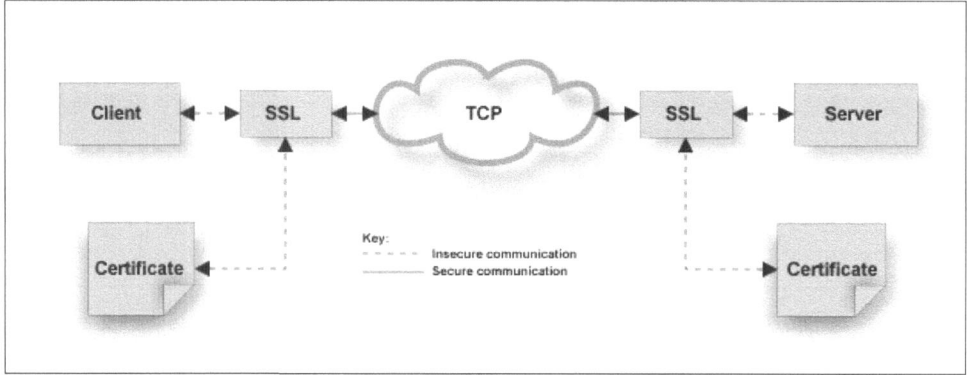

Figure 193:   WCP Encryption – Source SAG

8.4   EntireX Broker

8.4.1   EntireX Security

EntireX Security protects EntireX, Entire Broker and Broker Services. See also chapter 8, Security (SAF). It is available for z/OS, UNIX and Windows and installations must be done for the broker kernel and the broker stubs. For more information see Software AG's documentation webMethods EntireX, Security Solutions in EntireX.

8.5   Network

To secure the network between the host and the client, the network folks in your organization must be involved.

Some organizations use Internet Protocol Security (IPsec) to encrypt safely. It operates in the upper layers of the TCP/IP model and applications do not need to be specifically designed to use IPsec. It is fast because it encrypts on hardware and not on software level.

Other security options are Secure Sockets Layer (SSL), Transport Layer Security (TLS) and Secure Shell (SSH). The use of TLS/SSL must be designed into an application to protect the application protocols.

8.6   Entire Net-Work (WCP) LUW V7.3.4

8.6.1   Encryption V1.1.2

Encryption is a Software AG product option that provides support for the Secure Socket Layer (SSL) management that is provided for and installed on both mainframe and Linux, UNIX, Windows (LUW). See Figure 193: WCP Encryption – Source SAG

8.7   Entire Net-Work (WCL) Client V1.3.3

Entire Net-Work 7 also supports communications using Secure Sockets Layer (SSL). This support is provided using SSL protocol target entries in the Software AG Directory Server.

The SSL Toolkit is not included on the installation CD and must be separately requested at Software AG.

8.8   Event Replicator Target Adapter

The Event Replicator Target Adapter is used to transform Adabas data to the relational database management system (RDBMS). For security reasons, you must include the company's security group to make sure that sensitive data received from EntireX Broker in message queues, for example, is protected.

8.9   Adabas ADASCR on Linux, Unix, Windows

Similar to the mainframe, Adabas Security and the related security utility ADASCR is part of Adabas without additional costs and provides selective user access and update protection at a file, field, and field value level.

Performance problems with the feature 'Security by Value' are not known on the open system

Adabas is also using the UNIX group concept and Adabas access can be restricted to only assigned groups..

8.10   Natural Security

8.10.1   NSC

Natural Security is available on mainframes, UNIX, OpenVMS and Windows platforms. A full version is normally installed to protect the following Natural components:

- Users
- Libraries
- Links Between Users and Libraries
- DDMs/Files
- Utilities
- Applications
- Other Object Types
- Profile Parameters

On those Windows platforms which are not suited to the stand-alone operation of Natural, NSC is installed as a runtime-only version.

8.10.2   Natural SAF Security

Natural SAF Security is used in conjunction with Natural Security (NSC) and with an SAF-compliant external security system – see introduction to chapter 8.

- Add-on to NSC
- SAF-compliant (RACF, CA-ACF2, CA Top Secret)
- SYSSAFOS (defined in NSC)
- SAF interfaces: NSFNPAS, NSFNPASZ, NSFNPAX

Using Natural SAF Security, there is no need to define users in Natural Security and in the external security system.

8.11   Non-Adabas on Linux, Unix, Windows

Each relational database management system has its own security. Please contact the relevant database or security administration group in your company for more information.

9 Appendix

9.1 Subscription DB – ADARUN parameters

The user of the following parameters has 57 subscriptions spread across 4 LPARs running on 8 separate Replication STCs.

See also Appendix 9.2, Reptor – ADARUN parameters.

```
ADARUN DBID=205,DEVICE=3390,SVC=224
ADARUN LP=300000
ADARUN LWKP2=15000              LENGTH OF WORK PART2
*
***** DELTA SAVE PARAMETERS
*
ADARUN DSF=YES
*
***  PARAMETERS FOR ADABAS REPLICATION SERVICES (REPTOR) FOLLOW  ***
*
ADARUN LRPL=200M                REPLICATION POOL FOR NUCLEUS
ADARUN REPLICATION=YES          REPLICATION SET TO YES FOR THIS DATABASE
ADARUN RPLSORT=LAST             SORT ALL UPDTES BETWN ETS BY FILE/ISN/TRAN
ADARUN RPWARNINCREMENT=5        SHOW NEW WARNING MESSAGE EVERY AT %% INCR
ADARUN RPWARNINTERVAL=30        SECS WARNING WILL BE SUPPRESSED
ADARUN RPWARNMESSAGELIMIT=10    WHEN PERSISTENT OVERFLOW - MAX WARNINGS
ADARUN RPWARNPERCENT=70         %% OF RPL TO START ISSUING WARNINGS
ADARUN LBP=650M                 LENGTH OF BUFFER POOL WAS 550M 5/19/07
ADARUN LDEUQP=5000              LENGTH OF UNIQUE DESCRIPTOR POOL
ADARUN LFIOP=60M                LENGTH OF ASYNC. BUFFER FLUSH POOL
*                               - WAS 50M 5/19/07
ADARUN NU=2500                  NUMBER OF USERS WAS 1725 08/18/2007
ADARUN NH=100000                NUMBER OF HQE'S WAS 25K 6/24/06
*
* MODIFICATION OF THE ABOVE PARMS REQUIRES CF CACHE SIZE CHANGE
*
ADARUN PROGRAM=ADANUC
ADARUN PLOGRQ=YES               --> PLOGS ARE REQUIRED
ADARUN OPENRQ=NO                --> NO OPEN REQUIRED
ADARUN UTIONLY=NO               --> NOT A UTILITY ONLY SESSION
ADARUN NC=500                   NUMBER OF CQE'S WAS 300 8/23/03
ADARUN NT=90                    NUMBER OF THREADS WAS 105 08/23/03
ADARUN LFP=1M                   LENGTH OF FI POOL  FROM 800000 6/21/03
ADARUN LWP=7000000              LENGTH OF WORK POOL WAS 6M 11/22/08
ADARUN LI=50000                 LENGTH OF TBI POOL WAS 30K 11/03/07
ADARUN LOCAL=NO                 NET-WORK DATABASE
ADARUN LQ=350000                LENGTH OF TBLES POOL WAS 260K - 6/4/05
ADARUN LS=61000                 LENGTH OF SORT AREA
ADARUN LU=200000                IUB LENGTH (MAX)
ADARUN READONLY=NO              READ ONLY NUCLEUS
ADARUN INTNAS=900               ISSUE CKPT EVERY 5 MIN   .ACS 9/06/03

ADARUN CT=900                   COMMAND TIMEOUT INTERVAL
ADARUN TT=900                   TRANSACTION TIMEOUT INTERVAL WAS 600
ADARUN TNAA=1800                INACTIVITY TIMEOUT INTERVAL WAS 900
ADARUN TNAE=1800                INACTIVITY TIMEOUT INTERVAL (ETBT)
ADARUN TNAX=100000              INACTIVITY TIMEOUT INTERVAL (EXUU)
ADARUN NAB=400                  ATTACHED BUFFERS WAS 250  8/23/03
ADARUN LCP=2000                 ---> SECURITY POOL SIZE
ADARUN NSISN=101                ---> ISNS PER TBI ELEMENT
ADARUN FMXIO=6                  PARALLEL I/O OPERATIONS WAS 30 8/22/03
*
* NUCLEUS POOLS
*
* DATABASE/USER LIMITS
*
ADARUN NQCID=80                 ---> MAX NUMBER CIDS/USER
ADARUN NISNHQ=5000              ---> MAX HELD/USER(< 25% NH)WAS 3500 6/24/06
```

```
ADARUN TLSCMD=300                    ---> TIME LIMIT FOR SX COMMAND
*
* PROTECTION LOGGING
*
ADARUN PLOGDEV=8393
ADARUN NPLOG=4
ADARUN PLOGSIZE=30000
*
* COMMAND LOGGING
*
ADARUN LOGGING=YES
ADARUN LOGCB=YES                     LOG BASIC ADALOG RECORD + ACB
ADARUN LOGFB=NO                      LOG BASIC ADALOG RECORD + FB
ADARUN LOGRB=NO                      LOG BASIC ADALOG RECORD + RB
ADARUN LOGSB=YES                     LOG BASIC ADALOG RECORD + SB
ADARUN LOGVB=YES                     LOG BASIC ADALOG RECORD + VB
ADARUN LOGIB=NO                      LOG BASIC ADALOG RECORD + IB
ADARUN LOGIO=YES                     LOG BASIC ADALOG RECORD + I/O COUNTS
ADARUN LOGUX=YES                     LOG UB EXTENSION
*
* USER EXITS
*
ADARUN UEX4=DBALGRY8
ADARUN UEX8=UEXIT08                  USER EXIT8
ADARUN UEX12=UEXIT12                 USER EXIT12
ADARUN DSFEX1=DSFEXIT                DELTA SAVE USER EXIT TO SUBMIT
*
* DYNAMIC CACHE
*ADARUN CACHE=YES
ADARUN CACTIVATE=YES
ADARUN CSTORAGE=VIRTUAL64
ADARUN CASSOMAXS=200M
ADARUN CSTORAGE=VIRTUAL64
ADARUN CDATAMAXS=200M
ADARUN CDEMAND=0
ADARUN CFILE=(77,,,V)
ADARUN CFILE=(151,,,V)
ADARUN CDISPSTAT=NO
ADARUN CMAXCSPS=1
ADARUN CRETRY=900
*
ADARUN CLOGLAYOUT=5
*
*            * * * NEW V7.1.3 PARAMETERS - ADDED-07/06/2002 * * *
** I/O **
ADARUN ASYTVS=YES                    ASYNC,PER VOL=NO
ADARUN AOSLOG=YES                    WTO ON EACH AOS/DBS COM
ADARUN PGFIX=YES
*
** ADABAS TRANSACTION MANAGER **
ADARUN DTP=NO                        ASYNC TRAN MANADARUN LDTP=0          LEN OF ATM AREA
*
** FASTPATH **
ADARUN FASTPATH=YES         AFP EXIT PART OF NUCLEUS
*
*** VISTA PARMS    ***
ADARUN VISTA=YES
*
*   PARALLEL SERVICES PARMS FOLLOW
*
ADARUN NUCID=0                       DBID+INSTANCE
ADARUN CLUCACHESIZE=446000K          ASM CACHE STRUCTURE (FROM ADACOM)
ADARUN CLULOCKSIZE=85M               ASM CACHE STRUCTURE (FROM ADACOM)
ADARUN LRDP=0                        LENGTH OF REDO POOL
*
ADARUN DIRRATIO=951                  DIRECTORY RATIO
ADARUN ELEMENTRATIO=100              ELEMENT RATIO
ADARUN MXMSG=300                     MAX COMMUNICATION TIME BETWEEN NUCS
ADARUN MXCANCEL=600                  NUCLEI WILL WAIT FOR CANCEL CONFIRM
ADARUN CLOGMRG=NO                    AUTOMATICALLY MERGE CLOG AT CLCOPY?
*
ADARUN RPLCONNECTCOUNT=60     --> TRY RECONNECT 60 TIMES
ADARUN RPLCONNECTINTERVAL=60  --> TRY RECONNECT AFTER 60 SECONDS
```

Figure 194:   ADARUN Parameters Subscription Database

9.2   Reptor – ADARUN parameters

The user of the following parameters has 57 subscriptions spread across 4 LPARs running on 8 separate Replication STCs. They run 8 STCs to balance the workload and because MQ is LPAR-specific they are forced to stay on certain LPARs. They publish approximately 80 million total messages a week.

They have no backlog of Reptor messages (never SLOG) but that may be due to the speed of the MQ QMgr's which consume the messages. In the event an MQ queue was to go down, they made all their SLOGs 65,000 cylinders. They calculated this would hold 4 hours of live replication against their biggest subscription (their worst case scenario). If MQ was down longer than 4 hours they would then need to run the Replay function.

```
ADARUN DBID=931,DEVICE=8393,SVC=224
ADARUN LP=65000
ADARUN LWKP2=10000            LENGTH OF WORK PART2 ADDED 9/6/03
*
* REPLICATION
*
ADARUN LRPL=600M
ADARUN RPLPARMS=FILE
ADARUN RPWARNPERCENT=70
ADARUN RPWARNMESSAGELIMIT=10
ADARUN RPWARNINTERVAL=20
ADARUN RPWARNINCREMENT=5      SHOW NEW WARNING MESSAGE EVERY AT %% INCRE
*
ADARUN PROGRAM=ADANUC
ADARUN VISTA=NO
ADARUN DSF=NO                 --> NO DELTA SAVE REQUIRED
ADARUN PLOGRQ=SEL             --> PLOG REQUIRED
ADARUN OPENRQ=NO              --> NO OPEN REQUIRED
ADARUN UTIONLY=NO             --> NOT A UTILITY ONLY SESSION
ADARUN READONLY=NO            READ ONLY NUCLEUS
ADARUN INTNAS=900             ISSUE SYNS 60 CKPT 15 MIN  .ACS 9/06/03
ADARUN LOCAL=NO               --> MODIFIED BY JNA, PREV-VAL=YES
ADARUN FASTPATH=NO            -->
*
* NUCLEUS POOLS
*
ADARUN NC=200                 NUMBER OF CQE'S
ADARUN NH=20000               NUMBER OF HQE'S
ADARUN NT=18                  NUMBER OF THREADS
ADARUN NU=750                 NUMBER OF USERS
ADARUN LBP=100000000          LENGTH OF BUFFER POOL
ADARUN LFIOP=25000000         LENGTH OF ASYNC BUFFE FLUSH POOL
ADARUN TFLUSH=0               BUF FLUSH DURATION - 0 WHEN LFIOP IS USED
ADARUN LFP=600000             LENGTH OF FI POOL
ADARUN LWP=4000000            LENGTH OF WORK POOL
ADARUN LS=60000               LENGTH OF SORT AREA
ADARUN LI=10000               LENGTH OF TBI POOL
ADARUN LQ=100000              LENGTH OF TBLES POOL
ADARUN LU=200000              IUB LENGTH (MAX)
ADARUN NAB=820                NUMBER OF ATTACHED BUFFERS
ADARUN LCP=2000               ---> SECURITY POOL SIZE
ADARUN NSISN=51               ---> ISNS PER TBI ELEMENT
ADARUN LDEUQP=250000          USED BY SLOGGING TO 'LABEL' MSG COMPONENTS
*                             WAS 100K 08/18/2007
*
* TIME LIMITS
*
```

```
ADARUN CT=3600                    COMMAND TIMEOUT INTERVAL
ADARUN TT=1800                    TRANSACTION TIMEOUT INTERVAL
ADARUN TNAA=900                   INACTIVITY TIMEOUT INTERVAL (ACCU)
ADARUN TNAE=600                   INACTIVITY TIMEOUT INTERVAL (ETBT)
ADARUN TNAX=100000                INACTIVITY TIMEOUT INTERVAL (EXUU)
*
* DATABASE/USER LIMITS
*
ADARUN NQCID=40                   ---> MAX NUMBER CIDS/USER
ADARUN NISNHQ=5000                ---> MAX HELD/USER (< 25% NH)
ADARUN TLSCMD=300                 ---> TIME LIMIT FOR SX COMMAND
*
* PROTECTION LOGGING
*
ADARUN NPLOG=2
ADARUN PLOGDEV=8393
ADARUN PLOGSIZE=1500
*
* COMMAND LOGGING
*
ADARUN LOGGING=YES                RMG 8/2/2004
ADARUN NCLOG=2
ADARUN CLOGDEV=3390
ADARUN CLOGSIZE=40500
ADARUN CLOGLAYOUT=5
ADARUN LOGCB=YES                  LOG BASIC ADALOG RECORD + ACB
ADARUN LOGFB=NO                   LOG BASIC ADALOG RECORD + FB
ADARUN LOGRB=NO                   LOG BASIC ADALOG RECORD + RB
ADARUN LOGSB=YES                  LOG BASIC ADALOG RECORD + SB
ADARUN LOGVB=YES                  LOG BASIC ADALOG RECORD + VB
ADARUN LOGIB=NO                   LOG BASIC ADALOG RECORD + IB
ADARUN LOGIO=YES                  LOG BASIC ADALOG RECORD + I/O COUNTS
ADARUN LOGUX=YES                  LOG BASIC ADALOG RECORD + I/O COUNTS
*
* DYNAMIC CACHE
*
ADARUN CACHE=YES
ADARUN CACTIVATE=YES
ADARUN CSTORAGE=VIRTUAL64
ADARUN CASSOMAXS=100M
ADARUN CSTORAGE=VIRTUAL64
ADARUN CDATAMAXS=400M
ADARUN CFILE=(30,1,B,V)ADARUN CDISPSTAT=NO
ADARUN CMAXCSPS=1
*
* USER EXITS
*
ADARUN UEX12=UEXIT12              USER EXIT2
*
*** BUFFERFLUSHING ****
*
ADARUN ASYTVS=YES                 ASYNC,PER VOL/RABN
ADARUN FMXIO=6                    PARALLEL I/O OPERATIONS LIMIT FOR LFIOP
*
ADARUN RPLCONNECTCOUNT=60     --> TRY RECONNECT 60 TIMES
ADARUN RPLCONNECTINTERVAL=60  --> TRY RECONNECT AFTER 60 SECONDS
```

Figure 195:   ADARUN Parameters Reptor

9.3   Definitions Target DB – Windows

9.3.1   Parameters – db251.ini

```
#
# C:\ProgramData\Software AG\Adabas\\db251\DB251.INI
# Last Update: Tue Nov 30 10:26:23 2010
#
[CONTAINER]
  ASSO1                  = d:\sag\containers\ASSO1.251
  ASSO2                  = d:\sag\containers\ASSO2.251
  DATA1                  = e:\sag\containers\DATA1.251
  NUCCLG                 = "D:\SAG\Adabas\db251\NUCCLG"
  NUCPLG                 = "D:\SAG\Adabas\db251\NUCPLG"
  SORT1                  = e:\SAG\containers\SORT1.251
  SORT2                  = d:\SAG\containers\SORT2.251
  TEMP1                  = e:\SAG\containers\TEMP1.251
  WORK1                  = e:\sag\containers\WORK1.251
[CONTAINER-END]

[DB_PARAMETER]
  [ACTION_DBA]
  [ACTION_DBA-END]

  [ADANUC_STARTED]
    ACTI                 = YES
    ACTION_ROUTINE       = ada_nsta
  [ADANUC_STARTED-END]

  [ADANUC_TERMINATED]
    ACTION               = YES
    ACTION_ROUTINE       = ada_nsto
  [ADANUC_TERMINATED-END]

  [DELETE_CHECKPOINTS]
    ACTION               = YES
    ACTION_ROUTINE       = ada_dlcp
    MINIMUM              = 100
  [DELETE_CHECKPOINTS-END]

  [INCREASE_ASSO]
    ACTION               = NO
    ACTION_ROUTINE       = ada_iass
    EXTEND_RATE          = 10
    MESSAGE              = (I=40,W=20,E=10,F=5)
    MINIMUM             = 15
  [INCREASE_ASSO-END]

  [INCREASE_DATA]
    ACTION               = NO
    ACTION_ROUTINE       = ada_idat
    EXTEND_RATE          = 10
    MESSAGE              = (I=40,W=20,E=10,F=5)
    MINIMUM             = 15
  [INCREASE_DATA-END]

  [INCREASE_LBP]
    ACTION               = NO
    ACTION_ROUTINE       = ada_inuc
    MESSAGE             = (E=101)
  [INCREASE_LBP-END]

  [INCREASE_LS]
    ACTION               = NO
    ACTION_ROUTINE       = ada_inuc
    MESSAGE             = (I=50,W=80,E=101)
  [INCREASE_LS-END]

  [INCREASE_LWP]
    ACTION               = NO
    ACTION_ROUTINE       = ada_inuc
    MESSAGE             = (E=101)
  [INCREASE_LWP-END]
```

```
    [INCREASE_NH]
      ACTION                  = NO
      ACTION_ROUTINE          = ada_inuc
      MESSAGE                 = (I=50,W=80,E=101)
    [INCREASE_NH-END]

    [INCREASE_NT]
      ACTION                  = NO
      ACTION_ROUTINE          = ada_inuc
      MESSAGE                 = (I=90)
    [INCREASE_NT-END]

    [INCREASE_NU]
      ACTION                  = NO
      ACTION_ROUTINE          = ada_inuc
      MESSAGE                 = (I=80,W=101)
    [INCREASE_NU-END]

    [OFFLINE_CHECKPOINTS]
      MESSAGE                 = (I=50,W=20,E=5,F=2)
    [OFFLINE_CHECKPOINTS-END]

    [RECOVER_LOST_BLOCKS]
      ACTION                  = YES
      ACTION_ROUTINE          = ada_rlst
    [RECOVER_LOST_BLOCKS-END]

    [REORDER_FILE]
      ACTION                  = NO
      ACTION_ROUTINE          = ada_reor
      MAXIMUM                 = 12
      MESSAGE                 = (I=10,W=16,E=24,F=30)
    [REORDER_FILE-END]

    [SAVE_DB]
      ACTION                  = YES
      ACTION_ROUTINE          = ada_svdb
    [SAVE_DB-END]

    [TERMINATE_ADANUC]
      ABORT                   = 12
      CANCEL                  = 12
      SHUTDOWN                = 0
    [TERMINATE_ADANUC-END]
[DB_PARAMETER-END]

[ENVIRONMENT]
[ENVIRONMENT-END]

[NUCPARMS]
  AR_CONFLICT             = CONTINUE
  BFIO_PARALLEL_LIMIT     = 0
  CLOGBMAX                = 4096
  CLOGLAYOUT              = 5
  LAB                     = 16777216
  LABX                    = 20971520
  LBP                     = 104857600
  LOGGING                 =
  LPXA                    = 10
  LWP                     = 3145728
  MGC                     = 50
  NCL                     = 50
  NISNHQ                  = 90000
  NOBI
  NOPLOG
  NT                      = 20
  NU                      = 100
  OPTIONS                 =
  READ_PARALLEL_LIMITS    =
  TNAA                    = 3000
  TNAE                    = 3000
  TNAX                    = 3000
  TT                      = 900
  USEREXITS               =
  WRITE_LIMIT             = 25
[NUCPARMS-END]
```

Figure 196:   Adabas for Windows Parameters db251.ini

9.3.2   High Water Marks

```
%ADAOPR-I-STARTED,      24-FEB-2011 14:47:40, Version 6.2.1.01 (Windows)
Database 251, startup at 15-FEB-2011 13:22:53

ADANUC Version 6.2.1.01, PID 4688

                        ADANUC Version 6.2.1.01
          Database 251        High Water Marks      on 24-FEB-2011 14:47:35
Area/Entry               Size    In Use  High Water    %       Date/Time
----------               ----    ------  ----------    -       ---------
User Queue                100         2           2    2 17-FEB-2011 16:23:35
Command Queue               -         1           2    - 15-FEB-2011 14:21:15
Hold Queue                  -         1          51    - 15-FEB-2011 14:21:05
Client Queue               50         9           9   18 17-FEB-2011 16:20:55
HQ User Limit          90,000         -          51    0 15-FEB-2011 14:21:05
Threads                    20         2           3   15 17-FEB-2011 16:24:15
Workpool            3,145,728         0     786,448   25 15-FEB-2011 13:22:54
  ISN Sort            393,216         -           0    0
  Complex Search      393,216         -           0    0
Attached Buffer    16,777,216    36,864      36,864    0 24-FEB-2011 08:50:19
ATBX      (MB)             20         0           0    0
Buffer Pool       419,430,400 415,856,640 418,732,032 99 15-FEB-2011 13:22:54
Protection Area       332,790
  Active Area          99,837         -           4    0 15-FEB-2011 15:00:05
Group Commit               50         1           1    2 15-FEB-2011 13:48:05
Transaction Time          900         -          10    1 24-FEB-2011 14:45:35
```

Figure 197:   Adabas for Windows High Water Marks

9.3.3   Activities

```
                        ADANUC Version 6.2.1.01
          Database 251           Activity           on 25-FEB-2011 08:01:15


I/O Activity                 Total  Throwbacks                        Total
------------                 -----  ----------                        -----
Buffer Pool              2,068,217  Waiting for UQ context                0
WORK Read                        2  Waiting for ISN                       0
WORK Write                 357,029  ET Sync                               0
PLOG Write                       0  DWP Overflow                          0
NUCTMP                          48
NUCSRT                           0


Pool Hit Rate                Total  Interrupts        Current          Total
-------------                -----  ----------        -------          -----
Buffer Pool                  93.7%  WP Space Wait           0              0
Format pool                    99%
```

Figure 198:   Adabas for Windows ADANUC Activities

9.3.4   Buffer Pool Statistics

```
                          ADANUC Version 6.2.1.01
           Database 251   Buffer Pool Statistics   on 25-FEB-2011 08:01:15


Buffer Pool Size    :   419,430,400

Pool Allocation                        RABNs present
---------------                        -------------
Current     ( 98%) :   412,060,672     ASSO              :        10,713
Highwater   ( 99%) :   418,732,032     DATA              :        15,112
Internal    (  4%) :    19,037,184     WORK              :             0
Workpool    (  0%) :     2,453,504     NUCTMP            :             0
                                       NUCSRT            :             0


I/O Statistics                         Buffer Flushes
---------------                        -------------
Logical Reads     :    16,794,440      Total             :           447
Physical Reads    :     1,049,708      To Free Space     :             0
Pool Hit Rate     :          93.7%

                                       Write Limit  ( 5%):    20,971,500
Physical Writes   :     1,018,509      Modified     ( 4%):    19,899,392
```

Figure 199:   Adabas for Windows Buffer Pool Statistics

9.4 Test Results

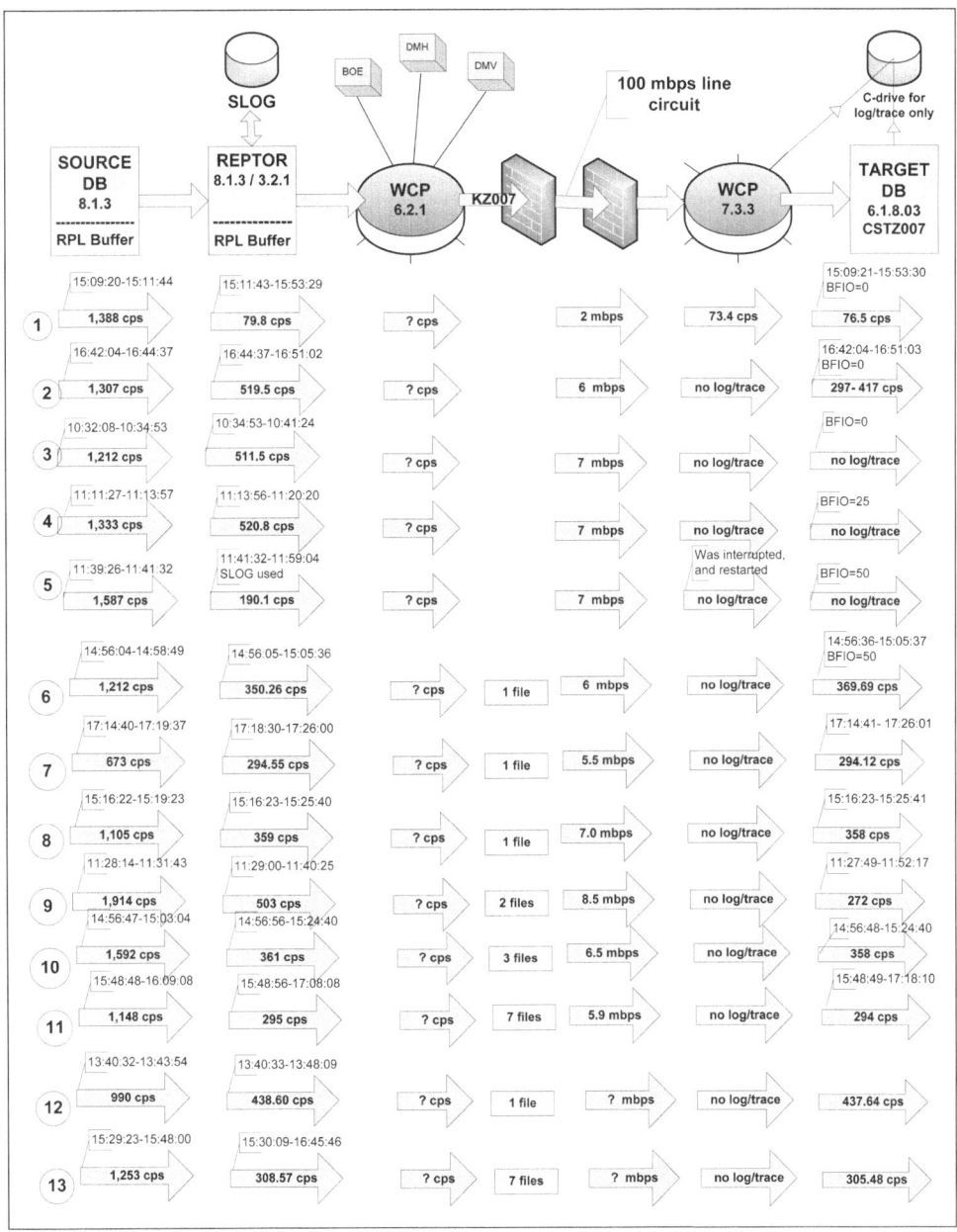

Figure 200: Replication Process – Number of Commands per Second (cps)

Test #	Date	Source Database						Replicator Engine			
		Duration Program Start	Duration Program Stop	Dur Sec	CPU Time min.sec. hs	Adabas N2-Cmds	Cmds per Second	Start	Stop	Se-conds	Cmds per Second
1	9/9/2010	15:09:20	15:11:44	144	00.09.42	200,000	1,388.89	15:11:43	15:53:29	2,506	79.81
2	9/9/2010	16:42:04	16:44:37	153	00.10.15	200,000	1,307.19	16:44:37	16:51:02	385	519.48
3	9/17/2010	10:32:10	10:34:53	163	00.10.12	200,000	1,226.99	10:34:53	10:41:24	391	511.51
4	9/17/2010	11:11:28	11:13:57	149	00.09.54	200,000	1,342.28	11:13:56	11:20:20	384	520.83
5	9/17/2010	11:39:28	11:41:32	124	00.09.38	200,000	1,612.90	11:41:32	11:59:04	1,052	190.11
6	9/20/2010	14:56:04	14:58:49	165	00.10.52	200,000	1,212.12	14:56:05	15:05:36	571	350.26
7	9/20/2010	17:14:40	17:19:37	297	00.10.16	200,000	673.40	17:14:41	17:26:00	679	294.55
8	9/21/2010	15:16:22	15:19:23	181	00.09.96	200,000	1,104.97	15:16:23	15:25:40	557	359.07
						F144 / F227					
9	9/24/2010	11:28:14	11:31:43	209	00.10.19	200,000	956.94	11:29:00	11:40:25	685	291.97
9	9/24/2010	11:28:14	11:31:43	209	00.10.39	200,000	956.94	11:28:26	11:42:16	830	240.96
9	9/24/2010	11:28:14	11:31:43	209		400,000	1,913.88	11:29:00	11:42:16	796	502.51
						F144 / F227 / F228					
10	9/24/2010	14:56:47	15:03:03	376	00.10.50	200,000	531.91	14:56:56	15:24:37	1,661	120.41
10	9/24/2010	14:57:04	15:03:04	360	00.10.58	200,000	555.56	14:59:26	15:24:40	1,514	132.10
10	9/24/2010	14:57:04	15:03:02	358	00.10.60	200,000	558.66	14:57:17	15:24:34	1,637	122.17
10	9/24/2010	14:56:47	15:03:04	377		600,000	1,591.51	14:56:56	15:24:40	1,664	360.58
						F144 / F227 / F228 / F229 / F230 / F231 / F232					
11	9/27/2010	15:48:48	16:08:52	1,204	00.12.54	200,000	166.11	15:48:56	17:06:35	4,659	42.93
11	9/27/2010	15:48:51	16:09:08	1,217	00.12.62	200,000	164.34	15:48:57	17:07:29	4,712	42.44
11	9/27/2010	15:49:03	16:09:18	1,215	00.12.50	200,000	164.61	15:51:23	17:08:08	4,605	43.43
11	9/27/2010	15:49:07	16:09:17	1,210	00.12.52	200,000	165.29	15:51:38	17:08:05	4,587	43.60
11	9/27/2010	15:49:07	16:09:11	1,204	00.12.49	200,000	166.11	15:49:08	17:07:43	4,715	42.42
11	9/27/2010	15:49:07	16:09:17	1,210	00.12.54	200,000	165.29	15:49:09	17:08:06	4,737	42.22
11	9/27/2010	15:49:07	16:08:37	1,170	00.12.51	200,000	170.94	15:49:10	17:05:36	4,586	43.61
11	9/27/2010	15:48:48	16:09:18	1,230		1,400,000	1,138.21	15:48:56	17:08:08	4,752	294.61
						F144					
12	10/8/2010	13:40:32	13:43:54	202	00.10.07	200,000	990.10	13:40:33	13:48:09	456	438.60
						F144 / F227 / F228 / F229 / F230 / F231 / F232					
13	10/8/2010	15:29:23	15:46:36	1,033	00.11.16	200,000	193.61	15:30:09	16:39:41	4,172	47.94
13	10/8/2010	15:29:39	15:48:00	1,101	00.11.16	200,000	181.65	15:30:12	16:45:46	4,534	44.11
13	10/8/2010	15:29:40	15:47:57	1,097	00.11.18	200,000	182.32	15:30:16	16:45:37	4,521	44.24
13	10/8/2010	15:29:40	15:47:56	1,096	00.11.23	200,000	182.48	15:30:21	16:45:34	4,513	44.32
13	10/8/2010	15:29:40	15:47:49	1,089	00.11.21	200,000	183.65	15:30:23	16:45:01	4,478	44.66
13	10/8/2010	15:29:40	15:47:50	1,090	00.11.24	200,000	183.49	15:30:26	16:45:11	4,485	44.59
13	10/8/2010	15:29:49	15:47:32	1,063	00.11.20	200,000	188.15	15:30:28	16:43:44	4,396	45.50
13	10/8/2010	15:29:23	15:48:00	1,117		1,400,000	1,253.36	15:30:09	16:45:46	4,537	308.57

Figure 201:   Replication Process – Number of Commands per Second –Spreadsheet 1

100 Mbps Line / Circuit		WCP Windows				Target Database CSTZ007				Comments			
Test #	Used Mbps	Start	Stop	Seconds	Cmds per Second	Start	Stop	Seconds	Cmds per Second	WCP trace	Ada Cmd Log	BFIO	SLOG used
1	2.0	n/a	n/a	V612	73.40	15:09:21	15:53:30	2,649	75.50	Yes	Yes	0	No
2	6.0	n/a	n/a	V612	0.00	16:42:04	16:51:03	539	371.06	No	Yes	0	No
3	7.0	n/a	n/a	V612	0.00	10:32:08	10:41:24	556	359.71	No	No	0	No
4	7.0	n/a	n/a	V612	0.00	11:11:27	11:20:20	533	375.23	No	No	25	No
5	7.0	n/a	n/a	V612	0.00	11:39:26	11:59:04	1,178	169.78	No	No	50	Yes
6	6.0	n/a	n/a	V621	0.00	14:56:36	15:05:37	541	369.69	No	Yes	50	No
7	5.5	n/a	n/a	V621	0.00	17:14:41	17:26:01	680	294.12	No	Yes	0	No
8	7.0	n/a	n/a	V621	0.00	15:16:23	15:25:41	558	358.42	No	Yes	0	No
9		n/a	n/a	F 144		11:27:49	11:40:25	756	264.55	No	Yes		
9		n/a	n/a	F 227		11:29:57	11:52:17	1,340	149.25	No	Yes		
9	8.5				Total:	11:27:49	11:52:17	1,468	272.48				
10		n/a	n/a	F 144		14:56:48	15:24:37	1,669	119.83	No	Yes	0	Yes
10		n/a	n/a	F 227		14:58:12	15:24:41	1,589	125.87	No	Yes	0	yes
10		n/a	n/a	F 228		14:58:12	15:24:41	1,589	125.87	No	Yes	0	yes
10	6.5				Total:	14:56:48	15:24:40	1,672	358.85				
11		n/a	n/a	F 144		15:49:13	17:05:38	4,585	43.62	No	Yes	0	Yes
11		n/a	n/a	F 227		15:48:49	17:07:30	4,721	42.36	No	Yes	0	Yes
11		n/a	n/a	F 228		15:50:27	17:08:10	4,663	42.89	No	Yes	0	Yes
11		n/a	n/a	F 229		15:50:47	17:08:06	4,639	43.11	No	Yes	0	Yes
11		n/a	n/a	F 230		15:50:45	17:07:44	4,619	43.30	No	Yes	0	Yes
11		n/a	n/a	F 231		15:50:47	17:08:07	4,640	43.10	No	Yes	0	Yes
11		n/a	n/a	F 232		15:50:46	17:05:38	4,492	44.52	No	Yes	0	Yes
11	5.9	na	n/a		Total:	15:48:49	17:08:10	4,761	294.06	No	Yes	0	Yes
12	0	n/a	n/a	F 144		13:40:33	13:48:10	457	437.64	No	Yes	0	No
13		n/a	n/a	F 144		15:29:24	16:39:42	4,218	47.42	No	Yes	0	Yes
13		n/a	n/a	F 227		15:30:45	16:45:47	4,502	44.42	No	Yes	0	Yes
13		n/a	n/a	F 228		15:30:46	16:45:38	4,492	44.52	No	Yes	0	Yes
13		n/a	n/a	F 229		15:30:47	16:45:35	4,488	44.56	No	Yes	0	Yes
13		n/a	n/a	F 230		15:30:50	16:45:02	4,452	44.92	No	Yes	0	Yes
13		n/a	n/a	F 231		15:30:49	16:45:13	4,464	44.80	No	Yes	0	Yes
13		n/a	n/a	F 232		15:32:20	16:43:45	4,285	46.67	No	Yes	0	Yes
13	0	na	n/a		Total:	15:29:24	16:45:47	4,583	305.48	No	Yes	0	Yes

Figure 202: Replication Process – Number of Commands per Second – Spreadsheet 2

9.5   Natural Monitor Programs

9.5.1   Ping Target Database

```
0010 DEFINE DATA LOCAL
0020 1 FILE44 VIEW OF ST-RI-CNTRB-LINE
0030   2 LOG-COUNTER
0040   2 ENTITY
0050 1 #OP (A1)   INIT <'S'>   /* for UDB USR1040N  S=set G=get
0060 1 #DB (N5)   INIT <251>   /* for UDB
0070 1 #RC (I4)
0080 *
0090 END-DEFINE
0100 *** ------------------
0110 INPUT #DB                 /* DB to be checked
0120 *** ------------------
0130 ON ERROR
0140   IF *ERROR-NR = 3148
0150     WRITE (0) NOTITLE 'ERROR: Database' #DB 'or Net-Work is down'
0160       TERMINATE 12
0170   ELSE
0180     WRITE (0) NOTITLE 'Other Adabas Error' *ERROR-NR
0190       TERMINATE 16
0200   END-IF
0210 END-ERROR
0220 ** --------------------
0230 CALLNAT 'USR1040N' #OP #DB #RC
0240 ** --------------------
0250 R1. READ (1) FILE44 BY ISN
0260 * DISPLAY LOG-COUNTER ENTITY *ISN(R1.)
0270   WRITE (0) NOTITLE 'DB' #DB 'and Net-Work are up and running'
0280 END-READ
0290 IF *COUNTER (R1.) = 0
0300   WRITE (0) NOTITLE
0310     'DB' #DB 'is up and running - but file 44 is empty'
0320 END-IF
0330 END
```

Figure 203:   Monitor – Natural Program Ping Target Database

9.5.2   Check Messages on DDPRINT

```
** ----------------------------------------------------------------------
**            EVENT REPLICATOR Performance Project
** RPL-P001: Read the nucleus statistics and log file
** Input:    CMWKF01 - READ WORK 1
**           REPLICATOR reports
**           Mainframe: DIETER.REPTOR.DDPRINT.JAN2011.OUTLIST
**           Windows:   Z:\Replicator\REPTOR_stat_JAN2011.txt
** Ouput:    Report
** Process:  Check the RPL statistics for:
**           - ADAF* messages
**           - HWM > 75 %
** Array:    FNR(1:999) - RSP and CNT (1:255)
**
** Date        Name    Reason for changes
** ----------  ------  --------------------------------------------------
** 2009-02-18  DSTORR  Copied from Adabas Performance Project PER-P001
** 2009-04-13  DSTORR  DDPRINT has no longer an ASA character
**
** ----------------------------------------------------------------------
DEFINE DATA LOCAL
** -- Input Work File
1 #ADALOG-LINE       (A133)
1 REDEFINE #ADALOG-LINE
* 2 #ADALOG-LINE-ASA  (A001)
  2 #ADALOG-LINE-TEXT (A133)
**
1 #OUTPUT-LINE       (A120)
1 REDEFINE #OUTPUT-LINE
  2 #SEQ             (N6)
  2 #BLANK           (A2)
  2 #TEXT            (A112)
**
1 #FNR               (0:999)   /* FNR = OFFSET IN TABLE
  2 #RSP             (N3/1:255)
  2 #CNT             (N6/1:255)
1 #I1                (N4)      /* FNR INDEX
1 #I2                (N4)      /* RSP/CNT INDEX
1 #RC                (L) INIT <FALSE>
1 #HWM               (L) INIT <FALSE>
** --
01 #ASTERISK    (A120)
01 #LC          (N6)           /* line count
01 #I-FNR-ALP   (A3)
01 #I-FNR-NUM   (N3)
01 #I-RSP-ALP   (A3)
01 #I-RSP-NUM   (N3)
**
END-DEFINE
**
IF *MACHINE-CLASS NE 'MAINFRAME'
  DEFINE WORK FILE 1 'Z:\Replicator\rpltmpm2_stat_20090413.txt'
  DEFINE WORK FILE 2 'Z:\Replicator\RPL-P100_stat_rep_200990413_new.txt'
END-IF
**
ON ERROR
  *ERROR-TA := 'PER-PERR'
END-ERROR
**
** ----------------------------------------
** -- Initialization
** ----------------------------------------
** --
#LC := 0
#ASTERISK := '********************************************************'
FOR #I1 = 0 TO 999        /* fill resp codes 1-255
  FOR #I2 = 1 TO 255
```

```
    #RSP(#I1,#I2) := #I2
  END-FOR
END-FOR
**
** ---------------------------------------
** -- Read statistics and fill array
** ---------------------------------------
** --
RW1.
READ WORK 1 #ADALOG-LINE        /* read one ADALOG
** --        Check Error Lines
  IF  SUBSTRING(#ADALOG-LINE-TEXT,01,12) = 'Start date= ' OR
      SUBSTRING(#ADALOG-LINE-TEXT,10,06) = 'ADAF54' OR
      SUBSTRING(#ADALOG-LINE-TEXT,01,06) = 'ADAF18' OR
      SUBSTRING(#ADALOG-LINE-TEXT,10,06) = 'ADAFCQ' OR
      SUBSTRING(#ADALOG-LINE-TEXT,10,06) = 'ADAF2A' OR
      SUBSTRING(#ADALOG-LINE-TEXT,10,06) = 'ADAF2D' OR
      SUBSTRING(#ADALOG-LINE-TEXT,10,06) = 'ADAF2B' OR
      SUBSTRING(#ADALOG-LINE-TEXT,01,06) = 'ADAF54' OR
      SUBSTRING(#ADALOG-LINE-TEXT,10,06) = 'ADAF8Y'
    ADD 1 TO #LC
    #SEQ := #LC
    #TEXT := #ADALOG-LINE-TEXT
    WRITE WORK FILE 2 #OUTPUT-LINE
  END-IF
** -------------- CHECK AND COUNT RSP CODES --------
  IF SUBSTRING(#ADALOG-LINE-TEXT,01,06) = 'ADAF18'
    #RC := TRUE
    #I-FNR-ALP := SUBSTRING(#ADALOG-LINE-TEXT,36,03)
    IF #I-FNR-ALP = ' '     /* avoid table offset blank
      #I-FNR-ALP := '000'
    END-IF
    #I-FNR-NUM := VAL(#I-FNR-ALP)
    #I1 := #I-FNR-NUM
    FOR #I2 = 1 TO 255
      #I-RSP-ALP := SUBSTRING(#ADALOG-LINE-TEXT,46,03)
      #I-RSP-NUM := VAL(#I-RSP-ALP)
      IF #RSP(#I1,#I2) = #I-RSP-NUM /* RSP
        ADD 1 TO #CNT(#I1,#I2)
**        WRITE 'FNR:' #I1 'RC:' #RSP(#I1,#I2) #CNT(#I1,#I2)
      END-IF
    END-FOR
  END-IF
**   ---------- check High-Water-Marks > 75 % ---------
  IF  SUBSTRING(#ADALOG-LINE-TEXT,01,17) = 'AB  -POOL    NAB='
      AND SUBSTRING(#ADALOG-LINE-TEXT,42,02) GT '75'
    ADD 1 TO #LC
    #TEXT := #ADALOG-LINE-TEXT
    WRITE WORK FILE 2 #ASTERISK
    WRITE WORK FILE 2 #OUTPUT-LINE
    WRITE WORK FILE 2 #ASTERISK
    #HWM := TRUE
  END-IF
**
  IF  SUBSTRING(#ADALOG-LINE-TEXT,01,17) = 'RPL -POOL    LRPL='
      AND SUBSTRING(#ADALOG-LINE-TEXT,42,02) GT '75'
    ADD 1 TO #LC
    #TEXT := #ADALOG-LINE-TEXT
    WRITE WORK FILE 2 #ASTERISK
    WRITE WORK FILE 2 #OUTPUT-LINE
    WRITE WORK FILE 2 #ASTERISK
    #HWM := TRUE
  END-IF
**
  ESCAPE TOP
END-WORK
** ------- Print response code array --------------
*
FOR #I1 = 0 TO 999
  FOR #I2 = 1 TO 255
```

```
     IF #CNT(#I1,#I2) GT 0
       COMPRESS 'FNR/RSP/CNT' #I1 #RSP(#I1,#I2) #CNT(#I1,#I2)
          INTO #OUTPUT-LINE
**        #SEQ := 0
        WRITE WORK FILE 2 #OUTPUT-LINE
      END-IF
  END-FOR
END-FOR
**
IF #HWM = TRUE
  WRITE WORK FILE 2 #ASTERISK
  #OUTPUT-LINE := 'Please check the high-water-marks!'
  WRITE WORK FILE 2 #OUTPUT-LINE
  WRITE WORK FILE 2 #ASTERISK
END-IF
**
IF #RC = TRUE
  WRITE WORK FILE 2 #ASTERISK
  #OUTPUT-LINE := 'Please check the ADABAS response codes!'
  WRITE WORK FILE 2 #OUTPUT-LINE
  WRITE WORK FILE 2 #ASTERISK
END-IF
**
IF #HWM = TRUE OR #RC = TRUE
  IF *MACHINE-CLASS EQ 'MAINFRAME'
    TERMINATE 12
  END-IF
ELSE
  WRITE WORK FILE 2 #ASTERISK
  COMPRESS *PROGRAM ': no errors found in DDPRINT!'
    INTO #OUTPUT-LINE LEAVING NO SPACE
  WRITE WORK FILE 2 #OUTPUT-LINE
  WRITE WORK FILE 2 #ASTERISK
END-IF
**
END
```

Figure 204: Monitor – Natural Program Check DDPRINT Messages

9.5.3 RPL and NAB Buffer Overflow

```
0010 ** --------------------------------------------------------------------
0020 ** DWSLOGHW: Check High Water Mark of Replicator Engine
0030 **           This program reads the AOS high-water marks
0040 **           checks for Replication (RPL)
0050 ** Input:   CMWKF01 - READ WORK 1 -- AOS High Water Marks
0060 ** Ouput:   CMWKF02 - WRITE WORK 2 -- AOS HWM
0070 **
0080 **           LIB: PDSTUTIL (prod); DIETER (devl)
0090 ** Date      Name    Reason for changes
0100 ** ---------- ------  ------------------------------------------------
0110 ** 2009-01-26  STDWS    CREATED
0120 ** 2009-02-25  STDWS    changed to write work file 2
0130 ** 2009-02-26  STDWS    ASA not read on mainframe but on Windows
0140 ** 2009-03-19  STDWS    HWM check from 50% to 65%
0150 **
0160 ** --------------------------------------------------------------------
0170 DEFINE DATA LOCAL
0180 1 #ADAREP-LINE      (A133)
0190 1 REDEFINE #ADAREP-LINE
0200   2 #ADAREP-LINE-ASA   (A001)
0210   2 #ADAREP-LINE-TEXT  (A132)
0220 **
0230 1 #ARRAY             (A79/1:50)
0240 1 #START             (L) INIT <FALSE>
```

```
0250 1 #I                    (I4)          /* array counter
0260 1 #HWM-MSG              (A79) INIT <'NAB or RPL reached 65%'>
0270 **
0280 END-DEFINE
0290 **
0300 **
0310 IF *MACHINE-CLASS NE 'MAINFRAME'
0320   DEFINE WORK FILE 1 'Z:\Replicator\DB134_HWM_20090226.txt'
0330   DEFINE WORK FILE 2 'Z:\Replicator\dwsloghw.db134_HWM_20090226.txt'
0340 END-IF
0350 **
0360 ** -------------------------------
0370 ** -- Read reports and fill matrix
0380 ** -------------------------------
0390 #I := 1
0400 RW. READ WORK 1 #ADAREP-LINE
0410 ** --
0420   DISPLAY #ADAREP-LINE (AL=79)
0430   IF SUBSTRING(#ADAREP-LINE-TEXT,1,6) = 'DATA H'
0440     #START := TRUE
0450     ESCAPE TOP   /* (RW.)
0460   END-IF
0470   IF SUBSTRING(#ADAREP-LINE-TEXT,1,11) =
0480      'DATA ,,,FIN'
0490     ESCAPE BOTTOM (RW.)
0500   END-IF
0510 **
0520   IF #START = TRUE
0530     #ARRAY(#I) := #ADAREP-LINE-TEXT
0540     ADD 1 TO #I
0550   END-IF
0560 *
0570 END-WORK
0580 **
0590 F1. FOR #I = 1 TO 30
0600   IF #ARRAY(#I) = ' ' OR
0610      SUBSTRING(#ARRAY(#I),1,13) = ' PF1----- PF2'
0620     ESCAPE BOTTOM (F1.)
0630   END-IF
0640   WRITE WORK FILE 2 #ARRAY(#I)
0650 END-FOR /* F1.
0660 **
0670 #F2. FOR #I = 1 TO 30
0680   IF  SUBSTRING(#ARRAY(#I),1,20) = 'Attached Buffer(NAB)' OR
0690       SUBSTRING(#ARRAY(#I),1,20) = 'Replication      (RPL)'
0700 *    SUBSTRING(#ARRAY(#I),1,20) = 'Command Queue   (NC) ' OR
0710 *    SUBSTRING(#ARRAY(#I),1,20) = 'Format Pool     (LFP)' OR
0720 *    SUBSTRING(#ARRAY(#I),1,20) = 'Hold Queue      (NH) ' OR
0730 *    SUBSTRING(#ARRAY(#I),1,20) = 'ISN-List Table (LI) ' OR
0740 *    SUBSTRING(#ARRAY(#I),1,20) = 'Seq. Cmd. Table(LQ) ' OR
0750 *    SUBSTRING(#ARRAY(#I),1,20) = 'User Queue      (NU) ' OR
0760 *    SUBSTRING(#ARRAY(#I),1,20) = 'Unique DE Pool (DUQ)' OR
0770 *    SUBSTRING(#ARRAY(#I),1,20) = 'Security Pool   (LCP)' OR
0780 *    SUBSTRING(#ARRAY(#I),1,20) = 'UQ File List    (UQF)' OR
0790 *    SUBSTRING(#ARRAY(#I),1,20) = 'ATM Trans. IDs (XID)' OR
0800 *    SUBSTRING(#ARRAY(#I),1,20) = 'Work Pool       (LWP)' OR
0810 *    SUBSTRING(#ARRAY(#I),1,20) = 'Redo Pool       (LRDP' OR
0820     IF SUBSTRING(#ARRAY(#I),51,02) GT '65'
0830       WRITE WORK FILE 2 #HWM-MSG
0840       TERMINATE 12
0850     END-IF
0860   END-IF
0870 END-FOR /* (F2.)
0880 ** --
0890 END
***** End of list *****
```

Figure 205:   Monitor – Natural Program RPL and NAB Overflow

9.5.4   SLOG Check on Reptor

```
0010 ** -----------------------------------------------------------------
0020 ** DWSLOGCK: Check SLOG of Replicator Engine
0030 **           This program reads the AOS/Replicator Statistics
0040 **           checks for queued values and send message to ......
0050 ** Input:   CMWKF01 - READ WORK 1 -- AOS/Replicator Statistics
0060 ** Ouput:   CMPRT01 - WRITE (2)
0070 **           FORMAT(2) LS=80 PS=40
0080 *
0090 ** Date        Name    Reason for changes
0100 ** ----------  ------  -----------------------------------------------
0110 ** 2009-01-05  STDWS   created
0120 ** 2010-03-10  STDWS   updated for AOS813 - different display
0130 **                     was: Destination slog cnt ..
0140 **                     now: On file ..
0150 **
0160 ** -----------------------------------------------------------------
0170 DEFINE DATA LOCAL
0180 1 #ADAREP-LINE      (A121)
0190 1 REDEFINE #ADAREP-LINE
0200   2 #ADAREP-LINE-ASA  (A001)
0210   2 #ADAREP-LINE-TEXT (A120)
0220 **
0230 1 #ARRAY            (A79/1:30)
0240 1 #START            (L) INIT <FALSE>
0250 1 #I                (I4)         /* array counter
0260 **
0270 END-DEFINE
0280 **
0290 **
0300 IF *MACHINE-CLASS NE 'MAINFRAME'
0310   DEFINE WORK FILE 1 'Z:\ADAREP\adabas_slogrep.txt'
0320 END-IF
0330 **
0340 DEFINE PRINTER (1) OUTPUT 'CMPRT01'     /* needs to suppress
0350 DEFINE PRINTER (2) OUTPUT 'CCONTROL'    /* the ASA sign
0360 FORMAT(2) LS=80 PS=40
0370 **
0380 ** -------------------------------
0390 ** -- Read reports and fill matrix
0400 ** -------------------------------
0410 #I := 1
0420 RW. READ WORK 1 #ADAREP-LINE
0430 ** --
0440   IF SUBSTRING(#ADAREP-LINE-TEXT,1,6) = 'DATA B'
0450     #START := TRUE
0460     ESCAPE TOP   /* (RW.)
0470   END-IF
0480 **
0490   IF #START = TRUE
0500     #ARRAY(#I) := #ADAREP-LINE-TEXT
0510     ADD 1 TO #I
0520   END-IF
0530 *
0540   IF SUBSTRING(#ADAREP-LINE-TEXT,2,23) =
0550       'Destination slog cnt ..'
0560     ESCAPE BOTTOM (RW.)
0570   END-IF
0580 *
0590 END-WORK
0600 **
0610 F1. FOR #I = 1 TO 30
0620   IF #ARRAY(#I) = ' '
0630     ESCAPE BOTTOM (F1.)
0640   END-IF
0650   WRITE (2) #ARRAY(#I)
0660 END-FOR /* (F1.)
0670 **
```

```
0680 #F2. FOR #I = 1 TO 30
0690   IF SUBSTRING(#ARRAY(#I),2,11) = 'On file ..'
0700     IF SUBSTRING(#ARRAY(#I),12,14) = ' '
0710       WRITE (2) NOTITLE
0720         // '*'(20)
0730          / 'SLOG is empty'
0740          / '*'(20)
0750     ELSE
0760       WRITE (2) NOTITLE
0770         // '*' '-'(38) '*'
0780          / #ARRAY(#I) (AL=25)
0790          / 'SLOG is not empty - open the destination'
0800          / '*' '-'(38) '*'
0810       TERMINATE 12                    /* for CC check
0820     END-IF
0830   END-IF
0840 END-FOR /* (F2.)
0850 ** --
0860 END
***** End of list *****
```

Figure 206:   Monitor – Natural Program SLOG Check Reptor

9.5.5   Compare two SLOGs

```
0010 ** ----------------------------------------------------------------------
0020 ** DWSLOGC2: Compare two SLOGs of Replicator Engine
0030 **           This program reads the AOS/Replicator Statistics
0040 **           checks for queued values and send message to ......
0050 ** Input:    CMWKF01 - READ WORK 1 -- AOS/Replicator Statistics old
0060 **           CMWKF02 - READ WORK 2 -- AOS/Replicator Statistics new
0070 ** Ouput:    CMPRT01 - WRITE (2)
0080 **           FORMAT(2) LS=80 PS=40
0090 **
0100 ** Libs :    PDSTUTIL (prod) - DIETER (devl)
0110 **
0120 ** Date         Name    Reason for changes
0130 ** ----------   ------  ---------------------------------------------
0140 ** 2009-01-14   STDWS   copied from DWSLOGCK and changed to read and com-
0150 **                      pare two SLOG reports
0160 ** 2009-02-04   STDWS   changed comments: SLOG is being drained
0170 **
0180 ** ----------------------------------------------------------------------
0190 DEFINE DATA LOCAL
0200 1 #ADAREP-LINE-1         (A121)
0210 1 REDEFINE #ADAREP-LINE-1
0220   2 #ADAREP-LINE-ASA-1   (A001)
0230   2 #ADAREP-LINE-TEXT-1  (A120)
0240 **
0250 1 #ADAREP-LINE-2         (A121)
0260 1 REDEFINE #ADAREP-LINE-2
0270   2 #ADAREP-LINE-ASA-2   (A001)
0280   2 #ADAREP-LINE-TEXT-2  (A120)
0290 **
0300 1 #ARRAY-1               (A79/1:30)
0310 1 #START-1               (L) INIT <FALSE>
0320 1 #I1                    (I4)        /* array counter
0330 **
0340 1 #ARRAY-2               (A79/1:30)
0350 1 #START-2               (L) INIT <FALSE>
0360 1 #I2                    (I4)        /* array counter
0370 **
0380 END-DEFINE
0390 **
0400 **
```

```
0410 IF *MACHINE-CLASS NE 'MAINFRAME'
0420   DEFINE WORK FILE 1 'Z:\ADAREP\adabas_slogrep_20090105.txt'
0430   DEFINE WORK FILE 2 'Z:\ADAREP\adabas_slogrep_20090116.txt'
0440 END-IF
0450 **
0460 IF *MACHINE-CLASS EQ 'MAINFRAME'
0470   DEFINE PRINTER (1) OUTPUT 'CMPRT01'          /* needs to suppress
0480   DEFINE PRINTER (2) OUTPUT 'CCONTROL'         /* the ASA sign
0490 END-IF
0500 **
0510 IF *MACHINE-CLASS EQ 'MAINFRAME'
0520   FORMAT(2) LS=80 PS=50
0530 ELSE
0540   FORMAT(0) LS=80 PS=50
0550 END-IF
0560 **
0570 ** -----------------------------------
0580 ** -- Read SLOG report 1 and fill matrix
0590 ** -----------------------------------
0600 #I1 := 1
0610 RW1. READ WORK 1 #ADAREP-LINE-1
0620 ** --
0630   IF SUBSTRING(#ADAREP-LINE-TEXT-1,1,6) = 'DATA B'
0640     #START-1 := TRUE
0650     ESCAPE TOP   /* (RW1.)
0660   END-IF
0670   IF SUBSTRING(#ADAREP-LINE-TEXT-1,2,32) =
0680       'For individual replay dbid/token'
0690     ESCAPE BOTTOM (RW1.)
0700   END-IF
0710 **
0720   IF #START-1 = TRUE
0730     #ARRAY-1(#I1) := #ADAREP-LINE-TEXT-1
0740     ADD 1 TO #I1
0750   END-IF
0760 *
0770 END-WORK /* (RW1.)
0780 **
0790 F1. FOR #I1 = 1 TO 30
0800   IF #ARRAY-1(#I1) = ' '
0810     ESCAPE BOTTOM (F1.)
0820   END-IF
0830   IF *MACHINE-CLASS EQ 'MAINFRAME'
0840     WRITE (2) #ARRAY-1(#I1)
0850   ELSE
0860     WRITE (0) #ARRAY-1(#I1)
0870   END-IF
0880 END-FOR /* (F1.)
0890 **
0900 ** -----------------------------------
0910 ** -- Read SLOG report 2 and fill matrix
0920 ** -----------------------------------
0930 #I2 := 1
0940 RW2. READ WORK 2 #ADAREP-LINE-2
0950 ** --
0960   IF SUBSTRING(#ADAREP-LINE-TEXT-2,1,6) = 'DATA B'
0970     #START-2 := TRUE
0980     ESCAPE TOP   /* (RW2.)
0990   END-IF
1000   IF SUBSTRING(#ADAREP-LINE-TEXT-2,2,32) =
1010       'For individual replay dbid/token'
1020     ESCAPE BOTTOM (RW2.)
1030   END-IF
1040 **
1050   IF #START-2 = TRUE
1060     #ARRAY-2(#I2) := #ADAREP-LINE-TEXT-2
1070     ADD 1 TO #I2
1080   END-IF
1090 *
1100 END-WORK /* (RW2.)
1110 **
```

```
1120 F2. FOR #I2 = 1 TO 30
1130   IF #ARRAY-2(#I2) = ' '
1140     ESCAPE BOTTOM (F2.)
1150   END-IF
1160   IF *MACHINE-CLASS EQ 'MAINFRAME'
1170     WRITE (2) #ARRAY-2(#I2)
1180   ELSE
1190     WRITE (0) #ARRAY-2(#I2)
1200   END-IF
1210 END-FOR /* (F2.)
1220 ** ------------------------------------
1230 ** Compare both arrays
1240 ** ------------------------------------
1250 F3. FOR #I1 = 1 TO 30
1260 ** -
1270   IF SUBSTRING(#ARRAY-1(#I1),2,17) = 'Items on file ...'
1280 ** -
1290     IF  SUBSTRING(#ARRAY-1(#I1),20,45) = ' ' AND
1300         SUBSTRING(#ARRAY-2(#I1),20,45) = ' '
1310       IF *MACHINE-CLASS EQ 'MAINFRAME'
1320         WRITE (2) NOTITLE
1330           // '*'(13)
1340           /  'SLOG is empty'
1350           /  '*'(13)
1360       ELSE
1370         WRITE (0) NOTITLE
1380           // '*'(13)
1390           /  'SLOG is empty'
1400           /  '*'(13)
1410       END-IF
1420       ESCAPE BOTTOM (F3.)
1430     END-IF
1440 ** -
1450     IF  SUBSTRING(#ARRAY-1(#I1),20,45) NE ' ' AND
1460         SUBSTRING(#ARRAY-2(#I1),20,45) EQ ' '
1470       IF *MACHINE-CLASS EQ 'MAINFRAME'
1480         WRITE (2) NOTITLE
1490           // '*'(34)
1500           /  'SLOG has been successfully emptied'
1510           /  '*'(34)
1520       ELSE
1530         WRITE (0) NOTITLE
1540           // '*'(34)
1550           /  'SLOG has been successfully emptied'
1560           /  '*'(34)
1570       END-IF
1580       ESCAPE BOTTOM (F3.)
1590     END-IF
1600 ** -
1610     IF  SUBSTRING(#ARRAY-1(#I1),20,45) GT ' ' AND
1620         SUBSTRING(#ARRAY-1(#I1),20,45) GT
1630         SUBSTRING(#ARRAY-2(#I1),20,45)
1640       IF *MACHINE-CLASS EQ 'MAINFRAME'
1650         WRITE (2) NOTITLE
1660           // '*'(46)
1670           /  'SLOG is being drained'
1680           /  '*'(46)
1690       ELSE
1700         WRITE (0) NOTITLE
1710           // '*'(46)
1720           /  'SLOG is being drained'
1730           /  '*'(46)
1740       END-IF
1750       ESCAPE BOTTOM (F3.)
1760     END-IF
1770 ** -
1780     IF  SUBSTRING(#ARRAY-1(#I1),20,45) NE ' ' AND
1790         SUBSTRING(#ARRAY-2(#I1),20,45) EQ ' '
1800       IF *MACHINE-CLASS EQ 'MAINFRAME'
1810         WRITE (2) NOTITLE
1820           // '*'(34)
```

```
1830                /  'SLOG has been successfully emptied'
1840                /  '*'(34)
1850          ELSE
1860            WRITE (0) NOTITLE
1870              // '*'(34)
1880              /  'SLOG has been successfully emptied'
1890              /  '*'(34)
1900          END-IF
1910          ESCAPE BOTTOM (F3.)
1920        END-IF
1930 ** -
1940      IF  SUBSTRING(#ARRAY-1(#I1),20,45) NE ' ' AND
1950            SUBSTRING(#ARRAY-1(#I1),20,45) EQ
1960            SUBSTRING(#ARRAY-2(#I1),20,45)
1970        IF *MACHINE-CLASS EQ 'MAINFRAME'
1980          WRITE (2) NOTITLE
1990              // '*'(34)
2000              /  'SLOG is not empty - open the destination manually'
2010              /  '*'(34)
2020        ELSE
2030          WRITE (0) NOTITLE
2040              // '*'(34)
2050              /  'SLOG is not empty - open the destination manually'
2060              /  '*'(34)
2070        END-IF
2080        TERMINATE 12
2090      END-IF
2100    END-IF
2110 END-FOR /* (F3.)
2120 ** --
2130 END
```

Figure 207:   Monitor – Natural Program Compare 2 SLOGs

9.5.6 Analyze WCP Log

The program RDWCPLOG (ReaD WCP Log) counts the number of Adabas commands per second in Entire Net-Work log of the client side.

```
Page    1                                             10-09-13  17:23:26

Adabas Calls
Total    per sec
    1        0 15:53:09.068 ba7660 LNK: (EA) ======= New ADABAS call ======= New ADABAS call ==
   77       76 15:53:10.005 ba7560 LNK: (EA) ======= New ADABAS call ======= New ADABAS call ==
  157       80 15:53:11.005 ba7560 LNK: (EA) ======= New ADABAS call ======= New ADABAS call ==
  236       79 15:53:12.005 ba7660 LNK: (EA) ======= New ADABAS call ======= New ADABAS call ==
  313       77 15:53:13.005 4b5ab0 LNK: (EA) ======= New ADABAS call ======= New ADABAS call ==
  393       80 15:53:14.005 4b5ab0 LNK: (EA) ======= New ADABAS call ======= New ADABAS call ==
  470       77 15:53:15.005 4b58b0 LNK: (EA) ======= New ADABAS call ======= New ADABAS call ==
  544       74 15:53:16.005 4b59b0 LNK: (EA) ======= New ADABAS call ======= New ADABAS call ==
  621       77 15:53:17.005 ba7660 LNK: (EA) ======= New ADABAS call ======= New ADABAS call ==
  702       81 15:53:18.005 ba7560 LNK: (EA) ======= New ADABAS call ======= New ADABAS call ==
  782       80 15:53:19.005 ba7560 LNK: (EA) ======= New ADABAS call ======= New ADABAS call ==
  861       79 15:53:20.005 ba7660 LNK: (EA) ======= New ADABAS call ======= New ADABAS call ==
  942       81 15:53:21.005 ba7560 LNK: (EA) ======= New ADABAS call ======= New ADABAS call ==
 1022       80 15:53:22.005 ba7560 LNK: (EA) ======= New ADABAS call ======= New ADABAS call ==
 1100       78 15:53:23.021 4b58b0 LNK: (EA) ======= New ADABAS call ======= New ADABAS call ==
 1179       79 15:53:24.005 4b59b0 LNK: (EA) ======= New ADABAS call ======= New ADABAS call ==
 1258       79 15:53:25.005 4b5ab0 LNK: (EA) ======= New ADABAS call ======= New ADABAS call ==
 1322       64 15:53:26.005 ba7560 LNK: (EA) ======= New ADABAS call ======= New ADABAS call ==
 1378       56 15:53:27.005 4b5ab0 LNK: (EA) ======= New ADABAS call ======= New ADABAS call ==
 1458       80 15:53:28.005 4b5ab0 LNK: (EA) ======= New ADABAS call ======= New ADABAS call ==
 1537       79 15:53:29.005 ba7560 LNK: (EA) ======= New ADABAS call ======= New ADABAS call ==
 1615       78 15:53:30.005 4b58b0 LNK: (EA) ======= New ADABAS call ======= New ADABAS call ==
```

Figure 208:   Monitor – Natural Program Analyze WCP Log

9.5.7   Checksum Program

The program CHECKSUM uses Natural's API to compare two Adabas files.

```
0010 * Sample CHECKSUM
0020 *   1 Provide DBIDs
0030 *   2 Provide file name in #FILE
0040 *   3 provide File Number in #FILE-NBR
0050 *   4 Provide file name in VIEW
0060 *   5 Provide a full DDM definition following VIEW
0070 *   6 Provide the LRECL in #DDM
0080 *
0090 * copy of CHECKSUM as CHKSM006 - File 6
0100 DEFINE DATA LOCAL
0110 1 #DB1 (N5)        INIT <187>                    /* <<<<< 1
0120 1 #DB2 (N5)        INIT <250>                    /* <<<<< 1
0130 1 #FILE-NBR (N5)   INIT <006>                    /* <<<<< 2
0140 1 #FILE (A32)      INIT <'ST-CALC-EDATE'>        /* <<<<< 2
0150 1 DDM   VIEW ST-MC-CALC-EDATE                    /* <<<<< 4
0160   2 LOG-COUNTER         (P15.0)                  /* <<<<< 5
0170   2 ENTITY              (A50)
0180   2 LAST-CHGD-DATE-TIME (A15)
0190   2 LAST-CHGD-USER      (A08)
0200   2 CALC-CODE           (A10)
0210   2 EFF-DATE            (A08)
0220   2 EFF-DATE-9C         (A08)
0230   2 EXP-DATE            (A08)
0240   2 DATA                (A250)
0250                    1 REDEFINE DDM
0260   2 #DDM (A365)                                  /* <<<<< 6
0270 1 #1023
0280   2 FUNC (A1)     INIT <"M">
0290   2 RC (N4)
0300   2 TIME (T)
0310   2 DATE (D)
0320   2 TS (B8)
0330   2 MS (P19)
0340 1 #1040
0350   2 OP (A1)       INIT <'S'>
0360   2 DB (N5)
0370   2 RC (I4)
0380 1 #4011
0390   2 FUNC (I4)
0400   2 CTX (B156)
0410   2 TEXT (A) DYNAMIC
0420   2 HASH (B20)
0430 1 #HASH (B20)
0440 1 #COUNT (P10)
0450 END-DEFINE
0460 *
0470 FORMAT SG=F
0480 *
0490 DEFINE SUBROUTINE HASH-RTN
0500 CALLNAT "USR1040N" #1040
0510 ASSIGN #4011.FUNC = 1
0520 CALLNAT "USR4011N" #4011
0530 ASSIGN #4011.FUNC = 2
0540 ASSIGN #1023.MS   = *CPU-TIME
0550 R.
0560 READ MULTI-FETCH ON DDM BY ISN
0570   ASSIGN #4011.TEXT = #DDM
0580   CALLNAT "USR4011N" #4011
0590 END-READ
0600 ASSIGN #4011.FUNC = 3
0610 CALLNAT "USR4011N" #4011
```

```
0620 ASSIGN #1023.MS = *CPU-TIME - #1023.MS
0630 CALLNAT "USR1023N" #1023
0640 DISPLAY 'DBID'     #1040.DB
0650         'Records'  *COUNTER (R.)
0660         'Checksum' #4011.HASH
0670         'CPU Time' #1023.TIME (EM=HH:II:SS.T)
0680 END-SUBROUTINE
0690 *
0700 AT TOP OF PAGE
0710   WRITE *DAT4U *TIME 'Started'
0720                    *PROGRAM
0730      10X 'Checksum Comparison'
0740    / 10T 'File' #FILE 1X 'File#:' #FILE-NBR
0750    /
0760 END-TOPPAGE
0770 ST.
0780 SET TIME
0790 *
0800 ASSIGN #1040.DB = #DB1
0810 PERFORM HASH-RTN
0820 ASSIGN #HASH = #4011.HASH
0830 ASSIGN #COUNT = *COUNTER (R.)
0840 *
0850 ASSIGN #1040.DB = #DB2
0860 PERFORM HASH-RTN
0870 *
0880 IF  *COUNTER (R.) = #COUNT
0890   THEN
0900     WRITE / T**COUNTER (R.) 'Counters match' (GRI)
0910   ELSE
0920     WRITE / T**COUNTER (R.) '>>>>>  Counters do not match  <<<<<' (REI)
0930 END-IF
0940 IF  #4011.HASH = #HASH
0950   THEN
0960     WRITE / T*#4011.HASH 'Checksums match' (GRI)
0970   ELSE
0980     WRITE / T*#4011.HASH '>>>>>  Checksums do not match  <<<<<' (REI)
0990 END-IF
1000 *
1010
1020
1030 WRITE *DAT4U *TIME 'Ended'
1040    / *TIMD (ST.) (EM=99:99:99'.'9)
1050 END
```

Figure 209:   Monitor – Natural Program Checksum

9.5.8 Compare Amount Fields

```
0010 * **************************************************************
0020 * VERIFY FILE 99 AFTER ADARES
0030 *
0040 * 11/19/2004 VPT
0050 * 09/23/2008 DWS added multi-fetch 100 to the read
0060 * 09/24/2008 DWS changed #multifetch as input value
0070 * 12/15/2008 DWS added display for elapsed time and cpu time
0080 *                cpu time for TSO and batch only
0090 * 12/22/2008 DWS corrected computation for *TIMD (hh:mm:ss.ms)
0100 * 01/05/2009 DWS changed #CTR with *COUNTER
0110 *                added fields LOG-COUNTER and #LOG-COUNTER
0120 * 01/13/2009 LRF CHANGE REPORTING DATE TO HAVE FOUR DIGIT YEAR AND IN
0130 *                FORMAT YYYY/MM/DD
0140 *
0150 * **************************************************************
0160 DEFINE DATA
0170 LOCAL
0180 1 CONTRIB VIEW OF ST-RI-CNTRB-LINE
0190   2 LOG-COUNTER
0200   2 POST-TAX-CNTRB-AMT
0210   2 PRE-TAX-CNTRB-AMT
0220   2 DB-POST-TAX-CNTRB-AMT
0230   2 DB-PRE-TAX-CNTRB-AMT
0240 1 #POST-TAX-CNTRB-AMT    (P12.2)
0250 1 #PRE-TAX-CNTRB-AMT     (P12.2)
0260 1 #DB-POST-TAX-CNTRB-AMT (P12.2)
0270 1 #DB-PRE-TAX-CNTRB-AMT  (P12.2)
0280 1 #LOG-COUNTER           (P15)
0290 1 #MULTIFETCH            (N4)
0300 1 #START-TIME            (A10)
0310 1 #START-DATE            (A10)
0320 1 #CPU-TIME-MS           (N7)         /* in units of 10 ms.
0330 1 #CPU-TIME-HH           (N2)
0340 1 #CPU-TIME-MM           (N2)
0350 1 #CPU-TIME-SS           (N3.2)
0360 1 #DATE10                (A10)
0370 END-DEFINE
0380 *
0390 INPUT #MULTIFETCH
0400 *
0410 ST. SET TIME
0420 *
0430 #START-TIME := *TIME
0440 #START-DATE := *DAT4U
0450 *
0460 AT TOP OF PAGE
0470   MOVE *DAT4I TO #DATE10
0480   EXAMINE FULL #DATE10 '-' REPLACE WITH '/'
0490   WRITE NOTITLE NOHDR 'PAGE: ' *PAGE-NUMBER 55T #DATE10 *TIME (AL=8)
0500 END-TOPPAGE
0510 R1. READ        MULTI-FETCH #MULTIFETCH CONTRIB
0520   ADD POST-TAX-CNTRB-AMT    TO #POST-TAX-CNTRB-AMT
0530   ADD PRE-TAX-CNTRB-AMT     TO #PRE-TAX-CNTRB-AMT
0540   ADD DB-POST-TAX-CNTRB-AMT TO #DB-POST-TAX-CNTRB-AMT
0550   ADD DB-PRE-TAX-CNTRB-AMT  TO #DB-PRE-TAX-CNTRB-AMT
0560   ADD LOG-COUNTER           TO #LOG-COUNTER
0570 END-READ
0580 *
0590 WRITE 'CONTRIBUTION FILE CHECK SUMMARY'
0600 WRITE
0610   2X  'POST-TAX-CNTRB-AMT'
0620   25T #POST-TAX-CNTRB-AMT (EM=ZZZ,ZZZ,ZZZ,ZZ9.99)
0630   / 2X 'PRE-TAX-CNTRB-AMT'
```

```
0640    25T #PRE-TAX-CNTRB-AMT (EM=ZZZ,ZZZ,ZZZ,ZZ9.99)
0650    / 2X 'DB-POST-TAX-CNTRB-AMT'
0660    25T #DB-POST-TAX-CNTRB-AMT (EM=ZZZ,ZZZ,ZZZ,ZZ9.99)
0670    / 2X 'DB-PRE-TAX-CNTRB-AMT'
0680    25T #DB-PRE-TAX-CNTRB-AMT (EM=ZZZ,ZZZ,ZZZ,ZZ9.99)
0690    / 2X 'LOG-COUNTER'
0700    24T #LOG-COUNTER         (EM=ZZZ,ZZZ,ZZZ,ZZZ,ZZ9)
0710    //
0720  **01T 'Records Read: '   16T #CTR (EM=ZZZ,ZZZ,ZZZ,ZZ9)
0730    01T 'Records Read: '   16T *COUNTER (R1.) (EM=ZZZ,ZZZ,ZZZ,ZZ9)
0740    35T 'With Multifetch =' 54T #MULTIFETCH (EM=Z,ZZ9)
0750    /
0760  *
0770  #CPU-TIME-MS := *TIMD(ST.)
0780  ** #CPU-TIME-MS := 189830      /* must be CPU 3min 9.83sec for tests
0790  *
0800  COMPUTE #CPU-TIME-SS = #CPU-TIME-MS * 0.001
0810  COMPUTE #CPU-TIME-MM = #CPU-TIME-MS * 0.001 / 60
0820  COMPUTE #CPU-TIME-HH = #CPU-TIME-MS * 0.001 / 3600
0830  *
0840  COMPUTE #CPU-TIME-MM = #CPU-TIME-MM - (#CPU-TIME-HH * 60)
0850  COMPUTE #CPU-TIME-SS = #CPU-TIME-SS - (#CPU-TIME-MM * 60)
0860  COMPUTE #CPU-TIME-MS = #CPU-TIME-MS - (#CPU-TIME-SS * 60)
0870  *
0880  WRITE 01T 'Times          ' 19T 'HH:MM:SS.T' 35T 'MM/DD/YYYY'
0890    /    01T '-------------' 19T '----------' 35T '----------'
0900    /    01T 'Start Time..:' 19T #START-TIME 35T #START-DATE
0910    /    01T 'END TIME....:' 19T *TIME       35T *DAT4U
0920    /    01T 'Elapsed Time:' 19T *TIMD(ST.) (EM=99:99:99'.'9)
0930    //   01T '-----------------------------------------'
0940    //
0950    01T 'CPU time in milliseconds:'
0960    27T #CPU-TIME-MS (EM=Z,ZZZ,ZZ9)
0970    /
0980    01T 'CPU:'
0990    06T #CPU-TIME-HH (EM=99)
1000    09T 'hours'
1010    15T #CPU-TIME-MM (EM=99)
1020    18T 'min'
1030    22T #CPU-TIME-SS (EM=99.99)
1040    28T 'sec'
1050    /                        /* only tso and batch
1060  *
1070  FETCH RETURN 'USR4004P'      /* display dynamic parms
1080  END
```

Figure 210: Monitor – Natural Program Compare Amount Fields

9.5.9   Parse Adabas Report for RPL Flag

```
** ----------------------------------------------------------------------
** DWSRPLRP: Checks Adabas report for active and inactive replication
**           and creates the following list:
**           FNR   RPL     STATUS     TDB   DSBI
**           ----  ----    --------   ---   ----
**           1     NO      n/a
**           4     YES     active     302   Off
**           9     YES     inactive   302   On
**
** Input:    CMWKF01 - READ WORK 1 -- Adabas report NOFDT,NOSTD
** Ouput:    CMPRT01 - WRITE (1)
*
** Date       Name     Reason for changes
** ---------- -------  -------------------------------------------------
** 2010/02/11 DIETER   created
** 2010/11/15 DIETER   updated for DSBI (log
BI)
**
** ----------------------------------------------------------------------
DEFINE DATA LOCAL
1 #ADAREP-LINE          (A121)
1 REDEFINE #ADAREP-LINE
  2 #ADAREP-LINE-ASA    (A001)
  2 #ADAREP-LINE-TEXT   (A120)
*
1 #FIRST-LINE    (A80)
*
1 #WF2-LINE      (A080)
1 REDEFINE #WF2-LINE
  2 #WF2-FNR       (A04)
  2 #WF2-SPACE1    (A02)
  2 #WF2-RPL       (A03)
  2 #WF2-SPACE2    (A02)
  2 #WF2-ACT-INACT (A08)
  2 #WF2-SPACE3    (A02)
  2 #WF2-TDB       (A03)
  2 #WF2-SPACE4    (A02)
  2 #WF2-DSBI      (A03)     /* before images
**
1 #WF3-OUTPUT    (A080)        /* for work file 3
**
1 #FILE                  (A04/1:999)
1 #RPL                   (A03/1:999)
1 #ACT-INACT             (A08/1:999)
1 #DSBI                  (A03/1:999)
1 #TDB                   (A04/1:999)
1 #I1                    (I4)          /* array counter
1 #NEW-FILE              (L)
**
END-DEFINE
**
**
IF *MACHINE-CLASS NE 'MAINFRAME'
  DEFINE WORK FILE 1 'H:\ADAREP\ADAREP39_20100216.txt'
  DEFINE WORK FILE 2 'H:\ADAREP\adabas-rplactive-rep-20100211.txt'
END-IF
**
IF *MACHINE-CLASS EQ 'MAINFRAME'
  DEFINE PRINTER (1) OUTPUT 'CMPRT01'
END-IF
**
IF *MACHINE-CLASS EQ 'MAINFRAME'
  FORMAT(1) LS=80 PS=50
END-IF
**
** ---------------------------------------------------
** -- Initialize table - all files are not replicated
** ---------------------------------------------------
FOR #I1 = 1 TO 999
  #FILE     (#I1) := ' '
  #RPL      (#I1) := 'NO'
```

```
  #ACT-INACT (#I1) := 'n/a'
  #DSBI      (#I)  := 'OFF'
  #TDB       (#I1) := ' '
END-FOR
#FILE      (1) := 'FNR'
#RPL       (1) := 'RPL'
#ACT-INACT (1) := 'STATUS'
#TDB       (1) := 'TDB'
#DSBI      (1) := 'DSBI'
#FILE      (2) := '----'
#RPL       (2) := '---'
#ACT-INACT (2) := '--------'
#TDB       (2) := '---'
#DSBI      (2) := '----'
**
** -----------------------------------
** -- Read ADAREP report and fill matrix
** -----------------------------------
#I1 := 2
RW1. READ WORK 1 #ADAREP-LINE
** --
  IF SUBSTRING(#ADAREP-LINE-TEXT,1,15) = 'A D A R E P   V'
    #FIRST-LINE := SUBSTRING(#ADAREP-LINE-TEXT,1,80)
    ESCAPE TOP   /* (RW1.)
  END-IF
**
  IF SUBSTRING(#ADAREP-LINE-TEXT,1,7) = '* File '
    #NEW-FILE := TRUE
    ADD 1 TO #I1
    MOVE SUBSTRING(#ADAREP-LINE-TEXT,10,3) TO #FILE(#I1)
    ESCAPE TOP   /* (RW1.)
  END-IF
*
  IF SUBSTRING(#ADAREP-LINE-TEXT,1,20) = 'File is replicated: '
    #RPL (#I1) := 'YES'
    ESCAPE TOP   /* (RW1.)
  END-IF
*
  IF SUBSTRING(#ADAREP-LINE-TEXT,1,41) =
     '  Replication is inactive for this file '
    #ACT-INACT (#I1) := 'inactive'
    ESCAPE TOP   /* (RW1.)
  END-IF
*
  IF SUBSTRING(#ADAREP-LINE-TEXT,1,23) =
     '  Replicator target ID '
    #TDB (#I1) := SUBSTRING(#ADAREP-LINE-TEXT,43,4)
    ESCAPE TOP   /* (RW1.)
  END-IF
*
  IF SUBSTRING(#ADAREP-LINE-TEXT,1,44) =
     '  Collect before images of updates   = Yes '
    #DSBI (#I1) := 'On'
    ESCAPE TOP   /* (RW1.)
  END-IF
*
  IF SUBSTRING(#ADAREP-LINE-TEXT,1,44) =
     '  Collect before images of updates   = No  '
    #DSBI (#I1) := 'Off'
    ESCAPE TOP   /* (RW1.)
  END-IF
END-WORK /* (RW1.)
**                                                       .
** -------------------------------------------
** -- Write report out of matrix
** -------------------------------------------
**
IF *MACHINE-CLASS EQ 'MAINFRAME'
  WRITE (1) NOTITLE NOHDR
    01T '-'(78)
    /
    01T *DATN (EM=9999-99-99) *TIME (AL=8)
    30T 'Adabas Replicator Report'
    68T 'Page' *PAGE-NUMBER (1)
    /
```

```
      01T *PROGRAM
      30T ' '
      68T *LIBRARY-ID
      /
      01T '-'(78)
      /
      01T #FIRST-LINE (AL=79)
ELSE
   #WF2-LINE :=
      '----------------------------------------------------------------
   WRITE WORK FILE 2 #WF2-LINE
*
*    01T *DATN (EM=9999-99-99) *TIME (AL=8)
*    30T 'Adabas Replicator Report'
*    68T 'Page' *PAGE-NUMBER (0)
*    /
*    01T *PROGRAM
*    30T ' '
*    68T *LIBRARY-ID
*    /
*    01T '-'(78)
*    /
   #WF2-LINE := #FIRST-LINE
   WRITE WORK FILE 2 #WF2-LINE
   #WF2-LINE :=
      '----------------------------------------------------------------
   WRITE WORK FILE 2 #WF2-LINE
   #WF2-LINE := ' '
*
END-IF
**
F1. FOR #I1 = 1 TO 999
   IF #FILE(#I1) = ' '
     ESCAPE BOTTOM (F1.)
   END-IF
   IF *MACHINE-CLASS EQ 'MAINFRAME'
     WRITE (1)
       01T #FILE(#I1)
       06T #RPL(#I1)
       10T #ACT-INACT (#I1)
       20T #TDB (#I1)
       26T #DSBI(#I1)
   ELSE
     #WF2-FNR        := #FILE(#I1)
     #WF2-SPACE1     := ' '
     #WF2-RPL        := #RPL(#I1)
     #WF2-SPACE2     := ' '
     #WF2-ACT-INACT  := #ACT-INACT(#I1)
     #WF2-SPACE3     := ' '
     #WF2-TDB        := #TDB(#I1)
     #WF2-SPACE4     := ' '
     #WF2-DSBI       := #DSBI(#I1)
     WRITE WORK FILE 2 #WF2-LINE
   END-IF
END-FOR /* (F1.)
**  ----------------------------------------------------
**  Write Work File 3 with ADADBS commands
**  ADADBS REPLICATION FILE=006,ON,TARGET=302,DSBI=OFF
**  ----------------------------------------------------
F2. FOR #I1 = 1 TO 999
   IF #RPL(#I1) = 'YES' AND #ACT-INACT(#I1) = 'inactive'
     COMPRESS
       'ADADBS REPLICATION FILE='
       #FILE(#I1)
       ',ON,TARGET='
       #TDB(#I1)
       ',DSBI=OFF'
       INTO #WF3-OUTPUT LEAVING NO SPACE
     WRITE WORK FILE 3 #WF3-OUTPUT
   END-IF
END-FOR /* F2.
END
```

Figure 211:   Monitor – Natural Program Parse ADAREP for RPL Flag

9.5.10 Determine Highest ISN Currently Used

```
* -----------------------------------------------------------------------
* ISNHIGH
* This is a common module which finds the highest ISN currently
* used in files
*
* Date          Author            Comments
* ----------    ---------------   ----------------------------------------
* Early 1999  Lewis Pritchard New Module
* 2011/01/28  Dieter Storr    adapted for a client
* 2011/03/25  Larry Frazin    modified to look for all files in a
*                             specified database requested by INPUT
*                             Statement. Does a direct call LF to
*                             determine file exists, and if exists
*                             follows with a 2nd direct call L1 with
*                             'S' in CB-COP2 to get the first unused
*                             ISN, subtract 1 from the results, and
*                             the results is the last used ISN. Note:
*                             is not necessarily the highest ISN
*                             record loaded.
*
* --------------------------------------------------------------
DEFINE DATA LOCAL
1 #HIGHEST-ISN    (P10)
/***********************************************************************
/*  COPIED FROM USR1043P LIBRARY SYSEXT
/*  This program serves as example how to design a user-defined
/*  program to call 'USR1043N'.
/***********************************************************************
LOCAL
 1 CONTROL-BLOCK   (A80)
 1 REDEFINE CONTROL-BLOCK
   2 CB-RESERVED  (B02)     /* Reserved
   2 REDEFINE CB-RESERVED
     3 FIRST-BYTE (B01)     /* H'30' for 2 byte files
   2 CB-CMD       (A02)     /* Command code
   2 CB-CID       (A04)     /* Command ID
   2 CB-FILE      (B02)     /* 2 byte file number
   2 REDEFINE CB-FILE
     3 CB-DBID     (B01)    /* Data base ID
     3 CB-FNR      (B01)    /* File number
   2 CB-RSP       (B02)     /* Response code / 2 byte DBID
   2 REDEFINE CB-RSP
     3 CB-DBID-ALT(B02)     /* Data base ID (alternate)
   2 CB-ISN       (B04)     /* ISN
   2 CB-ISL       (B04)     /* ISN lower limit
   2 CB-ISQ       (B04)     /* ISN quantity
   2 CB-FBL       (B02)     /* Format buffer length
   2 CB-RBL       (B02)     /* Record buffer length
   2 CB-SBL       (B02)     /* Search buffer length
   2 CB-VBL       (B02)     /* Value  buffer length
   2 CB-IBL       (B02)     /* ISN    buffer length
   2 CB-COP1      (A01)     /* Command option 1
   2 CB-COP2      (A01)     /* Command option 2
   2 CB-ADD1      (A08)     /* Additions 1
   2 CB-ADD2      (A04)     /* Additions 2
   2 REDEFINE CB-ADD2
     3 CB-ADD2-2X (A02)
     3 CB-SUB-CODE(B02)     /* Sub Code results
   2 CB-ADD3      (A08)     /* Additions 3
   2 CB-ADD4      (A08)     /* Additions 4
   2 CB-ADD5      (A08)     /* Additions 5
   2 CB-CT        (A04)     /* Command time
   2 CB-UA        (A04)     /* User area
 /*
```

```
 1 FORMAT-BUFFER (A1000)      /* LENGTH OF BUFFER CAN BE MODIFIED
 1 REDEFINE FORMAT-BUFFER
   2 FORMAT-ADDR (A01)
 /*
 1 RECORD-BUFFER (A5000)      /* LENGTH OF BUFFER CAN BE MODIFIED
 1 REDEFINE RECORD-BUFFER
   2 RECORD-ADDR (A01)
 /*
 1 SEARCH-BUFFER (A1000)      /* LENGTH OF BUFFER CAN BE MODIFIED
 1 REDEFINE SEARCH-BUFFER
   2 SEARCH-ADDR (A01)
 /*
 1 VALUE-BUFFER  (A1000)      /* LENGTH OF BUFFER CAN BE MODIFIED
 1 REDEFINE VALUE-BUFFER
   2 VALUE-ADDR  (A01)
 /*
 1 ISN-BUFFER    (A1000)      /* LENGTH OF BUFFER CAN BE MODIFIED
 1 REDEFINE ISN-BUFFER
   2 ISN-ADDR    (A01)
 /*
 1 RESPONSE      (I04)
*
 1 #FILE-NR      (N05)
 1 #X            (A02)
 1 #DBID         (N05)
 1 #FIRST-FILE   (N05)
 1 #NO-OF-FILES  (N04)
END-DEFINE
*
INPUT 'Enter DBID:'  #DBID
      'Starting FNR:' #FIRST-FILE
      'No. of files:' #NO-OF-FILES
*
IF #DBID = 0
   REINPUT 'DBID is 0, please enter a non-zero value'
END-IF
*
IF #FIRST-FILE = 0
   #FIRST-FILE := 1
   WRITE 'First file was not provided, assumed start with file 1'
END-IF
*
IF #NO-OF-FILES = 0
   #NO-OF-FILES := 10
   WRITE 'No. of files was not provided, assume next 10 files from 1st'
         'file will be displayed'
END-IF
MOVE ALL H'00' TO CONTROL-BLOCK
MOVE     H'30' TO FIRST-BYTE
MOVE       'OP' TO CB-CMD
MOVE 5000 TO CB-RBL
MOVE 1000 TO CB-ISL CB-FBL CB-SBL CB-VBL CB-IBL
MOVE 'ACC=.' TO RECORD-BUFFER
RESET CB-ADD1 CB-ADD2 CB-ADD3 CB-ADD4 CB-ADD5
PERFORM CALL-ADABAS
*
* <----------------------- start here
* WRITE 'OP CMD RC:' RESPONSE
*
FOR #FILE-NR FROM #FIRST-FILE TO #NO-OF-FILES
*
CB-FILE := #FILE-NR
CB-CMD  := 'LF'
CB-COP2 := 'S'
*
PERFORM CALL-ADABAS
IF RESPONSE = 17 OR = 200
   ESCAPE TOP
END-IF
```

```
R.  REPEAT
      CB-CMD := 'L1'
      CB-COP2:= 'F'
     PERFORM CALL-ADABAS
      DECIDE FOR FIRST CONDITION
        WHEN RESPONSE = 17 OR = 113 OR = 200
             ESCAPE BOTTOM (R.)
        WHEN RESPONSE = 0
             IGNORE
        WHEN NONE
             WRITE '=' RESPONSE 'FNR:' #FILE-NR
      END-DECIDE
*
         #HIGHEST-ISN    := CB-ISN
         #HIGHEST-ISN    := #HIGHEST-ISN - 1
         WRITE 'DBID:' #DBID 'FNR:' #FILE-NR 'HIGHEST ISN:' #HIGHEST-ISN
         ESCAPE BOTTOM
     END-REPEAT
END-FOR
*
* -----------------------------------------------------------
DEFINE SUBROUTINE CALL-ADABAS
*
MOVE #DBID TO CB-DBID-ALT
*
CALLNAT 'USR1043N'
  CONTROL-BLOCK
  FORMAT-ADDR
  RECORD-ADDR
  SEARCH-ADDR
  VALUE-ADDR
  ISN-ADDR
  RESPONSE
*
DECIDE FOR FIRST CONDITION
WHEN RESPONSE = 17
   WRITE 'THIS FILE DOESN"T EXIST:' #FILE-NR
WHEN RESPONSE = 113
   WRITE 'THIS ISN DOESN"T EXIST:'  #FILE-NR
WHEN RESPONSE = 200
   WRITE 'No access to this file:'  #FILE-NR
WHEN RESPONSE NE 0
  WRITE 'ADABAS Response Code:' RESPONSE '=' CB-CMD 'FNR:' #FILE-NR
      / 'sc:' CB-SUB-CODE
WHEN NONE
  IGNORE
END-DECIDE
END-SUBROUTINE
* -----------------------------------------------------------
END
```

Figure 212:   Monitor – Natural Program ISNHIGH – Check Highest ISN

9.5.11   RPL30REP – SLOG Check

```
** ---------------------------------------------------------------------
**            EVENT REPLICATOR Performance Project
** RPL30REP: Read the Adabas report of file 30, DB312, created by
**            SYSAOS in batch
** Input:    CMWKF01 - READ WORK 1
**            SYSAOS report of file 30 (SLOG)
**            Mainframe: ST.ADADBA.REPF30.DB312
**            Windows:   Z:\Replicator\xxx.txt
** Output:   CMWKF02 - WRITE WORK 2
**            Mainframe: DIETER.RPFF30.DB312
**            Windows:   Z:\Replicator\zzz.txt
** Process:  Check the Adabas SLOG ADAREP report for:
**            - High record usage
**            - High space usage
** Array:    Relevant Adabas Report lines: REPLINES(1:99)
**
** Date         Name    Reason for changes
** ----------   ------  --------------------------------------------------
** 2010-12-16  DSTORR   created
**
** ---------------------------------------------------------------------
DEFINE DATA LOCAL
** -- Input Work File
1 #INPUT            (A133)
1 REDEFINE #INPUT
  2 #ASA            (A01)
  2 #ADALOG-LINE    (A132)
1 #INFO-LINE        (A080)
** -- Output Work File
1 #REPLINES         (A133/1:500)
1 #FOUND1           (N2)
1 #FOUND2           (N2)
1 #FOUND3           (N2)
1 #FOUND4           (N2)
1 #FOUND5           (N2)
1 #FOUND6           (N2)
1 #FOUND7           (N2)
1 #I                (P10)
1 #START-REP        (L)
*
END-DEFINE
**
IF *MACHINE-CLASS NE 'MAINFRAME'        /** for tests on a PC
  DEFINE WORK FILE 1 'Z:\Replicator\**'
  DEFINE WORK FILE 2 'Z:\Replicator\**'
END-IF
**
ON ERROR
  *ERROR-TA := 'PER-PERR'
END-ERROR
**
** -----------------------------------------
** -- Read statistics and fill array
** -----------------------------------------
** --
#START-REP := FALSE
RW1.
READ WORK 1 #ADALOG-LINE
** --
  IF #START-REP = FALSE
    EXAMINE #ADALOG-LINE FOR '***** A D A B A S  BASIC  SERVICES *****'
      GIVING #FOUND1
```

```
     IF #FOUND1 GT 0
       #START-REP := TRUE
       #I := 1
       #REPLINES(#I) := #ADALOG-LINE
       ADD 1 TO #I
       ESCAPE TOP /* (RW1.)
     END-IF
   END-IF
*
   IF #START-REP = TRUE
     EXAMINE #ADALOG-LINE FOR '- Display File Layout -'
       GIVING #FOUND2
     IF #FOUND2 GT 0
       #START-REP := TRUE
       #REPLINES(#I) := #ADALOG-LINE
       ADD 1 TO #I
       ESCAPE TOP /* (RW1.)
     END-IF
*
     EXAMINE #ADALOG-LINE FOR 'DATAI '
       GIVING #FOUND3
     IF #FOUND3 GT 0
       #START-REP := FALSE
       #REPLINES(#I) := #ADALOG-LINE
       ESCAPE BOTTOM /* (R1.)
     END-IF
*
     #REPLINES(#I) := #ADALOG-LINE
     ADD 1 TO #I
   END-IF
**
END-WORK
*
FOR1. FOR #I = 1 TO 500
   IF #REPLINES(#I) = ' '
     ESCAPE BOTTOM
   END-IF
   WRITE WORK FILE 2 #REPLINES(#I)
END-FOR  /* (FOR1.)
**
** -----------------------------------------------
** -- Check array for records loaded and space usage
** -----------------------------------------------
**
COMPRESS
   *DAT4I '-' *TIME '- Report of SLOG File 30 DB312 - ' *PROGRAM
   INTO #INFO-LINE
WRITE WORK FILE 3 #INFO-LINE
**
FOR2. FOR #I = 1 TO 500
   IF #REPLINES(#I) = ' '
     ESCAPE BOTTOM
   END-IF
**
   EXAMINE #REPLINES(#I) FOR 'Records loaded'
     GIVING #FOUND4
   IF #FOUND4 GT 0
     #INFO-LINE := SUBSTRING(#REPLINES(#I),4,32)
     WRITE WORK FILE 3 #INFO-LINE
   END-IF
**
   EXAMINE #REPLINES(#I) FOR 'ASSOI 3390 UII'
     GIVING #FOUND5
```

```
  IF #FOUND5 GT 0
    COMPRESS
      'UI space allocated (blk):'
      SUBSTRING(#REPLINES(#I),17,08)
      'UI space unused (blk):'
      SUBSTRING(#REPLINES(#I),63,08)
      INTO  #INFO-LINE
    WRITE WORK FILE 3 #INFO-LINE
  END-IF
**
  EXAMINE #REPLINES(#I) FOR 'ASSOI 3390 NII'
    GIVING #FOUND6
  IF #FOUND6 GT 0
    COMPRESS
      'NI space allocated (blk):'
      SUBSTRING(#REPLINES(#I),17,08)
      'NI space unused (blk):'
      SUBSTRING(#REPLINES(#I),63,08)
      INTO  #INFO-LINE
    WRITE WORK FILE 3 #INFO-LINE
  END-IF
**
  EXAMINE #REPLINES(#I) FOR 'DATAI 3390 DSI'
    GIVING #FOUND7
  IF #FOUND7 GT 0
    COMPRESS
      'DS space allocated (blk):'
      SUBSTRING(#REPLINES(#I),17,08)
      'DS space unused (blk):'
      SUBSTRING(#REPLINES(#I),63,08)
      INTO  #INFO-LINE
    WRITE WORK FILE 3 #INFO-LINE
  END-IF
END-FOR /* (FOR2.)
**
END
```

Figure 213: Monitor – Natural Program RPL30REP – SLOG Space Check

9.5.12 READF30P – Read SLOG Content

```
0010 ** --------------------------------------------------------------------
0020 ** READF30P:  READ SLOG, file 30 of Reptor DB 312
0030 **            Written by Dieter Storr - 14 December 2010
0040 ** --------------------------------------------------------------------
0050 DEFINE DATA LOCAL
0060 1 ST-SLOG VIEW OF ST-SLOG-312    /* DB312 fix
0070    2 AA-FIELD
0080    2 AB-FIELD
0090    2 AC-FIELD
0100    2 AD-FIELD
0110    2 AE-FIELD
0120    2 AF-FIELD
0130    2 AG-FIELD
0140    2 AH-FIELD                /* 250
0150    2 C*AN-FIELD
0160    2 AN-FIELD (1:10)
0170    2 AQ-FIELD
0180    2 C*AR-FIELD
0190    2 AR-FIELD (1:10)
0200    2 BA-FIELD
0210    2 C*BB-FIELD
0220    2 BB-FIELD (1:10)         /* A250
0230 *
0240 1 I          (P10)
0250 1 #PO        (N4)
0260 1 COUNT      (N4)
0270 1 BB-OUT     (A16)
0280 1 #FILE-COUNT (N4)
0290 1 #READ-COUNT (N10)
0300 1 #STRING    (A50)
0310 1 #LOOP      (N05)
0320 1 #DELAY     (I2) INIT <1>
0330 *
0340 END-DEFINE
0350 **
0360 AT TOP OF PAGE
0370    WRITE '      File Name      ISN SLOG'
0380    /    '-------------------- --------'
0390    /
0400 END-TOPPAGE
0410 **
0420 R1. READ          ST-SLOG BY ISN STARTING FROM 1
0430    EXAMINE BB-FIELD(2) FOR 'ST-' GIVING POSITION IN #PO
0440    IF #PO GT 0 THEN
0450      MOVE SUBSTRING(BB-FIELD(2),#PO) TO BB-OUT
0460       WRITE BB-OUT *ISN
0470    END-IF
0480    ADD 1 TO #READ-COUNT
     ***
0600 END-READ
0610 IF *COUNTER (R1.) = 0
0620    WRITE (0) 'No records found in SLOG file 30 in DB 312'
0630 ELSE
0640    WRITE (0) 'Number of transactions in SLOG:' #READ-COUNT
0650 END-IF
0660 END
```

Figure 214:   Monitor – Natural Program READF30P – Read SLOG Content

9.5.13 RPL-P002 – Compare File Components

```
0010 ** ------------------------------------------------------------------------
0020 **            EVENT REPLICATOR Performance Project
0030 ** RPL-P002: Read the Adabas Report from the mainframe
0040 **            Read the Adabas Report from the server
0050 ** Input:    CMWKF01 - READ WORK 1
0060 **            CMWKF02 - READ WORK 2
0070 **            REPLICATOR reports
0080 **            Mainframe: ST.DBA.TDC.RPLPMPMB.DDPRINT.FEB0109.OUTLIST
0090 **            Windows:   Z:\Replicator\RPLPMPMB_stat_20090201.txt
0100 ** Ouput:    CMWKF03 - WRITE WORK 3 - EXCEL format
0110 ** Process:  Get the values for
0120 **             - DBID or Database
0130 **             - File
0140 **             - Records loaded
0150 **             - TOP ISN or Top ISN
0160 **             - MAXISN or Maximum ISN expected
0170 **
0180 ** Array:    DBID(1:999) - FNR (1:999)
0190 **
0200 ** Date       Name    Reason for changes
0210 ** ----------  ------  ------------------------------------------------
0220 ** 2011-01-26  DSTORR  created
0230 **
0240 ** ------------------------------------------------------------------------
0250 DEFINE DATA LOCAL
0260 ** -- Input Work File
0270 1 #ADAREP-LINE      (A133)
0280 **
0290 1 #OUTPUT-LINE      (A120)
0300 **
0310 1 #DBID1            (A03)
0320 1 #DBID2            (A03)
0330 1 #RECLOD-DB1       (A12/1:999)      /* FNR is offset
0340 1 #RECLOD-DB2       (A12/1:999)
0350 1 #TOPISN-DB1       (A12/1:999)      /* FNR is offset
0360 1 #TOPISN-DB2       (A12/1:999)
0370 1 #MAXISN-DB1       (A12/1:999)      /* FNR is offset
0380 1 #MAXISN-DB2       (A12/1:999)
0390 ** --
0400 01 #I-FNR-ALP   (A3)
0410 01 #I-FNR-NUM   (N3)
0420 01 #I           (N6)
0430 *
0440 **
0450 END-DEFINE
0460 **
0470 IF *MACHINE-CLASS NE 'MAINFRAME'
0480   DEFINE WORK FILE 1 'Z:\ADAREP\ADAREP39_FILE_RPL_20110127.txt'  /* DB039
0490   DEFINE WORK FILE 2 'Z:\ADAREP\CST008 DB 251 ADAREP 20110127.txt'  /* DB251
0500   DEFINE WORK FILE 3 'Z:\ADAREP\DB039_DB251_COMPARISON_20110127.txt' /* out
0510 END-IF
0520 **
0530 ON ERROR
0540   *ERROR-TA := 'PER-PERR'
0550 END-ERROR
0560 **
0570 ** -----------------------------------------
0580 ** -- Read Adarep Mainframe and fill array
0590 ** -----------------------------------------
0600 ** --
0610 RW1.
0620 READ WORK 1 #ADAREP-LINE       /* read one ADAREP mainframe
0630 ** --
0640   IF  SUBSTRING(#ADAREP-LINE,02,32) = 'A D A R E P   V8.1  SM3   DBID ='
0650     #DBID1 := SUBSTRING(#ADAREP-LINE,37,3)
0660     ESCAPE TOP
0670   END-IF
```

```
0680   IF  SUBSTRING(#ADAREP-LINE,02,09) = '* File   '    /* keep the blanks
0690     #I-FNR-ALP := SUBSTRING(#ADAREP-LINE,11,3)
0700     #I-FNR-NUM := VAL(#I-FNR-ALP)
0710   END-IF
0720   IF  SUBSTRING(#ADAREP-LINE,02,20) = 'TOP-ISN              ='
0730     #TOPISN-DB1(#I-FNR-NUM) := SUBSTRING(#ADAREP-LINE,24,12)
0740   END-IF
0750   IF  SUBSTRING(#ADAREP-LINE,02,20) = 'MAX-ISN Expected   ='
0760     #MAXISN-DB1(#I-FNR-NUM) := SUBSTRING(#ADAREP-LINE,24,12)
0770   END-IF
0780   IF  SUBSTRING(#ADAREP-LINE,02,20) = 'Records Loaded     ='
0790     #RECLOD-DB1(#I-FNR-NUM) := SUBSTRING(#ADAREP-LINE,24,12)
0800   END-IF
0810 END-WORK
0820 **
0830 ** --------------- 2nd report
0840 RW2.
0850 READ WORK 2 #ADAREP-LINE      /* read one ADAREP server
0860 ** --
0870   IF  SUBSTRING(#ADAREP-LINE,01,24) = '%ADAREP-I-DBON, database'
0880     #DBID2 := SUBSTRING(#ADAREP-LINE,26,3)
0890     ESCAPE TOP
0900   END-IF
0910   IF  SUBSTRING(#ADAREP-LINE,13,07) = ', File '
0920     #I-FNR-ALP := SUBSTRING(#ADAREP-LINE,22,3)
0930     #I-FNR-NUM := VAL(#I-FNR-ALP)
0940     ESCAPE TOP
0950   END-IF
0960   IF  SUBSTRING(#ADAREP-LINE,01,09) = 'Top ISN: '
0970     #TOPISN-DB2(#I-FNR-NUM) := SUBSTRING(#ADAREP-LINE,20,12)
0980   END-IF
0990   IF  SUBSTRING(#ADAREP-LINE,37,21) = 'Maximum ISN expected:'
1000     #MAXISN-DB2(#I-FNR-NUM) := SUBSTRING(#ADAREP-LINE,68,12)
1010   END-IF
1020   IF  SUBSTRING(#ADAREP-LINE,01,15) = 'Records loaded:'
1030     #RECLOD-DB2(#I-FNR-NUM) := SUBSTRING(#ADAREP-LINE,20,12)
1040   END-IF
1050 *
1060 END-WORK
1070 **
1080 COMPRESS FULL
1090   'FILE-NR'
1100   ' TOPISN'   #DBID1
1110   '  TOPISN'  #DBID2
1120   '  RECLOD'  #DBID1
1130   '  RECLOD'  #DBID2
1140   '  MAXISN'  #DBID1
1150   '  MAXISN'  #DBID2
1160   INTO #OUTPUT-LINE
1170 WRITE WORK 3 #OUTPUT-LINE
1180 **
1190 COMPRESS FULL
1200   '------- ---------- ---------- ---------- ---------- ---------- ----------'
1210
1220   INTO #OUTPUT-LINE
1230 WRITE WORK 3 #OUTPUT-LINE
1240 **
1250 F1.
1260 FOR #I = 1 TO 999
1270   IF  #TOPISN-DB1(#I) = ' ' AND
1280       #TOPISN-DB2(#I) = ' ' AND
1290       #RECLOD-DB1(#I) = ' ' AND
1300       #RECLOD-DB2(#I) = ' ' AND
1310       #MAXISN-DB1(#I) = ' ' AND
1320       #MAXISN-DB2(#I) = ' '
1330     ESCAPE TOP
1340   END-IF
1350   COMPRESS FULL
1360     #I
1370     #TOPISN-DB1(#I)
```

```
1380     #TOPISN-DB2(#I)
1390     #RECLOD-DB1(#I)
1400     #RECLOD-DB2(#I)
1410     #MAXISN-DB1(#I)
1420     #MAXISN-DB2(#I)
1430     INTO #OUTPUT-LINE
1440   WRITE WORK 3 #OUTPUT-LINE
1450 END-FOR
1460 END
```

Figure 215:   Monitor – Natural Program RPL-P002 – Compare File Components

9.6   WCP Log Windows

```
15:53:08.630 ba7560 LNK: (EA) ======= New ADABAS call ======= New ADABAS call =======
15:53:08.630 ba7560 LNK: (EA) - ACB content Length=80/0x50 Buffer=0xbe68a8
    0000:  3040D5F2 44CC6660 009000FB 000306DE  0@ÕòDÌf`...û...Þ   . N2...-........
    0010:  00000000 00000000 02CB0333 00000000  .........Ë.3....   ...............
    0020:  00004040 40404040 40404040 40404040  ..@@@@@@@@@@@@@@   ..
    0030:  40404040 40404040 40404040 40404040  @@@@@@@@@@@@@@@@
    0040:  00000000 00000000 00000000 00000000  ................   ...............
15:53:08.630 ba7560 LNK: (EA) - EACB content Length=68/0x44 Buffer=0x140fec0
    0000:  0101FB00 04180001 CB023303 00000000  ..û.....Ë.3....   ...............
    0010:  00000000 00000000 0000885C 00000000  ...........\....   ...........h*....
    0020:  60EA0000 02001800 C0DC4200 C0DC4200  `ê......ÀÛB.ÀÛB.   -.......{...{...
    0030:  C68EB2A8 E50C8606 D9C5D7D3 00000000  ÆŽ²¨å.†.ÙÀ×Ó....   F..yV.f.REPL....
    0040:  00000000                             ....              ....
15:53:08.630 ba7560 LNK: (FIRST) thread block 00BE24D0
15:53:08.630 ba7560 LNK: (FIRST) thread block 00BE24D0
15:53:08.630 ba7560 LNK: Set ID - thread 00BE24D0
15:53:08.630 ba7560 LNK: Set ID ADAID_T Length=24/0x18 Buffer=0x140fee4
    0000:  02001800 C0DC4200 C0DC4200 C68EB2A8  ....ÀÛB.ÀÛB.ÆŽ²¨   {...{...F..y
    0010:  E50C8606 D9C5D7D3                     å.†.ÙÀ×Ó          V.f.REPL
15:53:08.630 ba7560 LNK: Set ID - UID <ÀÛB>
15:53:08.630 ba7560 LNK: (SU) UID len 3 MAX 64
15:53:08.630 ba7560 LNK: (SU) UID-dmp Length=3/0x3 Buffer=0x140fcac
    0000:  C0DC42                               ÀÛB               {..
15:53:08.630 ba7560 LNK: (SU) Reusing last UID 004BBFEC
15:53:08.630 ba7560 LNK: (EA) - Call, DBID 251
15:53:08.630 ba7560 LNK: (AC) Alloc CTX (00BBA1E8-004BBFF4)
15:53:08.630 ba7560 LNK: (AC) Alloc CTX (00BBA1E8-004BBFF4|251-251)
15:53:08.630 ba7560 LNK: (AC) CTX-dmp Length=28/0x1c Buffer=0xbba1e8
    0000:  F4BF4B00 F4BF4B00 00000000 00000000  ô¿K.ô¿K.........   4...4...........
    0010:  01000000 FB000000 04000000           .....û.......     ...........
15:53:08.630 ba7560 LNK: (AC) Reusing CTX 00BBA1E8 DBID 251
15:53:08.630 ba7560 LNK: (EA) - THREAD content with Buffer Addresses Length=11484/0x2cdc Buf-
fer=0xbe24d0
    0000:  6B000000 00000000 ECBF4B00 B851BE00  k.......ì¿K..Q½.   ,..............
    0010:  C052BE00 FB000000 02001800 C0DC4200  ÀR½.û.......ÀÛB.   {...........{...
    0020:  C0DC4200 C68EB2A8 E50C8606 D9C5D7D3  ÀÛB.ÆŽ²¨å.†.ÙÀ×Ó   {...F..yV.f.REPL
    0030:  00000000 00000000 00000000 00000000  ................   ...............
    LINES 0040-2B80 SAME AS LINE 0030
    2B90:  00000000 00000000 A868BE00 F868BE00  ........¨h½.øh½.   .......y...8...
    2BA0:  C36BBE00 00000000 00000000 00000000  Ãk½............   C,.............
    2BB0:  00000000 00000000 00000000 00000000  ................   ...............
    2BC0:  00000000 00000000 00000000 00000000  ................   ...............
    2BD0:  00000000 00000000 00000000 C853BE00  ............ÈS½.   ............H...
    2BE0:  04000000 00000000 00000000 00000000  ................   ...............
    2BF0:  00000000 00000000 00000000 00000000  ................   ...............
    LINES 2C00-2CB0 SAME AS LINE 2BF0
    2CC0:  00000000 00000000 00000000 362E312E  ............6.1.   ...............
    2CD0:  382E3033 00000000 0000000F           8.03.......       ...............
15:53:08.630 ba7560 LCL: ======= Start LCL call ======= Start LCL call =======
15:53:08.630 ba7560 LCL: pThb 00BE24D0
15:53:08.630 ba7560 LCL: (CVT-IN) EBCDIC -> ASCII conversion required
15:53:08.630 ba7560 LCL: (CVT-IN) BYTE ORDER conversion required
15:53:08.630 ba7560 LCL: (CVT-IN) CB in Length=80/0x50 Buffer=0xbe68a8
    0000:  3040D5F2 44CC6660 00900094 000306DE  0@ÕòDÌf`..."..Þ   . N2...-...m....
    0010:  00000000 00000000 02CB0333 00000000  .........Ë.3....   ...............
    0020:  00004040 40404040 40404040 40404040  ..@@@@@@@@@@@@@@   ..
```

```
     0030:   40404040 40404040 40404040 40404040   @@@@@@@@@@@@@@@@
     0040:   00000000 00000000 00000000 00000000   ................  ................
15:53:08.630 ba7560 LCL: (CVT-IN) CB out Length=80/0x50 Buffer=0xbe68a8
     0000:   30404E32 6066CC44 90009400 DE060300   0@N2`fÌD..".Þ...   . +.-.....m....
     0010:   00000000 00000000 CB023303 00000000   ........Ë.3.....  ................
     0020:   00002020 20202020 20202020 20202020   ..                ................
     0030:   20202020 20202020 20202020 20202020                      ................
     0040:   00000000 00000000 00000000 00000000   ................  ................
15:53:08.630 ba7560 LCL: pCb 00BE68A8
15:53:08.630 ba7560 LCL: CB (IN) Length=80/0x50 Buffer=0xbe68a8
     0000:   30404E32 6066CC44 90009400 DE060300   0@N2`fÌD..".Þ...   . +.-.....m....
     0010:   00000000 00000000 CB023303 00000000   ........Ë.3.....  ................
     0020:   00002020 20202020 20202020 20202020   ..                ................
     0030:   20202020 20202020 20202020 20202020                      ................
     0040:   00000000 00000000 00000000 00000000   ................  ................
15:53:08.630 ba7560 LCL: set_ada_id_done to CE_TRUE
15:53:08.630 ba7560 LCL: DBID 251 DBINFO at 00BE5F8C
15:53:08.630 ba7560 LCL: DBID 251 found at 00BE5F8C
15:53:08.630 ba7560 LCL: DBINFO: dbid 251 usripc hdl 00BE6010
15:53:08.630 ba7560 LCL: hash index 19, command N2
15:53:08.630 ba7560 LCL: s2s4: input bitmap  0003
15:53:08.630 ba7560 LCL:      output bitmap  0003
15:53:08.630 ba7560 LCL: s1s3: input bitmap  0003
15:53:08.630 ba7560 LCL:      output bitmap  0003
15:53:08.630 ba7560 LCL: s2s4: input bitmap  0000
15:53:08.630 ba7560 LCL:      output bitmap  0000
15:53:08.630 ba7560 LCL: Used buffer bits: <IN> 03 <OUT> 00
15:53:08.630 ba7560 LCL: verify: buffer mask 0003
15:53:08.630 ba7560 LCL: command type 2
15:53:08.630 ba7560 LCL: writeusr: DBID 251
15:53:08.630 ba7560 LCL: (I): major = 6, minor = 1, sml = 8, pl = 3
15:53:08.630 ba7560 LCL: openusr: DBID 251 valid_vers = 1
15:53:08.630 ba7560 LCL: Input FB Length=715/0x2cb Buffer=0xbe68f8
     0000:   C1C16BF8 6BD76BC1 C26BF5F0 6BC16BC1   ÁÁk⌀k×ÁÁkⵋkÁkÁ    AA,8,P,AB,50,A,A
     0010:   C36BF1F5 6BC16BC1 C46BF86B C16BC1C5   ÃkñⵋkÁÁkⵋkÁÁk    C,15,A,AD,8,A,AE
     0020:   6BF16BC1 6BC1C66B F16BC16B D4C16BF1   kñkÁkÁÆkñkÁkÔÁkñ   ,1,A,AF,1,A,MA,1
     0030:   6BC16BD4 C26BF1F0 6BC16BC1 C96BF1F0   kÁkÔÁkñⵋkÁÉkñⵋ    ,A,MB,10,A,AI,10
     0040:   6BC16BC1 D16BF1F0 6BC16BC1 D26BF16B   kÁkÁÑkñⵋkÁÒkñk    ,A,AJ,10,A,AK,1,
     0050:   C16BC1D3 6BF16BC1 6BC1D46B F16BC16B   ÁkÁÓkñⵋkÁÔkñkⵋ    A,AL,1,A,AM,1,A,
     0060:   C1D56BF8 6BC16BC1 D66BF26B C16BC4E6   ÁÕkⵋkÁkÁÖkⵈkÁkÄæ  AN,8,A,AO,2,A,DW
     0070:   6BF46BC1 6BC1D76B F1F06BC1 6BC1D86B   k×kÁⵋkñðkÁⵋkⵋk    ,4,A,AP,10,A,AQ,
     0080:   F16BC16B C1D96BF9 6BC16BC1 E26BF3F0   ñkÁkÁÙküⵋkÁⵋkⵓð   1,A,AR,9,A,AS,30
     0090:   6BC16BC1 E36BF3F0 6BC16BC1 E46BF66B   kÁkÁⵓⵓðkÁⵋkⵖk     ,A,AT,30,A,AU,6,
     00A0:   C16BC1E5 6BF26BC1 6BC1E66B F1F06BC1   ÁkÁⵕkⵈⵋkÁⵖkñðkÁ    A,AV,2,A,AW,10,A
     00B0:   C1E76B6B F16BC16B C1E86BF1 F06BC16B   ÁⵗkkñkⵋkÁⵘkñðkⵋk  ,AX,1,A,AY,10,A,
     00C0:   C1E96BF2 6BC16BC2 C16BF86B D76BC2C2   ÁⵙkⵈkÁkⵄⵋkⵋk×kⵄⵄ  AZ,2,A,BA,8,P,BB
     00D0:   6BF1F06B C16BC2C3 6BF16BC1 6BC2C46B   kñðkÁkⵄⵓkñⵋkⵄⵖk   ,10,A,BC,1,A,BD,
     00E0:   F76BD76B C2C56BF1 F06BC16B C2C66BF1   ÷k×kⵄⵕkññðkⵋkⵄⵖkñ  7,P,BE,10,A,BF,1
     00F0:   6BC16BC2 C76BF1F0 6BC16BC2 C86BF46B   kÁkⵄⵗkñðkÁkⵄⵘk×k   ,A,BG,10,A,BH,4,
     0100:   C16BC2C9 6BF46BE4 6BC2D16B F76BD76B   Ákⵄⵙk×kⵤkⵄⵑk÷k×k   A,BI,4,U,BJ,7,P,
     0110:   C2D26BF4 6BE46BC2 D36BF76B D76BC5C3   ⵄⵒk×kⵤkⵄⵓkñ÷k×kⵕⵓ  BK,4,U,BL,7,P,EC
     0120:   6BF46BE4 6BC5C46B F76BD76B C5C56BF4   k×kⵤkⵕⵖk÷k×kⵕⵕk×   ,4,U,ED,7,P,EE,4
     0130:   6BE46BC5 C66BF76B D76BC5C7 6BF46BE4   kⵤkⵕⵖkñ÷k×kⵕⵗkⵈk×  ,U,EF,7,P,EG,4,U
     0140:   6BC5C86B F76BD76B C5C96BF4 6BE46BC5   kⵕⵘkñ÷k×kⵕⵙk×kⵤkⵕ  ,EH,7,P,EI,4,U,E
     0150:   D16BF76B D76BC2D4 6BF86BC1 6BC2D56B   ⵑkñ÷k×kⵄⵔkⵋkⵋk⵵ⵑk  J,7,P,BM,8,A,BN,
     0160:   F86BC16B C2D66BF8 6BC16BC2 D76BF56B   ⵋkⵋkⵄⵖkⵋkⵋkⵄ×kⵌk   8,A,BO,8,A,BP,5,
     0170:   C16BC2D8 6BF56BC1 6BC2D96B F86BC16B   ÁkⵄⵘkⵌkÁkⵄⵙkⵋkⵋk   A,BQ,5,A,BR,8,A,
     0180:   C4E46BF1 6BC16BC2 E26BF56B E46BC2E3   Äⵤkñⵋkⵋkⵄⵈkⵌkⵤkⵄⵓ  DU,1,A,BS,5,U,BT
     0190:   6BF66BE4 6BC4C16B F26BC16B C5C26BF1   kⵖkⵤkⵄⵋkⵈⵋkⵕⵄkñ    ,6,U,DA,2,A,EB,1
     01A0:   6BC16BC2 E46BF16B C16BC26B C5C36BC1   kⵋkⵄⵤkñkⵋkⵄkⵕⵓkⵋ  ,A,BU,1,A,BX,1,A
     01B0:   6BC2E86B F1F06BC1 6BC2E96B F1F36BC1   kⵄⵘkññðkⵋkⵄⵙkñⵓⵋ  ,BY,10,A,BZ,13,A
     01C0:   6BC3C16B F16BC16B C3C26BF6 6BC16BC3   kⵓⵋkñⵋkⵓⵄkⵖⵋkⵋⵓ   ,CA,1,A,CB,6,A,C
     01D0:   C3D86BF6 6BC16BC4 C36BC3C4 6BC16BC1   ⵓⵘkⵖⵋkⵄⵓkⵓⵖkⵋkⵋ   C,2,U,CD,10,A,CE
     01E0:   6BF16BC1 6BC3C66B F16BC16B C3C76BC1   kñkⵋkⵓⵖkñⵋkⵓⵗkⵋ   ,1,A,CF,1,A,CG,1
     01F0:   6BC16BC3 C86BF16B C16BC3C9 6BF1F06B   kⵋⵓⵘkñⵋkⵓⵙkññð     ,A,CH,1,A,CI,10,
     0200:   C16BC3D1 6BF86BC1 6BC3D26B F86BC16B   Ákⵓⵑkⵋkⵋkⵓⵒkⵋkⵋk   A,CJ,8,A,CK,8,A,
     0210:   C3D36BF1 6BC16BC3 D46BF46B E46BC3D5   ⵓⵓkñkⵋkⵓⵖk×kⵤkⵓⵕ  CL,1,A,CM,4,U,CN
     0220:   6BF1F8F0 6BC16BC3 D66BF86B C16BC3D7   kññⵋðkⵋkⵓⵖkⵋkⵋkⵓ×  ,180,A,CO,8,A,CP
     0230:   6BF1F56B C16BC3D8 6BF16BC1 6BC3D96B   kñⵌkÁkⵓⵘkñⵋkⵓⵙk   ,15,A,CQ,1,A,CR,
     0240:   F16BC16B C3E26BF1 F06BC16B C1C76BC1   ñkⵋkⵓⵈkññðkⵋkÁⵗkⵋ  1,A,CS,10,A,AG,4
     0250:   6BE46BC1 C86BF76B D76BC2E5 6BF46BE4   kⵤkÁⵘkñ÷k×kⵄⵕk×kⵤ  ,U,AH,7,P,BV,4,U
     0260:   6BC2E66B F76BD76B C3E36BF4 6BE46BE9   kⵄⵖkñ÷k×kⵓⵓk×kⵤkⵙ  ,BW,7,P,CT,4,U,Z
     0270:   C16BF76B D76BC4C3 6BF46BE4 6BC4C46B   Ák÷k×kⵄⵓk×kⵤkⵄⵖk   A,7,P,DC,4,U,DD,
     0280:   F76BD76B C4C76BF4 6BE46BC4 D46BF76B   ÷k×kⵄⵗk×kⵤkⵄⵔkñ÷k  7,P,DG,4,U,DM,7,
     0290:   6BC4D96B F46BE46B C4D86BF1 6BF16BC4   kⵄⵙk×kⵤkⵄⵘkñkñkⵄ   P,DR,4,U,DY,7,P,
     02A0:   C3E46BF1 6BC16BC3 E56BF1F0 6BC16BC3   ⵓⵤkñkⵋkⵓⵕkññðkⵋkⵓ  CU,1,A,CV,10,A,C
     02B0:   E66BF86B C76BC3E7 6BF86BC7 6BC3E86B   ⵖkⵋkⵗkⵓⵗkⵋkⵗkⵓⵘk   W,8,G,CX,8,G,CY,
     02C0:   F86BC16B C3E96BF8 6BC14B         ⵋkⵋkⵓⵙkⵋkⵋ         8,A,CZ,8,A.
15:53:08.630 ba7560 LCL: CB alignment gap is 1 bytes
```

```
15:53:08.630 ba7560 LCL: Now check RB/IB
15:53:08.630 ba7560 LCL: Input RB Length=819/0x333 Buffer=0xbe6bc3
       0000:   00000000 0000005F D9C9F2F8 F9F3F7F6   .......ÙÉòøùó÷ö    .......RI289376

(snip) obfuscated record buffer data

       0320:   000000F2 F0F0F3F0 F9F0F1F2 F0F0F3F0   ...òðˠóðùˠˠòˠˠˠð   ...2003090120030
       0330:   F9F3F0                                ùóð                          930
15:53:08.630 ba7560 LCL: lTotal = 1679, cb_offset = 780, rda_b_lng = 1679
15:53:08.630 ba7560 LCL: ADABAS user-queue handle = 0
15:53:08.630 ba7560 LCL: viowriteusr: DBID 251
15:53:08.630 ba7560 LCL: viowriteusr: attached buffer header flags 3
15:53:08.630 ba7560 LCL: viowriteusr: processing ACB request on DBID 251 converting to ACBX
15:53:08.630 ba7560 LCL: MP USRIPC WRITE X (251-00BE6010-5-0140FC60-0|-1609486212|12461264)
15:53:08.630 ba7560 LCL: writeusr: final response 0
15:53:08.630 ba7560 LCL: readusr: DBID 251
15:53:08.630 ba7560 LCL: vioreadusr: DBID 251 iIovCnt 2
15:53:08.630 ba7560 LCL: vioreadusr: attached buffer header flags 3
15:53:08.630 ba7560 LCL: vioreadusr: processing ACBX request on DBID 251 converting back to ACB
15:53:08.630 ba7560 LCL: MP USRIPC READ X (251-00BE6010-2-0140FC90-0|64|12476360)
15:53:08.630 ba7560 LCL: vioreadusr: copy buffer back for an ACB/ACBX request on DBID 251
15:53:08.630 ba7560 LCL: convert_to_acb: DBID 251
15:53:08.630 ba7560 LCL: len_user_abd= 8
15:53:08.630 ba7560 LCL: pdst pointing to first ATB buffer address 0269F9C8
15:53:08.630 ba7560 LCL: CB (IN) Length=80/0x50 Buffer=0xbe68a8
       0000:   30404E32 6066CC44 90009400 DE060300   0@N2`fÌD..".Þ...   . +.-....m.....
       0010:   00000000 00000000 CB023303 00000000   ........Ë.3.....   ..............
       0020:   00002020 20202020 20202020 20202020   ..                 ..............
       0030:   20202020 20202020 20202020 20202020                      ..............
       0040:   00000000 00000000 00000000 00000000   ................   ..............
15:53:08.630 ba7560 LCL: acbx before copy: rsp= 0
15:53:08.630 ba7560 LCL: acb after copy: acb rsp= 0
15:53:08.630 ba7560 LCL: receiving atb package representing an acb acbx conversion request
15:53:08.630 ba7560 LCL: ACBX cmd_code (N2)
15:53:08.630 ba7560 LCL: pabd (0269F968)  - # of abds    (2 )
15:53:08.630 ba7560 LCL: num_rb (1) - num_fb (1)- num_sb (0)- num_vb (0)- num_ib (0)
15:53:08.630 ba7560 LCL:    abdid (F)
15:53:08.630 ba7560 LCL: ABD dump Length=48/0x30 Buffer=0x269f968
       0000:   30004732 46004900 00000000 00000000   0.G2F.I.........   ..............
       0010:   CB020000 00000000 CB020000 00000000   Ë.......Ë.......   ..............
       0020:   00000000 00000000 00000000 F868BE00   ...........øh¾.     ...........8...
15:53:08.630 ba7560 LCL: FB (out) Length=64/0x40 Buffer=0x269f9c8
       0000:   41412C38 2C502C41 422C3530 2C412C41   AA,8,P,AB,50,A,A   .....&........
       0010:   432C3135 2C412C41 442C382C 412C4145   C,15,A,AD,8,A,AE   ..............
       0020:   2C312C41 2C41462C 312C412C 4D412C31   ,1,A,AF,1,A,MA,1   ...........(...
       0030:   2C412C4D 422C3130 2C412C41 492C3130   ,A,MB,10,A,AI,10   ...(..........
15:53:08.630 ba7560 LCL: ADABAS(rcv) UQ-handle (0)
15:53:08.630 ba7560 LCL: CB (OUT) Length=80/0x50 Buffer=0xbe68a8
       0000:   00404E32 6066CC44 90940000 DE060300   .@N2`fÌD."..Þ...   . +.-....m.....
       0010:   00000000 00000000 CB023303 00000000   ........Ë.3.....   ..............
       0020:   00002020 20202020 20202020 41010000   ..                A...             ..............
       0030:   20202020 20202020 20202020 20202020                      ..............
       0040:   00000000 00000000 00000000 00000000   ................   ..............
15:53:08.630 ba7560 LCL: final rc 0 CB 0
15:53:08.630 ba7560 LCL: (CVT-OUT) EBCDIC -> ASCII conversion required
15:53:08.630 ba7560 LCL: (CVT-OUT) BYTE ORDER conversion required
15:53:08.630 ba7560 LCL: (CVT-OUT) CB in Length=80/0x50 Buffer=0xbe68a8
       0000:   00404E32 6066CC44 90940000 DE060300   .@N2`fÌD."..Þ...   . +.-....m.....
       0010:   00000000 00000000 CB023303 00000000   ........Ë.3.....   ..............
       0020:   00002020 20202020 20202020 41010000   ..                A...             ..............
       0030:   20202020 20202020 20202020 20202020                      ..............
       0040:   00000000 00000000 00000000 00000000   ................   ..............
15:53:08.630 ba7560 LCL: (CVT-OUT) CB out Length=80/0x50 Buffer=0xbe68a8
       0000:   0040D5F2 44CC6660 94900000 000306DE   .@ÕÒDÌf`".....Þ    . N2...-m.....
       0010:   00000000 00000000 02CB0333 00000000   .........Ë.3....   ..............
       0020:   40404040 40404040 01410000 01410000   .@@@@@@@@.A..      ..    ....
       0030:   40404040 40404040 40404040 40404040   @@@@@@@@@@@@@@@@    ..............
       0040:   00000000 00000000 00000000 00000000   ................   ..............
15:53:08.630 ba7560 LCL: ======  LCL call finished =====  LCL call finished ======
15:53:08.630 ba7560 LNK: (EA) - EACB content Length=68/0x44 Buffer=0x140fec0
       0000:   0101FB00 04180001 CB023303 00000000   ..û.....Ë.3.....   ..............
       0010:   00003303 00000000 0000885C 00000000   ..3.......\....    .........h*...
       0020:   60EA0000 02001800 C0DC4200 C0DC4200   `ê......ÀÛB.ÀÛB.    -.......{...{...
       0030:   C68EB2A8 E50C8606 D9C5D7D3 00000000   ÆŽ²¨å.†.ÙÅ×Ó....    F..yV.f.REPL....
       0040:   00000000                              ....               ....
15:53:08.630 ba7560 LNK: (EA) Call DBID 251 - Local Complete
15:53:08.630 ba7560 LNK: (EA) ====== Returning CMD(EBCDIC): 0x'd5f2'Response: 0; RC: 0 ======
15:53:08.630 ba7560 ============ calling A1 local extended_adabas DBID=251 rc=0 ============
```

```
15:53:08.630 ba7560 LocalRequest OUT: Dump of reply ACB block
       0000:  0040D5F2 44CC6660 00900000 000306DE  *.@ÕòDÌf`.......Þ*
       0010:  00000000 00000000 02CB0333 00000000  *.........Ë.3....*
       0020:  00004040 40404040 40404040 01410000  *..@@@@@@@@@@.A..*
       0030:  40404040 40404040 40404040 40404040  *@@@@@@@@@@@@@@@@*
       0040:  00000000 00000000 00000000 00000000  *...............*
15:53:08.630 ba7560 LocalRequest OUT: Dump of reply EAB block
       0000:  0101FB00 04180001 CB023303 00000000  *..û.....Ë.3.....*
       0010:  00003303 00000000 0000885C 00000000  *..3........\....*
       0020:  60EA0000 02001800 C0DC4200 C0DC4200  *`ê......ÀÜB.ÀÜB.*
       0030:  C68EB2A8 E50C8606 D9C5D7D3 00000000  *ÆŽ²¨å.†.ÙÅ×Ó....*
       0040:  00000000                             *....*
15:53:08.630 ba7560 LocalRequest OUT: Returned Rbl=819 Ibl=0
15:53:08.630 ba7560 LocalRequest OUT: Reply RB is
       0000:  00000000 0000005F D9C9F2F8 F9F3F7F6  *......_ÙÉø╩ó÷ö*
       0010:  F0F3F240 40404040 40404040 40404040  *ðóò@@@@@@@@@@@@*


(snip) obfuscated record buffer data

       0320:  000000F2 F0F0F3F0 F9F0F1F2 F0F0F3F0  *...òðóðùðñòðñðóð*
       0330:  F9F3F0                               *ùóð          *
15:53:08.630 ba7560 =========WORK UNIT DBID=251 REPLY CLASSIC=========
15:53:08.630 ba7560 ProcessClassicRep pQNE=0xba9ff8
15:53:08.630 ba7560 -----------RDA SENDIG MESSAGE MsgReference=0xbcdc9c Length=144------------
---
15:53:08.630 ba7560 Buffer=0
       0000:  00900001 9F0E0000             *....Ÿ...      *
15:53:08.630 ba7560 Buffer=1
       0000:  44000000 00000004 315BC800 C68E9484  *D.......1[È.ÆŽ",*
       0010:  4B5A3030 37202020 4144414E 37532020  *KZ007   ADAN7S  *
       0020:  00000000 00000000 00000000 00000040  *...............@*
       0030:  03330000 00000090 00000000 00000000  *.3..............*
15:53:08.630 ba7560 Buffer=2
       0000:  0040D5F2 44CC6660 00900000 000306DE  *.@ÕòDÌf`.......Þ*
       0010:  00000000 00000000 02CB0333 00000000  *.........Ë.3....*
       0020:  00004040 40404040 40404040 01410000  *..@@@@@@@@@@.A..*
       0030:  40404040 40404040 40404040 40404040  *@@@@@@@@@@@@@@@@*
       0040:  00000000 00000000 00000000 00000000  *...............*
15:53:08.630 ba7560 <XtsSendMessageByRt> Reference=0xbcdc9c ThreadRef=0x0 Buffer=0x140fe5c
Length=8 Type=0
15:53:08.630 ba7560 MsgReference=0xbcdc9c Type=Persistent kept for reusage
15:53:08.630 ba7560 Enter CommBlock=0xbd0254 ++Owners=2 From:CheckBlockEntry
15:53:08.630 ba7560 <XtsSendMessageByRt> TargetName=NETWORK_ADAN7S TargetId=0x7e000003 Refer-
ence=0xbcdc9c RoutId=0x0 MsgNo=0 Length=152 Interval=0 ms
15:53:08.630 ba7560 PSend Server=NETWORK_ADAN7S TargetId=0x7e000003 ConId=17 Payload=152 Time-
out=60000
15:53:08.630 ba7560 SEND ConId=17 Length=152/0x98 Buffer=0x140dce4
       0000:  00900001 9F0E0000 44000000 00000004  ....Ÿ...D.......  ................
       0010:  315BC800 C68E9484 4B5A3030 37202020  1[È.ÆŽ",KZ007     .$H.F.md.!......
       0020:  4144414E 37532020 00000000 00000000  ADAN7S ........   ...+..........
       0030:  00000000 00000040 03330000 00000090  .......@.3......  ..............
       0040:  00000000 00000000 0040D5F2 44CC6660  .........@ÕòDÌf`  ........ N2...-
       0050:  00900000 000306DE 00000000 00000000  .......Þ........  ..............
       0060:  02CB0333 00000000 00004040 40404040  .Ë.3......@@@@@@  ..........
       0070:  40404040 01410000 40404040 40404040  @@@@.A..@@@@@@@@  ....
       0080:  40404040 40404040 00000000 00000000  @@@@@@@@........  ..............
       0090:  00000000 00000000                    ........          ........
15:53:08.630 ba7560 TcpSend Socket=340 Length=152 Timeout=60000
15:53:08.630 ba7560 PSend Server=NETWORK_ADAN7S TargetId=0x7e000003 ConId=17 TotalLength=152
exiting ...
15:53:08.630 ba7560 Exit CommBlock=0xbd0254 --Owners=1 From:CommonSendMessageByRT
15:53:08.630 ba7560 FreeCAF=0xbe6830
15:53:08.630 4b8240 TcpReceive Socket=340 Length=1686
15:53:08.630 4b8240 RECEIVE ConId=17 Length=1686/0x696 Buffer=0xbd02f8
       0000:  068E0001 000E0000 42000040 00FB0004  .Ž......B..@.û..  ...............
       0010:  315BC800 C68E9484 4144414E 37532020  1[È.ÆŽ",ADAN7S     .$H.F.md...+...
       0020:  4B5A3030 37202020 00040300 C68EB2A8  KZ007   ....ÆŽ²¨  .!........F..y
       0030:  E50C8606 0000030B D9C5D7D3 0000068E  å.†.....ÙÅ×Ó...Ž  V.f.....REPL....
       0040:  00000000 00000000 C1C16BF8 6BD76BC1  ........ÁÁkøk×kÁ  ........AA,8,P,A
       0050:  C26BF5F0 6BC16BC1 C36BF1F5 6BC16BC1  ÂkõðkÁkÁÃkñ₅kÁkÁ  B,50,A,AC,15,A,A
       0060:  C46BF86B C16BC1C5 6BF16BC1 6BC1C66B  ÄkøkÁkÁÅkñkÁkÁÆk  D,8,A,AE,1,A,AF,
       0070:  F16BC16B D4C16BF1 6BC16BD4 C26BF1F0  ñkÁkÔÁkñkÁkÔÂkñð  1,A,MA,1,A,MB,10
       0080:  6BC16BC1 C96BF1F0 6BC16BC1 D16BF1F0  kÁkÁÉkñðkÁkÁÑkñð  ,A,AI,10,A,AJ,10
       0090:  6BC16BC1 D26BF16B C16BC1D3 6BF16BC1  kÁkÁÒkñkÁkÁÓkñkÁ  ,A,AK,1,A,AL,1,A
       00A0:  6BC1D46B C16BC1D5 6BF16BC1 6BC16BC1  kÁÔkÁkÁÕkøkÁkÁkÁ  ,AM,1,A,AN,8,A,A
       00B0:  D66BF26B C16BC4E6 6BF46BC1 6BC1D76B  ÖkòkÁkÄækøkÁkÁ×k  O,2,A,DW,4,A,AP,
       00C0:  F1F06BC1 6BC1D86B F16BC16B C1D96BF9  ñðkÁkÁØkñkÁkÁÙkù  10,A,AQ,1,A,AR,9
       00D0:  6BC16BC1 E26BF3F0 6BC16BC1 E36BF3F0  kÁkÁâkóðkÁkÁãkóð  ,A,AS,30,A,AT,30
```

```
00E0:   6BC16BC1 E46BF66B C16BC1E5 6BF26BC1   kÁkÄäkökÁkÁàkòkÁ   ,A,AU,6,A,AV,2,A
00F0:   6BC1E66B F1F06BC1 6BC1E76B F16BC16B   kÆækñðkÁkÁÇkñkÁk   ,AW,10,A,AX,1,A,
0100:   C1E86BF1 F06BC16B C1E96BF2 6BC16BC2   ÁèkñðkÁkÁékòkÁkÂ   AY,10,A,AZ,2,A,B
0110:   C16BF86B D76BC2C2 6BF1F06B C16BC2C3   Ákøk×kÂÂkñðkÁkÂÂ   A,8,P,BB,10,A,BC
0120:   6BF16BC1 6BC2C46B F76BD76B C2C56BF1   kñkÁkÂÂk÷k×kÂÂkñ   ,1,A,BD,7,P,BE,1
0130:   F06BC16B C2C66BF1 6BC16BC2 C76BF1F0   ðkÁkÂÆkñkÁkÂÇkñð   0,A,BF,1,A,BG,10
0140:   6BC16BC2 C86BF46B C16BC2C9 6BF46BE4   kÁkÂÈkôkÁkÂÉkôkä   ,A,BH,4,A,BI,4,U
0150:   6BC2D16B F76BD76B C2D26BF4 6BE46BC2   kÂÑk÷k×kÂÔkôkäkÂ   ,BJ,7,P,BK,4,U,B
0160:   D36BF76B D76BC5C3 6BF46BE4 6BC5C46B   Ók÷k×kÂÅkôkäkÄÅk   L,7,P,EC,4,U,ED,
0170:   F76BD76B C5C56BF4 6BE46BC5 C66BF76B   ÷k×kÂÅkôkäkÂÆk÷k   7,P,EE,4,U,EF,7,
0180:   D76BC5C7 6BF46BE4 6BC5C86B F76BD76B   ×kÂÅkôkäkÂÈk÷k×k   P,EG,4,U,EH,7,P,
0190:   C5C96BF4 6BE46BC5 D16BF76B D76BC2D4   ÂÉkôkäkÂÑk÷k×kÂÔ   EI,4,U,EJ,7,P,BM
01A0:   6BF86BC1 6BC2D56B F86BC16B C2D66BF8   køkÁkÂÕkøkÁkÂÖkø   ,8,A,BN,8,A,BO,8
01B0:   6BC16BC2 D76BBF5B C16BC2D8 6BF56BC1   kÁkÂ×kökÁkÂØkõkÁ   ,A,BP,5,A,BQ,5,A
01C0:   6BC2D96B F86BC16B C4E46BF1 6BC16BC2   kÂÙkøkÁkÄäkñkÁkÂ   ,BR,8,A,DU,1,A,B
01D0:   E26BF56B E46BC2E3 6BF66BE4 6BC4C16B   âkökäkÂãkôkäkÄÁk   S,5,U,BT,6,U,DA,
01E0:   F26BC16B C5C26BF1 6BC16BC2 E46BF16B   òkÁkÂÂkñkÁkÂäkñk   2,A,EB,1,A,BU,1,
01F0:   C16BC2E7 6BF16BC1 6BC2E86B F1F06BC1   ÁkÂçkñkÁkÂèkñðkÁ   A,BX,1,A,BY,10,A
0200:   6BC2E96B F1F36BC1 6BC3C16B F16BC16B   kÂékñókÁkÃÁkñkÁk   ,BZ,13,A,CA,1,A,
0210:   C3C26BF6 6BC16BC3 C36BF26B E46BC3C4   ÃÂkökÁkÃÃkòkäkÃÄ   CB,6,A,CC,2,U,CD
0220:   6BF1F06B C16BC3C5 6BF16BC3 C66BF16B   kñðkÁkÃÂkñkÁkÂÆk   ,10,A,CE,1,A,CF,
0230:   F16BC16B C3C76BF1 6BC16BC3 C86BF16B   ñkÁkÂÇkñkÁkÂÈkñk   1,A,CG,1,A,CH,1,
0240:   C16BC3C9 6BF1F06B C16BC3D1 6BF86BC1   ÁkÂÉkñðkÁkÂÑkøkÁ   A,CI,10,A,CJ,8,A
0250:   6BC3D26B F86BC16B C3D36BF1 6BC16BC3   kÂÔkøkÁkÂÓkñkÁkÂ   ,CK,8,A,CL,1,A,C
0260:   D46BF46B E46BC3D5 6BF1F8F0 6BC16BC3   ÔkôkäkÂÕkñøðkÁkÂ   M,4,U,CN,180,A,C
0270:   D66BF86B C16BC3D7 6BF1F56B C16BC3D8   ÖkøkÁkÂ×kñõkÁkÂØ   O,8,A,CP,15,A,CQ
0280:   6BF16BC1 6BC3D96B F16BC16B C3E26BF1   kñkÁkÂÙkñkÁkÂâkñ   ,1,A,CR,1,A,CS,1
0290:   F06BC16B C1C76BF4 6BE46BC1 C86BF76B   ðkÁkÂÇkôkäkÂÈk÷k   0,A,AG,4,U,AH,7,
02A0:   D76BC2E5 6BF46BE4 6BC2E66B F76BD76B   ×kÂåkôkäkÂÆkñk÷k   P,BV,4,U,BW,7,P,
02B0:   C3E36BF4 6BE46BC9 C16BF76B D76BC4C3   ÂãkôkäkÂÉkÁk÷k×k   CT,4,U,ZA,7,P,DC
02C0:   6BF46BE4 6BC4C46B F76BD76B C4C76BF4   kôkäkÂÄk÷k×kÂÇkô   ,4,U,DD,7,P,DG,4
02D0:   6BE46BC4 D46BF76B D76BC4D9 6BF46BE4   käkÂÔk÷k×kÂÙkôkä   ,U,DM,7,P,DR,4,U
02E0:   6BC4E86B F76BD76B C3E46BF1 6BC16BC3   kÂèk÷k×kÂäkñkÁkÂ   ,DY,7,P,CU,1,A,C
02F0:   E56BF1F0 6BC16BC3 E66BF86B C76BC3E7   âkñðkÁkÂÆækøkÂÇkÂç   V,10,A,CW,8,G,CX
0300:   6BF86BC7 6BC3E86B F86BC16B C3E96BF8   køkÂÇkÂèkøkÁkÂékø   ,8,G,CY,8,A,CZ,8
0310:   6BC14B30 40D5F244 CC666000 9000FB00   kÁK@ÕòÐÌf`...û.   ,A.. N2...-.....
0320:   0306DF00 00000000 00000002 CB033300   ..ß.......Ë.3.
0330:   00000000 00404040 40404040 40404040   .....@@@@@@@@@@   .....
0340:   40404040 40404040 40404040 40404040   @@@@@@@@@@@@@@@@
0350:   40404000 00000000 00000000 00000000   @@@.............   ..............
0360:   00000000 00000000 00005FD9 C9F2F8F9   ........._ÜÉòøù   ..........RI289
```

(snip) obfuscated data

```
0680:   1C000000 0000F2F0 F0F3F0F9 F0F1F2F0   ......òðõóðùðñòð   ......2003090120
0690:   F0F3F0F9 F3F0                         ðóðùóð              030930
```

15:53:08.630 4b8240 ProcessBuffer DrvBlock=0xbcdc34 ConId=17 posting 1686 bytes
15:53:08.630 4b8240 RECEIVE_EVENT Server=NETWORK_ADAN7S TargetId=0x7e00003 ConId=17
Length=1686 Raw Request
15:53:08.630 4b8240 RECEIVE_EVENT Server=NETWORK_ADAN7S TargetId=0x7e00003 Reference=0xbcdc9c
Length=1686 Raw Request delivered
15:53:08.630 4b8240 ------------RECV RDA MESSAGE MsgReference=0xbcdc9c-------------
15:53:08.630 4b8240 RDACallBack: Dump of RDA MESSAGE
```
0000:   068E0001 000E0000 42000040 00FB0004   *.Ž......B..@.û..*
```

(snip) obfuscated data

```
0680:   1C000000 0000F2F0 F0F3F0F9 F0F1F2F0   *......òðõóðùðñòð*
0690:   F0F3F0F9 F3F0                         *ðóðùóð            *
```

15:53:08.630 4b8240 FIND NQE By MsgReference=0xbcdc9c
15:53:08.630 4b8240 FIND NQE pNQE=0xba9ff8 MsgReference=0xbcdc9c NControl=0xca NodeName=ADAN7S
15:53:08.630 4b8240 FIND NQE->GOT IT
15:53:08.630 4b8240 >>>>>>>>>>>>>> RDA DBID=251 REQUEST <<<<<<<<<<<<<<<<
15:53:08.630 4b8240 ADABAS Request from classic node=ADAN7S DBID=251 TID=ÆŽž̈ä†PID=D9C5D7D3
15:53:08.630 4b8240 AllocateCAF=0xbe6830
15:53:08.630 4b8240 QueueRdaAdabasRequest: Dump of ACB
```
0000:   3040D5F2 44CC6660 009000FB 000306DF   *0@ÕòÐÌf`...û...ß*
0010:   00000000 00000000 02CB0333 00000000   *.........Ë.3....*
0020:   00004040 40404040 40404040 40404040   *..@@@@@@@@@@@@@@*
0030:   40404040 40404040 40404040 40404040   *@@@@@@@@@@@@@@@@*
0040:   00000000 00000000 00000000 00000000   *................*
```
15:53:08.630 4b8240 Rbl=819 Fbl=715 Sbl=0 Vbl=0 Ibl=0
15:53:08.630 4b8240 Dump of FB
```
0000:   C1C16BF8 6BD76BC1 C26BF5F0 6BC16BC1   *ÁÁkøk×kÁkÂkõðkÁkÁ*
0010:   C36BF1F5 6BC16BC1 C46BF86B C16BC1C5   *Ãkñõkõðk ÁÄkøkÁkÁÅ*
0020:   6BF16BC1 6BC1C66B F16BC16B D4C16BF1   *kñkÁkÁÆkñkÁkÔÁkñ*
0030:   6BC16BD4 C26BF1F0 6BC16BC1 C96BF1F0   *kÁkÔÂkñðkÁkÁÉkñð*
0040:   6BC16BC1 D16BF1F0 6BC16BC1 D26BF16B   *kÁkÁÑkñðkÁkÁÔkñk*
0050:   C16BC1D3 6BF16BC1 6BC1D46B F16BC16B   *ÁkÁÓkñkÁkÁÔkñkÁk*
```

```
      0060:  C1D56BF8 6BC16BC1 D66BF26B C16BC4E6  *ÁÕkøkÁkÁÖkòkÁkÄæ*
      0070:  6BF46BC1 6BC1D76B F1F06BC1 6BC1D86B  *kôkÁkÁ×kñðkÁkÁØk*
      0080:  F16BC16B C1D96BF9 6BC16BC1 E26BF3F0  *ñkÁkÁÙkùkÁkÁâkóð*
      0090:  6BC16BC1 E36BF3F0 6BC16BC1 E46BF66B  *kÁkÁãkóðkÁkÁäkök*
      00A0:  C16BC1E5 6BF26BC1 6BC1E66B F1F06BC1  *ÁkÁåkòkÁkÁækñðkÁ*
      00B0:  6BC1E76B F16BC16B C1E86BF1 F06BC16B  *kÁçkñkÁkÁèkñðkÁk*
      00C0:  C1E96BF2 6BC16BC2 C16BF86B D76BC2C2  *ÁékòkÁkÂÁkøk×kÂÂ*
      00D0:  6BF1F06B C16BC2C3 6BF16BC1 6BC2C46B  *kñðkÁkÂÂkñkÁkÂÄk*
      00E0:  F76BD76B C2C56BF1 F06BC16B C2C66BF1  *÷k×kÂÂkñðkÁkÂÆkñ*
      00F0:  6BC16BC2 C76BF1F0 6BC16BC2 C86BF46B  *kÁkÂÇkñðkÁkÂÈkök*
      0100:  C16BC2C9 6BF46BE4 6BC2D16B F76BD76B  *ÁkÂÉkòkäkÁÑk÷k×k*
      0110:  C2D26BF4 6BE46BC2 D36BF76B D76BC5C3  *ÂÒkôkäkÁÓk÷k×kÂÂ*
      0120:  6BF46BE4 6BC5C46B F76BD76B C5C56BF4  *kôkäkÁÂk÷k×kÁÂkö*
      0130:  6BE46BC5 C66BF76B D76BC5C7 6BF46BE4  *käkÁÆk÷k×kÁÂkòkä*
      0140:  6BC5C86B F76BD76B C5C96BF4 6BE46BC5  *kÁÈk÷k×kÁÂkòkäkÁ*
      0150:  D16BF76B D76BC2D4 6BF86BC1 6BC2D56B  *Ñk÷k×kÁÔkøkÁkÁÕk*
      0160:  F86BC16B C2D66BF8 6BC16BC2 D76BF56B  *økÁkÁÖkøkÁkÂ×kök*
      0170:  C16BC2D8 6BF56BC1 6BC2D96B F86BC16B  *ÁkÁØkökÁkÁÙkøkÁk*
      0180:  C4E46BF1 6BC16BC2 E26BF56B E46BC2E3  *ÄäkñkÁkÁÂkòkäkÁã*
      0190:  6BF66BE4 6BC4C16B F26BC16B C5C26BF1  *kökäkÁÁkòkÁkÁÂkñ*
      01A0:  6BC16BC2 E46BF16B C16BC2E7 6BF16BC1  *kÁkÁäkñkÁkÁçkñkÁ*
      01B0:  6BC2E86B F1F06BC1 6BC2E96B F1F36BC1  *kÁèkñðkÁkÁékñóKÁ*
      01C0:  6BC3C16B F16BC16B C3C26BF6 6BC16BC3  *kÂÁkñkÁkÁÂkökÁkÁÂ*
      01D0:  C36BF26B E46BC3C4 6BF1F06B C16BC3C5  *ÂkòkäkÁÄkñðkÁkÁÂ*
      01E0:  6BF16BC1 6BC3C66B F16BC16B C3C76BF1  *kñkÁkÁÂkñkÁkÁÂkñ*
      01F0:  6BC16BC3 C86BF16B C16BC3C9 6BF1F06B  *kÁkÁÈkñkÁkÁÂkñðk*
      0200:  C16BC3D1 6BF86BC1 6BC3D26B F86BC16B  *kÁÑkøkÁkÁÒkøkÁk*
      0210:  C3D36BF1 6BC16BC3 D46BF46B E46BC3D5  *ÁÓkñkÁkÁÔkôkäkÁÕ*
      0220:  6BF1F8F0 6BC16BC3 D66BF86B C16BC3D7  *kñøðkÁkÁÖkøkÁkÂ×*
      0230:  6BF1F56B C16BC3D8 6BF16BC1 6BC3D96B  *kñõkÁkÁØkñkÁkÁÙk*
      0240:  F16BC16B C3E26BF1 F06BC16B C1C76BF4  *ñkÁkÁâkñðkÁkÁÇkô*
      0250:  6BE46BC1 C86BF76B D76BC2E5 6BF46BE4  *käkÁÈk÷k×kÁÂkôkä*
      0260:  6BC2E66B F76BD76B C3E36BF4 6BE46BE9  *kÁækñk÷k×kÁÂkôké*
      0270:  C16BF76B D76BC4C3 6BF46BE4 6BC4C46B  *Ák÷k×kÁÁkôkäkÁÄk*
      0280:  F76BD76B C4C76BF4 6BE46BC4 D46BF76B  *÷k×kÁÇkôkäkÁÔk÷k*
      0290:  D76BC4D9 6BF46BE4 6BC4C86B F76BD76B  *×kÁÙkôkäkÁÈk÷k×*
      02A0:  C3E46BF1 6BC16BC3 E56BF1F0 6BC16BC3  *ÁäkñkÁkÁÂkñðkÁkÁ*
      02B0:  E66BF86B C76BC3E7 6BF86BC7 6BC3E86B  *ækøkÇkÁçkøkÇkÁèk*
      02C0:  F86BC16B C3E96BF8 6BC14B            *økÁkÁékøkÁK    *
15:53:08.630 4b8240 Dump of RB
      0000:  00000000 0000005F D9C9F2F8 F9F3F8F1  *......._ÙÉò2ù óøñ*

(snip) obfuscated data

      0320:  000000F2 F0F0F3F0 F9F0F1F2 F0F0F3F0  *...òððóðùðñòððóð*
      0330:  F9F3F0                               *ùóð              *
15:53:08.630 4b5ab0 ==========A1 WORKING THREAD=1 DBID=251 REQ LOCAL==========
15:53:08.630 4b8240 ReadSyncRoutine DrvBlock=0xbcdc34 ConId=17 Timeout=-1
15:53:08.630 4b5ab0 LocalRequest IN: Dump of EAB block
      0000:  0101FB00 04180001 CB023303 00000000  *..û.....Ë.3.....*
      0010:  00000000 00000000 0000885C 00000000  *..........\....*
      0020:  60EA0000 02001800 C0DC4200 C0DC4200  *`ê......ÀÜB.ÀÜB.*
      0030:  C68EB2A8 E50C8606 D9C5D7D3 00000000  *ÆŽ²¨å.†.ÙÅ×Ó....*
      0040:  00000000                             *....          *
15:53:08.630 4b8240 TcpReceive Socket=340 Length=8192 submitted
15:53:08.630 4b5ab0 LocalRequest IN: Dump of ACB
      0000:  3040D5F2 44CC6660 009000FB 000306DF  *0@ÕòDÏf`...û...ß*
      0010:  00000000 00000000 02CB0333 00000000  *.........Ë.3....*
      0020:  00004040 40404040 40404040 40404040  *..@@@@@@@@@@@@@@*
      0030:  40404040 40404040 40404040 40404040  *@@@@@@@@@@@@@@@@*
      0040:  00000000 00000000 00000000 00000000  *................*
15:53:08.630 4b5ab0 LocalRequest: Rbl=819 Fbl=715 Sbl=0 Vbl=0 Ibl=0
15:53:08.630 4b5ab0 LocalRequest IN: Dump of FB
      0000:  C1C16BF8 6BD76BC1 C26BF5F0 6BC16BC1  *ÁÁkøk×kÁÂkõðkÁkÁ*
      0010:  C36BF1F5 6BC16BC1 C46BF86B C16BC1C5  *Ákñõkñ kÁkÁÄkøkÁkÁÂ*

(snip) obfuscated data

      0310:  F2F1F23E FDFA1619 36004F44 4D1C0000  *òñò>ýú..6.ODM...*
      0320:  000000F2 F0F0F3F0 F9F0F1F2 F0F0F3F0  *...òððóðùðñòððóð*
      0330:  F9F3F0                               *ùóð              *
15:53:08.646 4b5ab0 LNK: (FIRST) thread block 00BD5168
15:53:08.646 4b5ab0 LNK: (EA) ADALNKX Version: 6.2.1.23 - Build-Number 0 and ARCH BYTE 0x'21'
15:53:08.646 4b5ab0 LNK: ADALNKX Compilation Date: Oct  1 2008 Time: 15:18:31
15:53:08.646 4b5ab0 LNK: (EA) ======= New ADABAS call ======= New ADABAS call =======
15:53:08.646 4b5ab0 LNK: (EA) - ACB content Length=80/0x50 Buffer=0xbe68a8
      0000:  3040D5F2 44CC6660 009000FB 000306DF  0@ÕòDÏf`...û...ß   . N2...-........
      0010:  00000000 00000000 02CB0333 00000000  .........Ë.3....   ...............
      0020:  00004040 40404040 40404040 40404040  ..@@@@@@@@@@@@@@    ..
```

```
    0030:  40404040 40404040 40404040 40404040    @@@@@@@@@@@@@@@@    ................
    0040:  00000000 00000000 00000000 00000000    ................    ................
15:53:08.646 4b5ab0 LNK: (EA) - EACB content Length=68/0x44 Buffer=0xeffec0
    0000:  0101FB00 04180001 CB023303 00000000    ..û.....Ë.3.....    ................
    0010:  00000000 00000000 0000885C 00000000    ...........\....    ..........h*....
    0020:  60EA0000 02001800 C0DC4200 C0DC4200    `ê......ÀÜB.ÀÜB.    -.......{...{..
    0030:  C68EB2A8 E50C8606 D9C5D7D3 00000000    ÆŽ²¨å.†.ÙÀ×Ó....    F..yV.f.REPL....
    0040:  00000000                               ....                ....
15:53:08.646 4b5ab0 LNK: (FIRST) thread block 00BD5168
15:53:08.646 4b5ab0 LNK: (FIRST) thread block 00BD5168
15:53:08.646 4b5ab0 LNK: Set ID - thread 00BD5168
15:53:08.646 4b5ab0 LNK: Set ID ADAID_T Length=24/0x18 Buffer=0xeffee4
    0000:  02001800 C0DC4200 C0DC4200 C68EB2A8    ....ÀÜB.ÀÜB.ÆŽ²¨    ....{...{...F..y
    0010:  E50C8606 D9C5D7D3                       å.†.ÙÀ×Ó            V.f.REPL
15:53:08.646 4b5ab0 LNK: Set ID - UID <ÀÜB>
15:53:08.646 4b5ab0 LNK: (SU) UID len 3 MAX 64
15:53:08.646 4b5ab0 LNK: (SU) UID-dmp Length=3/0x3 Buffer=0xeffcac
    0000:  C0DC42                                 ÀÜB                 {..
15:53:08.646 4b5ab0 LNK: (SU) Reusing last UID 004BBFEC
15:53:08.646 4b5ab0 LNK: (EA) - Call, DBID 251
15:53:08.646 4b5ab0 LNK: (AC) Alloc CTX (00BBA1E8-004BBFF4)
15:53:08.646 4b5ab0 LNK: (AC) Alloc CTX (00BBA1E8-004BBFF4|251-251)
15:53:08.646 4b5ab0 LNK: (AC) CTX-dmp Length=28/0x1c Buffer=0xbba1e8
    0000:  F4BF4B00 F4BF4B00 00000000 00000000    ô¿K.ô¿K.........    4...4..........
    0010:  01000000 FB000000 04000000              ....û.......        ...........
15:53:08.646 4b5ab0 LNK: (AC) Reusing CTX 00BBA1E8 DBID 251
15:53:08.646 4b5ab0 LNK: (EA) - THREAD content with Buffer Addresses Length=11484/0x2cdc Buf-
fer=0xbd5168
    0000:  6B000000 00000000 ECBF4B00 F8D8BC00    k.......ì¿K.øØ¼.    ,..........8Q..
    0010:  00DDBC00 FB000000 02001800 C0DC4200    .Ý¼.û.......ÀÜB.    .............{..
    0020:  C0DC4200 C68EB2A8 E50C8606 D9C5D7D3    ÀÜB.ÆŽ²¨å.†.ÙÀ×Ó    {...F..yV.f.REPL
    0030:  00000000 00000000 00000000 00000000    ................    ................
       LINES 0040-2B80 SAME AS LINE 0030
    2B90:  00000000 00000000 A868BE00 F868BE00    ........¨h¾.øh¾.    ........y...8...
    2BA0:  C36BBE00 00000000 00000000 00000000    Ãk¾............    C,.............
    2BB0:  00000000 00000000 00000000 00000000    ................    ................
    2BC0:  00000000 00000000 00000000 00000000    ................    ................
    2BD0:  00000000 00000000 00000000 282DBD00    ............(-½.    ................
    2BE0:  04000000 00000000 00000000 00000000    ................    ................
    2BF0:  00000000 00000000 00000000 00000000    ................    ................
       LINES 2C00-2CB0 SAME AS LINE 2BF0
    2CC0:  00000000 00000000 00000000 362E312E    ............6.1.    ................
    2CD0:  382E3033 00000000 0000000F              8.03........        ...........
15:53:08.646 4b5ab0 LCL: ======== Start LCL call ======= Start LCL call ========
15:53:08.646 4b5ab0 LCL: pThb 00BD5168
15:53:08.646 4b5ab0 LCL: (CVT-IN) EBCDIC -> ASCII conversion required
15:53:08.646 4b5ab0 LCL: (CVT-IN) BYTE ORDER conversion required
15:53:08.646 4b5ab0 LCL: (CVT-IN) CB in Length=80/0x50 Buffer=0xbe68a8
    0000:  3040D5F2 44CC6660 00900094 000306DF    0@Õò Dì f`..."...ß    . N2...-...m....
    0010:  00000000 00000000 02CB0333 00000000    .........Ë.3....    ................
```

Figure 216:   Monitor – WCP Log Windows

9.7   ADARPL Replay S0C4 Dump

```
A D A R P L    V8.1  SM1   DBID = 00134  Started        2010-12-23  14:51:27


  Parameters:
  -----------


  ADARPL REPLAY TOKEN=15825
  ADARPL RPLTARGETID=312
  ADARPL LRPL=600000K

  Initialization handshake for Reptor 312 successful, token = 15825
     Replay Type  : Synchronized
     Token created: 2010-12-23 14:49:20.59
     ADARPL from date/time : 2010-12-20 02:00:00.00
     ADARPL to date/time   : 2010-12-23 14:49:22.01
     Subscription(s) involved:
     S134006   S134007   S134008   S134009
     S134010   S134011   S134012   S134013
     S134014   S134015   S134016   S134017
     S134018   S134019   S134020   S134021
     S134022   S134023   S134024   S134025
     S134026   S134027   S134028   S134029
     S134030   S134031   S134032   S134033
     S134034   S134035   S134036   S134037
     S134038   S134039   S134040   S134041
     S134042   S134043   S134044   S134045
     S134046   S134047   S134048   S134049
     S134050   S134051   S134052   S134053
     S134054   S134055   S134056   S134057
     S134058   S134059   S134060   S134061
     S134062   S134063   S134064   S134065
     S134066   S134067   S134068   S134069
     S134070   S134071   S134072   S134073
     S134074   S134075   S134076   S134077
     S134078   S134079   S134080   S134081
     S134082   S134083   S134084   S134085
     S134086   S134087   S134088   S134089
     S134090   S134091   S134092   S134093
     S134094   S134095   S134096   S134097
     S134098   S134099   S134103   S134104
     S134105   S134106   S134107   S134108
     S134109   S134110   S134111   S134112
     S134113   S134116   S134118   S134119
     S134120   S134121   S134122   S134125
     S134130   S134131   S134132   S134133
     S134135   S134137   S134138   S134139
     S134140   S134141   S134142   S134145
     S134146   S134147   S134148   S134149
     S134150   S134151   S134152   S134153
     S134154   S134158   S134159   S134160
     S134162   S134163   S134164   S134165
     S134166   S134167   S134168   S134170
     S134171   S134173   S134175   S134176
     S134177   S134180   S134181   S134182
     S134183   S134184   S134185   S134186
     S134195   S134196   S134197   S134198
     S134200   S134207   S134210   S134211
     S134212   S134214   S134216   S134221
     S134223   S134224   S134226   S134241
     S134242   S134243   S134249   S134260
     S134270   S134271   S134280   S134326
     S134327   S134344   S134401
```

```
Destination(s) involved:
D251006   D251007   D251008   D251009
D251010   D251011   D251012   D251013
D251014   D251015   D251016   D251017
D251018   D251019   D251020   D251021
D251022   D251023   D251024   D251025
D251026   D251027   D251028   D251029
D251030   D251031   D251032   D251033
D251034   D251035   D251036   D251037
D251038   D251039   D251040   D251041
D251042   D251043   D251044   D251045
D251046   D251047   D251048   D251049
D251050   D251051   D251052   D251053
D251054   D251055   D251056   D251057
D251058   D251059   D251060   D251061
D251062   D251063   D251064   D251065
D251066   D251067   D251068   D251069
D251070   D251071   D251072   D251073
D251074   D251075   D251076   D251077
D251078   D251079   D251080   D251081
D251082   D251083   D251084   D251085
D251086   D251087   D251088   D251089
D251090   D251091   D251092   D251093
D251094   D251095   D251096   D251097
D251098   D251099   D251103   D251104
D251105   D251106   D251107   D251108
D251109   D251110   D251111   D251112
D251113   D251116   D251118   D251119
D251120   D251121   D251122   D251125
D251130   D251131   D251132   D251133
D251135   D251137   D251138   D251139
D251140   D251141   D251142   D251145
D251146   D251147   D251148   D251149
D251150   D251151   D251152   D251153
D251154   D251158   D251159   D251160
D251162   D251163   D251164   D251165
D251166   D251167   D251168   D251170
D251171   D251173   D251175   D251176
D251177   D251180   D251181   D251182
D251183   D251184   D251185   D251186
D251195   D251196   D251197   D251198
D251200   D251207   D251210   D251211
D251212   D251214   D251216   D251221
D251223   D251224   D251226   D251241
D251242   D251243   D251249   D251260
D251270   D251271   D251280   D251326
D251327   D251344   D251401
File(s) involved:
      6       7       8       9      10      11
     12      13      14      15      16      17
     18      19      20      21      22      23
     24      25      26      27      28      29
     30      31      32      33      34      35
     36      37      38      39      40      41
     42      43      44      45      46      47
     48      49      50      51      52      53
     54      55      56      57      58      59
     60      61      62      63      64      65
     66      67      68      69      70      71
     72      73      74      75      76      77
     78      79      80      81      82      83
     84      85      86      87      88      89
     90      91      92      93      94      95
     96      97      98      99     103     104
```

```
      105   106   107   108   109   110
      111   112   113   116   118   119
      120   121   122   125   130   131
      132   133   135   137   138   139
      140   141   142   145   146   147
      148   149   150   151   152   153
      154   158   159   160   162   163
      164   165   166   167   168   170
      171   173   175   176   177   180
      181   182   183   184   185   186
      195   196   197   198   200   207
      210   211   212   214   216   221
      223   224   226   241   242   243
      249   260   270   271   280   326
      327   344   401
14:51:28  IEF403I STREPLAA - STARTED - TIME=14.51.28
14:51:29  +ABONL-28:  REPORT MEMBER CREATION FAILED, RC = 0000015C, DSN = SYSD.
14:51:29  +ABONL-18:  NO DATABASE FILES ELIGIBLE FOR SELECTION
14:51:29  +ABONL-10:  ABEND-AID WILL USE ABENDAID DD INSTEAD
14:51:29  +AB401        ===== ABEND-AID =====
14:51:29      REPORT WRITTEN TO: ABENDAID.JOB-STREPLAA STEP-ST1        .........
14:51:29      ABEND CODE=S0C4
14:51:29        ACCESS YOUR ABEND-AID REPORTS BY EXECUTING SYSTEM
14:51:29        COMMAND "AA" FROM ANYWHERE IN ISPF.
14:51:30  IAT1600 JOB STREPLAA (JOB48202) LINES EXCEEDED
14:51:33  IAT1600 JOB STREPLAA (JOB48202) LINES EXCEEDED BY 16,000
14:51:54  IAT1600 JOB STREPLAA (JOB48202) LINES EXCEEDED BY 32,000
14:51:54  IAT1600 JOB STREPLAA (JOB48202) LINES EXCEEDED BY 48,000
14:51:54  IAT1600 JOB STREPLAA (JOB48202) LINES EXCEEDED BY 64,000
14:51:54  IAT1600 JOB STREPLAA (JOB48202) LINES EXCEEDED BY 80,000
(snip)
14:51:57  SYSTEM COMPLETION CODE=0C4   REASON CODE=00000010
14:51:57    TIME=14.51.28  SEQ=04250  CPU=0000  ASID=01DB
14:51:57    PSW AT TIME OF ERROR  078D0000    8004FF54  ILC 4  INTC 10
14:51:57      ACTIVE LOAD MODULE           ADDRESS=00049C00  OFFSET=00006354
14:51:57      NAME=ADARPL
14:51:57      DATA AT PSW  0004FF4E - B21658F0  A99C50F0  3000187F
14:51:57      GR 0: 00000000_0000007A  1: 00000000_00000290
14:51:57         2: 00000000_8004FF50  3: 00000000_6F50589C
14:51:57         4: 00000000_00000000  5: 00000000_0004DFC4
14:51:57         6: 00000000_00000012  7: 00000000_6F492AD0
14:51:57         8: 00000000_00052D96  9: 00000000_0004FEF0
14:51:57         A: 00000000_80049C00  B: 00000000_0004AC00
14:51:57         C: 00000000_0004BC00  D: 00000000_0004DC00
14:51:57         E: 00000000_4AA0A008  F: 00000001_6F492830
14:51:57    END OF SYMPTOM DUMP
14:51:57  IEF450I STREPLAA ST1 REPLAY - ABEND=S0C4 U0000 REASON=00000010
14:51:57          TIME=14.51.57
14:51:57  IEF404I STREPLAA - ENDED - TIME=14.51.57
```

Figure 217:   RPL S0C4 Dump

9.8   Assembler Programs

9.8.1   Sleep/Wait

```
DIETER.ASM.SOURCE(SLEEP)

********************************* Top of Data *********************************
* THIS PROGRAM PERFORMS A TIMED WAIT. ITS PURPOSE IS TO HALT EXECUTION
* FOR A GIVEN PERIOD OF TIME. THE PERIOD OF TIME IS CODED ON THE EXEC
* STATEMENT IN HH:MM:SS.TH FORMAT (WHERE HH IS HOURS,
* MM IS MINUTES, SS IS SECONDS, T IS TENTHS OF A SECOND, H IS
* HUNDRETHES OF A SECOND.
*
* EXAMPLE:
* //SLEEP01  EXEC PGM=SLEEP,PARM='00:10:00.00'
*
* THIS WILL CAUSE A WAIT OF 10 MINUTES IN THE JOB.
*
* IF THIS PROGRAM ABENDS WITH A U0999 ABEND CODE, IT MEANS THAT THE
* TIME VALUE WAS NOT SUPPLIED IN A VALID FORMAT (HH:MM:SS:TH).
******************************************************************************
SLEEP    START 0
         STM  14,12,12(13)
         BALR 12,0
         USING *,12
         LR 10,13
         LA 13,SAVE
         ST 13,8(10)
         ST 10,4(13)
         L  5,0(1)
         USING  PARM,5
         CLC REQLEN,PARMLEN           COMPARE PARMLEN W/REQUIRED LENGTH
         MVI LOCATE,C'1'
         BNE NOTOK                    IF NOT EQUAL, BRANCH TO NOT OK
         CLC PARMVAL+2(1),COLON       LOOK FOR COLON BETWEEN HR& MIN
         MVI LOCATE,C'2'
         BNE NOTOK                    IF NOT EQUAL, BRANCH TO NOT OK
         CLC PARMVAL+5(1),COLON       LOOK FOR COLON BETWEEN MIN & SEC
         MVI LOCATE,C'3'
         BNE NOTOK                    IF NOT EQUAL, BRANCH TO NOT OK
         CLC PARMVAL+8(1),PERIOD      LOOK FOR DECIMAL POINT AFTER SEC
         MVI LOCATE,C'4'
         BNE NOTOK                    IF NOT EQUAL, BRANCH TO NOT OK
         MVC INTRVAL(2),PARMVAL
         MVC INTRVAL+2(2),PARMVAL+3
         MVC INTRVAL+4(2),PARMVAL+6
         MVC INTRVAL+6(2),PARMVAL+9
* ----------------------------------
*        PRINT PARM INFO
* ----------------------------------
DRUCK    EQU    *
         MVC    TEXT,=CL80' '
         MVC    TEXT(11),PARMVAL
         MVC    TEXT+12(17),=C'= PARAMETER VALUE'
         OPEN   (PRINT,OUTPUT)
         PUT    PRINT,TEXT
         CLOSE  (PRINT)
         B    WAIT
NOTOK    ABEND  X'3E7',DUMP,STEP
WAIT     STIMER WAIT,DINTVL=INTRVAL
END      EQU *
         L 13,4(13)
         LM  14,12,12(13)
         LA 15,0
         BR 14
```

```
* -------------------
*   DEFINITIONS
* -----------------
          DS     D
PRINT     DCB    DDNAME=DDPRINT,                                              *
                 MACRF=PM,                                                    *
                 BLKSIZE=800,LRECL=80,                                        *
                 DSORG=PS
TEXT      DS     CL80
          DS     D
SAVE      DS     18F
ALIGN     DS     0D
INTRVAL   DC     ZL8'00050000'
REQLEN    DC     XL2'B'
LOCATE    DC     X'00'
COLON     DC     C':'
PERIOD    DC     C'.'
PARM      DSECT
PARMLEN   DS     BL2
PARMVAL   DS     CL11
          END




//STSLEEP  JOB (ST345T,ST01,ST),'DIETER',TIME=1440,
//*        RESTART=GO,
//         MSGCLASS=2,NOTIFY=&SYSUID,LINES=9999        ,TYPRUN=SCAN
//*MAIN    CLASS=P10,USER=DIETER
//* -----------------------------------------
//ASMHCL   EXEC ASMHCL,PRINT=*
//C.SYSIN    DD DISP=SHR,DSN=DIETER.ASM.SOURCE(SLEEP)
//L.SYSLMOD  DD DISP=SHR,DSN=DIETER.ASM.LOADLIB
//L.SYSIN    DD *
 NAME SLEEP2(R)
/*
//GO       EXEC PGM=SLEEP2,PARM='00:00:30.00'
//STEPLIB  DD  DISP=SHR,DSN=DIETER.ASM.LOADLIB
//DDPRINT  DD  SYSOUT=*
//SYSUDUMP DD  DUMMY
//ABENDAID DD  SYSOUT=*
//
```

Figure 218:   Assembler Program Sleep/Wait

9.8.2   Get Dataset Name

```
//STGETDSN JOB (ST345T,ST01,ST),'STDWS',TIME=1440,
//*         RESTART=GO,
//          MSGCLASS=2,NOTIFY=&SYSUID,LINES=9999      ,TYPRUN=SCAN
//*MAIN     CLASS=P10,USER=STADBA
//* ------------------------------------------
//ASMHCL    EXEC ASMHCL,PRINT=*
//C.SYSIN    DD DISP=SHR,DSN=DIETER.ASM.SOURCE(GETDSN)
//L.SYSLMOD  DD DISP=SHR,DSN=DIETER.ASM.LOADLIB
//L.SYSIN    DD *
 NAME GETDSN(R)
/*
//GO        EXEC PGM=GETDSN,PARM='PDFOUT  '
//STEPLIB   DD  DISP=SHR,DSN=DIETER.ASM.LOADLIB
//PDFOUT    DD  DISP=SHR,DSN=*.STEPLIB
//SYSPRINT  DD  SYSOUT=*
//OUTPUT    DD  SYSOUT=*
NAME GETDSN(R)
/*
//GO        EXEC PGM=GETDSN,PARM='PDFOUT  '
//STEPLIB   DD  DISP=SHR,DSN=DIETER.ASM.LOADLIB
//PDFOUT    DD  DISP=SHR,DSN=*.STEPLIB
//SYSPRINT  DD  SYSOUT=*
//OUTPUT    DD  SYSOUT=*
//SYSUDUMP  DD  DUMMY
//ABENDAID  DD  SYSOUT=*
//

* ----------------------------------------------------------------
* GETDSN    (using RDJFCB)
* Obtain the DDNAME - can be used in a Natural program
* CALL 'GETDSN'                 this assembler routine
*       'ddname  '              ddname of the dataset (8 bytes)
*       RDJFCB-AREA             area for job file control block (A176)
*                               first 44 bytes is the dataset name
* Dieter Storr -- 8 August 2008
* ----------------------------------------------------------------
*
R0        EQU  0
R1        EQU  1
R2        EQU  2                (A) CALL TYPE
R3        EQU  3                (A) DBID
R4        EQU  4                (A) ADABAS MSG/OPERCOM
R5        EQU  5                (A) CACHE RELEASE COUNT TABLE
R6        EQU  6                NUMBER OF TABLE ENTRIES
R7        EQU  7                (A) PRINT LINE
R8        EQU  8
R9        EQU  9
R10       EQU  10
R11       EQU  11
R12       EQU  12
R13       EQU  13
R14       EQU  14
R15       EQU  15
          EJECT
*
** ----------------------------------------------------------------
*                         MAIN CONTROL SECTION                    *
** ----------------------------------------------------------------
*
GETDSN    CSECT
*
GETDSN    AMODE 24
GETDSN    RMODE 24
```

```
*
         STM   R14,R12,12(R13)        STORE CALLER'S REGS
         LR    R12,R15                LOAD MY ENTRY ADDR IN REG12
         USING GETDSN,R12             USE REG12 AS MY BASE REG
         ST    R13,SAVEAREA+4         STORE CALLER'S SAVE AREA ADDR
         LA    R15,SAVEAREA           GET MY SAVE AREA ADDRESS
         ST    R15,8(R13)             STORE IT IN CALLER'S SAVE AREA
         LR    R13,R15                LOAD MY SAVE AREA ADDR IN REG13
*
*        USING JFCB,R10               USE REG10 FOR DSECT JFCB
         LM    R2,R4,0(R1)            GET PARM ADDRESSES
         MVC   INDCB+40(8),2(R2)      * MODIFY DCB(DDNAME) length
*        LA    R4,JFCBAREA            * CREATE EXLST
*        ST    R4,DCBEXLST            * CREATE EXLST
*        MVI   DCBEXLST,X'87'         * CREATE EXLST
         RDJFCB (INDCB,INPUT)         * READ JOB FILE CONTROL BLOCK
         LTR   R15,R15
         BNZ   NODSN
*
HAVEDSN  DS    0H
         MVC   TEXT(08),2(R2)
         MVC   TEXT+10(10),=CL10'DSN FOUND!'
         B     DRUCK
NODSN    DS    0H
         MVC   TEXT(08),2(R2)
         MVC   TEXT+10(14),=CL14'DSN NOT FOUND!'
         B     DRUCK
*
* ----------------------------------
*        PRINT PARM INFO
* ----------------------------------
DRUCK    EQU   *
         MVC   TEXT+30(44),JFCBAREA
         OPEN  (PRINT,OUTPUT)
         PUT   PRINT,TEXT
         CLOSE (PRINT)
*
RETURN   DS    0H
         L     R13,SAVEAREA+4         ADRESSE SAVE-AEREA CALLER->REG13
         LM    R14,R12,12(R13)        RESTORE CALLER VALUES
         XR    R15,R15                CLEAR R15
         BR    R14                    EXIT
         EJECT
** ----------------------------------------------------------------
*                DEFINITIONS, WORK AND SAVE AREAS
** ----------------------------------------------------------------
         DS    D
SAVEAREA DS    18F                    STANDARD REGISTER SAVE AREA
TEXT     DS    CL80
         DS    D
PRINT    DCB   DDNAME=OUTPUT,MACRF=PM,LRECL=80,DSORG=PS
         DS    D
INDCB    DCB   DSORG=PS,MACRF=R,EXLST=DCBEXLST,DDNAME=########
         DS    0F
DCBEXLST DC    X'87',AL3(JFCBAREA)
JFCBAREA DC    176X'00'
         LTORG
*                JFCBDSNM= DATASET NAME 44 BYTES
*jfcb    DSECT
*        IEFJFCBN
         END GETDSN
****************************** Bottom of Data ******************************
```

Figure 219:   RPL S0C4 Dump

9.9   EntireX V8.0.1 Parameters

These parameters are used for Natural RPC Servers and not for replication.

```
**********************************************************************
*                                                                    *
*          EntireX Broker Attribute File v8.0.1                      *
*                                                                    *
**********************************************************************
**                                                                  **
** DEVLETBM EXB Attribute File                                      **
**                                                                  **
**********************************************************************
** Changes                                                          **
** --Date-- UserID ----------Description-------------------------- **
** 07/09/10 DCBA50 Add SMF records #215 with ACCOUNTING-VERSION = 3. **
** 04/20/10 DCBA50 Increase NCQE from 30 to 60 and therefore        **
**                          NABS from 73280 to 146560.              **
** 04/07/10 DCBA50 Set up ETB237 for EntireX 8.0.1                  **
**                                                                  **
**********************************************************************
*
DEFAULTS = BROKER
  BROKER-ID                    = ETB237

  ACCOUNTING                   = 215
  ACCOUNTING-VERSION           = 3
  AUTOLOGON                    = YES
  DYNAMIC-MEMORY-MANAGEMENT    = YES
  ICU-CONVERSION               = NO
  MAX-MEMORY                   = UNLIM
  MAX-MESSAGE-LENGTH           = 10000000
* NUM-LONG-BUFFER              = 75000 /* num-long/short should not be
* NUM-SHORT-BUFFER             =  5000 /* needed because of dynamic mem
  NUM-WORKER                   = 10
* PSTORE                       = COLD
* PSTORE-TYPE                  = ADABAS
* PUBLISH-AND-SUBSCRIBE        = YES
  SECURITY                     = YES
* STORE                        = BROKER
* SUBSCRIBER-STORE             = PSTORE
  TRACE-LEVEL                  = 0
  TRANSPORT                    = NET-TCP

* DEFAULTS = ADABAS
* DBID                         = nnn
* FNR                          = 3

DEFAULTS = DIV
  DIV = "DEFINE STORE ETBSTORE
        DDNAME STORE01
        DATASPACE NAME STORE01
        DATASPACE PAGES 6000
        ATTRIBUTE CELL COUNT 1500
        HASH MODULUS 13
        HASH CELL COUNT 15
        CELL POOL NAME CPBLOB01 SIZE 256   COUNT 4000
        CELL POOL NAME CPBLOB02 SIZE 4096  COUNT 300
        CELL POOL NAME CPBLOB03 SIZE 16384 COUNT 100"

DEFAULTS = NET
  ADASVC                       = 241
  EXTENDED-ACB-SUPPORT         = YES * Adabas v8 and above
* FORCE                        = YES * default is NO
  IUBL                         = 10005000
  LOCAL                        = NO
```

```
  NABS                        = 146560
  NCQE                        = 60
  NODE                        = 237
  RESTART                     = YES
  RETRY-LIMIT                 = UNLIM
  RETRY-TIME                  = 1M
  TIME                        = 120

DEFAULTS = SECURITY
* CHECK-IP-ADDRESS            = NO
  ERRTXT-MODULE               = NA2MSG0
* IGNORE-STOKEN               = NO
* INCLUDE-CLASS               = YES
* INCLUDE-NAME                = YES
* INCLUDE-SERVICE             = YES
* PROPAGATE-TRUSTED-USERID    = NO  * default is YES
  SAF-CLASS                   = NBKSAG
* SECURITY-LEVEL              = AUTHORIZATION
* TRACE-LEVEL                 = 3   * default is 0
  TRUSTED-USERID              = YES * default is YES
* UNIVERSAL                   = NO
* WARN-MODE                   = NO
  PASSWORD-TO-UPPER-CASE      = YES
  USERID-TO-UPPER-CASE        = YES


* DEFAULTS = SSL
* CONNECTION-NONACT           = 1H
* PORT                        = 22223
* VERIFY-CLIENT               = NO
* KEY-LABEL                   = ETBCERT
* TRUST-STORE                 = [USER-ID/]RING-NAME

DEFAULTS = TCP
  PORT                        = 18237

DEFAULTS = SERVICE
  CONV-NONACT                 = 5M
* DEFERRED                    = YES * default is NO
  SERVER-NONACT               = 10M
  TRANSLATION                 = SAGTCHA

  CLASS = ETB,    SERVER = Tutorial, SERVICE = CvUnitOfWork
  CLASS = GAME,   SERVER = CHESS,    SERVICE = MAIL
* CLASS = JMS,    SERVER = *,        SERVICE = *, TRANSLATION = NONE
* CLASS = *,      SERVER = *,        SERVICE = *, DEFERRED    = NO


**
*****  STRS RPC Services
**

DEFAULTS = SERVICE
  CONV-NONACT                 = 5M
* DEFERRED                    = YES * default is NO
  MAX-MESSAGE-LENGTH          = 10000000
  SERVER-NONACT               = 1M
  TRANSLATION                 = SAGTCHA

  CLASS = RPC,   SERVER = RPCR01,   SERVICE = CALLNAT
  CLASS = RPC,   SERVER = RPCR02,   SERVICE = CALLNAT
  CLASS = RPC,   SERVER = RPCR03,   SERVICE = CALLNAT
  CLASS = RPC,   SERVER = RPCR04,   SERVICE = CALLNAT
  CLASS = RPC,   SERVER = RPCR05,   SERVICE = CALLNAT
  CLASS = RPC,   SERVER = RPC001,   SERVICE = CALLNAT
  CLASS = RPC,   SERVER = RPC002,   SERVICE = CALLNAT
  CLASS = RPC,   SERVER = RPC003,   SERVICE = CALLNAT
  CLASS = RPC,   SERVER = RPC004,   SERVICE = CALLNAT
  CLASS = RPC,   SERVER = RPC005,   SERVICE = CALLNAT
  CLASS = RPC,   SERVER = RPC006,   SERVICE = CALLNAT
  CLASS = RPC,   SERVER = RPC007,   SERVICE = CALLNAT
```

```
   CLASS = RPC,    SERVER = RPC008,    SERVICE = CALLNAT
   CLASS = RPC,    SERVER = RPC009,    SERVICE = CALLNAT
   CLASS = RPC,    SERVER = RPC010,    SERVICE = CALLNAT
   CLASS = RPC,    SERVER = RPC011,    SERVICE = CALLNAT
   CLASS = RPC,    SERVER = RPC012,    SERVICE = CALLNAT
   CLASS = RPC,    SERVER = RPC013,    SERVICE = CALLNAT
   CLASS = RPC,    SERVER = RPC014,    SERVICE = CALLNAT
   CLASS = RPC,    SERVER = RPC015,    SERVICE = CALLNAT
   CLASS = RPC,    SERVER = RPC016,    SERVICE = CALLNAT
   CLASS = RPC,    SERVER = RPC017,    SERVICE = CALLNAT
   CLASS = RPC,    SERVER = RPC018,    SERVICE = CALLNAT
   CLASS = RPC,    SERVER = RPC019,    SERVICE = CALLNAT
   CLASS = RPC,    SERVER = RPC020,    SERVICE = CALLNAT
   CLASS = RPC,    SERVER = RPC021,    SERVICE = CALLNAT
   CLASS = RPC,    SERVER = RPC022,    SERVICE = CALLNAT
   CLASS = RPC,    SERVER = RPC023,    SERVICE = CALLNAT
   CLASS = RPC,    SERVER = RPC024,    SERVICE = CALLNAT
   CLASS = RPC,    SERVER = RPC025,    SERVICE = CALLNAT

DEFAULTS = TOPIC
* ALLOW-DURABLE                = YES
  PUBLICATION-LIFETIME         = 6D
  TRANSLATION                  = SAGTCHA
  TOPIC                        = *

******************** END **********************************************
```

Figure 220:   EntireX V8.01 Parameters

Bibliography

Adams, Mike and others (2010), EMC Techbooks V1.5, EMC SRDF/A and SRDF/A Multi-Session Consistency on z/OS

http://www-03.ibm.com/systems/storage/disk/ess/

IBM, Enterprise Storage Server Family

http://documentation.softwareag.com/adabas/ada823mfr/adamf/overview.htm

Software AG (2011), Adabas 8.2.3 for Mainframes

Software AG (2010), Adabas 6.2 SP1 for Open Systems

Software AG (2011), Entire Net-Work 6.2.2 for Mainframes

Software AG (2010), Entire Net-Work .3.4 for Open Systems

Software AG (2010), Entire Net-Work Client 1.3.3

Software AG (2010), Adabas SAF Security Kernel 8.1.2

Software AG (2010), Adabas SAF Security 8.1.2

Software AG (2011), Event Replicator for Adabas on Mainframes 3.3.2

http://documentation.softwareag.com/natural/nat427mf/overview.htm

Software AG (2011), Natural 4.2.7 for Mainframes

Software AG (2011), Natural Security 4.2.7 for Mainframes

Software AG (2011), Natural SAF Security 4.2.7 for Mainframes

http://documentation.softwareag.com/webmethods/wmsuites/wmsuite8-2_fcs/EntireX/8-2_EntireX/overview.htm

Software AG (2011), webMethods EntireX 8.2 for different platforms

http://storrconsulting.com/sc200.html

Storr, Dieter W. (1995), Effizienter DB-Einsatz von ADABAS, (Efficient Database Usage of Adabas), Second Edition (German)

Storr, Dieter W. (2009), Experiences with Event Replicator for Adabas, Article in TECHniques, Issue 3, 2009, Software AG

Storr, Dieter W. (2010), Optimize for Infrastructure, Article in TECHniques, Issue 2, 2010, Software AG

Sybase (2001), Disaster Recovery with Sybase Replication Server, High Availability through Warm Standby – A Sybase White Paper

Index